Peter Robinson

a portrait of his work

Peter Robinson

a portrait of his work

edited by
Tom Phillips

Shearsman Books

First published in the United Kingdom in 2021 by
Shearsman Books Ltd
50 Westons Hill Drive
Emersons Green
BRISTOL
BS16 7DF

Shearsman Books Ltd Registered Office
30–31 St. James Place, Mangotsfield, Bristol BS16 9JB
(this address not for correspondence)

ISBN 978-1-84861-744-5

Copyright © 2021 by the authors.

ACKNOWLEDGEMENTS
Martin Dodsworth's '*Dormiveglia* and Values' was originally published in *English: Journal of the English Association*, Volume 67, Issue 259, Winter 2018: our thanks to the editors for allowing it to be republished here.

Contents

Foreword: Accepting Vulnerability / 9
Elaine Randell

Introduction: A Tectonic Biography / 19
Tom Phillips

Chapter 1
Of but not in Liverpool / 32
Tony Crowley

Chapter 2
Not Feeling at Home: The Hidden Injuries of Class / 54
Matthew Sperling

Chapter 3
'Onward, glancing back again': Cambridge / 68
Ian Brinton

Chapter 4
The View from Somewhere / 87
Piers Pennington

Chapter 5
European Integration / 106
Adam Piette

Chapter 6
An Italian Peter Robinson / 124
Anna Saroldi

Chapter 7
Dormiveglia and Values / 149
Martin Dodsworth

Chapter 8
Losing and Finding: Japanese Poetry / 171
Andrew Houwen

Chapter 9
Topophilia in Tohoku / 192
Miki Iwata

Chapter 10
'Understanding relations':
An Anglo-American Reading / 210
Alison Stone

Chapter 11
Objects in the World / 229
James Peake

Chapter 12
Bringing It All Back Home / 257
Peter Carpenter

Bibliography 1971–2020 / 273
Derek Slade

Notes on Contributors / 316

A note on referencing

References to frequently cited works by Peter Robinson use the abbreviations given below together with the relevant page numbers. All other works cited are referenced in full in the footnotes. Where poems don't appear in the *Collected Poems* or the reference is to an earlier version of a poem which is substantially different to the version in *CP*, the reference is given to its original publication.

TC	*The Constitutionals: A Fiction* (Reading: Two Rivers Press, 2019)
RE	*Ravishing Europa* (Tonbridge: Worple Press, 2019)
CP	*Collected Poems 1976–2016* (Bristol: Shearsman Books, 2017)
STR	*September in the Rain: A Novel* (Newbury: Holland House Books, 2016)
BM	*Buried Music* (Bristol: Shearsman Books, 2015)
TDW	*The Draft Will* (Tokyo: Isobar Press, 2015)
FDB	*Foreigners, Drunks and Babies* (Reading: Two Rivers Press, 2013)
TRS	*The Returning Sky* (Bristol: Shearsman Books, 2012)
STS	*Spirits of the Stair: Selected Aphorisms* (Exeter: Shearsman Books, 2009)
TLG	*The Look of Goodbye* (Exeter: Shearsman Books, 2008)
TAP	*Talk about Poetry: Conversations on the Art* (Exeter: Shearsman Books, 2007)
GC	*Ghost Characters* (Nottingham: Shoestring Press, 2006)
UD	*Untitled Deeds* (Cambridge: Salt, 2004)
SP	*Selected Poems 1976–2001* (Manchester: Carcanet Press, 2003)
ATT	*About Time Too* (Manchester: Carcanet Press, 2001)
LF	*Lost and Found* (Manchester: Carcanet Press, 1997)
EF	*Entertaining Fates* (Manchester: Carcanet Press, 1992)
TOL	*This Other Life* (Manchester: Carcanet Press, 1988)
OA	*Overdrawn Account* (London: Many Press, 1980)

Foreword:
Accepting Vulnerability

Elaine Randell

During his Nobel Banquet Speech at the City Hall, Stockholm, on 10 December 1950, William Faulkner said:

> I believe that man will not merely endure: he will prevail. He is immortal, not because he alone among creatures has an inexhaustible voice, but because he has a soul, a spirit capable of compassion and sacrifice and endurance. The poet's, the writer's, duty is to write about these things. It is his privilege to help man endure by lifting his heart, by reminding him of the courage and honor and hope and pride and compassion and pity and sacrifice which have been the glory of his past. The poet's voice need not merely be the record of man, it can be one of the props, the pillars to help him endure and prevail.[1]

Strong and complicated emotions and compassion are conveyed in the writings of Peter Robinson, born three years after these words were uttered, so as to embrace a commonality of what it is to be human. His poetry has a unique sense of honesty, clarity and openness that carries the reader into a domain with renewed sensibility where feelings are neither avoided nor managed, but exposed in their naked states. The reader is not, however, abandoned to flounder in dissonance, for there is resolution in the work which has a capacity to excavate territory within ourselves that prods us towards a keener appreciation – not only of what we may have overlooked, but also what we can share and utilise for ourselves. In studying the practice of language and place within the poems, these prefatory remarks will consider how the directness of the work operates throughout.

His poetry and prose make no deliberate attempts to obscure or cloud feelings and observations, but carefully enable readers to source their own resonances and to take them back for further reflection. The poet suffered a benign brain tumor removal in May 1993, at a time of

---

[1] *The Faulkner Reader* (New York, NY: Random House, 1954), 3-4 (4).

upheaval and transition when his first marriage was ending, as here in the third section of 'Hearing Difficulties':

> 'God help you' comes from overseas.
> It means *the very best of luck*
> in the English of a Japanese;
> and it's true you need it when
>
> a consultant pats you on the knee
> offering some courage,
> lays his hands on you and says,
> 'You'll be wondering soon: why me?'

The impact of this near-death experience upon him and his writing, particularly in relation to the mining of ideas bringing a further empathic tonality to the work, cannot be underestimated:

> But I was thinking: Well, why not?
> What would they mean, the hours of boredom
> and jokes about a poet going deaf,
> all things being equal in sickness and in death,
> if not that here's just another of those people?
>
> So when you tell him we're getting a divorce
> (letting him know as a matter of course)
> he replies, 'It never rains but it pours.'[2]

The poet's use of self-perception and awareness is never a vehicle for a moral high ground, a common feature in people who have survived near-death experiences. 'A gratitude and thankfulness for continued life coupled with a loss of the fear of death' is unsurprisingly reported in *Psychology Today*,[3] and 'There is a new awareness of meaning and purpose in their lives. A new sense of self with increased self-esteem is reported. Experiencers also show a marked change in their attitude, not only toward their life but toward others as well. They tend to be more open, caring, and loving. However, they may also reexamine their existing relationships, ending some that are now not compatible with

---

[2] *CP*, 170-1.
[3] *Psychology Today*, web: https://www.psychologytoday.com/intl

their new beliefs and attitudes.' Robinson's 1997 collection *Lost & Found* speaks to just such experiences of difficult transition.

Refreshingly, this poet's work does not shelter under unnecessarily muddled techniques or fancy footwork. He speaks of the everyday from a secure base – and that is compelling. The poet has inevitably absorbed differing aspects of the cultures around him: Christianity, a life in Japan, the world of his employment in academia, as in the first stanza of 'To the Quick', which finds him thinking of his childhood from far away in place and time: '*Quick* was a word troubled me that much / on Sundays when a kid at church. / My father, in his surplice, said: / "and He shall come to judge both the quick and the dead."'[4] The poetry resonates with reason, faith and love; it uses the Japanese ideas of *wabi* (transient and stark beauty), *sabi* (the beauty of natural patina and aging), and *yūgen* (profound grace and subtlety). Aspects of Christianity shine through the work with its known and long-established problems, but also its compassionate and secure predictability, which underpinned the poet's childhood: 'Someone explained it meant: the living. / I'll have thought to keep moving / was how we avoid such a fate /when mum said, "Quick, quick, or you're going to be late!"' The inner world of the poet when a child, raised in a vicarage where routines and rhythms of the church year are marked with frequent celebrations of birth and death, provides the occasion for these early misunderstandings in 'To The Quick', a poem published almost two decades after his operation:

> But, now it's a Sunday, what distresses
> are gust-beaten grasses
> and stubborn leaves crinkled from autumn
> clinging through that quickness with the chill still to come.

Whether this refers forward to the 'chill still to come' of his mother and father remembered here, or of his own future and inevitable death, what resonates here is that drawn-out final line.

Such a chill and a closeness to that quickness had indeed come when, diagnosed with the brain tumour in 1992, he was thrown upon the kindness of strangers and on his deep knowledge of Roy Fisher's poetry:

---

[4] *CP*, 355.

When crises come, they throw us back upon whatever reserves and resources we may have stored away – and so it was for me in the early years of the 1990s living in Japan where I couldn't really speak the language, going through the accelerating break-up of that same relationship (by then a marriage) which stretched back to Bradford's social sciences library, and on top of it all waiting to undergo major surgery for the removal of a brain tumour. The years spent compulsively reading Fisher's writings had left many echoes in the back of my head; so finally I let them act as a set of magnets for other words and phrases: 'A Well-Made Crisis', its title from the third of Fisher's 'Seven Attempted Moves'.[5]

Fisher's importance for, and influence upon, this poet is key. In his 1999 interview with Ted Slade, Peter defines Fisher's impact as follows: 'I read the productions of a sensibility that either gives me something that I don't have in my equipment at all, or which unearths things in my experience and sensibility that I wasn't aware of having. Whereas the poetry I enjoy tends to nudge me in stimulating ways I recognise, his poetry positively elbows me out of my habitual thought patterns.'[6] Such nudging indeed describes the impact of Robinson's own work as in the reflections on his near-death experience and evident vulnerability in its rawness evoked above in the dialogue with a consultant in 'Hearing Difficulties'.

Nowhere more keenly is vulnerability, adversity and also the sense of shame explored and examined than in Peter Robinson's first novel, *September in the Rain* (2016), described as follows by Jonathan Coe on the jacket: 'The patient beauties of his poetry are carried over seamlessly into this, his first work of fiction.' The novel is a fictionalised account of a traumatic incident endured by Peter's partner in Italy, and witnessed at gunpoint by the poet, while they were travelling together. The author underlines for us that this is a work of fiction.

Words are fingerprints for Peter and at page six he uses the word 'shivering' for the second time within a few lines:

> You're shivering still with your arms clasped about you, long straight dark hair parted in the middle but falling forward and closing around the head to hide your features. A few traces of the red mud cling in the lank brown strands. You're wearing

---
[5] *TDW*, 87.
[6] *TAP*, 18.

> my shapeless, crumpled summer jacket, its shoulders and back darkened from the soaking. Other night workers and travellers are swivelling round and glancing towards you. They're talking about those *ragazzi inglesi*, making guesses about what must have happened outside in the rain. You sip at the coffee, holding the small white cup near your face with both hands.[7]

The conscious shock echoing within the character's core is evident. The writer takes us, carefully, alongside and within the defenceless victim at every turn. It is an accomplishment. Robinson takes us towards his complex feelings for his partner and her silent admonition of both him and his presence; we are left in no doubt where the pain is. While she is expecting to be examined by a police doctor, life carries on as usual. The banality of everyday life continues in the face of trauma. The uncertainty within the couple's relationship in the aftermath of events and before is palpable. Robinson has confirmed that his poems are often 'responses to the circumstances in which I find myself.'

September in the Rain sets out events and feelings in some detail after the shocking assault upon the Mary character in Italy and the eventual total collapse of the couple's relationship, articulated with the utmost care and revealed in its naked states:

> Trying to do the right thing, I took the road that appeared at least to make sense or two of our lives. Yet, after all those years of making amends, all the attempts at an ordinary existence, all the second chances that you allowed, it was as if the only way either of us could truly get away from that violence was by getting away from each other; as if our relationship was to violence itself and not to the other person.[8]

In the beautiful title poem to *Ravishing Europa* (2019), Robinson's most recent collection of poems compiled in the midst of the on-going Brexit crisis, he appears to tour Europe via significant memories. Dedicated to 'O', presumably his second wife Ornella Trevisan, it is evident that the trauma of those events in Italy, when his then girlfriend endured that rape, remains present to his mind:

---

[7] *STR*, 6.
[8] *STR*, 264.

> After staying up, oh, far too late
> for a televised debate
> and sickened at the bickering,
> I'm reminded of Europa
> by some more mendacious bullshit –
> then gone to bed, succumb
> again to sorry memories...
> They bring back lying with the victim
> of a far-off rape, a
> ravishing, like the ones depicted
> in occidental summer twilight
> on its sunset lands.[9]

Perhaps the title *Vanishing Europa* would also have been an apt one for these poems about a painfully returned sense of responsibility, grief, and loss.

In 'Postcards from Bern', Robinson recalls again 'Scargill's V-shaped chapel' which inspired him so clearly as a young man, taken there on parish holidays: 'Brought by bus with the parish young wives / or Mother's Union, we'd first glimpse, / brave above pines across the Wharfe valley, / its chapel's inverted V'. Scargill House, with its glorious chapel designed by George Pace, an ecclesiastical architect, in 1958–1961, remains still a Christian conference centre, its style evidently reminiscent of some Swiss Protestant church architecture:

> The wood scents from a church interior
> call up Scargill's V-shaped chapel.
> I'm catching my breath by its graveyard at Thun.
> Away across the lake
> an echo of Von Kleist's last cry
> couldn't shift a cloud above
> our young couple's sky.[10]

Geoffrey Hill, much admired by Robinson, said, 'the idea that you write to glorify or to make glorious the art of expressiveness seems to me, spot on.' In an interview with Ted Slade in 1999, while speaking about early

---
[9] *RE*, 8.
[10] *RE*, 86-7.

influences that inspired him to write poetry, Robinson confides that in early childhood he was 'singing poems by William Blake and George Herbert and William Cowper, before I knew what they were.' A deep sense of glory, in its true meaning, that of both wonder and splendour is apparent in much of Robinson's poetry. It is well known that hymns and music relating to worship have influence on our lives and continue to do so throughout; they use the power of poetry and strong music to convey convictions, stir the affections and, in the past, strengthen moral resolve. Few of us recall being stirred by a sermon or words from any leader of faith, but many of us recall the words and music of a hymn. Indeed, putting music to words imparts a power that lyrics are hard put to achieve on their own. This is a power that encourages us to let our guard down and show our feelings, our vulnerability, and reaches us when little else can.

In the 2013 book of short stories, *Foreigners, Drunks and Babies*, Robinson writes of events that closely resemble his own travels from the North of England via Italy to Japan. It is of significance that he does not own them entirely but uses potential fictional characters:

> That corner of a person he had never been, the one who felt guilty about how he'd treated her, the one he had lived with all this time, she had abolished it with her generous words. It was like being given back a bit of your integrity, something he had lost, or had been taken from him, somewhere down the way. That was what other people could do; they could restore, could repair some things of you. It was what she had done, even if unawares.[11]

An aphorism is defined by the Oxford Dictionary as 'a pithy observation which contains a general truth'. In his *Spirits of the Stair: Selected Aphorisms,* (2009), Robinson is perhaps giving 'advice to a young poet and notes to self'. However, these short prose writings are also exemplars of Robinson's light lyrical ear and voice. He acknowledges the influence of his childhood in the church. He explains in the Afterword: 'It's not, of course, that I knew nothing of aphorisms when that began to happen. Brought up in a vicarage, attending Sunday school and church services each week, I had come early into contact with the aphoristically

---

[11] *FDB*, 176.

memorable parables and sayings of Jesus Christ.'[12] Writers may find some particularly resonate for them, as when he suggests that the 'very thing that prompts you to start a piece of writing may be just what you'll have to leave behind to finish it.'

> Two types of poetic occasion: emotion recollected while you're feeling it; emotion that comes back to you months later with significance you weren't aware of at the time. In each case, you'll have had to wait for the lived prompting to evolve as a form of words and phrases with direction and implication. Yet in the first case it's better to try and forget you've promised yourself that 'there's a poem here', while in the second you can be thankful that something was germinating without you even being aware of it.[13]

The early poem 'Tokens of Affection', in which a couple move house, expresses tenderness regarding change, and emotions are noted, but they are neither imposed nor foisted: 'In cracks between the floorboards / forgotten things, discovered again, / are thrown away.'[14] In the preface to *In the Circumstances: About Poems and Poets* Robinson states a belief in 'poetry as a response to other lives and the otherness of those lives.'[15] In an interview with Ian Samson, he replies to one question: 'There's a thread of poetry associated with the familiar style, that is full of other people and their differences: from before Ben Jonson to Frank O'Hara and beyond. Those kinds of poem which take place between people are ones I'm particularly drawn to',[16] as can be heard at the end of this same section from 'Tokens of Affection':

> I've placed, for safe keeping,
> my postcards in the pressure cooker.
> You sweep the floor
> like eating the pattern off your plate.[17]

---

[12] *STS*, Afterword, 147.
[13] *STS*, aphorism 209, 46.
[14] *CP,* 59.
[15] Robinson, *In the Circumstances: About Poems and Poets* (Oxford: Oxford University Press, 1992), vii.
[16] *TAP*, 21.
[17] *CP*, 59.

An exploration of human vulnerability is at the core of *The Constitutionals*, the writer's recently published book which, although described as a fiction, is more of a poetic work of internal reference. The book explores the thoughts and ideas of a man feeling debilitated and emotionally deserted by illness. His discomfort is exacerbated by his observations of his local neighbourhood and his perception of it as a contaminated and contagious tapestry of the horror of neoliberalism. The man, Crusoe, walks the local streets, understandably preoccupied with ideas about recovery and rescue, not only for himself but for the world. A central leitmotif of this stunningly beautifully composed novel reflects the poet's empathy, based on his own experiences, with illness and how it feels for life to go on without you:

> drugged with painkiller and feverishly sweating, unable to eat or digest what I was fatefully trying to keep down. The sun would come up and decline in the sky. The days would follow each other, counted like clouds above the rooftops through our back-bedroom window. The distant noise of life beginning again, going by, whether inside the house or out, it would reach me like the flies upon a horse's face.[18]

The Constitutionals describes how the main character of the book, Crusoe, pursues his travels to enhance his physical health. In so doing he 'catches an embedded metaphor in the idea of taking the body politic for a walk as well'. The novel depicts the state of the nation: 'This is why the visual arts are so much more closely locked into the tastes of the times – I found myself speculating – and their radicalism can so often feel like a sop for the beneficiaries of zero hours contracts and raids on pension schemes by absconding captains of merchandising.'[19] *The Constitutionals* is about accepting vulnerability, using compassion and rapport, couched within a format of detailed observation uniquely Robinson's own.

Interaction between others, between things, that's where the richness is in Robinson's best work. In writing we cannot help but make personal contact with others. A part of us is given up to another in commitment to paper and something more than real occurs in words. Shelley asserted that 'the mind of the creator is itself the image

---
[18] *TC*, 17-18
[19] *TC*, 199.

of all other minds'. This is a glimpse at the collective unconscious, which Jung recognised as being apparent in moments of crisis or great wonder. In his poetry, Peter Robinson accepts and permits his vulnerability and therefore encourages us, his readers, to do the same by tapping into our primal fears of loss and abandonment. The reward is to find enrichment within that intimate sharing, a finding of the self and the finding of our selves not alone but with others.

Introduction:
A Tectonic Biography

Tom Phillips

As Roy Fisher observed, Peter Robinson's work can be likened to 'a listening device, alert to the moments when the tectonic plates of mental experience slide quietly one beneath another to create paradoxes and complexities that call for poems to be made.'[1] This description will be familiar to readers of Robinson's work: it has often been cited by publishers and reviewers alike. The perspective it opens on that work is also a productive one in that it draws attention both to some of the poetry's key themes and the questions Robinson raises and explores with regards to the relationship between writing, reading and other forms of experience and, indeed, to how poems come to be made in the first place.

To some extent, of course, the paradoxes and complexities which call for Robinson to make his poems are evident in the resultant poems. And these poems provide us with as much of the biographical detail as we need to know. We know, for example, that many of the poems in *Lost and Found* relate to Robinson's move to Japan while those in *The Returning Sky* relate to his repatriation to the UK some eighteen years later. More specifically, 'The Passersby' from *Buried Music* evidently refers to a visit – or probably visits – to London (and elsewhere) in the aftermath of the 2008 financial crash and Robinson's responses to that particular crisis as an incoming economic returnee who's been back long enough to gauge the shift – tectonic in its own way – that both capital and the capital have undergone.[2]

In saying as much, I'm aware this might also suggest that a biography isn't necessary.

And again to an extent, that's true. Robinson's *Collected Poems* is not a *roman à clef*. The experience of reading, say, 'Graveyard Life' is not necessarily enhanced by knowing that the occasion for this poem – at which I was present, as the dedication indicates – was an afternoon

---

[1] Adam Piette & Katy Price (eds.), *The Salt Companion to Peter Robinson* (Cambridge: Salt Publishing, 2007), 22.
[2] *CP*, 424-8.

walk through the cemetery at the eponymous Cemetery Junction in Reading or that, when we spotted the Muntjac deer and photographer amongst the gravestones, we happened to be discussing national identity in the context of a PhD that I was just beginning. My own reading of that poem is inevitably inflected by that knowledge, but it's not necessary for anyone else to know that to find meaning and value there.[3]

At the same time, however, Fisher's reference to the movement of tectonic plates also suggests an approach to a biography which might identify some of the transitions that underlie Robinson's writing – whatever form it might take – and provide an introduction to the more detailed textual and contextual analyses which follow.

1

Born in Salford, Lancashire, on 18 February 1953, Peter Robinson spent his earliest years in Pendlebury and Daveyhulme, where his father was a curate in the Church of England. He then lived in vicarages in Liverpool from 1956 to 1962 and from 1967 to 1971 – that is, from the ages of three to nine and from fourteen to eighteen. The five years between were spent in Wigan. These shifts – tectonic or otherwise – were due to his father's being allotted one parish then another, and Robinson remembers them very clearly as times when he experienced being on his own and repeatedly trying to make sense of and form attachments to new surroundings:

> With the last two moves, in 1962 and 1967, there was also the problem of settling into new schools with classes that were already formed. There was, in the final move too, what now seems a long period (but may not have been) of not having any friends at all. This is one of the things, childhood illnesses the other, that helped make a reader and an artist of me, I imagine – the need to give myself inner direction so as not to be lost in places and days.[4]

---

[3] *CP*, 355.
[4] Interview with Peter Robinson, conducted via email, early 2017.

In the same interview, Robinson notes that art and music came into the household via his mother's side of the family. His maternal grandfather was a photographer and played the violin, his maternal grandmother was a pianist, while his mother's younger sister went to art school and married a fellow watercolourist. Growing up in vicarages, regularly attending church and joining the church choir at the age of eight also meant that he was more than familiar with church music and was first introduced to English poetry through *Hymns Ancient & Modern*. His own early efforts at music-making – the piano tuition which provides the material for the short story 'Music Lessons'[5] – were not particularly encouraging (he was better at theory than practice), but they did lead to a subsequent return to piano-playing and to his taking up the guitar in his teens. Aside from a foray into writing around the age of ten, when he filled several school exercise books with war stories before abandoning the idea, it was painting and drawing for which Robinson showed the most enthusiasm and in which he seems to have displayed the most talent. Indeed, he was not to try writing again until he moved back to Liverpool in 1967. Here, as he has recounted in the short memoir 'Becoming a Reader',[6] he was encouraged by his English teachers Peter Stott and Alan Hodgkinson and began writing 'some odd attempts at satires about religion and society'.[7] Reading Woolf and Joyce in the sixth form inspired experiments with modernist prose while ballad stanzas written in the style of Blake and Coleridge began to acquire an ironic, more twentieth-century twist after he was introduced to Eliot and Pound. These *Mauberley*-esque stanzas earned him a prize for poetry in the final year at school.

Robinson wasn't in the first generation of his family to go into tertiary education: his mother and father – who were the first in theirs – met at the University of Durham in 1947–48 when she was studying geography and he theology in preparation for taking up his calling to the church. It was expected that their four children would all go to university and Robinson applied to Durham, with York as his second choice. He ended up taking up an offer from the latter, initially to

---

[5] The story, published in the collection *Foreigners, Drunks & Babies*, is fiction but also autobiographical.
[6] *TDW*, 68-76.
[7] Interview and personal correspondence with Peter Robinson, early 2017. All subsequent quotations are taken from this interview and correspondence unless otherwise stated.

read for a joint English and History degree before switching, during his second term, to a solely English one. He was, though, able to maintain an on-going interest in art, studying a paper on Rubens and Rembrandt with Richard Verdi as well as an introduction to modernist poetry and Ezra Pound led by David Moody. Despite his own somewhat lower expectations, Robinson was awarded a First and the opportunity to do research. On this occasion, the choice was between an MA in the history of art at the Courtauld Institute in London or a PhD on Ezra Pound and the visual arts at Cambridge.

Accepted by both, Robinson opted for Cambridge and moved south for the first time, living in London and working as a porter at the National Hospital for Nervous Diseases. With money saved from this job, he and his girlfriend, Rosemary Laxton, were able to make a hitchhiking trip to Italy in the weeks before Robinson was due to start on his PhD. It was during this trip that the sexual assault on his girlfriend which Robinson was forced to witness at gunpoint took place. As the poet has written, this was 'probably the decisive event in my earlier life and the one that has inflected, one way or another, everything else that has happened since.'

Returning to England, Robinson moved to Cambridge to begin work on his PhD and encounter what was – and still is – an educational centre of the 'establishment'. This, too, represented a shift – a social one – which, like the move south to London, placed Robinson even further away from both his 'primal landscape' in the north and his background in the particular stratum of the middle classes reserved for what used to be referred to as the 'genteel poor' (in which the clergy and their families were habitually included). These geographical and social shifts overlapped with the profound psychological and emotional shock of the sexual assault and led to both personal and professional repercussions.

Robinson's work on his PhD was, he says, 'troubled' and he abandoned his original topic of Pound and painting in favour of the contemporary poets Roy Fisher, Donald Davie and Charles Tomlinson. During the first year, he lived in lodgings in Cambridge while Rosemary Laxton continued to work at a children's home in Little Venice, London, and the two only saw each other at weekends and during vacations. The following year brought a little more stability as she was able to join him in Cambridge and they rented an attic flat together.

Robinson was also becoming increasingly involved in the city's poetry scene, co-editing the seven issues of *Perfect Bound* (1976-79), meeting poets including Roy Fisher, Jeremy Prynne and John Matthias, and writing some of the early 'domestic interior' poems which would surface in his 1979 privately printed pamphlet *A Part of Rosemary Laxton*.

These attempts at stability and forming attachments, however, were interrupted by a series of removals as the couple, who had first met during the summer of 1971, moved from one flat to another, bought a house together and then found themselves living in and out of friends' spare rooms while they waited for it to be renovated. In 1979, the year of their marriage, there was a tectonic shift in the public sphere as well when Margaret Thatcher's Conservative government came to power with clear intentions of dismantling any notion of an existing consensus in favour of neoliberalism and an economy driven by the free market. Amongst its policies was a significant reduction in university funding.

By 1981, with his doctoral funding having run out, but with the PhD still not quite awarded, Robinson was facing another displacement, this time to West Wales where he was offered a temporary lectureship at the University of Aberystwyth. This also meant regular twelve-hour cross-country journeys to visit his wife in south London where she too had taken up a new job – in a hospice in Sydenham – and the couple had taken out a mortgage on a small house in Forest Hill. Even though the poet that he had replaced in the post at Aberystwyth, Jeremy Hooker, seemed unlikely to return, there was little prospect of Robinson's employment there extending beyond two years, let alone becoming permanent – thanks to the funding cuts being introduced by the recently elected Thatcher government – and he left after eighteen months in June 1982, around the time that the Falklands War ended.

A part-time teaching position then took Robinson back to Cambridge where he also reconnected with the city's poetry scene, organising events for the 1983 Cambridge Poetry Festival and chairing the festival committee in 1985. It was in the summer of 1981 and at Easter 1982 that he twice met Vittorio Sereni, not long before the Italian poet's death in 1983. These meetings resulted in work beginning in earnest on the translation project with Marcus Perryman which would culminate, twenty-six years after it was begun, in the publication of *The Selected Poetry and Prose of Vittorio Sereni* in 2006. By the mid-1980s, Robinson's own poetry had appeared in a series of pamphlets and books, beginning with *The Benefit Forms* in 1978, and in 1988 he was awarded the Cheltenham Prize for Literature for his first volume with Carcanet, *This Other Life*. He had also edited a collection of critical essays about Geoffrey Hill, co-founded the magazine *Numbers* and co-curated the 1988 Poetry International at London's South Bank Centre.

Securing a permanent job in the British academic world, however, was proving difficult and this, combined with difficulties in his marriage, resulted in what would be another decisive tectonic shift. Robinson was offered a year's work at Kyoto University, followed by a one-year research fellowship, and he and his wife decided that he should take up the offer, not only for financial reasons, but also as an opportunity to take stock and, if things went well personally and professionally, to consider starting a family. Robinson describes this period as follows:

> Struggling to get some kind of foothold in the British academic world during the 1980s was the kind of experience I ought to have foreseen, though it proved much more draining and demoralizing than it might have done. At interviews I was – as Eric Griffiths put it – always the bridesmaid, never the bride. Going to live and work in Japan was not predicted at all, and I remember Michael Hofmann expressing surprise that one such as me should do such a thing.

As a further complication, Robinson had met Ornella Trevisan in June 1984 and, in his own words, 'become rather infatuated in a fashion that definitely wouldn't have happened were our situation more secure in terms of my employment, our sentimental life, and habitation'. Although his feelings for her had not diminished, he was at least trying to put them behind him in the hope of saving his marriage and this too fed into his decision to accept the offer from Kyoto.

Robinson flew to Japan for the first time in March 1989. It was to be the start of what would become an eighteen-year stay. The first two of these were spent in Kyoto, where he taught in the English department of the university before moving to Tohoku University in Sendai, some two hundred miles north-east of Tokyo on the island of Honshu:

> The sense of tectonic shifts both public and private began early in my years away. When I left England, the plane flew over Alaska to get to Japan, because Soviet airspace was not open to capitalist airlines. Mrs Thatcher seemed firmly in post. Within a year, she was out of power, the Berlin Wall had fallen, China had experienced public protest on a large scale, and within another

the Soviet Union had collapsed. In the space of a further year, my marriage had also more or less gone west and I had been diagnosed with what proved to be a benign brain tumour.

Robinson returned to England in November 1992 to consult with specialists at Addenbrookes Hospital in Cambridge. Because the tumour was non-malignant, however, the operation to remove it wasn't deemed urgent and wasn't scheduled until the following May. Now estranged from his first wife, Robinson spent most of the intervening six months in Parma in northern Italy – the hometown of Ornella Trevisan. Whilst there, he received the news that, because he was unable to renew his annual contract with Tohuku University in person, he would lose his job in Japan, and that his wife was filing for divorce on the grounds of abandonment, with Ornella cited as co-respondent.

The eight-hour operation to remove the brain tumour took place at Addenbrookes on 12 May 1993. By then, the intervention of colleagues in Sendai had ensured that Robinson's contract would be renewed for the academic year beginning in September of that same year, and he spent the summer convalescing from surgery before returning to Japan in the autumn. Over the course of the next two years in Sendai, the divorce was finalised – by mutual 'no fault' consent, as it turned out – and he married Ornella as soon as he was free to do so. By then their first daughter Matilde had been born.

He was to stay working at Tohuku University until 2005 before spending his final two years as a professor at the Kyoto Women's University. It was during this time that he continued working on translations of Italian poets, as well as publishing his own poetry in two collections from Carcanet – 1997's *Lost and Found* and 2001's *About Time Too* – as well as the *Selected Poems,* which appeared in 2003. It may have been his witnessing the aftermath of the Great Hanshin Earthquake in 1995, whilst visiting friends at Kobe Women's College, and his writing about it that prompted Roy Fisher to make the oft-quoted observation about 'tectonic shifts' cited at the beginning of this chapter.

Talking about this period, Robinson says:

> It was in Japan that, oddly enough, I really started to make contact with Europe as a reality of familiar people ... My familiarity, never more than patchy and passive, with other languages – French, German, Italian, Spanish and Japanese, for

instance – also grew through reading, translating poetry, and meeting native speakers ... The university had provided us with satellite TV on our mountain overlooking the Pacific Ocean, and so we would watch the news on France 2, ZDF, CNN as well as NHK, BBC and others. I've never felt so complexly in touch and able to sense the divergences of view – as in 2003 at the time of the second Iraq War when we could hear what the French thought of it at the same time as American, British and other outlets.

This might also be considered a tectonic shift in the sense that, although he was still publishing poetry in the UK and remained in contact with UK-based poets such as Roy Fisher and Charles Tomlinson, he was no longer directly involved in the country's poetry scene – in the same way that he had been when co-organising the South Bank's Poetry International with Maura Dooley, for example – and this had initiated the change in perspective that Robinson describes above. In turn, this would lead to greater involvement with writers and greater engagement with readers in other countries and Robinson's participation in events across Europe, as well as in Japan and the USA. It would also result in poems of his being translated into Dutch, German, Italian, Romanian, Spanish, Bulgarian and Japanese. Thus, while Todd Swift described him as 'a major English poet' in the autumn 2012 issue of *Poetry Review*, it would perhaps have been more accurate to leave it at 'a major poet': the 'English' might be factually correct, but it rather suggests a variety of Englishness which doesn't at all fit with Robinson's internationalist outlook.

By 2005, however, it was starting to look as if a return to the UK might be possible. Although an application for the A.C. Bradley chair at the University of Glasgow proved unsuccessful, Robinson eventually secured an offer of a professorship at the University of Reading. The Japanese Ministry of Education had also begun to exert pressure on the country's public university system to reduce spending and Robinson had been advised to get a job at a private university instead – which is one of the reasons behind his move back to Kyoto for the last two years of his time in Japan. This renewed uncertainty about employment combined with family circumstances – both his and Ornella's parents were aging, their daughters were moving into secondary education – and a desire to overcome resentments attending his departure from the UK in the 1980s due to the political culture of the country's academic institutions at the time to make the prospect of returning seem an attractive one.

Robinson arrived in the UK to take up the professorship at Reading just as the financial system was about to crash. While he was in Japan, he had already experienced the after-effects of the land bubble bursting and seen how funds were draining away from towns and villages in northern Japan and how politics had become a matter of cleaning up the banks and re-stimulating the economy (a politics which would become all too familiar after 2008). 'Coming back to Britain,' he says

> was a curious experience in many ways. Returning meant buying a house in the Thames valley in the last days of the boom that wasn't supposed to be one – which plunged me into mortgage debt, from which I won't be free until firmly into my 70s, and the only thing that can be said for the subsequent bust that wasn't supposed to happen either is that it has issued in a period of minimal interest rates similar to those in Japan while we were there, which has made the debt less burdensome than it might otherwise have been, so far at least. We returned to what seemed an unsustainable credit culture.

Indeed, many of the things that those of us who lived in the UK got used to during the 1990s and 2000s seemed odd, if not wholly irresponsible (0% balance transfers on credit cards, cold calls from credit companies) and, when the financial crash finally happened in October 2008, it seemed to Robinson that another tectonic shift had taken place – a shift which would prompt many of the poems published in 2012's *The Returning Sky*, as well as in 2015's *Buried Music* and *For the Small Mercies* (the volume of new poems contained within 2017's *Collected Poems*).

Robinson and his family have now lived in Reading for more than a decade. As well as his work at the university, he has become the poetry editor for the Reading-based publisher Two Rivers Press and has continued to develop connections across Europe and in the USA. In 2016, he was the keynote speaker at a conference in Montenegro on writing and place at which he spoke about how art is one of the means by which we construct our idea of home.

That was on 23 June. The following morning the result of the Brexit referendum was announced and he gave a poetry reading in a restaurant in the Montenegrin city of Nikšić at which he read some of the poems that would subsequently appear in *Ravishing Europa* (2019).

Another tectonic shift had taken place. 'In some ways,' Robinson says

> the Brexit moment was simply the consequence of the failure either to respond to the [2008] crash in a more radically constructive way, or to disperse the public pain for private loss more equably. Yet whether *its* consequences will provide the political impetus to address the underlying problems in ways that can have positive results over the mid to longer term is far from clear. Again, I've found myself prompted to write by the ironies and paradoxes of what has been happening. The poems I've been writing over the last year or so, and the two political pieces, 'Balkan Diary' and 'Respecting a Decision', are probably the most overtly engaged things I've ever done. This is, of course, very much an on-going story, so perhaps it's best to leave the narrative of my life here – with the thought that we are not likely to be relieved from living through 'interesting' times for quite some while yet.

2

Many of the subsequent chapters in this volume do, of course, refer to specific events and details from Robinson's biography. Many of them, in fact, focus on work produced in relation to some of the specific 'tectonic shifts' discussed above. Tony Crowley, for example, looks specifically at Robinson's changing poetic response to Liverpool over the course of his lifelong engagement with the city, from early poems reflecting on his upbringing there to those written after he moved away and during his subsequent return visits. Ian Brinton, on the other hand, details Robinson's years in Cambridge, when the poet first arrived in the south of England and a centre of the academic establishment. Andrew Houwen and Miki Iwata both examine the poems written after the economic migration to Japan while Peter Carpenter reflects on some of the first poems Robinson wrote on returning to England in 2007 and published in the collection *English Nettles* (Two Rivers Press, 2010). Anna Saroldi, Martin Dodsworth and Adam Piette, meanwhile, discuss Robinson's ongoing relationship with Italy and with Europe as a whole – a relationship initially traumatised by the sexual assault in northern Italy and now further troubled by the prospect of Brexit, a socio-political tectonic shift, foreshadowed, at least to some extent, in *For the Small Mercies*, and responded to more fully in *Ravishing Europa*, not to mention the growing number of poems which have followed the latter's 2019 publication by Worple Press.

Again, though, this is not because one needs to know all the details of the life in order to understand the work. As Robinson himself sees it, poetry – or non-exclusionary poetry, poetry which doesn't offer up or attempt to impose a ready-made worldview – comes into being through the relationship between the 'intensely singular' viewpoint of the poet, the lyric 'I', and 'the entire culture of techniques, expectations, assumptions' that arises from and constitutes the social practice of making art.[8] It's no accident that many of the following chapters illuminate the 'intensely singular' elements within the poems whilst, at the same time, drawing attention to how they connect into social practices – be they artistic, philosophical, ethical, political and so on. Matthew Sperling, for example, brings to light 'the hidden injuries of class' which striate many of the poems and aphorisms, while Piers Pennington engages directly with how Robinson's writing negotiates with the problem of perspective – a problem also examined in James Peake's discussion of the prose fiction.

Alison Stone, meanwhile, looks at Robinson's writing as social practice in relation to its responses to and dialogue with Anglo-American poetic traditions, consequently identifying connections which have hitherto been occluded or, at best, distorted and simplified, possibly because Robinson's physical presence in other geo-cultural spheres, namely Italy and Japan, has led to a playing down of his engagement with American poetry and specifically that whose roots might be found in the work of William Carlos Williams.

In addition to examining this fundamental question about the relationship between the 'intensely singular' and the social practice of art, however, this volume will also hopefully help to define Robinson's position within the international practice of art. Even while this book has been in preparation, Robinson's poetry has been translated into a number of languages that it hadn't been rendered in before and he is gaining readers in cultures where – it's possible to speculate – he wasn't expecting to do so. He has also continued to make connections with poets writing in other languages and an internationalism which might be traced to even some of the earliest poems is certainly emerging more

---

[8] *TAP*, 138

strongly in his latest work – and, indeed, other literary and academic activity.

At the same time, at least part of the stimulus for publishing this volume is the fact that, while Robinson is mostly known as a poet, his poetry is only one – albeit a major – strand of his work. The publication of the novel *September in the Rain* in 2016 and now, in 2019, *The Constitutionals*, together with the books of aphorisms, the 2013 short story collection *Foreigners, Drunks and Babies*, not to mention the series of major academic works beginning with 1992's *In the Circumstances*, indicate the breadth of his work as it has been expanding into other, albeit related territories – and that's something I hope that this collection of essays also reflects.

If anything, in fact, the idea behind this volume began from a wholly different place to where it has reached. The initial idea was to build on the already published critical work in *The Salt Companion*, edited by Adam Piette and Katy Price, which, having been published in 2007, inevitably left open the field of Robinson's work since his return to the UK in 2008.

When discussing possible subject areas with the contributors, however, a number of things became apparent – most notably, this ongoing question regarding the role of the autobiographical, the aesthetic and the 'realist' (for want of a better term) – of the intensely singular and the socially cultural – in the work; the traceable origins to earlier writing of ethical, literary and philosophical concerns that have surfaced more significantly in more recent poetry and prose; and the often-overlooked engagement with both political and financial realities as confronted by, on the one hand, an economic migrant in Japan and, on the other, a returning economic migrant in the UK. At the same time – and as is perhaps inevitable with books of this kind – its preparation has coincided with a range of publications in all genres which perhaps wouldn't have been foreseen when the original idea came about. If the financial crisis in 2008 fed into the work Robinson published immediately after his return to the UK from Japan, the consequences of the Brexit referendum have produced, not only the 2019 Worple collection *Ravishing Europa*, but also further as-yet-uncollected poems, academic papers relating to Europe and internationalism, translations into – amongst other tongues – Spanish, Romanian, Bulgarian and Macedonian, and the psychogeographic fiction *The Constitutionals*. Not to mention studies of the sound-sense of poetry and the poetry of money.

These things being so, as editor, I would very much like to thank all the contributors to this volume who have remained tirelessly patient with the changing scope of the book as a whole and my various insistencies about incorporating the new perspectives which Robinson's most recent work has been offering. Above all, of course, I would like to thank Peter Robinson himself for being such a generous and open 'subject' – both for me, as editor of the book, and for the individual contributors. It should also be noted that Derek Slade's efforts as bibliographer for this book have gone way beyond expectations and that his contribution represents the fullest and most detailed account of Robinson's work in all forms to date.

As Peter Carpenter observes of Robinson's practice in his chapter here, citing Elvis Costello: 'Every day he writes the book'.[9] Having seen this practice in operation on the streets of Sofia (as manifested ultimately in 'Wall-to-Wall' and 'Don Quixote in Sofia' in *Ravishing Europa*), I can safely say that he does. And that, perhaps, is the entry point for all the chapters that follow: chapters about a poet and a writer, for whom things start, not with the mythological or metaphorical, but with what actually happens to ourselves in this life.

---

[9] https://www.youtube.com/watch?v=AZc9IT7h-3U&list=RDAZc9IT7h-3U&start_radio=1&t=11

Chapter 1
Of but not in Liverpool

Tony Crowley

INTRODUCTION

Born in Salford in 1953, the son of an Anglican curate, Peter Robinson moved to Liverpool's North End when his father took his first parish at St. Andrew's, Litherland, in 1956. At that point, Liverpool was 'still a thriving seaport, still a semblance of the gateway to empire it had been'.[1] Six years later, his father was relocated to Wigan, less than twenty miles geographically, but a world away linguistically, culturally, and indeed in terms of the size of the town, before finally settling back in Liverpool in 1967, in St. Michael's, Garston, in the South End. This was an unusual physical passage, from dockland to dockland (Bootle and Garston are the northern and southern endpoints of Liverpool's dock system), by way of working-class Wigan. But travelling isn't simply movement from one place to another, since all journeying has a social and cultural aspect to it. In Robinson's case, the awkwardness of a childhood marked by the social distinction of respectability, underpinned by the impecuniousness that came with his father's role as an Anglican priest in impoverished tenancies, is encapsulated in the social and spatial translation from Wigan Grammar School to Liverpool College (a public school in Liverpool which took half-fees for clergymen's sons). In addition, by his own account, the trip home every day from Liverpool College to 'the working-class, dockside village slum of Garston',[2] raised 'the inescapable question of class and, more generally, a growing awareness of divisions'.[3] It was a journey (by bus, cycle and walking) that passed through some of Liverpool's pleasantest middle-class suburbs on the way back to the church house near to Garston gas works and the railway, a crossing that appears to have reinforced the strangeness of his social position and informed the sharp class-consciousness of the early poetry.

---

[1] Peter Robinson (ed.), *Liverpool Accents: Seven Poets and a City* (Liverpool: Liverpool University Press, 1996), 137.
[2] *Liverpool Accents*, 140.
[3] *Liverpool Accents*, 139.

Though he does not claim to be Liverpudlian, it is clear that Robinson was 'shaped by the city that went from pre-fabs to post-Beatles in my childhood and youth',[4] and that his experience engendered a complicated relationship with Liverpool. He reports, for example, that as a child he felt that it was 'a place to which I had become inseparably connected, yet without ever having the sense that it was somewhere I belonged'.[5] Nevertheless, although he was born on the other side of a major identity-divide (Salford), and has spent most of his life living away from Liverpool, there is no question as to his conscious affiliation to the place: 'in Japan people occasionally want to know what my home town is, and despite the doubt about birthplace, or where most years have been spent, I always answer: Liverpool'.[6] In this respect at least, Robinson, like many others formed by the city, has learned that you can take the person out of Liverpool, but you can't take Liverpool out of the person. And yet despite the poet's deep connection with Liverpool (his parents continued to live in the city after his father's retirement), I will suggest that the sense of being *of* but not *in* this particular place will prove to be key to an understanding of the poetry that I will consider in this chapter.

HOME IS WHERE THE ART BEGINS

In a reflection on his development as a young poet, Robinson has expressed his early 'conviction that art could be made out of what surrounded you'.[7] And it is certainly the case that there is an interiority to Robinson's Liverpool poetry at times that gives it an intense specificity and localism, even perhaps at the cost of appearing slightly obtuse. Two passages from 'In the Background' illustrate the point:

> The spectator of a constancy
> not my own, and changed I see
> whether the Crescent
> is boarded up or not, the leaves
> soggy in gutters

---

[4] *Liverpool Accents*, 141.
[5] *Liverpool Accents*, 138.
[6] *Liverpool Accents*, 141.
[7] *Liverpool Accents*, 139.

>   as they might have been
> another year,
>   all the same it's unfamiliar.

Both the syntax and format of the lines present difficulties of interpretation that sit oddly with the fact that 'the Crescent' is a row of working-class shops in Garston, a disjuncture of fact and representation that suggests a determination, to use Roy Fisher's phrase, to make this place strange. The shops themselves are close to another feature mentioned in the same poem:

> Copper-oxide-coloured ledge
> slung between two brick supports,
>   the bridge
> marks the line's trajectory,
> bisected by the avenue.[8]

In this case, the railway bridge that separates leafy Mather Avenue and Allerton from Garston is personally significant to the poet, in terms of his youthful wanderings in the city, and it is indeed an important marker in the social spatiality of Liverpool, yet the lack of contextualisation makes the references potentially enigmatic.

'A Short History', by contrast, links place, class and family in ways that allow the reader more immediate access and perhaps mark a shift away from defamiliarisation. The poem focuses on the father's role as vicar, and ties it to the dereliction of the city:

>   the service finished,
> we make back through the city's
> fringes, its vanished
> forestation, wrinkled asphalt:
> a drowsing land
> where grass can reach waist height
> on central reservations, sites
> of motor industries'
> loading bays no longer manned.[9]

---

[8] *CP,* 64-5.
[9] *CP,* 69.

The importance of the father's role in the local community is represented by his speaking at a gathering of the faithful ('woven emblems ruffled, unfurled'):

> uplifted faces dad addressed
> from a lorry's back, speech amplified:
> your authorised language
> to reiterate certain promises ...[10]

A clergyman 'invested with a mysterious importance'[11] clearly has social status, but such social distinction does not necessarily convert to cash value:

> That little extra earned from funerals
> or the Easter bonuses,
> dad, the making sacrifices,
> you know what it is to want money.[12]

Indeed, given the 'equivocal privilege of the large houses we would live in',[13] the family's genteel poverty caused a double difficulty: furnishing and heating a house whose size served to mark his father out from the very community he was meant to serve. Little surprise that such circumstances produced a family of 'edgy people growing apart'.[14]

The claustrophobic frustration of the situation is conveyed in the ironically titled 'Faith in the City' – also the title of the Church of England's report on the decay of British cities, published in 1985 and co-authored by David Sheppard, Bishop of Liverpool (the report offered a searing indictment of the social effects of Thatcherism). In this poem, the poet-speaker stands, again, on Garston Park:

> I'd watch a while the Sunday League game,
> clouds and my father's parish in its hollow;
> now across those pieces
> of a swallowed industrial village, I know

---

[10] *CP,* 70.

[11] *Liverpool Accents,* 139.

[12] *CP,* 71.

[13] *Liverpool Accents,* 139.

[14] *CP,* 71.

> I shan't reach a destination –
> for avenues proliferate
> taunting each approach, crossroads appear,
> beyond a cutting and the railway station
> distances congeal, it's late
> and front doors shut
> – or be an equal of the animated faces
> who pass by, indifferent here.[15]

There is an awkward lack of confidence expressed in these lines that matches the decline of the industrial village that has been swallowed by the effects of economic 'restructuring' and all it entailed. For the speaker, all that can be articulated is the knowledge that both moving and remaining appear equally negative. The parenthesis – extended so far as to be disruptive – emphasises that once begun, there will be no end to the journeying, only multiple possibilities that taunt, choices that daunt, lines that run together into the distance, lateness and closed doors. Meanwhile, staying offers only a sense of inferiority and an inability to match the 'animated faces' indifferently passing by (there is no Yeatsian haughty disdain for the 'vivid faces' of his fellow citizens in Robinson's work).

A sense of entrapment, and of 'shame / and guilty feeling, inner rage' is also conveyed in 'Plain Money', in which the speaker addresses the father, late-night drink in hand, staring at the wall:

> – Dad, what's out there in the darkness
> where the gasworks was? A by-pass
> abandoning your parish in its hollow,
> tail lights streaming elsewhere. Do you know:
> is it worse to be corrupted by too little
> or too much? Where does money go?[16]

Garston has always been peripheral to Liverpool and was incorporated in the city only in 1902, but the opening of the by-pass in 1984 effectively divided 'the village' and cut it off even further; it became a place to pass through on the way to somewhere else – 'tail lights streaming'. Given that, the son's question to the father appears ironic

---
[15] *CP,* 78.
[16] *CP,* 79.

– too little or much of what corrupts? Nevertheless, the question of the disappearance of money recurs in the poem:

> Entrusted with an errand – you remember –
> greedy for distant places, I had spent
> mum's change on foreign stamps ...
> [...]
>   Lying to evade repayment,
> I said I'd dropped her money in the street
> where, doubtless unbelieving, she had sent me
> back into the dusk to find it.[17]

The desire for otherness – the greed for distant places – in the form of those cultural artefacts from elsewhere, foreign stamps, is fulfilled only by way of a betrayal of the mother, whose punishment is to return the child to the very streets from which he wants to escape. But as is clear from many of the Liverpool poems, the need to leave effects a deep and puzzling breach which persists:

> Whatever was thus lost, I'd not recover
> there on Bootle's pavements, eyes cast down.

Whatever border had been crossed, the way back for the guilty, searching ('eyes cast down') child was not to be found in those streets, nor in 'framing stories' to explain the offence. And so, the child realises, 'I'd have to go back home and make repentance'. If this were the conclusion, the poem would be little more than a traditional 'first sin against the parents' vignette, but Robinson's poetry is ever restless and the verse ends:

> but passing outside the Pacific Hotel – saw
> a pool of someone's sick dried on the floor –
>
> which marked how near he'd reached towards its door.[18]

Sordid though it might be, the distraction of elsewhere (the Pacific Ocean) is what catches the attention of the child, as does the fact that

---

[17] CP, 77.
[18] CP, 78.

whoever had caused the mess had almost got to the door of the pub on Stanley Road, Bootle.

Liverpool was a distressed place in the 1970s and 80s; from a high point of 867,000 in 1937, its population fell from 610,000 in 1971 to 510,000 in 1981 and 452,000 in 1991. Unemployment, poverty, poor housing and general neglect blighted the city and forced people out – for work, for education, for opportunity. The awful decline of the city, from abundance to redundance, is captured in 'The Albert Dock', a reference to what was once a centre-point of Liverpool's seven miles of docks, but which by the 1970s lay abandoned and dilapidated. In the text the poet-speaker witnesses a performance by a Baptist band, 'playing at the nineteenth century' (when the dock was at its busiest), in order

> to make the dull red sandstone
> of converted warehouse dockland
> chime once more with confidence.

Put like that, of course, the attempt seems little more than absurd:

> But now I couldn't see the sense
> and leaning on black stanchion chains
> painted solid, asked what remains
> from when this port was in its hey-day.[19]

The chains painted solid is a beautiful detail, embodying the redundancy of so much of what constituted Liverpool's past. But the question that the poem raises is what remained,

> when shops are discounting all their stock
> and some haven't even a memory of work,
> when a thin film of our past's what you get,
> the city where we grew is in debt
> to Swiss banks and the Japanese.[20]

Reduced (notice the bare rhyme 'get' and 'debt') to borrowing from foreign banks to keep the city functioning, but ultimately broken by

---
[19] CP, 168.
[20] CP, 169.

the Thatcher government, Liverpool in the 1980s faced bankruptcy, a thin version of its past, and but a memory of work, with 'none of it making much sense any more'. As the poem asks, with its repetition of 'sense', what 'meaning' remains when a brutal form of economics takes priority over human lives? Very little is the answer, and when so little is left, small wonder that so many would leave.

INTERRUPTIONS

Donald Davie's 'Winter's Talents' is a poem about a winter's train journey through England in search of 'a feelingful voice':

> Dee-side and Mersey-side
> Lie up ahead, blocked off
> In freezing fog. To them
> The voice must speak. The rime
> Dies off in the chemical reek.
> Whose swag, whose chiselled cadence
> Crusts, or whose coral, in
> Garston, Halewood, Speke?[21]

The poem seems to dismiss Garston, Halewood, Speke (three contiguous but distinct areas of 'blocked off' Liverpool), since they are separated from 'the rime' by the 'reek' of the chemical works of Widnes. Interestingly, one of Robinson's central Liverpool poems that predates Davie's work, 'The Interrupted Views', also takes the narrative form of a rail journey into Liverpool.[22] But as noted earlier, for many, leaving Liverpool is easier than getting Liverpool to leave you. And whatever the source of the city's pull, it certainly seems to be the case that the Liverpudlian sense of exile is particularly acute. Yet once the physical and cultural border has been crossed, the act of returning 'home' is a tricky and sometimes difficult process, as the poem makes clear.

A view can be interrupted for various reasons, including something that inter-venes (comes between), or a break in perspective caused by dis-traction (pulling away). In Robinson's poem, there are several views that are interrupted as the work conveys a sense of discontinuity,

---

[21] Donald Davie, *Collected Poems* (Manchester: Carcanet, 2002), 390.
[22] *CP*, 40-1.

despite the apparently reassuring notion, in the form of the poem's epigraph, that 'the world is full of home'. Adrian Stokes's observation, however, raises an important question that lingers: if the world is full of home, if there is a sense in which 'Liverpool' is 'of all places',[23] then why is there a need to go back? This rather enigmatic opening is reinforced by an impersonal, distanced tone that works against the familiar idea of the self resting safely back where it belongs.

> Sunlight on the glass
> blazes this temporary blindness,
> the passenger's,
> who gathers himself
> to his thought of returning.

The poetic voice is descriptive rather than self-assertive and presents a momentary event, a flash of sunlight that blinds the passenger who appears oddly reluctant (he needs to gather himself even to the 'thought of returning'). His gaze registers the pace of the journey as the speed of the train mocks that once dominant mode of transport on which so much was built, the canal. In this case it is the Weaver Navigation that links to the Trent and Mersey canal and thereby to the river that linked Manchester and Liverpool (and thus Robinson's actual and claimed 'homes'). But history moves on as the lock brickwork gathers moss, the canal waters are 'almost still', and the view, like memory itself, becomes a blur before disappearing entirely.

This difficult opening is superseded by a shift in tone in which the personal voice rather grandiloquently announces that 'my coming back is like the sky. / No choice in that'. The inevitability of the return, of the sky, of the traveller is somewhat undermined, however, by the bathetic weakness of the sun and the 'cloud-grey' sky reflected on the 'wavelets' (the Mersey is full of sandbanks at this easterly point). The poem marks this fall in confidence with an abrupt declaration that constitutes a key expression of the returning poet's attitude towards Liverpool: 'desire infuses regret'. It is a sharp articulation of longing pouring into sadness, yet it is curiously open and unclear. Is this the desire to escape or to return? Is it grief at having left or for the need to go back? Such indeterminacy is emphasised by the reflective ending to

---

[23] *Liverpool Accents*, 137.

the verse in which the poem hints at the view of the fields and hills of Cheshire, the Wirral peninsula and, further, the mountains of North Wales that meets the rail passenger just before crossing the Mersey: 'A feeling for landscape / we call it.' There is a curious mix here of affect and distance, a confusion signalled by the recognition of the inadequacy of the phrase ('we call it') used to describe the poet's response.

Though landscape depends on distance and a measured perspective, it is often disrupted by the unexpected actualities of place:

> But I didn't expect
> the river's inimical chill.
> The carriage window
> reflects me so.

The unfriendly cold of the Mersey (the 'mæres ēa' in Anglo-Saxon – boundary river) brings the self to a moment of reflection (the window no longer the cause of 'temporary blindness'), which is but a prelude to another interruption:

> Then a latticework
> of girder, flickering,
> black on the water a long way beneath:
> the train is crossing the rail bridge;
> the view, interrupted,
> of home, my old home –
> a low shelf of alluvial deposit.

As anyone making this journey will know, there is a brief sight of Liverpool across the Mersey as the train slowly pulls out of Runcorn, a 1960s new town built to remedy the housing crisis of its old neighbour, and it passes over the rail bridge across the river. But the view is broken by a majestic relic of high industrialism – the bridge's 'latticework of girder'– contrasted here with the estuarine alluvium on which Liverpool sits (the nickname for people from Garston is 'mudmen'). If this is arrival, however, it is qualified, for this is 'home, my old home' – in other words, in a complicated way, home, and not home.

As the train, and poem, picks up speed again, space – physical geology – becomes place as the familiar waypoints register history:

> The airport control tower,
> derelict gasworks,
> these are the landmarks.

These human marks on the land were once important. The control tower belonged to the old Speke airport that opened in 1930, played a role as an RAF base in World War Two and reverted to civilian use thereafter. While the gasworks, which abutted his father's parish church and supplied gas to the docks, stood from the 1890s. Significantly, both became redundant (the airport moved down the road to become John Lennon Airport in 1986, though the iconic gasholders were removed only recently). For Robinson, nonetheless, they serve a crucial function:

> They put us in our place
> and wanting it, I come
> back to the ash heaps,
> the car dumps, each graffito
> taken as a welcome.
>
> Mute welcomes proliferate.

Landmarks allow us to understand where we are, but there is a subtle play of agency in these lines as the power of historical landmarks is acknowledged: 'they put us in our place'. The enjambment that follows, however, allows for a re-assertion of self as desire supersedes regret to facilitate the 'come back'. This return, though, is again complicated. 'Want' signals both lack and longing – the absence of 'our place' and the urge for it – but the energy of the desire is again deflated by the specifics of reality: ash heaps, car dumps, graffiti. True to form, the poem re-turns as, suffused with the excitement of home, the poetic persona over-interprets graffiti as a form of welcome. But of all forms, graffiti is the most redolent of locality and particular meaning – an insider's medium if ever there was one. And so the 'welcomes' (the word is rather anxiously repeated), if many, do not necessarily speak to the outsider and indeed are 'mute'. Having arrived, therefore, the poet-speaker is in an odd place, as the last line of the poem indicates:

> Home is the view I appropriate.

In one reading this is an act of confident self-assertion as the poetic persona becomes both declarative and proprietorial. But there is an uncertainty here that borders on failure and sets a seal on the doubts that have haunted the poem throughout. For it is not 'home' that is appropriated, but the 'view' that stands for 'home', which is a different thing entirely. What is more, as we have seen earlier in the poem, a 'view' requires perspective, being at one remove from the thing itself. And if this 'view' is the best there is, then it speaks to a complex relationship since a 'view' demands both distance (too near and you can't see it) and proximity (too far and it becomes invisible). In this regard, perhaps the best vantage point (or 'spec' as they say in Liverpool) is to be *of* but not *in* a place, but then this produces other difficulties, to which Robinson's Liverpool poetry constantly alludes. And in any case, as the title of the poem reminds us, even the best of views can be interrupted.

Reconciliation

In 'Between Fortunes', another travel poem – away from Liverpool, 'between South Lancashire / and Victoria Coach Station' – it is made clear that whatever else draws Robinson to his hometown, it isn't nostalgia:

> Nostalgia, a disease of the soul, tries
> vainly to return you home
> through conurbations; but the bus
> soldiers on...[24]

Originally coined to mean longing for familiar surroundings or homesickness of such acuteness that it merited medical treatment, 'nostalgia' later came to signify a sentimental evocation of a time either in the general past or within the lifetime of an individual. There is little room for such sentimentality in Robinson's work (indeed for any sentimentality), but there is another possible meaning for 'nostalgia', at least etymologically, which does fit the pattern traced in 'The Interrupted Views': the pain (αλγία) caused by the return home (νόστος). Yet elsewhere in the poetry, there are clear indications of a process of 'moving on' that involves a form of settlement with Liverpool.

---

[24] CP, 115.

In 'Confetti', for example, a wedding poem set in Garston, against doubters questioning his poetic vocation – '"*Who* do you think you are?" one said, / and "*What* are you trying to prove" another', Robinson is confident enough to keep a sense of perspective:

> Today, above a guesthouse breakfast,
> the glass-framed aerial photograph
> of match-works, boulevards, points and sidings,
> river-front docks, the church, was enough
> to bring home just how few they were.

Seen from a distance, Speke boulevard, Bryant and May, the railway, Garston docks and St. Michael's church, are small indeed – a couple of miles between them – and in and of themselves, unimportant enough. Once this point has been 'brought home', it allows for a reassertion of the significance of Robinson's craft (albeit in self-mocking terms).

> The *where* had seemed more permanent
> than me, who have outlived it all the same,
> a callow prodigal who came back
> to engraft flat vistas with some meaning.[25]

Physical spaces change – Speke boulevard is now the A561, the match-works is a set of offices, the railway, docks and St. Michael's are all much reduced in terms of traffic and surrounded by new-build, but what converts space into place is the human practice of meaning-making, of which poetry is one significant mode.

A similar moment of poetic assurance occurs in 'Platt Fields', a text that narrates a return to Manchester and the grandparents' house, of which nothing remains, except 'in my imagination', a conundrum that prompts the reflection:

> Then what was it supposed to mean
> if not that the life of streets has an end
> yet something else stretches beyond?[26]

---

[25] *CP*, 134.
[26] *CP*, 293.

The question might have been posed at the end of the first line, yet the run-on conveys a sense of confidence – almost inevitability – in the answer: that 'something else' remains beyond the physical. It may be the uncertainty of memory, since the child in the poem mistakes park railings for the cemetery in which his grandfather was buried – 'in fact, he'd been cremated, / his ashes at rest I don't know where' – or the 'glimpses' and 'glances' of imagination, but it persists.

Imagination is the site on which Liverpool past and present can meet and, in an odd sort of way, be reconciled (conciliāre – to bring together either physically or in thought or feeling). Thus in 'The Red Dusk', a crowd leaves a game at Anfield, home of Liverpool Football Club:

> in a city where you simply had to know
> who'd done what on any given Saturday
> at Anfield or away.[27]

Teasingly, the reference to popular culture is underpinned by metaphors so familiar as to be almost clichés: 'painting the town red', 'the referee was blind', 'you'll never walk alone'. Yet the red dusk of that specific evening is transposed by the poetic imagination to a historical moment of greater political significance:

> You remember: a sunset was blazing on the Mersey
> where the battleship *Potemkin* – let's say – lay
> at anchor through the policemen's strike…

The Liverpool Police Strike of 1919 ('The Loot' as it was known in the local vernacular) was part of the general social upheaval and political turmoil that followed the First World War and culminated in the General Strike. But it is only in the imaginary that the *Potemkin* dropped anchor in the Mersey, since it was the battleship *HMS Valiant* that the British state sent in response to the strike (as it had ordered *HMS Helga* to the Liffey during the Easter Rising in 1916). Poetry thus yanks these two Liverpool moments together in a fanciful if effective manner, before returning us (we can take it as red / read) to the crowd streaming away from the match:

---

[27] CP, 271.

Uplifted, carried forward by a dimmed red tide,
red-nosed, red-faced, we were each being sent
off into the late light of a vast inflamed eye.

This apparent if measured sense of ease with Liverpool also appears in 'Pier Head', in which past and present again meet. As we saw earlier in 'The Albert Dock', Liverpool's dockland had become a cipher for the general decay of the city by the 1970s. But partly in response to the riots of 1981, a section of the waterfront has been transformed with the building of two outstanding museums and the siting of The Tate Gallery at the Albert Dock. Both the Merseyside Maritime Museum and the Museum of Liverpool are dedicated to commemorating precisely the type of history that the poetic persona of 'Pier Head' recalls as he looks down on the dock from the vantage point of high culture:

From gallery space at the Albert Dock
I look down on red cobblestones,
bollards, lock gates, harbour walls,
reminded of the stateless persons
who clutched their Nansen passports
on a Cunard White Star liner,
Piet Mondrian aboard.[28]

Liverpool was, historically, a refugee port – from the Irish fleeing starvation in the nineteenth century to the Russians and East Europeans in the early twentieth century who embarked for the United States, League of Nations passports in hand. The conciliating link between these two worlds – art and this specific exodus of refugees (and it is remarkable how earlier refugee crises seem to have been banished from contemporary European political thinking) is Mondrian, who fled Paris in 1938 and, on 23 September 1940, left from Liverpool for New York on the White Star liner the *RMS Samaria*.

The wretchedness of 'stateless persons' clutching bits of paper that promised a better life (whatever the reality) is capped in the second stanza of the poem:

---

[28] *CP*, 500.

> It's not
> the leaving's a-grieving, but my thoughts
> of the *Arandora Star*, torpedoed,
> its exiled alien passenger list –
> all those whose final sight of land
> had been this homely shore.

The first two lines contain a half-hidden reference to the chorus of the well-known folksong (technically a forebitter) 'The Leaving of Liverpool': 'So, fare thee well, my own true love / And when I return united we will be / It's not the leaving of Liverpool that grieves me, / But my darling when I think of thee'. And in 'Pier Head', the source of grief is also not the leaving of Liverpool, but the bitterly incongruous and tragic fate of the passengers on the *Arandora Star*, mostly Italian and German internees en route to Canada, torpedoed by a German U-boat in 1940. And yet, despite the awfulness of this event, and indeed the desperation of the White Star refugees, it is notable that the poem ends with the epithet 'this homely shore'. This can of course be read as ironic, perhaps even sardonic, but I would read the poem otherwise: as a text that recognises Liverpool as the site of difficult, awkward, tragic history, but also as a place in which re-generation is possible and which is 'homely', if not quite home.

If, as I have argued, two of the many functions of poetry are to go beyond the physical and to conciliate, its capacity in this regard is tested by the death of a loved one, since there is no more forceful and indeed brutal reminder of the persistence of the meta-physical and the need for conjoining past and present than that. 'Like the Living End',[29] dedicated to Robinson's friend David Mather (1954–2010), is significant for my reading in its use of Liverpool as the provocation of memory, imagination and poetry itself. The poem begins with lines from Eliot's 'East Coker' – 'Home is where one starts from... / ... old stones that cannot be deciphered'[30] – an epigraph that takes us from what we know to a difficulty of interpretation, a problem that recurs in the last stanza. The poem itself, however, begins again with that insistent journey into Liverpool:

---

[29] *CP*, 411-16.
[30] T.S. Eliot, *Collected Poems 1909–1962* (London: Faber & Faber, 1974), 203.

> After all the journeying
> suddenly you see it: our river
> with its reaches in their estuary light,
> the sandbank outlines at low tide
> and streams flowing forward to Seaforth.

Unlike the prospect in 'The Interrupted Views', there is no blockage here, just the sudden moment at which the full sweep of 'our', shared, Mersey can be seen, as it streams from its upper reaches out towards the Irish Sea (note the way the pace of the lines and the alliteration of the last line draws our attention to the river 'flowing forward' sea-forth). The occasion of the return is a death:

> After all, the journeying
> that took you from yourself forever
> forever returns you, though not quite,
> home being never the same –
> but come here for a funeral
> you have it, don't you, that bereavement
> in every departure, like its foretaste,
> and each return a fostering
> of distances…[31]

Though the initial line of this second stanza is lexically the same as the first line of the poem, the medial caesura creates a sense of sameness but difference that is reinforced thematically in what follows. For the 'journeying' (rather than 'journey') that took the self away is also the 'journeying' of the return home, 'though not quite', because leaving is a type of bereavement, entailing grief and loss, and return entails the recognition of distance and thus difference because once left, home is 'never the same'.

There is an impersonal tone to this stanza, with the self referenced as 'you' throughout, which sits oddly with the cause of the return, the 'forever / forever' of a sudden death that brings 'you' 'here for a funeral'. But this changes in the next stanza, as the bridge, an impediment in 'The Interrupted Views', is over-come:

---

[31] *CP,* 411-2.

> Above the bridge, an easyJet
> plane descends to the renamed airport,
> and in its higher sky's
> releases, burdens being lifted
> from you into the uneventful air
> were shaming re-stirred memories
> of girls, Dave, drunken parties,
> those all-night games of Hearts …

There is a clear sense of release here, 'burdens being lifted', as the anxiety of the return is superseded by the memory of the dead friend and youthful misbehaviours, which becomes the point from which 'you can start again'. But because the dead,

> … can't go any more,
> are out of touch, I've come
> back to a map of unvisitable places.[32]

Thus begins a journey of conciliation; not a physical conjunction, since the places are now 'unvisitable', but emotional recollection, pleasures recalled, a shared love invoked. It is a journey that turns, towards its end, into Robinson's familiar walking across South Liverpool.

> Then I'd have to get out of the house again,
> traverse old love's domain
> across Mather, this Friday morning,
> then Menlove Avenue (another pun there)
> to Quarry Street and Newstead farm,
> built from warm sandstone cut out of its hill;
> it brings home all our pining.[33]

Even the street names play with language – Mather Avenue / David Mather, Menlove Avenue / love for the male friend, or the local joke directed at girls, 'men love havin' you'– as the walk takes in Allerton and Woolton, leafy suburbs both. Woolton quarry was the source of the local red sandstone used in many Liverpool buildings, including the last great Gothic Anglican Cathedral, and it is clearly a touch-stone

---
[32] *CP,* 412.
[33] *CP,* 414-5.

for Robinson – a material prompt to 'bring home' grief. The walk continues across Allerton golf course:

> The golf course in those grounds
> of its tumble-down estate
> has columns, plinths, an obelisk
> in the local sandstone
>
> [...]
>
> Uncanny in both senses,
> life histories among neglect
> at such dilapidations,
> old stones that cannot be deciphered
> have grown forgetful now,
> as if those years had never happened...[34]

'Uncanny' has several meanings, in fact – 'careless', 'unreliable', 'mysterious' (as in Emerson's comment on Stonehenge – 'again and again a fresh look at the uncanny stones'[35]), and, of course, the Freudian sense. For Freud, repetition can produce the uncanny and there is a classic example earlier in the poem when the poet-speaker unintentionally returns to his music teacher's house, 'momentarily lost / and driven here by accident'[36]). Likewise, the remains of the estate on the golf course are also uncanny in that they are both familiar and yet disturbing and puzzling – hence the repetition of the quotation from Eliot. Perhaps the profoundest sense of the uncanny in the poem, however, is the sudden death of Mather, since death at a stroke makes what was familiar strange, unknowable and indecipherable.

In lines that Robinson leaves out from 'East Coker' in the epigraph to 'Like the Living End', Eliot declares: 'As we grow older / The world becomes stranger, the pattern more complicated / Of dead and living'.[37] For Robinson, the answer to the enigma of the strange and complex

---

[34] *CP,* 415-6.
[35] Ralph Waldo Emerson, *Collected Works of Ralph Waldo Emerson*, vol. v, *English Traits*, ed. Philip Nicoloff, Robert E. Burkholder, Douglas Emory Wilson (Cambridge, MA & London: Harvard University Press, 1994), 157.
[36] *CP,* 413
[37] Eliot, *Collected Poems,* 203.

relations between the dead and the living, the past and the present, once due respect has been paid, is co-option:

(forgive me, forgive me I'm co-opting *you* now).

But what else can I do with our dead ones
as we become people from history too?

Like Liverpool's past, Mather's death is a spur to poetry, a provocation to 'try it one more time again'.[38]

In 'Like the Living End' Robinson's treatment of Liverpool is gentler, easier, 'reconciled' even. And a further example of this later stance occurs in 'The Spelk', a poem about a local word for a splinter which embodies the relationship between language, place and memory.

Like when a window pane just after sunset
flares and lets this spelk
(yes, that's the word) or rotten wood splinter
stick in the skin of my palm...

As in 'The Interrupted Views', sunlight on glass is the occasion of this memory, though the prompt is 'spelk', a northern dialectal word that would have been familiar to an older generation of Garston South (Liverpool) Enders, probably by dint of the closer proximity of 'the village' to Widnes (and Lancashire of old) than to the city centre. Whatever the provenance, however, 'spelk' is a magical word, crossing time – 'eras and epochs of kids' minor hurt / lit up by that word' – and conjuring up the place of memory:

I'm back on a bike that's slipped through a crack
in the terrace and shot down the brew
to ramshackle sheds, hen-coops, house-ends
where streets break apart into dirt.[39]

The link between language and place is reinforced here by 'crack' and 'brew', Liverpool words meaning 'alleyway' and 'hill' respectively,[40] but

---

[38] *CP,* 416.
[39] *CP,* 318.
[40] Tony Crowley, *The Liverpool English Dictionary on Historical Principles 1850-*

the power of the image lies in the speed of the slippage between present and past. It suggests the deep, unconscious link between words and the places where we learnt them, as shown in the final lines that repeat (not quite), the beginning of the poem:

> like when a window pane just after sunset
> flares and, without a thought, thoughts revert.[41]

Conclusion: Home and Away

As the theorists tell us, space isn't place, and the difference lies in meaning: places are spaces that have been made meaningful by human beings, through their active imposition of labour, cultural practices and values on specific physical contexts. One particular form of place that holds a privileged position in contemporary poetry, and indeed criticism, is 'home', though its status is often ambivalent, ranging from the comfort of being 'at home' to the sense of the unease created by the 'uncanny' (Freud's translation of 'unheimlich', 'unhomely'). In this chapter, I have attempted to consider the ways in which Peter Robinson uses Liverpool as a way of raising questions about 'home', particularly in relation to notions of space (distance and return), place (meaning, values) and belonging (ease and discomfort). I have argued that it is possible to trace a gradual conciliation with Liverpool in the poetry, but nevertheless the question of 'home' persists. Thus in 'Owning the Problem', Robinson has an epigraph from F.H. Bradley: 'and it is but grief to have come home if one cannot return to oneself'.[42] But there is much in Robinson's work that suggests that the reverse may also be true: 'it is but grief to have returned to oneself if one cannot come home'.

In 'Recovered Memory', the poet's 'younger daughter' asks, 'Dad, is there anywhere *you* feel's home?',[43] and the question remains unanswered, though, as noted in the introduction to this essay, 'Liverpool' is Robinson's recorded response. More interestingly, perhaps, it is possible that Robinson's treatment of Liverpool in the poetry – the walking across its distinct areas, the exploration of its

---

2015 (Liverpool: Liverpool University Press, 2017), s.v. crack, brew.
[41] *CP,* 319.
[42] *CP,* 359.
[43] *CP,* 352.

natural and social history, the respect for its culture and language – reveals a more general attitude to the practices that constitute 'home' as a place to be made rather than a space that exists (hence the possibility that 'the world is full of home'). In that sense, it could be said that for Robinson, being *of* but not *in* a place complements being *in* but not *of* a place, in that both allow for a profound understanding of the complexity of being home and away at one and the same time. It is the difficult and painful, tough and sharp, yet sometimes light and joyous, rendering of that complexity that distinguishes Robinson's restless but wonderfully sustained poetic achievement.

Chapter 2
Not Feeling at Home:
The Hidden Injuries of Class

Matthew Sperling

1

'If misery is handed down from generation to generation,' Peter Robinson writes in aphorism 40 in *Spirits of the Stair*, 'then it's no surprise that when I'm angry or depressed you hear the sounds of an eighteenth-century farm labourer who finds himself forced to beg for work in a factory slum.'[1]

The opening phrase puts us in the orbit of Philip Larkin's line, 'Man hands on misery to man', in 'This Be the Verse',[2] but makes the matter more tentative. Robinson takes Larkin's settled view on a truth about life as a possible line of thinking to be pursued and tested out instead. The tentativeness befits the tentative form of the prose aphorism (just as Larkin's ringing certainty befits his four-square tetrameters). The second half of Robinson's compound proposition ('If ... then ...') departs from Larkin's version of inherited misery by shifting the emphasis away from the familial and domestic ('They fuck you up, your mum and dad') and towards the social and economic. The comparison might at first seem incongruous, even distastefully so: surely the unhappy things in the life of someone who makes his living by teaching, reading and writing bear no comparison to those in a life of real penury and physical hardship? But the misery of the imagined ancestor comes not from hardship and toil in themselves, but rather from the enforced change in his situation. A life of farm labour is likely hard and limited in its freedoms, but could still be dignified in its oppression, and a source of self-respect within a community of shared values; the trouble comes when industrialisation disrupts this settled life with the degrading conditions and stern discipline of factory work.

So what is the equivalent of this in the life of a poet and academic? Aphorism 200 in the same book suggests one sort of answer:

---
[1] *STS*, 16.
[2] Philip Larkin, *The Complete Poems*, ed. Archie Burnett (London: Faber and Faber, 2012), 88.

> 'Whose creature are you?' asked a distinguished professor of literature as we sat down to lunch. 'And how is it you live?' Though in my mid-twenties, I was so naïve about how this world worked that the first question made no sense, and, when he explained, I could only reply that I was no one's. To the latter, I said I was making ends meet with bits of part-time teaching. Now, I realise, his questions were not of that kind at all. To the first I should have replied: 'Pray tell me, sir, whose dog are you?' And to the latter: 'Employment hazardous and wearisome!' But, on second thoughts, no, my clay-footed half-comprehension was by far the better way to get out of there alive.[3]

The young man that the writer once was finds himself in a world different from the one he was raised in. Not yet fluent in the codes of Oxbridge high-table wit, not understanding the rules of the game he has been invited to play, he assumes that the fault lies within himself and that he is, in some way, *wrong* ('naïve', 'clay-footed'). Later, from his retrospective position, he knows the rules of the game: rather than speaking with candour about the material conditions of one's life, one must flash back with apt quotations from Pope or Wordsworth, appropriately ironised to smooth over the sharp edges of early-career precarity. But the same knowledge gained with age enables him to see that the fault lay not within him but in the world itself; that the proving of his worth in the eyes of the distinguished professor would have come at too high a cost in damage to his own sense of dignity and self-respect. Better to 'get out of there alive', even if that impulse sends you away from Cambridge to a university position on the other side of the world in Japan.

The unhappiness of both the uprooted farm labourer and the baffled young poet-scholar results from what sociologists call *status incongruity*. The life they know has been disrupted by a move into a different context, with material conditions, values, codes and expectations different from those they are familiar with, and this has caused feelings of indignity, doubt and inadequacy which damage one's sense of self-worth. I have taken this formula from *The Hidden Injuries of Class*, Richard Sennett and Jonathan Cobb's study of the tangle of feelings provoked by post-war patterns of social mobility in the minds of people who were primarily its beneficiaries. In interviews

---

[3] *STS*, 24.

with and observations of American people who have moved out of the working class into the affluent middle class, Sennett and Cobb uncover and analyse the feelings of discontent, inadequacy and injured dignity that can attend this move, showing how 'an increase in material power and freedom of choice' is very often 'accompanied by a crisis in self-respect'.[4] In this view, the winners and the losers equally suffer the psychic wounds of living in a class society.

2

Robinson's *Collected Poems* opens, as did his *Selected Poems* of 2003, with the poem 'Worlds Apart', first published in *Perfect Bound* in 1976. Whether it is in fact the earliest written poem in the book is not clear, but it is now presented as the first poem in his oeuvre. This is a position of some importance. Other poets of recent years – think of Seamus Heaney's 'Digging', Geoffrey Hill's 'Genesis' or Ted Hughes's 'The Thought-Fox' – have selected a first poem for editions of their selected and collected works that figures as a self-conscious origin myth. That's not quite Peter Robinson's style, but 'Worlds Apart' nonetheless establishes some of the crucial concerns of his early poetry. In short order, at the beginning of the poem we get a snapshot of some urban topography; a sense of the effects of widespread unemployment on a group of people; a snippet of the idioms of the British pub, with its rituals of round-buying, camaraderie and so on, that also perhaps carries a wider implication about the repetitiveness and narrowness of a life constrained by a class-conditioned lack of freedom; a historical understanding of patterns of economic migration; and we're off!

> Sweltering brick
> and a smell of sticky tarmac,
> dazed, the ambience
> at the street corner,
> where men, they're jobless,
> were drawn out by sun,
> mused on far-off places,
> a next pint, 'the same again'.

---

[4] Richard Sennett and Jonathan Cobb, *The Hidden Injuries of Class* (New York, NY: W. W. Norton, 1993), 29.

> And some did go
> some thin dawn
>   from quiet, grey wharves
> out through the Manchester Ship Canal
> to Chicago.⁵

Out of this 'world', sketched in with a light touch, and yet thick in its description of how lives, livelihoods, places and circumstances interrelate, Robinson's grandfather steps forward in the fourth stanza, and the poem floats one of the major and vexing questions of British social history. How is it that members of the British working-classes have so often acted and voted against their own material interests? Why was there never a proletarian revolution?

Robinson's understanding of the psychological tangle of feelings that arises from people's relation to their own material and social circumstances is subtle enough to hint toward the reasons:

> A photograph displays him:
> sepia, jaundiced, thin.
> He voted Baldwin,
> would hardly accept the Co-op divvy.
> Who he was
>   in his suit and large trilby,
> hugging a white hen,
> his death and his own obfuscations
> have blurred.
>   It catches something:
> fixed, so proud, in his fenced-round
> plot of ground,
> thinking himself a propertied man.⁶

The grandfather who votes for the Conservative Prime Minister Stanley Baldwin even during the era of the General Strikes and the Trades Disputes Act in 1926–7, and who refuses the money that the mutualised Co-operative Party would pay back to him as a customer of its shops (and that a Conservative Chancellor, Neville Chamberlain, managed to tax), has taken from his experience of living in a class society the idea

---

⁵ *CP*, 21.
⁶ *CP*, 21-22.

that property-owners are more worthy of respect. Likewise, in his mind there are fine gradations of dignity to be found between different kinds of employment: 'An ads rep for a store, he'd say, / though only a door-to-door / vacuum cleaner salesman.' If the difference in dignity between selling physical commodities door to door and selling the abstract commodity of advertising space is enough to lie about, the difference between being a 'propertied man' or a mere worker is certainly enough to distort a realistic sense of one's self and social relations; the grandfather has so far internalised the idea that being middle class is superior to being working class that he thinks of himself as wealthy even to the extent of acting in ways that impede the improvement of his own conditions and rejecting money that is rightly his. The poem does its work in the gap between the Marxist ideas of class *in itself*, as an objective description of differences in income, wealth, occupation and so on between different people, and class *for itself*, as people's subjective awareness of themselves as members of a class with shared histories, interests and objectives. The danger here would be for the poem to adopt a superior, condescending view on this, imputing 'false consciousness' to the poet's less well educated elder, but Robinson avoids this danger by exercising a cautious sympathy for the imaginative project the grandfather is engaged in.

> Rule of thumb,
>   plain common sense
> he clings to, attaches some little order
> to his circumstances, patched
> with that easy romancing.[7]

And towards the end of the poem we are told, regarding the man's relation to his wife, that 'what he looks for / in those eyes / is her recognizing him'; that even with the 'obfuscations' and 'half-lies', 'his world suffices'.[8] To attach order to one's circumstances; to seek recognition in the face of the other; to make one's world into a liveable, sufficient space: the impulses sound somewhat similar to those that give rise to the wish to write a poem.

---

[7] *CP*, 22.
[8] *CP*, 23.

3

However much writers and intellectuals occupy an ambiguous class position (in Bourdieuan terms, they are a subordinated fraction of the dominant class), to make your living as a writer and university teacher represents a definite case of upward mobility for 'a vicar's son [...] brought up in a series of poor, urban parishes in the industrial north west of England' (not to mention someone descended from farm labourers).[9] Robinson has a nuanced view of his class origins: in his own account, he comes from 'a fairly cultured and artistic family', with both his parents the first in their families to have gone to university. As a vicar's son, he could attend Liverpool College, a Victorian-era public school that has since become an Academy, as a day boy on a clergy scholarship. His upbringing in poor neighbourhoods in the north-west therefore caused class alienation in both directions: he was both a little too middle-class to be at home among the poor children of his father's parishes and a little too provincial to be at home at Cambridge or in the literary world. 'I feel a sense of displacement practically all the time', Robinson has said. 'That's how I perceive the world.'[10]

The roots of this sense of displacement lie, for him, in his childhood experience of moving around frequently as his father was sent to new parishes and of always being set apart from the other children by the unasked-for status his father's vocation gave him:

> Vicarage children have a built-in sense that they don't quite belong: they get told it by the kids from the local church school, and if they are growing up in poor parishes, then there may well be wildly discrepant assumptions of class and cultural difference in the mix too. [...] Being the local vicar's son, and a bit clever, I got bullied and had to learn how to get away from dangerous people.[11]

These are experiences shared by many people, but what is unusual in Robinson's case is the precision with which this understanding of

---

[9] *TAP,* 9. See also the memoir, 'Liverpool … Of All Places' for more on the background of his childhood in Peter Robinson (ed.), *Liverpool Accents: Seven Poets and a City* (Liverpool: Liverpool University Press, 1996), 137-141.
[10] *TAP*, 84.
[11] *TAP*, 10 & 121.

class difference in childhood informs his adult sense of literary and intellectual life. His sense of not quite belonging, he says, 'produced a sense of protective detachment from situations that may have helped to stimulate a poet's stance towards the world'.[12]

Protective detachment means that if you don't fully belong to the society you are thrown into, if you can stand back from it a little bit, that society can't hurt you so much. In Robinson's account, this leads naturally into his positioning within the poetry world in a place of 'non-aligned formal eclecticism',[13] and his scepticism towards poetic schools, group allegiances, aesthetic factions and metropolitan cultural power-broking among his contemporaries. Discussing the neighbourhood bullies of his childhood, he regrets the fact that he 'didn't learn well enough [...] how to spot at sight an intellectual bully'; discussing his early relation to the Cambridge avant-garde, and to the Geoffrey Hill/Christopher Ricks axis of poetry and criticism, Robinson remarks how he 'had to put a certain distance between myself and both of those more secure circles of power and influence' (*to get out of there alive*, he might have added).[14] And the distance he has put between himself and the avant-garde was driven by reservations about the political claims made on its behalf and its class limitations. First, on the idea that the advanced poem ought to 'destabilise' the lyric self:

> I found myself growing more and more out of sympathy with this notion of what serious poets were meant to be about. Were they really destabilizing their own? It was supposed to be political, but where I grew up there were all sorts of social and personal problems, with political implications, that came from people having rather weak identities that were being fiercely buffeted by their social circumstances.[15]

Second, on the avant-garde politics of form:

> We're each of us to some degree or other complicit with those who have power. Writing a curiously asyntactical, dictionally heterogeneous, or oddly lineated bit of text has practically no

---

[12] *TAP*, 10.
[13] *TAP*, 11.
[14] *TAP*, 121-2.
[15] *TAP*, 62.

relation to that difficult fact. It can perhaps signal the desire to be less complicit; but it doesn't in itself make you any less so.[16]

In both cases, the highly developed codes shared by a group of highly educated and privileged people – aesthetic codes which are also behavioural codes – need to be rejected in order to protect the independence informed by early experience of the difficult and painful realities of class division.

There are artistic advantages to not belonging. If 'you are a provincial and a slow-starter with, as a result, little access to power and preferment', Robinson says, and if you can 'get used to the wilderness', it might be possible to 'thrive like the rosebay willowherb on a railway-line embankment'.[17] The sense of not belonging extends to Robinson's model of the literary line he is working in. When asked by an interviewer, 'Do you feel part of any English tradition?', his answer tellingly conflates the history of poetry with the history of regional labour:

> My mother's relatives were working people from the North East, and I feel affection for Basil Bunting. My father's brother wore himself out in the Birmingham car industry and Roy Fisher was the poet who most helped me find my way when young.[18]

The relation between the first and second halves of those two sentences doesn't need to be made explicit; tradition is found in the linkages between the histories of family, forms of working-class life, and literature. This is what shapes the influences on Robinson's early work: 'I [...] must have seen myself as attempting to find my way following a line of non-metropolitan, northern and north-midlands poets that would include Basil Bunting, Roy Fisher, Charles Tomlinson, and Donald Davie.'[19]

Robinson's way along this line couldn't help but be diverted by changes in British society since he started writing in the 1970s. The work of Tomlinson, Davie and Fisher – along with that of Geoffrey Hill, another early reference point for Robinson, and poets like Ted Hughes and Tony Harrison – was touched by their shared experience of being transplanted to a different class from that of their parents through

---

[16] *TAP,* 127.
[17] *TAP,* 122.
[18] *TAP,* 24.
[19] *TAP,* 40-41.

expanded educational possibilities. They all established themselves as poets during the era of the Welfare State, 1945–79. The literary narrative of post-war social mobility – what Douglas Dunn, writing about Tony Harrison, has called 'the scholarship boy's revenge' – is in some ways a familiar one. But things look different for a poet born in 1953, who is coming to maturity as a writer at the moment when the neoliberal era begins in Britain with the election of Margaret Thatcher and the relative social mobility of the post-war settlement begins to be eroded.

Throw in the defeat of organised labour, the privatisation of public services, the Majorite ambition to create a 'classless society' and the Blairite distancing of the Labour party from its socialist origins, and the outlook for a non-metropolitan poet exercised by class division does not look promising.

Note that the non-metropolitan writers Robinson names are also among the most internationalist English poets of their time. Robinson's deep engagement with poetry in several languages and time spent living in other countries is likewise following in their line. For the poet who doesn't belong, who experiences sharp alienation at living in a class-divided society, being abroad provides a sort of solution to the question of displacement by giving it a more obvious face:

> For a foreigner not to feel at home in Japan is normal. But not feeling at home in England where I didn't find a job, where my marriage went wrong, and where the political culture has been going through a long drawn out phase of moral and managerial self-deception, hypocrisy, and contempt for others … that's a different matter.[20]

There is a distinguished English tradition of writers from working-class backgrounds – think of D. H. Lawrence or Anthony Burgess – for whom exile was preferable; in Taormina or Monaco, one can simply be English in a way that is impossible while living and working in a native country where one is always classmarked by accent and habituation. If you don't feel at home, the best move is to head for a place where you will not be at home: 'you are freed at a stroke from the innumerable ways in which a native culture sets the agenda and delineates the pale of thought and feeling.'[21]

---

[20] *TAP*, 25-6.
[21] *TAP*, 14.

In *Minima Moralia*, Theodor Adorno tells us that 'it is part of morality not to be at home in one's home'.[22] Property ownership in an unequal society is a form of self-betrayal; shelter and comfort have become impossible in the knowledge of how your having them systematically denies them to other people; 'not to be at home in one's home' is therefore the only ethical response, though also self-wounding and self-defeating. ('Wrong life,' after all, 'cannot be lived rightly', as Adorno famously concludes this aphorism.) I quote the standard English translation by E. F. N. Jephcott, but Adorno's original German reads: 'es gehört zur Moral, nicht bei sich selber zu Hause zu sein' – which is more like, *it is part of morality not to be at home with oneself.* In this light, Robinson's experience of feeling 'a sense of displacement practically all the time', of maintaining 'a sense of protective detachment' from the world as his particular version of the 'poet's stance', is also a mode of last-ditch ethical response to the prevailing injustices of living in a class society.

4

So 'Sweltering brick / and a smell of sticky tarmac,' are the first two lines of Robinson's *Collected Poems*. Two pages further on, Robinson describes L. S. Lowry as a painter 'Enraptured by brick and dirty stone' ('A Homage'). And then we get: 'Set against the ochre brick-work' ('The Benefit Forms'); 'Moss on lock brickwork' ('The Interrupted Views'); 'Workmen pile chipped bricks / unevenly' ('Going Out to Vote'); 'a red brick house' ('Tokens of Affection'); 'the squat red brick' and 'Copper-oxide-coloured ledge / slung between two brick supports' ('In the Background')[23] … In the course of the next 500 pages, the words 'brick', 'bricks' or 'brick-work' occur fifty-five times – which is good going, considering that Robinson spent almost twenty of his middle years living in Japan, where bricks are almost never used as a construction material.

Robinson makes this territory distinctly his own in his awareness of how urban topography comes to be inscribed in people's mental lives. The bricks are bricks of the mind, as much as features of an empirical reality that could be mapped back onto any existing city. 'If this blank's

---

[22] Theodor Adorno, *Minima Moralia: Reflections on a Damaged Life*, trans. E. F. N. Jephcott (London: Verso, 2005), 39.
[23] *CP*, 23, 27, 40, 54, 60 & 63-64.

not written on, / then you read the brick like braille', as the closing lines of 'In the Background' have it.[24] The material forms of the rundown, the decaying, the de-funded, the derelict, the makeshift are the things from which a sense of the relation between the self and the social are made. 'They put us in our place', Robinson writes in 'The Interrupted Views', narrating a return to the landmarks of his childhood.[25]

The ambition to 'read the brick like braille' speaks to Robinson's sense of how thoroughly imbricated speech-acts are with the social fabric. An important text here is 'The Draft Will', a prose work included in *Untitled Deeds*, which, Robinson has said, 'began life as a memoir back in 1993-4' and was 'the first piece of writing in which I began to explore the ways that speech acts might impact, or have impacted, on my father's family'.[26] The grandfather who appears in 'Worlds Apart', written in the mid-1970s, reappears in this prose text of nearly twenty years later. It covers some of the same territory as 'Worlds Apart', only with a more self-conscious sense of the relation between the poet's speech-act in producing the text and the speech-acts of his ancestors; the poet is implicitly contrasted with the grandfather who 'won prizes for his poultry' rather than his poetry.[27] Section 17 of the text reproduces verbatim a document from the archive of Robinson's family history – 'This is the last will and testament of me Thomas Fisher Robinson'[28] – and pokes around in the story of illegitimate birth quietly lodged within it. But the speech-act is, in the terms of J. L. Austin, 'infelicitous': the deletions and insertions which have not been initialled invalidate it as a legal document, and the acts of witness and bequest that it attempts to perform thereby fail.

A poet like Tony Harrison would make much of the disparity between his own advanced literacy and such a botched utterance on the part of his working-class forebears. In Robinson's hands, the poet and the grandfather seem more to be working in the same territory: 'It was only a draft will, no more nor less able to make things happen than a poem.'[29] This is not to say that the will and a poem are *completely* unable to make things happen, but rather that they both fall short of

---

[24] *CP*, 66.
[25] *CP*, 40.
[26] *TAP*, 124.
[27] *UD*, 84.
[28] *UD*, 86.
[29] *UD*, 89.

the constituted authority of a legal document or the official utterances of a judge or vicar when performed in the right circumstances, and instead find a second-order ability to make things happen in the way in which one person's mental life can have an influence on another's.

Class is, among other things, a linguistic construct. Differences in wealth, income, occupation, opportunity, access to education and healthcare and so on are real facts in the world, but an empirical study of these things alone will only tell you so much about class, because class lives primarily in the ways in which people relate to, think and speak about these facts. This is where poetry has an advantage, in some ways, over sociology and other disciplines that might want to address the matter; if poetry is the most linguistically self-conscious of endeavours in writing, it is also the one that can work itself most subtly into the ways in which class is shaped by speech-acts.

Let us consider 'The Benefit Forms', the first of Robinson's poetic sequences to be preserved in *Collected Poems*. As much as the poem occupies the territory of social realism, setting up shop in the dole office during a period of high unemployment caused by deindustrialisation and the crushing of organised labour, its purview is also linguistic, giving us a wide range of examples of the ways in which 'bureaucracy's / clarity of name'[30] shapes, collides with, bullies and coerces the lives of ordinary people. In the first section, after the office opens and 'that class of person / inundates the place', a couple are impelled to answer questions in ways that deform the reality of their lives:

> He voices
> and she echoes
> guesses to questions
> misconceived.[31]

The same topic is approached from the opposite point of view a page later, when the 'you' who is the benefits inspector becomes the addressee: 'you want them / to sign a form that says they are lovers. / It's called co-habitation'.[32] And then the poet himself, or at least his first-person poetic avatar, is caught up in the same trap of language:

---

[30] *CP*, 31.
[31] *CP*, 25.
[32] *CP*, 26-7.

> 'Medium build,' the writing says
> 'for labouring' or thinned
> I am to 'something clerical'. [...]
>
> The trick of self-possession treats
> my lack of trade or skill
> to name and fit me into.
>
> Set against the ochre brick-work,
> that young man, I am,
> who misremembers
> where he's going.[33]

The words 'I am' are shifted from the positions in which we would expect to find them in idiomatic English – a feature of Robinson's writing that Eric Griffiths has named 'the egotistical demure'.[34] But the unusual positioning of the 'lyric I' here arises less from reticence about the overweening presence of the self in poetry and more from the ways in which the self is buffeted, knocked around and forced into awkward positions by its relation to the institutions of social power. The 'young man [...] misremembers / where he's going' only to the same extent to which he is alienated from where he comes from; returned to his home town after education had enabled him to leave it, he is now more suited to 'clerical' work than labouring. He has also misplaced his relationship to language:

> Then my turn comes.
> I've lost my tongue.
> Some say it degrades,
> but I don't know what to say.[35]

The lines are at once a confession of linguistic failure and a manipulation of poetic ambiguities handled with high sophistication. If, as Robinson has said, one of the effects of class alienation is that you 'feel a sense of

---

[33] *CP*, 27-8.
[34] Eric Griffiths, 'Blanks, Misgivings, Fallings from Us', in Adam Piette and Katy Price (ed.), *The Salt Companion to Peter Robinson* (Cambridge: Salt Publishing, 2007), 56.
[35] *CP*, 26

displacement practically all the time', it is here that the feeling is most painfully, but also most fruitfully felt, in the injuries of class sustained directly on the tongue.

Chapter 3
'Onward, glancing back again': Cambridge

Ian Brinton

In the early poem 'How He Changes'[1] Peter Robinson guides the reader through a mapping of how a work of art can be created. The opening recollections of a narrative from the past have a stilted and grey lifelessness as 'acquaintances spoken of / move dumbly'. His painter's eye notes that there is 'An ivory grey / blankness in their atmosphere' which chokes the free-running movement of recall. The progress towards objectivity is gradual as his focus concentrates, like a camera lens, upon particularities of landscape:

> No longer reminded
> of surnames, entanglements, jokes,
> he sees the road's curve,
> grass verges, old road-house
> anew.

That emphatic single-word line presents the reader with a flash of insight and, moving round the curve in the road, the persona evoked throughout the poem is prompted to take a route which eradicates the 'history' and 'remorse', both of which are personal reminiscences; indeed, they are taken 'right out of view'. The last stanza has a fuller sense of ease and sounds like the words of a man who has achieved his objective:

> He'd come round to recounting the story
> and found in his recall
> no trace of former entrapments.

Those entrapments, 'trammels' as Charles Olson called them in his poem 'As the Dead Prey Upon Us' in which he cried out to 'disentangle the nets of being', suggest the ill-defined world of sentimentality and nostalgia for a past which exists in mere vagueness. As the poetic

---
[1] *CP*, 35-36.

persona 'turns the first corner', with its nod in the direction of Eliot's 'Ash Wednesday', he sees now a past landscape in a less subjectively possessive way:

> What he sees
> – grass, leaves, roofs, chimneys –
> are only themselves
> and the sky like a blank drawing board
> stands out, indifferently blue.

This early poem was published in 1980's *Overdrawn Account* where it consisted of two sections. Robinson removed the second section for the 2003 *Selected Poems* and as one looks at the energetic movement forward in the first section one can see why that decision might have been taken. The first part of 'How He Changes' has echoes of Pierre Reverdy's 'Comme on change', a poem which opened with the request for someone else to tell the story. The opening line had a pleading tone for another voice to take responsibility for recounting or narrating the past:

> Qu'on nous raconte cette histoire
> Qu'on nous dise ce qui'il est devenu
>
> Let somebody tell the story
> Let somebody say what happened to him
>   (trans. Kenneth Rexroth)[2]

Reverdy's poem concluded with the poet voyaging alone into 'L'ombre sans écho' ['echoless shadow']. He has seen 'le ciel le mur la terre et l'eau' ['heaven, wall, earth, water'] and recognised that 'Ce n'était plus du tout le même / Au coin quand il s'est retourné' ['It's not the same at all any more / At the corner when he turns around']. As the poem's narrator turns his first corner in 'How He Changes', echoing that turning at the third stair in Eliot's poem, his vision is of clarity: grass, leaves, roofs, chimneys – an industrial landscape from childhood reminiscence but untainted by sentimental evocation. These objects are 'only themselves' and the sky stands out 'indifferently blue'.

---

[2] Pierre Reverdy, *Selected Poems* (London: Cape, 1973), 40-41.

The second section of 'How He Changes' as it appeared in *Overdrawn Account* offers a proximity to experience which is a far cry from the movement towards artistic distance felt for in section one. It opens with a detailed memory from childhood:

> Out in the open;
> dusk closing in;
> thin grass runs
> down the slope of the playing field
> to a row of small houses.³

Although here too there is an echo of the Reverdy poem in which 'La rue est noire' ['The street is black'] and 'La nuit vient doucement' ['Night comes softly'], the focus is upon an actual scene remembered. The use of a pronoun a few lines further on lends a Wordsworthian air to a childhood reminiscence:

> Stood on this rise
> he can feel vestiges
> of an obscured
> need to run back
> out of fear in the settling darkness,
> signified by the amber streetlamps
> now coming on.

This world of personal reminiscence sits uneasily after the objectivity pursued in section one of 'How He Changes', and it came to find a re-written location in the later novel of personal reminiscence, *September in the Rain*:

> No, running home to mum was not the answer. And picking up on the uneasy silence that followed, Alice let the topic drop. There and then, in the empty street, she took my arm. Side by side, as lovers do, towards her room, we walked – me gratefully taking a last glance back towards the houses, their laundry waving its offered surrender, and the street lights' globes of amber on their arching concrete poles.⁴

---
³ *OA*, 27.
⁴ *STR*, 96.

Perhaps it is that use of the word 'mum', as well as the domestic gestures of 'took my arm' and 'Side by side' accompanied by the naked response of gratitude, that evokes the personal nature of the reminiscence. If so, then the moving sense of attempting to give formal boundaries to a past long gone which Robinson achieves in the short autobiographical sketch, 'Hit the Road, Jack' (composed for the centenary of Linacre Infants and Junior School and published in 2015's *The Draft Will*) is reflective of an increased desire for an objective assessment of the past. The formality of the reconstruction is there in the precision of the writing as Robinson recalls the world of the early 1960s:

> There were two playgrounds, divided by a wall. The one on the left, if you were facing towards the Mersey, was for the Infants; the larger one on the right, for the Juniors.[5]

With the introduction of a class photograph, 'a black and white class photo that lay around unconsidered in my parents' house for years and years', the past tense shifts to the present as a long-gone world is brought back into focus and figures unmet for sixty years emerge out of a darkness:

> On my immediate left in the photograph is Barbara Penny. On the other side of her is Colin Wells. On the back row, three from the left is Billy Morrison. When the school's centenary was announced in Liverpool, with a call for memories and memorabilia, Billy heard about it from his family, found me on the Internet, and sent a message from British Columbia, in which he added some more names to the faces.

Prompted by the catalyst, the photograph, 'It comes back to me as I write that we learned how to tell the time in this class', and Ray Charles' song 'Hit the Road, Jack' emerges from the shadowy background of being a US number one and a UK number 6 hit in 1961:

> I can recall clearly standing on the asphalt of the playground of the Junior School at about home time thinking it would certainly hurt if you hit the road, and wondering why Jack would want to do it anyway.

---

[5] *TDW*, 63.

Similar to the way in which a photograph prompts the past to leak through into the present we become aware, as readers of 'Lawrie Park Avenue' in 2012's *The Returning Sky*, of an erased past shadowing forth into the clarity of the poem's present. That poem concludes with a reference to a deleted figure hovering in the background:

> But lacking such things to do with the past,
> like this figure he had painted out
> who fills the air with an indelible stain,
> there'd be no possibilities.
>
> They thicken into leaf, his flanking trees.
>
> Look, now, it's as plain as plain.[6]

The poem is dedicated '*Camille Pissarro, 1871*', and the palimpsest nature of the past seems to wink at the viewer of the French artist's early gouache sketch of 'The Avenue, Sydenham'. The sketch was made as an early study for the oil painting which hangs in the National Gallery and in it one can indeed see a female figure whose 'pentimenti could be seen / still on the gravel, advancing towards me, / as a darker stain': the past is in fact ineradicable.

This movement towards bringing out into the open a hidden sense of what lies lurking and potent in the past, what seems to be hidden waiting to be brought to light, informs Robinson's lifelong preoccupation with the work of Adrian Stokes. In 1981 he edited Stokes's *Collected Poems* for Carcanet Press and referred in his introduction to the art critic's attitude towards carving, highlighting its difference from the modelling involved in the making of sculpture. He suggested that the 'carver' responded to the 'otherness' of his stone and in doing so was 'looking for a form that is already present in the marble, to make what he imagines is already there reveal itself. In *Colour and Form*, Stokes had written:

> In old pictures, as well, sometimes the backgrounds of portraits seem to be the material upon which, we feel, the artist has worked and from which he has elicited his foreground forms.

---

[6] *CP*, 395.

> Thus the background possesses some significance apart from its negative role in showing up the figure. A certain tension and equality, the tension of the spread object, obtain throughout.[7]

This steady emergence of a form contained within a larger structure is what is hinted at in Robinson's early 'How He Changes' and we are prompted to recognise an echo of William Carlos Williams's enumeration of exactness in 'By the road to the contagious hospital'. That poem from 1923 had appeared in *Spring and All* and was immediately preceded by the statement 'THE WORLD IS NEW'. In Williams's picture of spring's newness (written almost precisely to distinguish it from Eliot's *The Waste Land* of the previous year) we read that 'One by one objects are defined' and they appear with the 'stark dignity of / entrance'. In 'How He Changes' Robinson's past emerges with a similar starkness of outline and what he sees is 'grass, leaves, roofs, chimneys', which are presented as 'only themselves'. It comes then as no surprise that in his introduction to Stokes's poems he should recognise the opportunity to 'condense and realise':

> His creative activity is a thinning out of the stone block. Conscious as he must be of the grain, the hardness and points of fracture in the block, he must be respectful of his material to coax from it a shape lying within, revealed by the flaking-off, the reducing process of stone carving.[8]

What appears important for Peter Robinson is what he also calls 'an emergence projected by the artist into the stone, minimizing the temporal element by visualizing it presented on an object's surface'. When Donald Davie reviewed this edition of Stokes's poems for the *Times Literary Supplement* in April 1982 he highlighted one poem for which he had some particular respect, 'At Night (I)'. Davie noted how Stokes had attempted to articulate the precise quality of sensuous experience and focused upon the way the poem gives life to the sound of suburban electric trains at night:

---

[7] *The Critical Writings of Adrian Stokes* (London: Thames & Hudson, 1978), Vol. II, 40.
[8] *The Collected Poems of Adrian Stokes* (Manchester: Carcanet Press, 1981), 6.

> These passing links of sound change to an upright thread
> Soar in joints and spokes that square the firmament [9]

In Stokes's poem sound seems to create a structure with the word 'upright' and the architectural sense is then promoted with 'soar', 'joints' and 'spokes' before the mathematical aspect of a building is presented with the verb 'square' with its echo of the concluding lines of Andrew Marvell's 'A Dialogue between the Soul and Body'. Davie links this movement with those recollections of stone building that kept up the spirits of Ezra Pound incarcerated in his Pisan cage:

> For Pound *in extremis*, in *The Pisan Cantos*, was stayed and comforted time and again by just what the young Stokes so compellingly purveyed – a well-curb, a coign of worked marble, some emblem out of Renaissance Rimini or Venice or Urbino, figurative or not, in either case magnificently enhanced by what Stokes first perceived and named as stone-bloom or stone-blossom (lichens and weathering and the soft attrition of human hands), the artefact splendidly expressive but not self-expressive, all *outward*, all – Stokes's own word – manifest.

This unearthing of what lies hidden, the disclosing of an objective world masked by the smoothness of a present existence, is central to another of Robinson's early poems from *Overdrawn Account*. It is no surprise that 'The Interrupted Views' has an epigraph quotation from Adrian Stokes, 'The world is full of home', as it focuses on a train journey undertaken by the author returning to his childhood home:

> Sunlight on the glass
> blazes this temporary blindness,
> the passenger's,
> who gathers himself
> to his thought of returning.[10]

The sense of being enclosed by his own mind with its foreseen world of nostalgic return is offered to us as a 'temporary blindness': a dazzling light on what is in effect an opaque flat surface. Windows that one

---

[9] Stokes, 70.
[10] *CP*, 40.

can look through can also be enclosures as this passenger concentrates upon what it means to return. Those objects of memory concerning the industrial landscape he is approaching ('Moss on lock brickwork / and the almost still waters') are 'blurred out' as if the tears of nostalgic reminiscence hide the concrete sense of the outside world. The poet's movement of sculpting, chipping away at the flatness of the self-enclosed vision, is carried forward with care and dawning awareness:

> So my coming back is like the sky.
> No choice in that.
> How weak sun's gilded
> the cloud-grey wavelets.
> Desire infuses regret.
> A feeling for landscape
> we call it.

The 'almost still waters' are now 'wavelets' while the nostalgic sense of narcissistic dream endures with the desire for return infusing regret at what will be perceived as change. The poet's ability to recognise this poison is caught with the irony of the phrase concerning a feeling for landscape, a generalised term of uncritical vagueness that might well be used by a writer for *Country Life*. The journey of discovering the otherness of the life to which he is returning is then glimpsed with 'a latticework / of girder, flickering, / black on the water a long way beneath' as the train crosses the rail bridge. The latticework acts as a still imprisoning mesh and the fixed sense of objective otherness is only arrived at in the next lines:

> The airport control tower,
> derelict gasworks,
> these are the landmarks.

And having chiselled out this visual awareness of what lies beneath the word 'home', Robinson recognises that the landmarks 'put us in our place' as he comes back to the 'ash heaps, / the car dumps, each graffito / taken as a welcome.' The personal nature of the journey is then stilled as a carving in the last line of the poem:

> Home is the view I appropriate.

Taken from early French, *à propre* (to oneself), the concluding word is the 17th century Latinate version of this idea of ownership: taking something to oneself which is an aspect of becoming aware of boundaries: lines between the self and the other. It is this sense of experience being placed within a continuum, our awareness of who we are in relation to what has gone before, that perhaps occurred to Georg Simmel in 1911 when he wrote about what it was like to have an adventure:

> An adventure is certainly part of our existence, directly contiguous with other parts which precede and follow it ... At the same time, however, in its deeper meaning, it occurs outside the usual continuity of this life.

When R. F. Langley used this quotation in a lecture given at Barracks Studio, Newcastle-under-Lyme, on the 6th of May 1995, he followed it by suggesting that episodes in ordinary life have their beginnings and ends determined by boundaries which are, in a way, mechanical and not organic (as would be the case with an island) since 'they are drawn by mutual pressure from both sides'. Simmel had written that what lifts an adventure out of the regular course of human destiny was a propelling force 'of a life forming from inside out'. Peter Robinson's sculptural poetry releases the picture which lies within and the clarity of 'The Interrupted Views' is revealed chip by chip as the train journey moves to its conclusion. In his 1995 lecture Langley had gone on to quote Adrian Stokes clearing his parents' house at Lower Stoneham, as recorded in 'Art and Literature' from 1964.

> Traces of our occupation were disappearing fast: many symbols of absence came together: the experience was painful, confused, and discoloured by the rush of time. I went finally into the garden where this mental state was shaped and limited by taking on the character of a thing. For, in the quietness of Saturday lunchtime, the gardener had left burning a steady bonfire that smouldered easily. It simplified the confused feelings I had felt in the house concerning 'the clean sweep'. But the spectacle was itself appealing because of the intense, directed and simple action it contained ... Such is a work of art vis-à-vis emotion. I was grateful to this bonfire as if to a remaining, administering person. It performed a ritual I felt

was needed: I took pleasure in the palpable image outside me of all I felt: IT, a concrete form, was my feelings, yet calm, noble, wrapt and also more vivid than they, without the confusion or successiveness of feelings: it was new and disinterested.

In a similar fashion Robinson's sharp awareness of the reality of the past emerges in 'The Interrupted Views' where the movement of the train journey acts like the sculptor's chisel. The steady focus upon what is actually there, unhindered by the sentimental fancies of distance, is also perhaps similar to what Roger Langley hoped to achieve in his journey of stillness recorded in the interview he gave with R. F. Walker. At dusk, having walked out from the village in which he lived, Langley stood still for an hour and a half by a track 'and no-one came anywhere near me':

> And it just occurred to me that I ought to stand without moving at all for that length of time and see what happened. Not even turning my head. A lot of rabbits came up and sat on my feet. And moths whipping about within inches of me. A feeling that you might get through to what was really there if you stripped off enough.[11]

This sense of the 'emergence' of reality and its importance to Peter Robinson's awareness of the rhythms and processes of life can be traced back to Stokes's assertion in *Colour and Form* that 'Carving creates a face for the stone, as agriculture for the earth, as man for woman. Modelling is more purely plastic creation: it makes things, does not elicit upon the surface, as a face, the significance of something that already exists.'[12]

It is this concern for chiselling out the reality that lies beneath the surface that so impressed Roy Fisher in his Preface to the *Salt Companion* volume. Having noted how unusual it was in English poetry nowadays 'to find a writer of Peter Robinson's sophistication occupying himself with what appears, at least, to be autobiography', Fisher referred to the dangers of using personal pronouns 'as chutes into a void where characters in a poem can be subjected to misrepresentation, manipulation or lies, destabilising the poem into harangue or the author's self-delusion'. He

---

[11] Tim Allen & Andrew Duncan (eds.), *Don't Start Me Talking, Interviews with Contemporary Poets*, (Cambridge: Salt Publishing, 2006), 254.
[12] *Critical Writings*, Vol. II, 22.

recognised that one of the fine characteristics of Robinson's poetry was its close relation to an understanding of Stokes's concern with carving stone:

> He appears to treat the 'I', 'you' and 'we' in as lapidary a fashion as the carefully layered words of his observations of scenery, weather and situations. Treating the pronouns in this way means they have to be given the stability and respect accorded to things.[13]

Throughout Robinson's early poems, especially those which recorded the years of childhood and the poet's upbringing in a financially careful vicar's family near Bootle, this lapidary sense of individuals within their landscapes is a powerful presence. In 'A Short History', from the 1988 collection *This Other Life*, it is as though we walk with the past below our feet discovering along the path monuments which pierce the soil to remind us of how, in Charles Olson's words, the dead 'prey upon us'. The poem introduces the reader to the trammels of the past and we are presented by the poet's painterly eye with 'first light / through gripping ivy', 'leaf shadow, / telephone wires on the ceiling', 'meshed stained glass' and 'woven emblems'.[14] The words seem to echo Robinson's close reading of Stokes, noting the emblematic effect which he imagined as the ability to make manifest through the fantasies projected onto the stone and the manner of its working a generalised symbol for the inner life of both epoch and individual. Introducing Stokes's poems he highlights how this inner life 'bespeaks the importance of psychoanalysis as a means to the substratum of art' which Stokes himself had drawn attention to in *Colour and Form*:

> Where lies the perennial strength of this fantasy? It is, of course, all the figures of the inner life, of the unconscious, that are shown as a fixture, as one harmonious family, steadfast, completed as an open rose, open, revealed.[15]

Having completed his first degree at York, Peter Robinson arrived in Cambridge to do research on Ezra Pound and the Visual Arts and

---

[13] Adam Piette & Katy Price (eds.), *The Salt Companion to Peter Robinson* (Cambridge: Salt Publishing, 2007), 21.
[14] *CP*, 69-71
[15] *The Salt Companion*, 23.

perhaps the choice of university for this research should come as no surprise since the York English Department had been largely staffed by Cambridge graduates from the early '60s. It was October 1975, some few months after Richard Burns's first Cambridge Poetry Festival had taken place in April, and Robinson continued working on his own poetry with a sense of purpose that was in 1978 to find a public platform in both *The Benefit Forms*, a pamphlet published by Richard Tabor with a grant from the Eastern Arts Association, and *Going Out to Vote*, a broadsheet produced by John Welch's Many Press. In response to reading the poetry of Roy Fisher, whose work Robinson later recalled elbowed him 'out of my habitual thought patterns', he now changed his area of research in order to focus on the modern world of Tomlinson, Fisher, Larkin and Donald Davie as well as his own poetry. At the same time he also became involved in the organisation of future Cambridge Poetry Festivals, acting as secretary to Paul Johnstone for the second one in 1977 and running the third one himself in 1979. In an interview with Nate Dorward, published in *Talk About Poetry: Conversations on the Art*,[16] when asked about *Perfect Bound*, the magazine he co-edited from those Cambridge years in the 1970s, he made clear that 'the magazine was not my personal plaything, and was not edited with the single-minded aim of promoting my vision of poetry at that date.' As a consequence of this determination that the magazine should not become associated simply with the so-called Cambridge School, the heterogeneous nature of the poems and prose published coincided to some extent with Robinson's sense of a distinction to be maintained between 'all the various things that were happening, and my private take on them.' As Robinson saw it, that sense of things going on may well have been what encouraged the Eastern Arts Association to think that sponsoring a magazine alongside the Cambridge English Faculty and the National Poetry Secretariat (attached to the Poetry Society in London) was an idea to be pursued. In the Nate Dorward interview Robinson gave an account of what had appeared in each issue and one can see from issue number one a scene being set for what would become one of the most interesting and wide-ranging small-press publications of the late 1970s:

> Issue One opened our account with 'The Land of Saint Martin' by J.H. Prynne. Then come two sections from 'The Art of

---

[16] *TAP,* 54-73.

Flight' by Allen Fisher, poems about the burning of the Crystal Palace that I was very taken by.

Then, picking out some things, there's a run of work by first-year graduate student poets: my poem 'World's Apart' which will come first in a future *Selected Poems*, 'Six Days' by Geoffrey Ward, and 'Driving Each Other' by John Wilkinson, there are six poems by Edwin Morgan, and 'After Christopher Wood' by John James. The reviews section contains pieces by Semmens on McClure, Ward on Dorn's *Gunslinger*, myself on Veronica Forrest-Thomson's *On the Periphery*, and Wilkinson on Crozier's *Residing*.

Issues four and five of the magazine were co-edited with Aidan Semmens, then a young undergraduate at Trinity College, and in his reminiscences put together for the online *Blackbox Manifold* issue 9, with its festschrift for Robinson's sixtieth birthday, Semmens recalled 'The smell of Cow Gum, the long nights fading into dawn, the first Graham Parker album playing over and over on Peter's record-player; the adventure of a rail trip to London to hire the IBM golf-ball typewriter on which we – mostly I, as a fluent touch-typist – would typeset the whole magazine.'

Responding to Nate Dorward's question concerning the lack of female contributors, Robinson suggested that since the magazine 'was experimental in its general leanings there was also the problem of finding women writers who would fit the bill. The prominence of Denise Levertov in issue two indicates how much she constituted a sort of rare ideal.' Semmens also commented on the gender issue when he followed the highlighting of an impressive list of contributors to issue four (Harry Guest, Peter Riley, John Welch, Gael Turnbull, Michael Haslam, Tom Raworth, Matthew Mead, Douglas Oliver, Ken Smith) with the suggestion that it was perhaps marred only by a gender imbalance 'that would be inconceivable today'. He then continued to suggest that

> I'd like to think I noticed it, with embarrassment, at the time but I can't honestly say whether I did or not, or whether Peter did; I am sure Wendy Mulford, who alone broke the male dominance of number five, did. Is it a defence to say that it was not until the following year, just after I left, that Trinity accepted its first woman undergraduate? Perhaps not, but it

is an indicator of the times (and society) we lived in. There were fewer women poets to choose from then ... Be that as it may, Wendy was in excellent company in *Perfect Bound* 5, being joined by John Riley, Ralph Hawkins, David Chaloner, Rod Mengham, Iain Sinclair, Edwin Morgan, Richard Burns – and, as a reviewer, J.H. Prynne. Though the magazine was now no longer either defined by or confined to Cambridge, it was still plainly our base.

In the fourth issue Peter Robinson wrote a review of Denise Riley's *Marxism For Infants* and Riley's own poems were to appear in issues six and seven respectively. However, there is no escaping the fact that the gap is there and in terms of feminism and avant-garde poetics Robinson was to suggest to Nate Dorward that the issues were too complex for the scope of the interview:

> There would be, for instance, the problem for me that definitions of avant-garde writing as 'destabilizing identity' would need qualification. It's certainly the case that this sort of slogan was what got put on various strategies then and for years to come. Actually, I found myself growing more and more out of sympathy with this notion of what serious poets were meant to be about. Were they really destabilizing their own? It was supposed to be political but where I grew up there were all sorts of social and personal problems, with political implications, that came from people having rather weak identities that were being fiercely buffeted by their social circumstances. I never felt myself in possession of one of the anathematised subjectivities that needed destabilizing, rather with masses of conflictual and contradictory experience and hurt that needed putting together and making sense of.

Towards the end of the run of *Perfect Bound* Robinson felt that he was moving away from 'an uneasy alliance with what has come to be called Cambridge School poetry and into as much of the entire field full of folk as I can manage to live with and appreciate'. It was during 1978, two years after the magazine publications of *The Benefit Forms*, that he started to write poems 'that seemed fully to strike my own note' and many of these were to find their way into the Many Press collection,

Overdrawn Account, two years later.

Since *Perfect Bound* had been so firmly Cambridge-based, Nate Dorward asked about the term 'Cambridge School' of poetry and Robinson's reply was a thoughtful distancing of himself from any such labelling:

> ...it's an elastic term stretching from a fairly loose affiliation of avant-garde poetries, to an inner circle of J. H. Prynne plus a few friends. It works to exclude poets who have perfectly good claims to be Cambridge poets, like Clive Wilmer, but who are rightly taken not to be Cambridge School poets, and of course it can exclude poets who passed through the town as undergraduates such as Michael Hofmann ... Hardly anyone who appears to belong to it likes the term, and some of those who don't belong seem to resent it. So I prefer to keep clear of the whole idea.

In the *Cambridge University Library Poetry Archives Newsletter*, Number 1, Autumn 2014, Prynne himself addressed this term 'Cambridge School':

> Terms like this or similar have already been put to use in some quarters, to describe a category of recent poetical production, principally since circa 1960 or earlier, associated in some way with Cambridge, often (but by no means always) with writers linked at some point to the University.
>
> Although the new Cambridge University Library Poetry Archive has provisionally adopted a very approximate formula such as this, to describe the central focus of its new collection, some caution is needed. A term like 'school' or 'group' often implies some kind of membership or coherent unity of purpose or practice, often with a recognisable set of characteristics and influential chief figures, possibly in distinct variance from other 'groups' or traditions.

The article, which was later presented as a short lecture to the Friends of the University Library, acknowledged that there had been a 'somewhat remarkable flowering of poetry writing and publishing' in Cambridge over the course of the last half-century and much of it had been adventurous. However, apart from the geographical tag, 'poetry of this adventurous tendency has been remarkably individual and various, following many different paths and career developments.' Prynne also referred to the fact that much of the so-termed 'new' poetry had appeared in magazines and small presses, lending perhaps an appearance of a restricted clientele. However, 'it's chiefly the economics of modern publishing that has caused these small-group arrangements to flourish, rather than any exclusive motivation' and poets 'from very different local origins and walks of life have been involved, in shifting friendships and informal alliances over a wide span of differences.'

Thinking over the enormous amount of adventurous new poetry being written in the 1970s, the Dorward/Robinson interview examined in some detail issues raised by the 1982 Andrew Motion/Blake Morrison anthology *Penguin Book of Contemporary British Poetry* which had included what came to be known as an infamous disclaimer for what was really going on. In the introduction it had been suggested that there was 'a stretch, occupying much of the 1960s and '70s, when very little – in England at any rate – seemed to be happening, when achievements in British poetry were overshadowed by those in drama and fiction, and when, despite the presence of strong individual writers, there was a lack of overall shape and direction.' Robinson's response to this wild assertion not only offers us an outline of the 1970s background to *Perfect Bound* but also highlights the sense of excitement of those years in which he was discovering his own voice:

> It's not really possible for me to give a thumbnail sketch of Seventies poetry in Britain. There was far too much going on and I was just trying to find out about it. There were many more magazines than now, many of the short-lived variety. There were lots of little presses that could produce good-looking books quite cheaply. John Welch's Many Press, for instance, was never more than a basement or attic venture with an occasional grant to do a slightly more substantial volume, like my first collection, but he published many people who are still writing strongly. The 1960s and the idea of underground culture had meant that there was no simple rule for dismissing a book on the basis of its publisher's name. There were both specialist poetry bookshops and general bookshops in university towns with reasonable poetry sections. Most of this has disappeared. I think that poetry

then seemed a very lively thing to be involved with, something that mattered a lot, and a field that was populated by valuable writers of various older generations who were to be respected and learned from. I was lucky enough to meet a few of them, who proved generous and supportive of the young as well.

The last issue of *Perfect Bound* offered a reflection of what was happening at the 1979 Cambridge Poetry Festival: Hans Magnus Enzensberger and Octavio Paz rubbed shoulders with Edmond Jabès and Michel Deguy; Denise Riley and Elaine Feinstein appeared alongside Tom Raworth and Matthew Mead. The full line-up for this last issue included also Nasos Vayenas, Marcus Perryman, Marina Tsvetayeva, Jeremy Reed, Matthew Sweeney, Christopher Meckel, Richard Hammersley, Tim Dooley, John Barrell, Thomas A. Clark, Adam Clarke-Williams, John Freeman, Aidan Semmens, Roberto Sanesi, Ralph Hawkins, Pier Paolo Pasolini and Anne Waldman. The festival was run by Robinson himself along with Alison Rimmer and it involved a big Saturday night event with an American presence: Allen Ginsberg, Anne Waldman and Kenneth Koch. It was hardly to be wondered at that almost all copies of that Issue 7 were sold at the time. The Dorward interview offers us a glimpse of what was going on:

> Ginsberg did the whole thing for a tiny fee plus flights on to his next festival. The idea was to present the widest range of poetries so as to attract as many constituencies as possible. There was an afternoon of Sound Poetry, a debate between Silkin and Davie about poetry and politics, big readings by Hans Magnus Enzensberger and Joseph Brodsky, Edmond Jabès with Rosemarie Waldrop translating, Michael Hamburger talking about Celan with an exhibition of his French wife's etchings…

In a short piece of prose written for *The Cambridge Review* 106, no. 2287 (1985), titled 'A Performing Art', Robinson re-created that infectious and exhilarating world of the festivals by recalling that when he had heard a poem that he liked he would then scour the festival bookstall, 'for the composed work has an ambivalent existence which seems satisfied neither by its utterance nor indeed its text alone':

Between text and utterance too the combinations of emphasis are extensive. You might learn something of what your poet thinks or assumes about these two states from the word used to describe the action of turning a poem from an arrangement of print into one of air.

That metamorphosis, a release from one form to another, sits closely with Robinson's own readings of Adrian Stokes and he later recalled the presence of Enzensberger at the 1979 festival in terms of cutting a shape in time:

> I can still quite clearly picture Hans Magnus Enzensberger at the third festival in June 1979 on stage in the darkened Corn Exchange at Cambridge. He was reading from his poem *The Sinking of the Titanic* in German and his own English translation. Enzensberger's face was extremely mobile: ingenuousness, sarcasm, disgust and pity passed across his features as he read. He had been in Italy and was wearing a white summer suit that seemed slightly luminous under the spotlights. When he reached the end of the poem where imaginary and symbolic passengers are swimming away from the ship, Enzensberger seemed to have turned the darkness of the Corn Exchange into an Atlantic Ocean.

Peter Robinson's development as a poet was closely bound up with this world of hard edges, and the new realities in-forming Cambridge poetry and the university scene became an interesting focus for a letter he wrote to Adam Clarke-Williams in early 1980:

> ...in Cambridge we do or did have a poetry 'scene' which sharply differentiated between self-consciously written linguistic speciality and the innocent, and stupidly, transparent – never realizing, I now think, that if the transparent does not exist (as how can it?) then the language of writers who do produce a transparent style must be as potentially significant in the hot-house linguistic light, as the self-possessed and much advertised version of the written. I think what I'm saying is that it is a mistake, but an easy one to make, to assume that the stylised manner of a Prynne or Stein, even Empson, is any more 'written'

than the styleless style of an Orwell, of Davie, or even Larkin – whose use of the words 'here' and 'there' is subtle and even devious. I am beginning to think that difficulty of an evident kind in language is completely misconceived; i.e. complexity of response can be rendered in an evident simplicity that proves contextually rich, rather than the reverse, which is hopeless, or the complex matching the complex, which is true but should be rare – rather than normal means of proceeding. My own experience suggests that what happens to us seems simple and proves complex. Things happen easily – why, how, where, and leading to and from what? is more difficult. The simple style that presents a surface over a mesh of difficulties – that speaks to me the apparent and the true features of our experience.[17]

Aidan Semmens recalled that when he knew Robinson in the mid-seventies 'his adult style [as a poet] was by then already well-formed, his gentle ironies and punning on common forms of speech perfectly tuned to wry personal and social observation in a way quite antithetical to the denser, more difficult, more Prynne-influenced work of near-contemporaries such as Geoffrey Ward and John Wilkinson'. The enduring presence of a past long gone is perhaps teased out by Robinson's wit in the 1970s rather than chiselled from stone, and one of his poems from the opening of the next decade weds his respect for Stokes with his overriding concern for a humane sense of the everyday. 'Editorial Footnote' takes its epigraph from a poem by Stokes, 'Cambridge', and its opening point is a visit he made to the art critic's drawing room at 20 Church Row, Hampstead. Embedded within the poem's centre there is the direct speech of the curator 'Please / find within unfinished drafts, last proofs', and it is almost as if Stokes, who had died some eight years beforehand, has been preserved inside the room; his presence is still felt by Robinson, both visitor and poet, as he notices

>   the slight depression
> in a chair cover, still as if
> he had just risen to leave and gone.[18]

---

[17] *Letters from Peter Robinson*, Blackbox Manifold 9 (2012).
[18] *CP*, 92.

Chapter 4
The View from Somewhere

Piers Pennington

The first paragraph of Peter Robinson's preface to his first book of critical essays, *In the Circumstances: About Poems and Poets* (1992), finds the author summarizing its chapters by emphasizing the fundamental question that his creative as well as his critical writing has attempted to fathom ever since: 'each considers the bearing [...] of contextual circumstance, of the world from which the poems arose and to which, in the first place, they returned'. Despite this initial focus upon 'the world', however, the following paragraph continues to elaborate Robinson's fascination with 'the idea of other lives in poems, and poetry as a response to other lives and the otherness of those lives', in a gently complicating way. 'The term "otherness" is often encountered in criticism and can be used to indicate ideas about the differentiation of perceiver and perceived [...] and the incorporation into artworks of relations with a perceived world,' Robinson points out: 'The ideas of poems as "other" and of various othernesses in poems are explored under the assumption that the differentiations involved [...] are continuously at risk'.[1] To be sure, this develops the generous – and necessary – attempt to recognise 'the world' beyond the poet and the poem. Even so, Robinson's introduction of a 'perceiver' and a 'perceived world' subtly acknowledges the inescapability of subjectivity: one reason, perhaps, why 'the differentiations involved [...] are continuously at risk'. And, as the presence of 'continuously at risk' intimates, there is no straightforward way of negotiating the tension between the 'perceiver' and 'the world', which runs through and stimulates all of Robinson's work.

Poetry, Poets, Readers: Making Things Happen (2002), for instance, Robinson's second book of critical essays, again explores questions of circumstance, but with an emphasis upon the claims of speech act theory – not only as it was initially set out by J. L. Austin, whose

---

[1] Peter Robinson, *In the Circumstances: About Poets and Poems* (Oxford: Clarendon Press, 1992), n. p. See also 'Through frosted glass', the poet's interview with Ian Sansom, from 1994, in *TAP,* esp. 21 and 26, for further reflections on 'otherness'.

How To Do Things With Words (1962) includes the famous caveat that in order to issue a performative utterance 'I must not be joking, for example, nor writing a poem',[2] but also as it was developed by John Searle, whose *Speech Acts: An Essay on the Philosophy of Language* (1969) opens by asking 'How do words relate to the world?'[3] Searle's later essay, 'The Logical Status of Fictional Discourse' (1975), provides an important point of departure for Robinson's opening chapter, in which he attempts to disprove W. H. Auden's infamous claim that 'poetry makes nothing happen'.[4] After taking issue with Searle's suggestion that 'newspaper accounts contain one class of illocutionary acts [...] and fictional literature contains another class of illocutionary acts', Robinson questions the philosopher's understanding of what he imagines Iris Murdoch, for instance, to be doing when she is writing a novel: 'She is pretending [...] to make an assertion, or acting as if she were making an assertion, or going through the motions of making an assertion, or imitating the making of an assertion,' Searle writes[5] – a statement that amplifies the implications of Austin's claim that 'I must not be [...] writing a poem'. Turning his attention to the reading of poetry, however, Robinson modulates these related interpretations by drawing a distinction between the recognition of 'pretending', on the one hand, and the recognition of 'the textual signs which inform us that it is a poem, a context in which such pretending inevitably goes on', on the other: 'you're doing something both complex and subtle, for you see the words simultaneously in two distinct ways', which means that 'we are able simultaneously to respond to the text in two distinct ways: *as if* these were real speech acts, and in the knowledge that they are not'.[6] Robinson continues to elaborate 'the textual signs

---

[2] J. L. Austin, *How To Do Things With Words*, ed. by J. O. Urmson and Marina Sbisà, 2nd edn. (Oxford: Clarendon Press, 1975), 9.
[3] John R. Searle, *Speech Acts: An Essay in the Philosophy of Language* (Cambridge: Cambridge University Press, 1969), 3.
[4] W. H. Auden, 'In Memory of W. B. Yeats', in *The English Auden: Poems, Essays and Dramatic Writings 1927–1939*, ed. Edward Mendelson (London: Faber and Faber, 1986), 242.
[5] John R. Searle, 'The Logical Status of Fictional Discourse', in *Expression and Meaning: Studies in the Theory of Speech Acts* (Cambridge: Cambridge University Press, 1979), 58-75 (63, 65).
[6] Peter Robinson, *Poetry, Poets, Readers: Making Things Happen* (Oxford: Clarendon Press, 2002), 10, 11. For related discussion, see Paul Hullah, '"Put In My Place": Arrangement of Self and World in Peter Robinson's Early Poems',

which inform us that it is a poem' later in the chapter, when he touches upon the differences between the genres. 'One distinction between much fiction and lyric poetry would involve the degree of expected naturalization,' he suggests: 'Many lyrics [...] work by keeping both naturalizing and disjunctive aspects of the reading experience in full view', while 'much fiction expects its readers to imagine a complete and continuous natural scene'.[7] The presence of the word 'naturalization' invokes another critic of poetry whose work is much concerned with the relation between words and the world. Veronica Forrest-Thomson introduces her understanding of 'naturalization' in her preface to *Poetic Artifice: A Theory of Twentieth-Century Poetry* (1978) as a critical rather than a creative process, though, suggesting that it constitutes 'an attempt to reduce the strangeness of poetic language and poetic organisation by making it intelligible, by translating it into a statement about the non-verbal external world, by making the Artifice appear natural'.[8] What is more, the citation from Ludwig Wittgenstein's *Zettel* (1967) that Robinson presents near the beginning of his chapter – 'Do not forget that a poem, even though it is composed in the language of information, is not used in the language game of giving information' – is also to be found in *Poetic Artifice*, even though it is clear to see that Robinson prefers representation to the artifice that Forrest-Thomson celebrates throughout her study.[9]

Robinson continues to discuss Wittgenstein in the opening chapter of his third collection of critical essays, *Twentieth Century Poetry: Selves and Situations* (2005), yet he opens the study by presenting two related questions from another philosopher, Thomas Nagel, which return to a familiar theme:

> We must turn our attention to the circumstances in which people act and by which they are formed, and we must

---

in *The Salt Companion to Peter Robinson*, ed. Adam Piette and Katy Price (Cambridge: Salt Publishing, 2007), 36-54 (37).
[7] Robinson, *Making Things Happen*, 21.
[8] Veronica Forrest-Thomson, *Poetic Artifice: A Theory of Twentieth-Century Poetry* (Manchester: Manchester University Press, 1978), xi.
[9] Ludwig Wittgenstein, *Zettel*, ed. G. E. M. Anscombe and G. H. von Wright, trans. G. E. M. Anscombe, 2nd edn. (Oxford: Blackwell, 1981), 27 (§160), cited by Robinson in *Making Things Happen*, 6, and Forrest-Thomson in *Poetic Artifice*, x.

change the question from 'How should we live, whatever the circumstances?' to 'Under what circumstances is it possible to live as we should?'[10]

The following paragraph finds the poet raising the possibility that 'the subjects of our attention can only be thought and felt about when experienced from somewhere beyond them – as if they could only be experienced, as it were, ecstatically', before quashing the suggestion by pointing out that, 'as the title of a previous book had it, we are always and inescapably "in the circumstances"'.[11] Nagel asks the questions in *Equality and Partiality* (1991), specifically in the chapter 'Kant's Test', which investigates the philosopher's 'categorical imperative' and comes to the conclusion that 'in one way or another it fails to heal the division of the self that results from the duality of standpoints' – namely, the 'personal' and the 'impersonal'.[12] In this respect, 'Kant's Test' continues to explore the relation between the subjective and the objective that Nagel addressed in his earlier book, *The View from Nowhere* (1986), which Robinson cites in one of the footnotes to his chapter, suggesting that it provides a complicating account of 'the self as necessarily conscious of being a body among other such bodies'.[13] Tellingly, the footnote accompanies the sentence from which Robinson's study takes its title. 'Nor can poets, both as and as not inscribed subjects of poems, be separable from the circumstances within which they both live and represent themselves as living,' the poet asserts: 'I am suggesting that however impersonal or transpersonal or non-personal an outlook any of us attempts to adopt, it must, nevertheless, be a view (that's to say, a self) from somewhere (in a situation)'.[14] As such, Robinson's understanding appears to have been written against *The View from Nowhere*, and its attempt to work out 'how to combine the perspective of a particular person inside the world with an objective view of that same world', even though his emphasis upon 'self' and 'situation' accords with the beginnings of Nagel's argument: 'we can't forget about those subjective starting points indefinitely', since

---

[10] Thomas Nagel, *Equality and Partiality* (New York and Oxford: Oxford University Press, 1991), 52.
[11] Peter Robinson, *Twentieth Century Poetry: Selves and Situations* (Oxford: Oxford University Press, 2005), 2.
[12] Nagel, *Equality and Partiality*, 52.
[13] Robinson, *Selves and Situations*, 4, note 10.
[14] Robinson, *Selves and Situations*, 4.

'we and our personal perspectives belong to the world'.[15] Nonetheless, the poet is sceptical of too great an emphasis upon self, as his subsequent citation of a passage from Wittgenstein's *Tractatus Logico-Philosophicus* (1922) suggests: 'Here we see that solipsism strictly carried out coincides with pure realism. The I in solipsism shrinks to an extensionless point and there remains the reality co-ordinated with it' – which ultimately means that the 'I' becomes '"the limit" of the world'.[16] Robinson's interest in 'solipsism' appears to have been prompted by a negative – and personal – review of his 1992 collection *Entertaining Fates*. Discussing the review in his interview with Ian Sansom, from 1994, Robinson points out that 'Timothy Harris thought he detected in *me*, not my work, what he called "a self-absorption amounting almost, if not in fact to, solipsism"', before relating the criticism to 'the difficulties involved in writing about intimate situations while wishing to preserve some degree of anonymity and privacy'.[17] Robinson attempts to elaborate the 'difficulties' in a later interview, with Marcus Perryman, from 1998. 'Timothy Harris's phrase [...] might be aiming at, but failing to hit through the *ad hominem*, a complexity of lyric poetry, and perhaps of art more generally,' he ventures: 'The equipment that can make you curious and responsive to the world is only going to be registering sensitively if you are attending closely to it'.[18] In a later interview still – with Katy Price, from 2003, one year after *Making Things Happen*, and two years before *Selves and Situations* – Robinson hints at a means of finally resolving the 'difficulties', by gesturing towards a distinction between subjectivity and solipsism. 'It may look as if some lyric poets are obsessed with their own lives, but that can be deceptive,' he cautions: 'If you put a first-person singular pronoun into a poem, it may well be making space

---

[15] Thomas Nagel, *The View from Nowhere* (New York & Oxford: OUP, 1986), 3, 6. Nagel's understanding of 'objectivity' resonates with Robinson's understanding of 'subjects [...] that could only be experienced [...] ecstatically', in this respect: 'An objective standpoint is created by leaving a more subjective, individual, or even just human perspective behind' (7).
[16] Ludwig Wittgenstein, *Tractatus Logico-Philosophicus*, trans. C. K. Ogden (London: Kegan Paul, Trench, Trubner & Co., 1922), 153 (5.64), cited by Robinson in *Selves and Situations*, 2.
[17] *TAP*, 22. See *PN Review 93*, 20.1 (September-October 1993) for Harris's review, and see *PN Review 94*, 20.2 (November-December 1993) for Robinson's letter in response.
[18] *TAP*, 33.

for other people' – since the opposite approach only results in the effects that Wittgenstein describes: 'If you leave it out, the entire text, whatever it appears to be about, will likely be an unmitigated self-projection'.[19]

As such, Robinson's understanding resonates – surprisingly, perhaps – with that of John Wilkinson, a contemporary at Cambridge, who makes a related point in 'Frostwork and the Mud Vision', his 2002 review of three anthologies of modern and contemporary poetry.[20] 'Reading the anthologies, it can feel as though the lyric poetry of the twentieth century has been harried past endurance by the problem of the first person singular, the lyric "I",' Wilkinson suggests: 'This cannot be evaded by extirpation of the cursed pronoun, for the depersonalised poem tends to then lay claim to an overweening authority'[21] – where the presence of the word 'depersonalised' similarly acknowledges the influence of Forrest-Thomson.[22] In contrast to the '"in your face" difficulty' that frequently accompanies the poetry of experiment, however, Robinson makes his preference for representation clear in his 1998 interview with Perryman, pointing out that 'I [...] like to have a situation or story that I'm addressing, even if quite obliquely, so that what the reader can be expected to notice is the setting, the scenery, the participants, the basic situation'.[23] Nonetheless, he continues to state that poems have to be 'many-faceted' in order 'to be [...] true to even quite restricted human situations', suggesting that 'the way to do that in art is, I think, to recess

---

[19] *TAP,* 104-05. Robinson subsequently formalised this understanding in aphorism 22 from *UD*: 'Put an "I" in a poem and I may make a space for others; leave it out and the whole thing is nothing but me' (7). Compare also aphorisms 68 and 69 (16) and Robinson's interview with Alex Pestell, from 2005, also in *TAP,* 131.

[20] Robinson reflects upon the publication of 'Going Out To Vote' in 'The life of a little magazine', his interview with Nate Dorward, from 2002 (*TAP,* 71-2).

[21] John Wilkinson, *The Lyric Touch: Essays on the Poetry of Excess* (Cambridge: Salt Publishing, 2007), 187.

[22] Forrest-Thomson, *Poetic Artifice*, 42.

[23] *TAP,* 31. See also Robinson's essay 'John James and *The White Stones* 71: Music, Rhyme, and Home', in *Poetry Wales*, 47.2 (Autumn 2011), 37-44, in which Robinson's apprehension of difficulty frequently turns upon questions of self and situation, and compare also J. H. Prynne's *The Oval Window: A New Annotated Edition*, ed. N. H. Reeve and Richard Kerridge (Hexham: Bloodaxe Books, 2018) for a sequence that explores a number of meanings of 'window'.

the complexity into the poetic structure, which can then be caught by reading and looking again at the composed words'.[24] Robinson's apprehension of a 'complexity' that is intrinsic to the 'poetic structure' anticipates his acknowledgement of 'naturalizing and disjunctive aspects', while his accompanying emphasis upon 'art' and 'reading and looking at the composed words' hints at the visual imagination that comes to the fore in his other art: the painting that he references throughout his poetry and that sometimes appears on the covers of his collections. Indeed, not only does the word 'artwork' appear in the preface to *In the Circumstances*, but Robinson's collocation of 'art' and 'words' is also to be found in *Making Things Happen*, when he elaborates the *'as if'* quality of literary discourse: 'The ability to respond in both ways simultaneously requires us to see all the words of the artwork under two distinct, though related, aspects'[25] – a statement that invokes the visual imagination, since 'aspect' ultimately derives from the Latin *specere*, meaning 'to look'. Significantly, it is in this respect that the two understandings of the two poets accord most closely. Wilkinson praises 'frostwork poets' in his review: 'frostwork' is 'window glass which is semi-opaque through its decoration', and he uses the term to describe 'poets whose writing exhibits a sustained balance between linguistic surface and reference to an external or internal world', before defining it as 'a perceptive and productive poetic artifice (to use Forrest-Thomson's term) operative in tension with an imparted reality'.[26] And despite his preference for representation, Robinson acknowledges its necessary interplay with artifice when he discusses his own work in strikingly comparable terms, again in his interview with Sansom: 'The poems are like frosted glass', he suggests, since 'they half reveal and half conceal their occasions'.[27]

In line with the focus upon 'circumstance' that runs throughout Robinson's criticism, almost all of the poems that have been preserved (and revised) in the 2017 edition of his *Collected Poems* appear to

---

[24] *TAP*, 31.
[25] Robinson, *Making Things Happen*, 11.
[26] Wilkinson, *The Lyric Touch*, 181, 186. Wilkinson does not acknowledge Robinson in the review, but his praise of W. S. Graham singles out features that similarly have a bearing upon Robinson's approach – not only his understanding that 'the dynamism of painting was enacted in the tension between surface artifice and referentiality', but also his frequent recourse to 'the poetic mode of address' (186, 187).
[27] *TAP*, 22. Compare also 21.

have been written *in propria persona*, exploring the various subtleties of self and situation that are bound up with a particular time or a particular place – an approach that gives the book as a whole the feel of an autobiography in verse. Indeed, a glance at the index reveals that three of the four entries in the first cluster of titles are addresses, in the form of house numbers and street names, while the fourth is a date, in the form of a day, a month, and a year.[28] Even so, a number of the other poems in the volume complicate Robinson's preference for representation, through their references to his other art. *Overdrawn Account*, for instance, the debut collection of 1980, opens with 'In the Background Details', a title that hints at a painter's perspective, while the first paragraph of the prose poem 'A Woman A Picture and A Poem' sees 'bright sunshine [...] break across the gap between cloudbanks and the tumuli'.[29] As such, the two compositions anticipate the recent 'Picturesque', which appears in the sequence of 'Ringstead Poems' that Robinson gathers in *For the Small Mercies*, the new collection that he presents at the end of the *Collected Poems*: 'You could paint this scene – that's what I said,' he remembers, as he perceives 'sun, bright on a reaped field, / golden with dark hedgerows framing it'.[30] Robinson touches upon the relation between poetry and painting in his interview of 2003. 'I still do the occasional picture when the mood takes me,' he confirms: 'Textures, surfaces, perspectives, points of view, figures and grounds, light and shadow – they all come into it.' But despite his understanding that 'the space of a poem seems quite a different proposition to that of a picture',[31] the influence of Robinson's visual imagination continues to make itself felt throughout his work, in a number of inconspicuous ways, as the presence of 'framing' in 'Picturesque' intimates. 'The Interrupted Views', for instance, another poem from *Overdrawn Account*, is prefaced with an epigraph from art critic Adrian Stokes's poem 'Home', which colours the poet's evocation

---

[28] *CP*, 513.
[29] *OA*, 7-10, 42. Robinson has subsequently revised 'In the Background Details', changing the title to 'In the Background' and placing it at the end of the *Overdrawn Account* section of the *Collected Poems* (63-6). Neil Corcoran discusses the poet's approach to painting in 'Chance and Circumstance: Painting in Peter Robinson's Poems', in *The Salt Companion to Peter Robinson*, 207-18.
[30] *CP*, 475.
[31] *TAP*, 95.

of an early return to his hometown of Liverpool: 'The world is full of home'.³² Robinson's opening lines attempt to capture the quality of the light – 'It's an occidental sun / blazes this temporary blindness, / white light in the glass', they originally read in *Overdrawn Account*,³³ having been revised for their appearance in the *Collected Poems*: 'Sunlight on the glass / blazes this temporary blindness' – and the poet proceeds to raise the possibility of a tension between artifice and representation by observing the 'carriage window' that 'reflects me so'. Train journeys across the country frequently call to mind Philip Larkin's 'Here' or 'The Whitsun Weddings', but Robinson's poem has a more direct precedent in 'Corner Seat', by Louis MacNeice, which not only singles out a 'face in the reflected train', but also acknowledges the inescapability of subjectivity: 'Windows between you and the world'.³⁴ Robinson then introduces a further complicating image, though, as 'a latticework / of girder, flickering' returns to the title, while also preparing for the final line, which accepts the inescapability of subjectivity by emphasizing the activity of perception: 'Home is the view I appropriate.'³⁵

The later 'Editorial Footnote', from *This Other Life*, the poet's second collection of 1988, is prefaced with another epigraph from Stokes – from 'Cambridge', the second and final section of his poem 'Buildings', which raises further questions of perspective: 'This window will see us out'.³⁶ Stokes's poem comes to its close by punning upon prepositions – 'Despite our looking through / This window will see us out' – and 'Editorial Footnote' appears to remember a day in Robinson's life as editor of *With All The Views*, his 1981 edition of Stokes's *Collected Poems*, as he finds himself in his subject's rooms, where he looks through his subject's papers and reports that 'the window / view that saw him

---

³² Adrian Stokes, 'Home', in *With All The Views: The Collected Poems of Adrian Stokes*, ed. Peter Robinson (Manchester: Carcanet New Press, 1981), 75.
³³ *OA*, 30.
³⁴ Louis MacNeice, 'Corner Seat', in *Collected Poems*, ed. Peter McDonald (London: Faber & Faber, 2007), 255. Intriguingly, windows are to be found throughout MacNeice's work, most notably in the earlier 'Snow', which opens with a similarly quotidian image: 'The room was suddenly rich and the great bay-window was / Spawning snow and pink roses against it' – and which also comes to its close by hinting at a more fundamental acknowledgement: 'There is more than glass between the snow and the huge roses' (24).
³⁵ *CP*, 40-1.
³⁶ Stokes, *With All The Views*, 39.

out excerpted trees' and is 'now / upholding still-life objects'.[37] The movement between the two epigraphs from Stokes is revelatory of the development in Robinson's approach, however: even though questions of 'home' recur throughout the poet's *oeuvre*, only a handful of 'windows' are to be found in *Overdrawn Account* – and, even then, they appear largely by implication. 'Waking, St Paul's Square', for instance, pays careful attention to the 'bell tent of light' that fills the morning room, before Robinson attempts to suggest the quality of the light, once again: 'Effect of the curtains', which are 'hardly less white / than the sphere of a Chinese / lampshade, and as still'.[38] A few pages later, 'Ear to the Night' finds the poet returning to the collocation of the 'lampshade' and the 'curtains', but at the other end of the day: 'By the ceiling's stamen, / pendulous, comes // a soft glimpse through curtains', he observes, as 'dark shimmers / at the window'.[39] The later 'Take Care of Things' finds Robinson going one stage further, however, since rather than simply looking at the world beyond the glass, he begins to develop its potential for artifice: 'The window box's marigolds, / beneath them, the frame', the poem begins, and Robinson proceeds to note that 'wrought-iron rails / with cherry trees in blossom are // inert', before pointing out that 'your green carboy / distorts them in uneven glass'[40] – where the 'frame' and the 'rails' anticipate the comparable shaping of the 'carboy'. Windows, by contrast, are to be found throughout *This Other Life*, and Robinson appears to acknowledge this important development in his approach by using a photograph of a shop's plate glass frontage on the cover of the original 1988 collection. What is more, 'A Short History', the opening poem, begins with lines that confirm the development by continuing to emphasise the glass's subtly distorting effects, in preparation for the magnified glimpses of autobiography that follow: 'Let me introduce first light / through gripping ivy round the window / which enlarges tendrils, leaf shadow, / telephone wires on the ceiling'[41] – and Robinson brings the poem's second verse paragraph to a close by singling out 'lace-curtained windows' that are 'still undisturbed', before opening the third with a related detail, which is bound up with his memories of his father's

---

[37] *CP,* 92.
[38] *CP,* 24.
[39] *CP,* 37.
[40] *CP,* 46.
[41] *CP,* 69.

vocation: 'We waited under meshed stained-glass / on walking days'.[42] Nonetheless, the most powerful early manifestation is to be found in '472 Claremont Road', one of the poems from the index's first cluster, which finds the poet returning to 'the house where my father was born', then notes 'tattered lace flapping from a broken window / in its dereliction', before remembering 'your mother's [...] face' by means of an image of glass that manages to reconcile the realism of representation with the stylisation of artifice: 'Try and see once more the buried features / wrinkle in a front door's frosted glass'.[43]

Gaston Bachelard, the French philosopher, touches upon windows in *The Poetics of Space*, his 1958 study of houses and perception. Having stated that '*the house's situation in the world* [...] gives us, quite concretely, a variation of the metaphysically summarised situation of man in the world', Bachelard turns his attention to light, postulating that 'a rather large dossier of literary documentation on the poetry of houses could be studied from the single angle of the lamp that glows in the window'.[44] Intriguingly, the painting that Robinson uses for the cover of the *Collected Poems* complements the philosopher's emphasis upon light, while remembering the earlier poems of *Overdrawn Account*, by presenting a detail from his 'Self-Portrait with Lampshade', from 1981. Bachelard returns to windows later in his study, though, in terms that are exemplary of the way in which they appear throughout the poems in Robinson's volume: 'Through the poet's window the house converses about immensity with the world'.[45] Indeed, the photograph on the back of the *Collected Poems* shows Robinson writing at a desk beneath a window that is partially illuminated by a bright shaft of angled sunlight, according with the existence that he describes in two compositions from *This Other Life*: 'The things we said today / I work on at the window', he remembers in 'Writing on the Quiet', before focusing upon the 'frame', while he proceeds to wonder 'who could spend a lifetime / or make a living at the window?' in the following 'Building Society'.[46] As 'The Interrupted Views' suggests, however, windows also come to the fore in Robinson's many poems about travel and abroad. 'Between Fortunes',

---

[42] *CP*, 70.
[43] *CP*, 74-5.
[44] Gaston Bachelard, *The Poetics of Space*, trans. Maria Jolas (Boston, MA: Beacon Press, 1994), 27-8, 33.
[45] Bachelard, *The Poetics of Space*, 69.
[46] *CP*, 101-2.

for instance, which appears to find the poet making the return journey from Liverpool, and which invokes 'The Whitsun Weddings' through its reference to 'ousted cooling towers',[47] gestures towards the artifice that is a consequence of the separation from circumstances: 'blinds are drawn to concentrate / travellers' eyes on the dazzling / half-transparent video screen', the poet reports, before contrasting the coach's 'wide-swept windscreen' with the 'black, reflective windows / in which each confected diversion / flickers', then characterizing his increasing distance from 'home' in the concluding suggestion that he is 'dispersed'.[48] More fundamentally, the many years that Robinson spent teaching in Japan, in '"exile"' or, as he also suggests, 'economic migration', forced him to modulate his approach to poetry: 'I suddenly started to experience environments and so on which had very little reverberation for me, were rather flat, so I had to find the reverberations'.[49] In this respect, it is significant that the poet's use of the image appears to reflect his feelings about his newfound circumstances. 'The boarded-up windows lent oppressiveness / to shady corners of a bare room's tokonoma',[50] Robinson writes in 'An Undetermined Heart', a poem from 1997's *Lost & Found* that appears to remember his arrival in Japan in 1989, while 'Maple Leaf' paints a similarly desolate picture in its opening lines: 'Maple leaf shapes in the frosted pane, / my kitchen door gives on to nothing'[51] – a recognition that not only contrasts with the 'features' that Robinson perceives in the 'frosted glass' of '472 Claremont Road', but that also anticipates the later 'Marking Time', from 2001's *About Time Too*, which observes 'fogged windows', before remembering that 'for days / the treacherous turned to wetness, / then froze, ice crazing a pane'.[52] Nonetheless, 'Maple Leaf' comes to a hopeful close, by reconciling the door's artifice with the title's suggestion of the natural world, as the light from the 'sun' means that 'each maple leaf shape in the frosted pane /

---

[47] Philip Larkin describes 'a cooling tower' in 'The Whitsun Weddings', in *Collected Poems*, ed. Anthony Thwaite, rev. edn. (London: The Marvell Press & Faber & Faber, 1990), 116.
[48] *CP*, 115-6.
[49] *TAP*, 14, 76. The first interview is with Ted Slade, from 1999, while the second is with Jane Davies from 2000.
[50] *CP*, 148.
[51] *CP*, 155.
[52] *CP*, 227.

glows palely with a borrowed green'[53] – where the half rhyme of 'pane' with 'green' emphasises the perception of congruity, while also managing to acknowledge the reality of their continuing separation. The poet's feeling of estrangement comes to the fore in 2006's *Ghost Characters*, though. 'Remembering February', from the first part of the book, is set at 'home', yet Robinson contrasts his situation with that of a 'foreigner who has done his share / of pining through townships [...] by windows, wondering where / the love of life ends if not at ocean',[54] in order to emphasise the similarities between the islands of the United Kingdom and those of Japan. What is more, the collocation of 'windows' and 'ocean' is also to be found in the title sequence: the opening section of 'Ghost Characters' remembers that 'we went where lido restaurants' / wall-high windows opened / onto waves and a trampled beach', while the closing section similarly remembers that 'we went where lido restaurants' / wall-high windows opened / on freshening breeze and overcast skies'[55] – where the movement from the 'waves' and the 'beach' to the 'breeze' and the 'skies' continues the approach of 'Maple Leaf', by creating a 'reverberation' through the poem's form.

Robinson moved back to the UK in 2007, however, to become Professor of English and American Literature at the University of Reading – and he subsequently assumed the role of Poetry Editor at the local Two Rivers Press in 2010, producing the anthology *Reading Poetry*, a gathering of poems about his adopted hometown, in 2011. The earlier 'On Van Gogh's *La Crau*', the final poem in *Entertaining Fates*, memorialises the reproduction of the famous painting that has accompanied the poet throughout his life. 'Above mantelpieces, year after year, / though walls or wallpapers / or views from closed windows / altered, it stayed there,' he writes, before emphasizing that 'home / would not be home without that picture', which 'startles the distanced, the returning eye'.[56] As such, the poem's final line anticipates the title of the first collection that Robinson published following his move, 2012's *The Returning Sky* – although a number of the poems in the collection had previously appeared in the shorter *English Nettles and Other Poems*, which was illustrated by Sally Castle and published by the Two Rivers Press in 2010. The collection's subject matter provides an opportunity

---

[53] *CP*, 156.
[54] *CP*, 239.
[55] *CP*, 246, 249.
[56] *CP*, 141-2.

for Robinson to develop the concerns of *Overdrawn Account*, particularly his interest in debts and related personal obligations, as the brief 'Credit Rating' makes clear: 'through the hazy screen I see [...] that rather than a cemetery / it's an estate agent's window'.[57] By contrast, the opening line of the immediately following 'Personal Credit' invokes Edward Thomas's 'Rain', as Robinson continues to explore the intricacies of purchasing – as opposed to renting or residing in – a house: 'Rain in the small hours, yet more rain / falls on roof and misted glass, / on the floor of a half-woken mind...'[58] – where the repetition of 'rain' at either end of the line confirms the allusion, even though the security of the 'roof and misted glass' are knowingly at odds with the 'bleak hut' and the many other uncertainties of Thomas's poem.[59] The house in question appears to be described in 'Double Portrait', the poem that Robinson suggestively writes after Dutch artist Frans Hals's painting of the same name, not only because Hals's 'Double Portrait of a Couple' (1622) displays its couple on a single canvas, in contrast to his usual practice of using two separate canvases, hinting at the new life that Robinson and his family are beginning together in the South East, but also because Robinson's poem remembers 'A Short History', by means of a particularly telling detail. 'Tendrils knocking at a window / insistently had wormed on through / gaps between aperture and frame', the poet observes in the second stanza, gesturing towards the natural world's complication of the house's separation, as well as the familiar understanding of 'setting down roots', in order to prepare for the following suggestion of the homeliness that is a consequence of living in the land of his mother tongue, once again: 'language seeps from crevices'.[60] Later in the collection, 'Mortgaged Time' appears to remember the poet's first impressions of his new house. 'An abandoned villa front / had row on row of shutters / dangling by their hinges,' he relates in another variation on the image that recurs throughout his work, hinting at a more subjective apprehension of enclosure: 'We'd found ourselves among the ruins / of a family's histories' – although 'a demolition process / was helped by rampant ivy', before a

---

[57] *CP*, 344.
[58] *CP*, 345.
[59] Edward Thomas, 'Rain', in *The Collected Poems and War Diary, 1917*, ed. R. George Thomas (London: Faber & Faber, 2004), 95. The opening lines of Thomas's poem read: 'Rain, midnight rain, nothing but the wild rain / On this bleak hut, and solitude, and me...'
[60] *CP*, 347.

further variation on the image invokes the new beginning: 'through [...] shard-edged windows, / a start of pigeon wings / took flight for open air'.[61] The pigeon – or the dove – symbolises both peace and love, and Robinson's poem ultimately paints a picture of continuation, since both the 'shard-edged windows' and the 'start of pigeon wings' remember '472 Claremont Road', with its 'tattered lace flapping from a broken window'.[62] Rather than attempting to return to the past by looking back through the frosted glass of memory, however, the broken windows raise the possibility of a direct connection with the present, once again – of being 'in the circumstances' in a more fundamental way than before.

In this respect, it is intriguing to find that *The Returning Sky*, like *English Nettles*, references a number of local place names: 'Whiteknights Park', for instance, names the poet's workplace, while '165 King's Road', another of the poems from the index's first cluster, names 'the address Rimbaud gave in *The Times*'.[63] In doing so, Robinson's collection looks forward to *Thomas Hardy: Places and Other Poems*, the selection of Hardy's work that he edited for the Two Rivers Press, in 2014. Discussing his reading of Hardy's poetry in the 'Afterword' to the book, Robinson points out that there are 'relatively few strictly *loco-descriptive* poems' that were 'exclusively inspired by specified, named places', although he continues to note that 'a number of poems [...] named places in them, or indicated the piece's location in a title, a subheading, or a note-like reference beneath the text'.[64] Robinson acknowledges the early influence of Hardy in his interview with Tom Phillips from 2006. 'He's a poet and novelist I read intensively when young,' he discloses: 'That sort of reading suffuses you in unpredictable ways because it's so formative or self-confirming.'[65] The collocation of 'formative or self-confirming' hints at the way in which inclinations have potential to harden into identities, while the collocation of 'poet and novelist' anticipates the most recent development in Robinson's career as a writer: although he included the prose poem 'A Woman A Picture and A Poem' – which acknowledges

---

[61] *CP*, 369-70.
[62] *CP*, 74.
[63] *CP*, 341. See also the notes to the poems in question, which provide further background, in *English Nettles and Other Poems* (Reading: Two Rivers Press, 2010), 54.
[64] Peter Robinson, 'Afterword: "For poetry of place"', in *Thomas Hardy: Places and Other Poems*, ed. Peter Robinson (Reading: Two Rivers Press, 2014), 52.
[65] *TAP*, 143.

Hardy – in *Overdrawn Account*, and although 2004's *Untitled Deeds* included pieces of prose, the publications of *Foreigners, Drunks and Babies: Eleven Stories* in 2013, *September in the Rain: A Novel* in 2016 and *The Constitutionals: A Fiction* in 2019 confirmed Robinson's status as a creative writer of fiction as well as poetry.

Robinson touches upon the differences between writing poetry and writing fiction in his interview with Alex Pestell from 2005: 'All that has to take place for poetry to make things happen is for those involved to read it as a form of fully meant and thoroughly embodied communication,' he suggests – where 'embodied' alludes to a statement from *Making Things Happen*: 'Poetry survives by being embodied in a reader'.[66] Turning his attention to fiction, however, Robinson suggests that novels are 'not usually communications of quite this kind', since 'poetry's relation to the fictive is both more thoroughgoing and more patently conventional', which ultimately means that 'poetry can be more directly about, and directed towards, lived and living occasions'.[67] Indeed, the former's brevity, together with its setting up of a speaker, who is frequently – but by no means always – pinned down to a particular time and place, enables a reader to take such compositions to heart, in contrast to the many selves and situations and the many times and places that the more expansive form of the novel usually combines.[68] Most fundamentally, though, Robinson intimates that the differences are primarily a consequence of form – or the 'textual signs' of 'a poem', as he puts it in *Making Things Happen*: the various patterns of poetry, most notably its lines and its stanzas, emphasise its distance from the discourses of the day, while the unbroken sentences of fiction have the potential to approximate to other forms of language (and the lived experience that they suggest) in a more straightforward way. In this respect, another passage from Searle's essay 'The Logical Status of Fictional Discourse' appears to be particularly apposite. 'The utterance acts in fiction are indistinguishable from the utterance acts of serious discourse, and it is for that reason that there is no textual property that will identify a stretch of discourse as a work of fiction,' Searle writes: 'It is the performance of the utterance act with

---

[66] Robinson, *Making Things Happen*, 37.
[67] *TAP*, 129.
[68] For a suggestive discussion of a contrasting approach, see Hans-Georg Gadamer, *Gadamer on Celan: 'Who Am I and Who Are You?' and Other Essays*, ed. and trans. Richard Heinemann and Bruce Krajewski (Albany, NY: State University of New York Press, 1997).

the intention of invoking the horizontal conventions that constitutes the pretended performance of the illocutionary act.'[69]

Even so, Robinson's understanding that 'poetry's relation to the fictive is more thoroughgoing and more patently conventional' is borne out by the conventions of the publishing industry. *Foreigners, Drunks and Babies* is prefaced by a 'customary disavowal' that, Robinson acknowledges, echoes the epigraph to the title story: '"there are no such people"'.[70] *September in the Rain*, by contrast, presents a fuller disclaimer, which takes into account the complexity of the novel's relation to the act of sexual violence that Robinson witnessed and initially attempted to work through in a sequence of poems from *This Other Life*. 'Although portions of *September in the Rain* are derived from real events, each character in it is a composite drawing upon several individuals and the author's imagination,' reads the note on the title page: 'Place and time have been adapted to suit the shape of the book, and with the exception of a few public figures, any resemblance to persons living or dead is coincidental' – before the final sentence goes one stage further by taking care to preclude the possibility of autobiography: 'The opinions expressed are those of the characters and should not be taken for ones held by the author.'[71] Such disclaimers are not usually to be found at the beginnings of books of poetry. Does this practice constitute a tacit recognition that poets in fact speak *in propria persona*, as the many references to the real people and real events from Robinson's life that appear throughout his *Collected Poems* intimate? Or is it, rather, a recognition of the fundamental impersonality of the medium of poetry, which results in its potential for tension between artifice and representation – and, accordingly, between voice and self – with the ultimate consequence that the attempt to speak *in propria persona* is necessarily a fiction? Roy Fisher calls attention to 'the figure representing the empirical Peter Robinson' in the passage from his essay

---

[69] Searle, 'The Logical Status of Fictional Discourse', 68. Compare the 'complete and continuous natural scene' of fiction that Robinson describes in *Making Things Happen* (21).

[70] *FDB*, n.p.

[71] *STR*, n.p. See also the similar 'Note' on the adjacent page, which finds Robinson repeating the point: 'When not invented, its characters resemble only in outline their originals, and are composed for fictional purposes' (n.p.). Compare also aphorism 29 for Robinson's earlier acknowledgement of the 'fictiveness of autobiography' (*UD*, 8).

that was excerpted as a blurb for *Untitled Deeds*,[72] while Robinson casts light upon the relation between the two understandings in his interview of 2003, immediately before hinting at the distinction between subjectivity and solipsism: 'The departure point of a poem may well be autobiographical, but the arrival can't be.'[73] Similarly, another passage from *Making Things Happen* suggests how voice is able to be reconciled with self. 'In English the word "act" has a curious double life because it means to pretend to do something and really to do it,' Robinson affirms: 'What this ambiguity tells us about how English speakers understand "acts" and "action" is that pretending to do something and really doing it are intimately related.'[74]

Regardless of genre, however, Robinson's creative imagination continues to work in the same way. 'Windscreen wiper blades making / sweeps at sheeting rain' appear in 'A September Night', the third poem in the sequence from *This Other Life*, while the opening 'There Again' similarly acknowledges 'the predictable returns of windscreen wipers'.[75] A further variation on the image is to be found in the prefatory chapter of *September in the Rain*, which is titled '20 September 1975', where it hints at the many uncertainties of the circumstances in which the couple find themselves following the incident, having made their way back to the shelter of a petrol station: 'The rain is still pouring in the blackness outside. Rivulets are coursing across the plate-glass windows, fusing and dividing as they run.'[76] Later, when they finally reach the police station in Como, they are greeted by 'a dusty-grey frontage with barred and meshed windows, on the opposite side of the street', before a closer inspection reveals further details: 'A film of grime covered the grilled windows'.[77] As such, the windows of the police station approach the closing lines of 'Vacant Possession', the penultimate poem in the earlier sequence, which finds the poet and his partner returning to her former residence and looking through 'jammed sash windows', only to notice that 'one barely visible, ghosted handprint / smears an un-cleaned, frosted-glass pane'.[78] By contrast, the final chapter of *September*

---

[72] Roy Fisher, 'Preface' to *The Salt Companion to Peter Robinson*, 21-25 (23).
[73] *TAP*, 104.
[74] Robinson, *Making Things Happen*, 20.
[75] *CP*, 82, 80.
[76] *STR*, 5.
[77] *STR*, 10.
[78] *CP*, 84.

in the Rain finds Richard – the male protagonist and narrator, who is a lecturer at an Art College in Winchester – back in Milan, on a research trip, where he has travelled to view 'La Lattante' (1865), a painting of an infant being fed, by the Italian artist Cletofonte Preti, for his forthcoming book. Robinson's description of the painting comes to its close with a familiar detail: 'The skin of her head, torso, left arm, and bare feet are lit by a very strong light source – a putative window beyond the right edge of the picture'.[79] The windows that appear throughout Robinson's poetry manifest the 'two distinct, though related, aspects' of *Making Things Happen*, by conditioning the perceptions of the world that the poet's subjectivity then conditions further. The 'light source' from the 'putative window' that Robinson imagines at the end of *September in the Rain* works in a comparably 'dual' way, however, since the promise of new life (and the accompanying new beginnings) that the painting celebrates only appears once the novel has acknowledged the continuing shadows of its lasting hurt.

---

[79] *STR*, 261.

Chapter 5
European Integration

Adam Piette

Peter Robinson's poetry has long engaged with the ways the mind adapts its sense of being at home in the world as political space, from the exploration of Englishness and British identity through the industrial crisis and emerging nationalist rhetoric of the mid-1970s in the early *Benefit Forms* poems, through the experience of exile in Japan and the weighing of attachments in the three 'homes' of Liverpool, Sendai and Parma of the collections from *Lost and Found* (1997) to *The Look of Goodbye* (2008). Many poems dwell on experiences of European cities, leaning heavily, through epigraph and allusion, on the work of European poets such as Saba, Sereni, Hölderlin, Goethe, Montale and so many others; Robinson's intense engagement with translation as theorist and practitioner has worked up a European aesthetics of transfer and transcultural communication, Englishing so many European poets from Pierre Reverdy to Luciano Erba and beyond.

Brexit has been a concern of his most recent work, with particular emphasis on the felt filiation between destructiveness in the private sphere (turning on the rape in Italy that has marked his life and work) and the destruction wreaked on the idea of a companionable, integrated Europe. This chapter will survey the contradictions, potential and struggles of poems about Europe and European history in Robinson's work before concentrating closely on the collection, *Ravishing Europa* (2019). It will attempt to track the poet's use of Adrian Stokes's thinking on integration to sketch a prolegomena about Europe as a psychic whole on the brink of being ravished by the hard right's bullying triumphalism. The run-up to the *Ravishing Europa* section will deal with important coordinates in Robinson's own sense of Europeanness: his links to Vittorio Sereni, reconnoitring Robinson's long history of scholarly and imaginative struggles with Italian art and poetry, especially with regard to Italian fascism and the Second World War. Robinson travelled to Italy in Pound's footsteps, but gave up a thesis on Pound and visual art – colouring complex feelings for his own personal family history (his father was a soldier in the Italian campaign) and the lines of resemblance drawn between Sereni's struggles within the guilt and compulsions of Mussolini's warfare state as soldier-poet and Robinson's own experience with the rape event in Italy. Adrian Stokes, as guide and theorist of European art, is another companionable spirit, enabling an optimism of the will through the dialectic of reparation (from paranoid to depressive aesthetic and psychic states) that structures the manner in which one might begin to feel one's way beyond the pessimism of the intellect. Robinson's explorations around a Stokesian poetry of reparation will be defined before moving to close readings of the Brexit poems and their gauging of the 'dark again' of European disintegration.[1]

Robinson's poetry has engaged with its own status as European modernist lyric through allusions, reflections and imbrications of various kinds. The allusions arrange complex weaves of comparison and contradistinction with regard to European poets and poems, allusions often signalled by epigraphs and voicing of respondents (to the poems' appeals) as dead or othered companions. The reflections arrange this audience of European companionate intelligences as co-present ego-figures, acting out and challenging the ego's reimagining of experience, in the tradition of Eliot's compound ghost. The imbrications form overlapping planes of allusion that introject secretively ambiguous tonal complexity into the singular experience, its place and time, a Wordsworthian recurrential logic fusing with European/Anglo-American modernist simultaneity and palimpsest layering. Italy stands as the site of this threefold compounding of web-like allusiveness, ego-figure work and overlapping planar space-time, in part because of its importance as a Poundian geo-psychological homeland for Renaissance demonstrations of art's powers. Robinson early on aimed to train as a painter, and as academic and poet he projected painterly casts of mind and language, picking up on Pound's redefinitions of early modern Italian artworks as contemporary statements of affect, aesthetic acts of self-portraiture and material conjuring of trans-historical environments. The allusiveness of the Cantos throws together onto a surface concrete and seemingly random expressions and impressions, clearly *there* in line and technique, but also multiple, as if forced together by a Mallarméan throw of the dice.

---

[1] I am indebted in my use of Adrian Stokes to the fine essay by David Pascoe, 'The rough with the smooth: Peter Robinson, Adrian Stokes, and the forms of reparation', *Salt Companion to Peter Robinson*, ed. Adam Piette and Katy Price (Cambridge: Salt Publishing, 2007), 104-121.

The conjunctions, clashing chances and collusions of spatio-temporal experiences have visual power because of the temporal imbrication, concrete memories made planar to become actively compositionally plastic and psychologically explosive as improvisatory and unconsciously driven. Robinson took the Poundian allusiveness, trained it upon lived occasions, an everydayness that is deceptive if taken too easily as singular lyrical experiencing of affective moments. The painterly multiple and planar effect is European-modernist as well as European in older traditions, for instance, in the early poem 'Looking Up', which features lovers in psychological estrangement from each other, locked into a domestic space that is connected to the world through the window looking up towards the skies.[2] As such it is an anti-aubade, diverting the troubadour form to register a tormented distancing; and it figures a Romantic type-scene, revisiting the situated lyricism of Baudelaire's prose poems with their city interiors, inaccessible clouds and skies and stories of troubled and conflictual love. The poem reads as an autobiographical statement of emotional moment, yet opens up with the re-airing of conventional tropes into a heartfelt balancing act negotiating the pain and bewilderment of troubled relationships. The lines track the daylight as it 'settles / adhesively' on the 'breakfast things', matching the poem's work sticking things together with syntax, illuminating (as the poem also does) the couple's interior in terms of 'those inventories of objects / which used to depress me, you said' – 'inventories of objects' was Juan Gris's phrase describing the still life representations of his analytic cubist work.[3] The move is characteristic of Robinson's addressee poetics, the 'you' both the partner whose mood is being coaxed back into conciliation with the poet, and the reader as fellow or angelic dead poet-companion, who is called upon as critic of the poem's own brokenly comic rerun of cubist and surrealist inventory lists.

The second section of the poem widens the allusive field and makes this a fully European lyric: having pictured the depressive lover, staring fixedly anywhere than at her partner within the 'small room' of the house and of the stanza, the poet's own gaze moves, desperately, for some comfort, towards the skies seen through the windows, the cloud tails flaking above 'early white sheets'. He glimpses a black plastic bag

---

[2] *CP,* 62.

[3] '[my pictures] are no longer those inventories of objects which used to depress me so much', Juan Gris, quoted in John Golding, *Cubism: A History and an Analysis, 1907-1914* (London: Harper & Row, 1968), 135.

flapping on lines beyond the roofs – it resembles a question mark, ironically exposing the deadening silence and fixity of the relationship, dogged by uncertainty and 'no questions'. The poem ends saying there are no answers either, but that is 'no problem', because variously 'the cirrus have refused them' – curiously adapting Wittgenstein's reflections on questions and answers in the *Tractatus* ('We feel that even if all possible scientific questions be answered, the problems of life have still not been touched at all. Of course there is then no question left, and just this is the answer').[4] The endings of Robinson poems have this characteristically eerie lift and rumble of significance, but obscured by difficult and liberating uncertainty and ambivalence. Here the comforts of the Romantic sublime are ironised down to an indifferent refusal to respond: this is a relationship that has to sort itself out. One might turn to Goethe's praise for Luke Howard's 1803 classification of clouds, cirrus the highest and most sublime of clouds, sign of the Father's responsiveness to lamb-like supplication.[5] The poem is 'variously' European, more clearly, in its connections to the aubade, alba and Tagelied tradition, and in its staging of a Donne-like room- and stanza-enclosed couple caught up in the conventions fashioning a cloudy poetics of strata, from the cumulus of the sheeted morning bedroom setting (cumulus means sheet) to the flaky perilously transient cirrus (meaning fibrous) of a permanent love bond always under refusal from the edict of the absent father in the skies. The cirrus are plural, plural as the allusive and planar cloudy strata of the air-as-poem.

I have gone into such detail to demonstrate Robinson's complex networking of European intertexts through the allusive work, casting objects (here the clouds) as uncertain ego-figures, flooding the small room of the poem with the light and phenomena from other times and days. The effect is a Europeanising of the domestic interiors and exteriors of the scenes, as sign of a various-minded allegiance to internationalist modernism and its revision of medieval, Romantic and lyrical tropes. The allusive weave of the poem is the motor, then, for the imbrication and planar layering of the temporal and cultural specificities of the

---

[4] Section 6.52 of Ludwig Wittgenstein, *Tractatus Logico-Philosophicus*, trans. C.K. Ogden (London: Kegan Paul, Trench, Trubner, 1922), 89.
[5] Goethe responded enthusiastically to Luke Howard's 1803 'Essay on the Modification of Clouds' with poems dedicated to the strata Howard had named. Cf. Richard Hamblyn, *The Invention of Clouds: How an Amateur Meteorologist Forged the Language of the Skies* (London: Picador, 2001).

occasions. This variousness matches the variety of responses to Europe we find in the pre-Brexit work: the several strands and sub-genres of the long engagement with Europe in the collections working towards an act of advocacy for a European modernist internationalism. We have the work that is set in European cities and landscapes, travelogue recordings of impressions, anguished interrogation of often traumatic experiences, responses to artworks and European poetry, political reflections on European history triggered by encounters. The travelogue poems include 'To the Dutch Italianists', exploring Dutch scapes in ways that seek to match Robinson's own domestic perspectives and everydayness to Dutch realism;[6] and the more recent 'Copenhagen' sequence,[7] which searches for Kierkegaardian analogues to the spooky temporal overlaps and imminence of angst-laden loss within feelings experienced in the city alongside (and addressed to) his companion. The two sequences, so far apart, exemplify the subtle rootedness – of Robinson's sense of the uses of poetry (intimate, philosophical, ethically searching) – in European culture, environment, intellectual tradition, and deep time.

The trauma poems are darker, combing the experiences within the cities and sites, as exercises in difficult multidirectional memory, seeking to represent the occluded violence of history on the continent. 'Bohemian Interlude' records, as in a notebook or diary, impressions of Prague haunted by Kafka disappeared by the city's touristy appropriation of him, and yet there as lost absence along with the Prague Jewish population murdered in the Holocaust (*CP*, 447).[8] 'Die Lilliputbahn' tracks elusive impressions of Vienna that register, at the edge of the imagination, the lost traces of the Jewish population killed in the Second World War: the allusion to this terrible history is kept quiet as the Robinson persona registers the quiet of the city as enclosing the silencing of 'a piece of [the city's] heart / during the seven German years'. The poem is dedicated to Diethard Leopold, son of the founder of the Leopold museum and now a trustee, who led an initiative to restore items in the museum's artworks – once owned by that lost Jewish population, acquired in the post-war. This act of restitution,

---

[6] *CP*, 126-7. Cf. also the three Dutch poems 'Ear to the Night', 'Finding the Range' and 'Autobiography' and the three sequences written about Amsterdam whilst his daughter Matilde went to university there, 'From Amsterdam', 'Provincialweg' and 'Provident Scenes' (*CP*, 440-6).
[7] *CP*, 487-90.
[8] *CP*, 447.

of reparation, places the poem's meditation, quietly, within European penitential history.⁹ The French sequence 'From the Dordogne' visits Oradour and other French sites in the region and correlates, at an extreme angle, the breakdown of his first marriage to Rosemary Laxton as poisoned by the aftermath of the rape event ('you said that we were only yoked / by violence together') to the obscene violence of the Second World War ('us left daunted to remember, / sharing it, *danger de mort*').¹⁰ The correlation is itself acknowledged as poisoned by violence since the poems yoke together the personal trauma with the trauma of the Oradour killed.

Poetry's own acts of imaginative comparison – Samuel Johnson defined metaphysical poetry's conceits as 'heterogeneous ideas [...] yoked by violence together' – is held to account, in an act of almost self-denying admission, as ineluctably driven by Europe's violent past.

The trauma poems are dominated by the rape sequence and the seven poems' broken moves to record the painful experience as a difficult enforced witnessing, again, of the violence; and part of the re-witnessing that is done in other Italian poems network the event into the fascist history of Italy. Historical trauma infiltrates so many of the Italian poems, from 'Feeding the Dead is Necessary', with its sensing of the dead's presence (the Austrian and Italian naval battles, the American soldiers who drowned in the lake, the killing of Mussolini after Salò) keyed in to Italian culture through the concealed allusions to Italian poetry,¹¹ through to 'White Lines' set in an Italy where a woodpecker's tapping is heard despite such noise and distraction as the lightning storm occurring later in the poem – whose 'arrowed forks and flare-flames', figured in the poet's mind partly as allusions to the war, become unavoidable as the poem progresses.¹² The lightning discharges seem to write across the sky 'like so many un-sourced quotations / escaped from the lost dead's un-thumbed tomes'. Something is being

---

⁹ Cf. the poem 'Raubkunst' (the German term for stolen art), *CP*, 276-8.
¹⁰ *CP*, 137-8. Robinson returns to Oradour with 'Twinned Villages' (*CP*, 467) about a visit to Tyneham, a ghost village in Dorset emptied of inhabitants by the army because of its firing ranges; the 'annihilation' recalls the French murders. The poem was printed in the anti-war collection, *The Arts of Peace*, edited by Robinson and Adrian Blamires and published by Two Rivers Press in 2014.
¹¹ *CP*, 95.
¹² *CP*, 285.

hidden within the clumsiness of the expression here, as though the analogy of lightning to war-dead voices or the voices of dead authors is being obscured in the act of its recall – and the next lines confirm this: 'because [the dead] can't remember us, / resentful, we've forgotten them'. The sense that post-war Italy may be forgetting its war dead, and also abandoning its links to its dead authors, is strong here, but has laced through it another more obscure anxiety. When Robinson's I-voice turns from the white of the lightning strikes to white lines on the nearby road, linked somehow to 'an obscure grief or shamefulness' formed from the dark, we are left with a sense of open secret. The last line speaks of 'allusive adverts': and allusion here is adverted to as signalling a personal trauma, a historical trauma, and a literary set of coordinates, all of them 'forgotten' in the scumbling act of shameful remembering. The poem's lightning may be alluding to Montale's 'Arsenio', which also features the poet experiencing the storm as an internal dialogue with his own possible death and psychological darkness. Such allusion is a gaming, nevertheless, with obscurities designed to conceal the shameful past and only cryptically to betray the act of concealment: the road and its white lines figuring the mind's darkening white lies to itself and to the dead. What is dead and yet rising like storm-cloud at the back of the mind is the rape, that occurred on a roadside on a night of lightning, and which strikes, again, like a charged act of warlike destruction within the psyche, forcing re-enactments, cycles of grief, shame, censorship, self-torment. The only thing quite comparable to this experiencing of the storm's violence is someone nursing wartime post-traumatic stress disorder; and the war imagery of the lightning sees artillery flashes in the sky coming in from the shameful (for Italy) Second World War. Shelley rises to semi-consciousness too: 'the cloud of mind is discharging its collected lightning', from his Preface to *Prometheus Unbound*, representing the mental power of English poetry inspired by and triggering European revolutionary energies. Written in Rome to imitate Aeschylus, Shelley's poem enacts that discharge of lightning. For Robinson, retracing Shelley's Anglo-Italian writing within European traditions, the discharging is far more ominous, darkened by history, the storm a re-wounding strike upon the mind's surfaces, the 'arrowed forks and flare-flames' like hellish war-weapons glimpsed at the edge of reason then repressed as soon as seen.

    A second major cluster of European poems looks back at Europe from expatriate perspectives, and these are linked allusively to the trope so common to Robinson's more political work, that of the rumours of violent or paradigmatic historical events from abroad, from an elsewhere at once geographical and psycho-cultural. 'News Abroad' remembers accompanying his partner in La Spezia when the Falklands War breaks out.[13] 'A Quiet Day' is set in Ornella Trevisan's flat in Parma, but registers the spectral impact of the bombs landing on Tripoli, a strike ordered by Reagan and using aircraft flying from British bases; and is addressed to 'someone / from the other life who knows', perhaps Sereni who had died three years before, or it may be Marcus Perryman (his co-translator) in Verona or someone in the UK: the mysterious and uncontacted addressee signals as much the otherness of the poet's peaceful lifetime and craft when set against history, as it intuits a dead centre of inward violence within the imagination that responds, with a mixture of persecutory paranoia and political outrage, to the news from abroad. Europe here is a geopolitical setting for Anglo-American neo-colonial violence in North Africa; yet Italy, in an odd reversal of the Italian war and rape poems, is here a refuge, a Parma for peace as much as it is a setting for an inward psychic struggle between warrior and pacific impulses. Similarly, 'Coverage' registers the first Iraq war on the World Service; 'Nabucco' reacts to the shelling of Dubrovnik in the war in ex-Yugoslavia from Verona. And once Robinson had moved to Japan, European events come from afar as from another time: 'More Aftershocks' senses the news from Assisi of an earthquake as though the tremors could be felt. 'January Sales' takes stock of the Asian Tigers stock market crash in wintry Japan.[14] These news poems sit side by side with work that registers the recurrence of imagery and affect that allude, as though recoded by screen memory, to the rape scene in Italy, its lightning flashes, the rain and gusts of wind, its dreadful road: its cryptic allusiveness is replayed in 'Above the Falls' where a gale through the gorge's trees (their arms 'upraised') is heard, fantastically, as a roar of allusions, 'freshly amplified this year ...' – again no more than this to break the silence.[15] 'This year' must be the anniversary of the event,

---

[13] *CP*, 96: the poem contains allusions to Sereni and Montale; cf. the discussion of the poem in the introduction to *The Salt Companion to Peter Robinson* (Salt, 2007). As Katy Price and I wrote then: 'Political events have the elusive quality of the dead, for Robinson – his poetry is haunted, always, by the reticent ghosts of current events, intuited beyond the horizon' (8-9).
[14] *CP*, 154, 158 & 237.
[15] *CP*, 244.

2000 being twenty-five years after the 1975 event, as if the weather were recreating the conditions in dark tune with the temporal turning and returning of the years. Characteristically, these rustling allusions also replay Wordsworth's 'Simplon Pass' ('Winds thwarting winds bewildered and forlorn') whilst at the same time quoting Josef Brodsky and, more distantly, Mandelstam.[16] The past is always variously personal, historical and cultural, with imbricative force that thickens and deepens the lived complexity of the reverberating memory. Bad weather in Japan is registered again in 'Typhoon Weather', which figures the same image of 'upraised arms':

> tormented trees
> flailed like arms of women
> fleeing a rape in some smoky canvas
> like the victim's upraised hands
> in Goya's picture of reprisals[17]

The upraised hands recall the picture used for the cover of Robinson's Carcanet *Selected Poems* (2003), Antonio del Pollaiuolo's *Apollo and Daphne* from Ovid's *Metamorphosis*. The personal is fused with the political, the Pollaiuolo and Goya's *El Tres de Mayo* bringing together the victim of personal assault and the victims of state violence. Countering the pain here, as well as softening the curiously cold quizzicality of the gaze, is the verbal music, signalled by the opening t-repetition and 'flailing'-'fleeing' play, connecting 'upraised' to 'reprisals'. They share four phonemes clustered in the same order around a comparable diphthong, a pleasing consonance that runs against the torment being depicted.

And this is what marks the work in its very engagement with political and personal acts of violence: the terms of possible resolution of the conflict and damage caused lie in the integrative processes

---

[16] 'A tree stands there rustling, as it were, with allusions', Brodsky, 'Of Grief and Reason', in *Of Grief and Reason: Essays* (New York: Straus & Giroux, 1995), 2. The Mandelstam sentence about history as the noise of time ('the noise and the germination of time') may therefore be in the background – cf. the Vera Komissarzhevskaya chapter of *The Noise of Time: The Prose of Osip Mandelstam*, trans. Clarence Brown (North Point Press: San Francisco, 1986), 109.
[17] *CP*, 245.

generated by the artwork (here the verbal music-making of the lines) even in the expression of that very damage. Paralleling the formal felicities of sound-repetition (acting as a Wordsworthian co-presence within the lines)[18] is the idea of a peaceable European integration[19] and a common culture sustained by the web of relations summoned through Robinson's allusions. Adrian Stokes, in the important chapter on the ego-figure in the 1958 'Greek Culture and the Ego', speaks of the ways art can mirror and match the shift from paranoid to depressive states of mind in the child as it moves from the disintegrating feelings structured around the contradictions of the part-object towards a new vision of the whole mother that brings internal and external objects together. The ego-figure stands in for the projections and introjections generated by the whole mother that enable integration to happen. For Stokes, that integration occurs in art through comparable 'aesthetic formal (integrative) values' that emerge from the strange contradiction of art: that it imposes distance so that we can appreciate the object as a whole and so reflect on our own singularity; and at the same time it consumes us into its zone with its enveloping effects. The dialectic of this contradiction resolves itself as process through a miming of the integration of warring part-objects within the whole mother: Stokes's example of this is the harmoniousness of sounds: 'in concerted sound, from accompaniment, we entertain a vivid sense of co-ordination *in process*, of sounds within sounds, harmony within melody and warring voices, of bits and polarities as they become a whole that is self-sufficient'.[20] That integrative process has its political analogue in the example provided to Robinson by Vittorio Sereni's negotiation of the shame and complicity of his own wartime experience in the Italian conscript army. As Robinson shows in his introduction to the edition of Sereni's work he co-translated and edited, Sereni stages an allegory

---

[18] 'the co-presence of something regular [...] tempering and restraining the passion by an intertexture of ordinary feeling [...] [throwing] a sort of half consciousness of unsubstantial existence over the whole composition' (1802 Preface to *Lyrical Ballads*).

[19] Not the full political concept of an integrated Europe exactly; rather the idea of spiritual unity. Robinson in communication to the author: 'I'm not a believer in the super-state Europe, or necessarily in the Euro as currently managed impoverishing further the south'.

[20] Adrian Stokes, *Critical Writings,* vol. III (London: Thames & Hudson, 1978), 97-8.

of Europe as a fragile space of 'peace and culture' in the *Diario d'Algeria* collection, written whilst on active service and as POW. Robinson quotes Leonardo Sciascia's judgement: 'there is evidently still in Sereni the sense of Europe's fragility ... but also an idea of Europe as *other* than the war, the violence, the Nazi-fascism. An idea, a myth, a utopia'.[21] In the fourth poem of 'Algerian Diary', Sereni, imagining a dead American soldier on the D-Day beaches, resists a fellow POW's plea to pray for Europe on the occasion of the Normandy landings because of the suffering war unleashes on armies and civilians, and because of his own entanglement within the army.[22] What he has instead is 'the music now: / of the tents that flap against the poles. / It's not the music of angels; it's my own / music only and enough –'. As Robinson puts it:

> These lines turn the move towards an aesthetic realm in which history can be resisted upon itself [...] The music of the tents is composed into the bitter harmonies of Sereni's lines, offering a truth to immediate surroundings where there had been distraction or illusion.[23]

The integrative music of his own work, as in the chance rhyming of 'upraised' and 'reprisals', plays a similar role in composing into the scenes of European violence and their difficult modes of 'appeal and admission' a registering of fidelity to the immediate surroundings that signals 'vitality', a being 'alive to the continent's fate' as well as a Kleinian integration, through seemingly marginal coordination and accompaniment, of those broken, damaged experiences into that other music along its lines, that other Europe of peace and culture.

This difficult integrative music can be registered in the first poem of the sequence 'The Late Returns', which recounts a visit to Lake Garda and Villa Igea at Gargagno where Lawrence finished *Sons and Lovers*, 'wild thyme / scenting olive-grove grass, crime / scenery come back to more than once'.[24] The observation comes out of the

---

[21] *The Selected Poetry and Prose of Vittorio Sereni: A Bilingual Edition*, ed. and trans. Peter Robinson and Marcus Perryman (Chicago: University of Chicago Press, 2006), 9.
[22] Cf. Sereni's own comments on this poem in the prose piece 'Algeria 44' in *Selected Poetry and Prose*, 289-91.
[23] *Selected Poetry and Prose of Vittorio Sereni*, 10.
[24] *CP*, 421. The title alludes to Lawrence's 'Twilight in Italy'.

blue and reserves its meaning until the end where the vision of his companion 'mirrored in lake shadow' triggers the comment that 'this beauty's unbearable as before / even if seen from its opposite shore'. 'As before' may signal allusion, as to Sereni's poem 'Un ritorno' which visualises a lake as 'an astonished / mirror of me a lacuna of the heart',[25] or previous poems by Robinson, as in 'Easter Break' which has the poet hearing 'self-destructive' waves and feeling like he is 'falling in another nightmare';[26] but something is still held back. The mystery of the lines only deepens if one remembers that Mussolini's Salò Republic fusing Italian and German fascism was set up at Gargagno, its HQ the Palazzo Feltrinelli; and that Mussolini was killed near Lake Como. What is hinted at is that Robinson had visited the lake with Rosemary Laxton and is here returning to the scene with Ornella Trevisan. The terrible event in 1975 occurred in the vicinity of Lake Como, so the territory is doubly haunted, by the fascist dictatorship that drew Sereni into its brutal circle and against whom Robinson's own father served in the Italian campaign, and by the act of sexual violence that fell upon a couple of cultural tourists on their way back from visits to Florence and Rome. But that double violence is countered by another doubling, the recurrence of visitation ('come back to more than once') that is accompanied, musically, by the recurrence of delicate sound patterning in and along the lines. As Robinson remarked on his key poem about the assault, 'There Again': 'It doesn't describe; it re-experiences it in its own terms, terms which try to draw upon the balms of sound and delicacy.'[27] The re-experiencing, the being 'there again' is made possible by formal-ethical acts of aesthetic integration which turn in particular on the 'balms of sound'.

The terms of 'The Late Returns' – 'wild thyme / scenting olive-grove grass, crime / scenery' – figure forth the return of sounds in the shift from Lawrence to crime scene in the full rhyme accentuated by the enjambment, the delicate balm of the sound-repetitions on aɪ, gr, sen-siːn, m/n. The confrontation between peaceable Italy and a space of violence is played out in the terms of the accompaniment ('thyme / scenting' rhyming delicately with 'crime / scenery') such that the peaceable balm of sound provides a governing counterpoint that holds the thing together

---

[25] Sereni, 'Un ritorno' *Selected Poetry and Prose*, 122.
[26] *CP*, 117.
[27] 1999 interview with Marcus Perryman, in *The Cortland Review* – http://www.cortlandreview.com/features/99/06/. Collected in *TAP*, 40-53 (43).

as potentially reparative, as integrative. That potentiality stands and falls on a reader's ethical tact and willingness to accept the language offered as pleasurable on the limited terms that the invitation to hear the balm-like sound-patterns sets up. Those limited terms are the subject of the poem's delicate act of appeal, there in the lines as a temporary judgement about the transient difficulty of responding to beauty at all in such a place, with such a topic: 'this beauty's unbearable as before / even if seen from its opposite shore' – the 'opposite shore' is at once the other side of Lake Garda and the other side of the poem, the phenomenological space of the reader. The poem acknowledges, then, how weak the claim to the balm of sound has to be when dealing with the brutal dynamic and aftermath of the re-experiencing of the violences. At the same time the b-repetitions ('beauty's unbearable as before') offer an auditory accompaniment to what is seen that secretly sustains the integrative counterpointing. Seeing again, being there again cannot repair the damage; but the work of art channelling reparative energies, that combine Stokesian integration as concerted sound with Sereni's peaceable counter-political music-making, may make up the difference, by singing of that other Europe, that other space of loving being, together again.

Turning now to the collection, *Ravishing Europa*, published in 2019: the poems chart thinking about European identity in the run-up to and aftermath of the Brexit vote on 23 June 2016. Robinson's views on Brexit are outlined in his contribution to the English Association pamphlet, *English After Brexit*, edited by Adrian Barlow. In his 'Balkan Diary', he states that the 'overwhelming feeling was of loss – not the lost vote, but what that loss implied'.[28] The essay meditates on the coincidence that he learnt the result whilst in the Balkans at a conference in Nikšić, Montenegro; and suggests the consequence of the vote, since it was such a close result, was the fracturing of the states of mind of British citizens, accompanied by threats to the Union with pressure on Scotland and Northern Ireland, and a disintegration of trust in the body politic. Psychologically, the vote would install itself within each and every citizen as an inner division of mind: 'because when a nation is divided its citizens rather than lining up neatly on each side of the split, find it running through their psyches'.

---

[28] Peter Robinson, 'Balkan Diary', *English After Brexit*, edited by Adrian Barlow (Leicester: English Association, 2016), 35-46; available here: http://www2.le.ac.uk/offices/english-association/news-1/out-now- english-after-brexit-ea-fellows-reflect-on-brexit-plus-peter-robinsons-balkan-diary

This 'Balkanising blow to recognition and incorporation of difference within ourselves' had resulted, for Robinson himself, in an 'inwardly Balkanised self', the fissure of the vote repeated in the divided states of the mind. The *Ravishing Europa* collection responds to this fragmenting effect of the 2016 referendum; and like 'Balkan Diary', relates the vote not only to the local divisions and enmities of the UK body politic (political warfare over the welfare state, austerity economics, Leaver 'nostalgia and resentment, blame and despair'), anti-immigration racism, post-Imperial break-up, Balkanising of the Union, the migrant crisis triggered by the Iraq war, the Syrian Civil War, and climate and political crises in Africa, but also to the emergence of a Brexiteer fiction of 'a *Sinn Féin* England in a neo-nationalist, potentially ex-UK' facing a Europe rhetorically stripped of all ideal or reparative form.

The first of the three sections of the collection are 2016 texts written in the immediate aftermath of the vote,[29] and they detail a range of feeling and thought related to the Balkanised identity now observing the fallout of the vote in the UK and in Europe. 'Belongings' is dated 3rd April, so is temporally situated just before the referendum, and puns on 'staying in Europe', telling the story of seeing two Belgian girls on a train from Milan, making their way to Turkey, reading Apollinaire – the poet reflecting on 'the in-two-minds of Europe' 'fighting it out through you'. 'Monterosso' registers the change in experiencing Italian swimmers at the seaside town that was Montale's childhood holiday home: the Balkanising effect has created a fractured temporal Europe in the mind. The poem responds to Montale's 'The Lemon Trees' and other Monterosso poems, exploring the return of the dead, the return of quotations, and reflecting on how changed the crowds on the beach are. 'Violated Landscape' reacts to those very words as graffito scrawled on a screen in front of a ghastly hotel built at Portovenere 'by Byron's grotto': and hints at the resemblances between the rape experience and aftershocks and the violation of the European idea. 'Women of Elche' listens to two Spanish friends, one in despair at the Euro crisis and crazy building regime, the other more stoical, both sustained by the figure of a palm tree, ambiguous symbols of salvation and peace rising above the inwardly Balkanised self. 'Lincolnshire Landscapes' is a brief sequence, using Richard Wollheim comparing Bernard Williams's thought to Dutch landscapes as epigraph, turning towards and away

---

[29] The collection's second and third sections are also year-gatherings, 2017 and 2018–19 poems respectively.

from Tennyson's Mablethorpe beach, gazing across the sea beyond Englishness towards the Europe being abandoned.[30] 'Out of Europe' figures an encounter with 'another ghost from Europe', someone who finds that the sound and sense of words bring small relief in purgatory – the addressed figure being glimpsed by the window of Waterstone's in Broad Street in Reading, seeming to wave goodbye, again the divisions of the post-referendum mind matching the ghosted temporal-psychological divisions of the life.[31] 'Post-Truth' looks at the word of the year in 2016, and evokes a Lazarus rebirth of the truth from the past self-abandoned to 'each diverse ruse' of the liars of the Leave campaign.[32] The title poem, 'Ravishing Europa', explores, through bitter reminders triggered by a television debate on the referendum, the painful outline of a possible rhyme between the Europa myth and the rape from years back that links, through the pun on rape, the yellow oil-bearing plant cultivated in fields in England, to the lies spread by Leave ideologues in the run-up to the vote. The Europa-related memories triggered by the Brexit debates include:

> a far-off rape, a
> ravishing, like the ones depicted
> in occidental summer twilight
> on its sunset lands.[33]

---

[30] *RE*, 3-4, 5, 7, 17 & 9.

[31] *RE*, 24. The figure may be Rosemary Laxton, who surprised the poet by attending the launch of *September in the Rain* at the bookshop, 10 September 2016.

[32] *RE*, 34. Leavers in the North of England were figured as 'those left behind', in the poem as 'the thing [the year] leaves behind'. 'Post-Truth' was first printed in the 50-page proceedings of the 'Brexit and the Democratic Intellect' symposium held 13-14 January 2017 at the University of Durham alongside 'Belongings', 'Balkan Trilogy', 'Lincolnshire Landscapes'. https://re-addurhamenglish.files.wordpress.com/2017/05/brexit_complete_ver-1-3.pdf. In his talk at the conference, 'Respecting a decision: the experts, the people, and the politicians', Robinson argues strongly that the referendum as run and defended by the Leave campaign is unworthy of respect, and manipulated genuine feelings for narrow interests: 'the thoughts and feelings, the anger and protest of each and every one of these voters is, I would suggest, what needs respecting – and it isn't respected by a successful cabal's bundling of divisive difference into a "mandate" derived from a bare majority' (29).

[33] *RE*, 8.

The 'Europa'-'off rape a' rhyme, the pun on rape, the twist of Leadsom's 'sunlit uplands' to 'sunset lands': Robinson is writing in a divided tongue, memories of the violence in Italy obscured in and by the same words that paint a 'ravishing' picture of a bogus England (rape fields lit by sunset). A dream of Europe has been violated, and England is shrinking into a projection of the last sunset of its Empire and nostalgic sense of nationhood. Robinson channels this double sense of the occasion through his own deep personal division between now and then: the poem moves on to consider the second marriage as a loving preserving of European bonds, of relationship and association.

If we look at the gathering accumulative effect of these 2016 Brexit poems, one sees a dark return of many of Robinson's European concerns, the double sense to Europe as violent in history and as peaceable transnational territory; loss of connection to the past in the ghost invocation of European figures such as Sereni and Montale; the depth of elegiac feeling for what is being lost, only recuperable in the act of stating other points of view (as beyond England from the shore towards old Europe); the felt relationship between the traumatic violence of the rape event and political acts of violence and the destructive annihilating effect of Brexit; the divisiveness of mind split between then and now, potential and actuality, ghost and substance matching the divisions of a polity at ideological civil war, Balkanising the witnessing mind and heart.

If we look closely at an important poem in the *Ravishing Europa* collection, the 'Balkan Trilogy' sequence, many of these themes are taken up and developed. Dedicated to the memory of Geoffrey Hill (whom Robinson did so much to promote with a key collection of essays),[34] the poem has a Sereni epigraph, 'prega per Europa', the POW's words in *Diario d'Algeria* discussed above. Its first section gazes on the rock outcrops above Dubrovnik and senses landscape features that 'point towards / past damage', signalling the contours of the rape landscape in Italy fused with the war-zones familiar to those who saw that landscape on the news in the Balkan wars of the 1990s, in particular the Siege of Dubrovnik of 1991.[35] The shame felt during the aftermath of the

---

[34] And whose very last poem, according to Alice Goodman, 'looks forward into the grim details of Britain's withdrawal from the European Union' [Alice Goodman, 'Poetry gives us a way of reading the world' (October 5, 2016), http://cofecomms.tumblr.com/post/151398012257/poetry-gives-us-a-way-of-reading-the-world]

[35] In the *English After Brexit* pamphlet, the experience behind the poem is

trauma is now triggered by Brexit itself, the 'risen shame' coincidental with 'hearing news that wrecks it', 'it' referring to the idea of shelter, 'wrecks it' rhyming the cause into witty being.[36] The last 'Herceg Novi' section finds some comfort in the 'spectral headlands' jutting from the 'isolated sea', yet is crossed by darker intimations: those headlands figure the British Isles now isolated from the long history of Europe despite Robinson feeling 'no less at home' in Balkan space. The ambiguity of those headlands, as both signalling a beautiful dream of Europe and the isolated UK, is the cost of the 'sensible inward migrations' that the poet is tempted by on this violent severing from European history – inward migration, after all, is the weak claim to resistance and ego-defence of non-exilic anti-fascists during the years of the Mussolini regime. Nevertheless, the Sereni/Stokes effect is here at work at the same time, along the same lines. Comparing himself to someone emerging from bereavement, the darts of starlings figuring renewed life,

> so from a balcony, soon after sunrise,
> no less at home, you see
> spectral headlands jutting in an isolated sea
> and can hardly believe your eyes.

The poem is dated 30 June 2016 so was written during the week following the vote: what Robinson cannot believe is the decision to enter into isolation, to confirm the death of the dream of Europe, to initiate disintegration and inward Balkanisation of the mind – part of the sense of the lines is that he cannot believe *what he finds out online and in the papers*. At the same time, Europe as dream space of integration is summoned in those same headlands, now a ghost space on the horizon. And furthermore, simultaneously, a third space is created by the lines, a differently political aesthetic zone, generated by the abba rhymes, by the interplay of flexible rhythms (dactylic tetrameter, fourteener) held together by alternate trimeters (the 4:3 of the first two lines matched by the 7 of the third, the final line reprising elements of lines two and three), most of all by the delicate balm of internal rhyming, so-soon-sunrise-see-spectral-isolated-sea; home-head-lands-hardly; and other

---

recorded: 'we walked some way around outside of the old castle walls [...] There Tom [Phillips] and I scanned the heights above the bay where Serbian and Montenegrin artillery had shelled the town in late 1991' (35-6).
[36] *RE*,11-12.

subtler sound-effects, like the way 'eyes' rhymes with 'sunrise' but also, conceptually with 'see' and therefore with 'sea'; or the quiet pun on 'believe', nesting resistance to the Leave campaign. The 'you' addressee is of course Robinson himself, and the 'eyes' signal the two I's of writing, the experiencing and writing selves, as well as punning on the ayes of the Yes vote, and more broadly to the divisions of mind and state. The effect is an extraordinarily rich compounding of the European thematics I have been developing: the ghostly accompanying European ego-figure so often addressed in the poems is here openly Robinson himself, split into pre- and post-Brexit identities. The post-traumatic sufferer finding short-lived and ambiguous solace in the music of integration is played out here with a return to the Sereni/Stokesian music of concerted sound, acknowledged as fitfully an act of inward migration, but proffered, still, as integrative and against the grain of a reckless abandonment of European solidarities.

Chapter 6
An Italian Peter Robinson

Anna Saroldi

As well as being an award-winning poet and a widely published critic, Peter Robinson now has an established reputation as a translator, from French, German and Japanese, but pre-eminently Italian poetry. He has put a vast amount of effort into translating from the beginning of his career, through the 1970s to the 1990s, but it was only later that his work in this area began to gain prominence and recognition, with two major translations published soon after the turn of the millennium: *The Selected Poetry and Prose of Vittorio Sereni*,[1] co-authored with Marcus Perryman, and *The Greener Meadow*,[2] a selected poems of Luciano Erba, which won the John Florio Prize, the prestigious award for translations from Italian into English. After the reception of these volumes, Robinson was recognised as a professional translator and commissioned to produce a volume of poems by Antonia Pozzi.[3]

The first seeds of the poet's relationship with Italy, however, are not linked to any poetic plan, but are instead connected to personal relationships. Despite the fact that Robinson is mostly known as a translator from Italian, this is not the first foreign language he learned and translated. He grew up in the North of England, where, as he remembers, no one among his acquaintances spoke any foreign languages. His father knew a little German because of his wartime military experience, but that was all. Robinson's passion for Italy initially stems from his father's biography: he has said that it was in fact 'my dad's reminiscences of his time in Italy travelling right up to Brunik in the Alto Adige before the Armistice that fired my interest in the place and its culture'.[4] His father, who became a clergyman, went to Italy as a member of the Intelligence

---

[1] Vittorio Sereni, *The Selected Poetry and Prose of Vittorio Sereni: A Bilingual Edition*, trans. Marcus Perryman and Peter Robinson (Chicago: University of Chicago Press, 2006).
[2] Luciano Erba, *The Greener Meadow*, poems selected, introduced and translated by Peter Robinson (Princeton: Princeton University Press, 2007).
[3] Antonia Pozzi, *Poems*, trans. Peter Robinson (Richmond: Oneworld Classics, 2011).
[4] *TAP*, 114.

Corps during the Second World War, and loved it. Italy was to him the land of war and wonder, and a number of firsts: the first time so far away from home, the first experience of opera, the first adventure for a boy who had always been protected by his parents. The father's memories thus gave Robinson a first positive impression of Italy. However, in school Robinson did not study Italian, but took Latin and French at O level, and a little German. When he started university at York, he studied 'English and Related Literature', which required him to take a foreign literature class. Robinson studied the French Symbolists, taught by writer Nicole Ward-Jouve, who was also his tutor.[5] The course introduced Robinson to the practice of reading poetry in European languages, an activity he has continued ever since. The first author he translated was Blaise Cendrars, attempting to render into English his *Au cœur du monde (fragment retrouvé)* in 1974, fascinated by its use of long and short lines.

The second factor that pushed Robinson towards Italy was his interest in the relationship between poetry and art. As a student of visual art and Ezra Pound, Italy had to be visited. This led to the events of summer 1975 when, while on holiday in Italy, Robinson and his then girlfriend found themselves hitchhiking in the rain, at night, on a deserted autostrada somewhere between Milan and Como. There, the rape of Robinson's girlfriend occurred, which he witnessed at gunpoint. This traumatic event inevitably changed his life and has continued to influence his writings. But so too did Italy itself in many other ways. The following years were those spent in Cambridge, where Robinson studied for his doctorate, during which he also dedicated himself to translation. Ward-Jouve had recommended him to read Apollinaire, and from there he discovered Reverdy for himself, who was at the time popular in the Cambridge poetry circles influenced by the New York school.[6] Robinson's first published translation was featured in a special issue of *Poetry and Audience* in 1977, consisting of three pieces by Reverdy, 'Mao-Tcha', 'The Name of The Wings' and 'On Ten Fingers' (the last two later included in *The Great Friend*).[7]

---

[5] For more on the role of Nicole Ward-Jouve in Robinson's education, see *TAP,* 52-54.

[6] Also because of Frank O'Hara's poem 'A Step Away from Them', ending with the lines 'My heart is in my / pocket, it is Poems by Pierre Reverdy', see Frank O'Hara, *The Collected Poems,* ed. D. Allen (New York, NY: Knopf, 1995), 257-58.

[7] Pierre Reverdy, 'Mao-Tcha', 'The Name of The Wings', 'On Ten Fingers',

Between 1977 and 1979, he published a number of other translations from Reverdy in various small magazines. Robinson kept working on him and accumulated quite a substantial amount of material, with the aim of publishing a selection of translated poems. This is an important characteristic of Robinson's work as a translator: the absolute majority of his projects are begun because of a personal interest and enthusiasm in the author, not under commission. Many, such as the Reverdy project, were never finalised, partly through the difficulty of finding a suitable publisher.

Robinson similarly undertook the translation of a book of short poems by the French poet Alain Delahaye, who had attended the Cambridge Poetry Festival in 1977. He translated the collection *L'être perdu*, an abstract kind of lyric poetry, influenced by Jaccottet and Bonnefoy.[8] This was Robinson's first experience as a translator collaborating with a living poet, and it did not turn out successfully. Robinson 'began to feel, rightly or wrongly, that he [Delahaye] was taking over the translations', with the effect of eliminating the 'Anglo-Saxon vigour' that Robinson was trying to impart to them, and for this reason the collaboration did not reach publication.[9]

At Cambridge, Robinson also first became acquainted with Italian poetry, and with Sereni in particular. As Robinson recalls, he 'encountered Sereni's name for the first time in 1979 and started to try and render some of his poems the following year'.[10] In him, Robinson found a more concrete poetic style than that of the French poets he knew, which dealt with recognisably actual experience, and a poet positively engaging with his translators. It marked a considerable shift in Robinson's poetic interests and reading, as he moved from a French *poésie pure*, with its idealism and minimalism, to a much more socially engaged poetry and a preference for specific and concrete language.[11] Robinson decided that the style he had found in Italian poetry was much more suited to him and could help him in his own writing. In the years between 1979 and 1989, there is a change of track in Robinson's poetry, as he becomes

---

trans. Peter Robinson, *Poetry and Audience*, 1977.
[8] Alain Delahaye, *L'être perdu* (Paris: Maeght, 1977).
[9] *TAP,* 16.
[10] *TAP,* 114.
[11] Peter Robinson, 'Vittorio Sereni nella vita di un poeta inglese', in *Vittorio Sereni. Un altro compleanno* (Milano: Ledizioni, 2014), 343-53, 346.

more 'eloquent', as Montale would put it.[12] He started expanding his vocabulary and using more structured syntax, distancing himself from those who believed in a more abstractly discontinuous style.

Around the same time, he put some tentative creative effort into coming to terms with the immediate experience of sexual violence, which resulted in the series of eight rape poems.[13] In 1987 a young Italian lector at Cambridge, Emanuela Tandello, contacted Robinson about a possible visit by Italian poets. Thus it was that both Robinson and Tandello collaborated on the 1988 Poetry International Festival in London, where they organised a joint reading with Franco Fortini and Amelia Rosselli, the latter's poems being collaboratively translated by them.[14] It had been more than a few years since Robinson had started translating Italian poetry: before the holiday in Italy in 1975, he had bought a copy of Ungaretti's *L'Allegria*, innocently thinking that he could manage to translate it, the poems being so short. His fellow Cambridge student Marcus Perryman helped him with Ungaretti, and this project developed a few years later into a fine-printed limited edition by Richard-Gabriel Rummonds's Verona-based Plain Wrapper Press.[15] Rummonds had published the very first limited edition of Sereni's *Stella Variabile*,[16] and, discovering that Robinson and Perryman were interested in translating him, organised a meeting between them. This encounter with Sereni marks Robinson's Italian turn.

Around 1981, Robinson had written a line in 'The Harm', 'clearly pleasing each other', consciously imitating Sereni's poem 'Un incubo' ('certo si piacciono, certo'),[17] read in the Oscar *Poesie scelte* edition brought to him from Italy by a friend. Tandello translated the line as 'il loro godimento così ovvio', but the poet asked her to replace it with

---

[12] *Ibid.*, 344.

[13] Of the eight poems, 'The Trial', was published just once in *This Other Life* and then abandoned as Robinson was not satisfied with it, and considered it 'too narrative'. The scene it recalls is now a part of his novel *September in the Rain*.

[14] The event is recalled in 'Italian Poets in London', *Bulletin of the Society for Italian Studies*, 21 (1988), 50-56. Robinson's summary of the festival is followed by two translations, respectively from Rosselli and Fortini, both by Robinson and Tandello.

[15] Giuseppe Ungaretti, *Six Poems*, trans. Peter Robinson and Marcus Perryman (Verona: Plain Wrapper, 1981).

[16] Vittorio Sereni, *Stella Variabile* (Verona: Amici del libro, 1979).

[17] Vittorio Sereni, *Poesie*, ed. Dante Isella (Milan: Mondadori, 1995), 134.

a word-for-word allusion to Sereni's poem. Robinson and Perryman met Sereni twice before his death, and the poem 'Towards Darkness' was inspired by their second and last meeting in Segrate and Milan. To Robinson, Sereni was a 'Godsend',[18] to the extent that he stated that 'non è esagerato dire che ho cominciato ad imparare la lingua [italiana], proprio per poter leggere poesie italiane e quelle di Sereni in particolare' ('it's not an exaggeration to say that I began to learn Italian really to read Italian poetry and Sereni in particular').[19] Robinson strongly felt the impulse not only to learn the language, but also to learn from him, and in the poem 'Towards Darkness' movingly asks: 'With your gratitude and reticence, / through obscure exits, guide me', echoing Sereni's own 'La malattia dell'olmo' ('Guidami tu, stella variabile, fin che puoi ...'), which he had already begun to translate. In a way, Robinson felt abandoned by Sereni's sudden death, which occurred in 1983: 'I have barely begun, and the work / so soon leads into silence' ('Towards Darkness').[20] Robinson and Perryman had invited Sereni and Fortini to the Cambridge Poetry Festival. Sadly, only Fortini and another Italian poet, Maurizio Cucchi, were able to attend.[21] Homages to Sereni began to become explicit in Robinson's poetry. In 'News Abroad' he uses the phrase 'from square to square',[22] consciously imitating Sereni's 'da una piazza all'altra' ('Saba'), and in fact he employs Sereni's phrase in his poem's Italian translation, just as he had asked to be done with 'The Harm'.

Robinson has also translated non-European poets. When teaching in Japan, he tried to learn Japanese and produced an edition of translated poems in collaboration with one of his students, Fumiko Horikawa: the collection *When I was at My Most Beautiful and Other Poems 1953–82*, by Noriko Ibaragi.[23] During those Japanese years, though, Robinson never abandoned Italian literature and was slowly working on an anthology of twentieth-century Italian poetry. The

---

[18] *TAP*, 25.
[19] Robinson, 'Vittorio Sereni nella vita di un poeta inglese', 343.
[20] *CP*, 97.
[21] Fortini had also joined the 1983 edition of Cambridge Poetry Festival, as recalled by Robinson in 'Franco Fortini in Cambridge', *The Fiction Magazine*, 2:2 (1983), 64-66. The article is followed by five translations of Fortini's poems by Robinson and Perryman.
[22] *CP*, 96.
[23] Noriko Ibaragi, *When I was at My Most Beautiful and Other Poems 1953–82*, trans. Peter Robinson and Fumiko Horikawa (Cambridge: Skate Press, 1992).

project was already well developed in the early nineties, but various personal obstacles stood in its way (most prominently Robinson's brain tumour and his divorce), as well as professional difficulties, such as those with the publisher who had initially supported an anthology of translated poetry. Robinson had to confront the proverbial British indifference towards translated literature (and poetry most of all) and the reluctance of publishers (at the time more rooted than today) to believe that such a project could sell in the British market. The initial plan was rather comprehensive, with two volumes stretching from Carducci to Veracini, and including the most renowned poets of the twentieth century alongside younger generations (represented, for instance, by Cucchi, Frabotta, Valduga, and Magrelli). All the poems were to be translated by Robinson himself, with Perryman's assistance; Robinson had already sketched renderings of at least a few poems by every author on the list (including some particularly challenging ones, such as Zanzotto), and had translated others more extensively (Montale, for instance).[24] The anthology was never completed, but the surviving typescripts clarify the extent to which Robinson has engaged with contemporary Italian poetry.

Today, Robinson has completed a manuscript of translations from Fortini (some of which are already published in *The Great Friend* and in *Modern Poetry in Translation*),[25] an author whom he had started working on thanks to Perryman and later kept translating on his own. In addition to a project on Giorgio Bassani's *Complete Poems* in collaboration with Roberta Antognini, he has written an essay on the so-called *linea lombarda*, and at the same time worked on a selection of poems from the three collections by Pietro De Marchi (b. 1958), a contemporary Swiss-based Italian poet who follows in the same line as Giorgio Orelli.[26] De Marchi lives in Zurich and his poetry often deals with the presence and reality of daily bilingualism, balancing itself between Italian and German, a situation of co-presence and the dialogue

---

[24] Robinson's translation of Montale's *Mottetti* appeared in *Modern Poetry in Translation*, 8 (1995), 179-86.
[25] Poems by Franco Fortini trans. Peter Robinson and Marcus Perryman, *Modern Poetry in Translation*, 9 (1996), 188-200.
[26] A previous English-language edition of poems from De Marchi's first two collections has been edited and translated by Marco Sonzogni: see Pietro De Marchi, *Here and not Elsewhere: Selected Poems 1990–2010* (Toronto: Guernica, 2012).

of languages and cultures that Robinson knows and understands well.

The Great Friend and Other Translated Poems

Despite the fact that the Italian anthology was never published, a smaller selection of his translations from different languages, *The Great Friend and Other Translated Poems,* was published by Worple Press (2002), featuring not only, but mostly, Italian poems, and illustrating Robinson's activity in the field. This publication divides his translating production into two parts, marking the end of his early career. It features various examples of the many different poets Robinson had privately worked on and was published just four years before the large Sereni collection, which had a much greater ambition and scope, wanting to introduce to the English-language audience a little-known foreign author by providing an almost complete translation of his poems. The Sereni translation is a fully public work, meant to be the compass and point of reference for any new reader in English who wants to learn something about Sereni and his oeuvre. *The Great Friend* is a more private work, a personal selection of beloved authors, assembled on purely personal criteria. *The Great Friend* also marks Robinson's willingness to be a part of a specific Italian poetic tradition. The format is quite unusual for British poetry publishing: not only, as Jacob Blakesley has shown, do British poets translate much less than, for instance, French and Italian ones,[27] but, if they do publish translations, they rarely choose the personal anthology format, opting instead for single-author volumes. Italian poets, on the other hand, are the most likely to be translators, and this for a specific, well-established format, that of the 'quaderno di traduzioni'.

The label comes from Eugenio Montale's homonymous collection, published in 1948, which '[diede] il nome a un genere letterario prettamente novecentesco e italiano' ('[gave] the name to a literary genre typically twentieth century and Italian').[28] This collection stands out for being published while the poet-translator was alive: before him, Ungaretti had done the same (but with a different title, *Traduzioni,*

---

[27] Jacob S. D. Blakesley, *A Sociological Approach to Poetry Translation. Modern European Poet-Translators* (New York: Routledge, 2019), 19.
[28] Jacob S. D. Blakesley, 'I Quaderni di traduzioni', *I quaderni di poesia,* 5 (2017), 13-25, 13.

1936),[29] but otherwise collections of translations by Italian poets had only been published posthumously (such as Carducci's *Versioni da antichi e moderni*, and Pascoli's *Traduzioni e riduzioni*).[30]

The choice of the word 'quaderno' intimates that the reader is accessing the private notebook of the author, the scrapbook where drafts are hidden. It does not give the impression of a completed work, but rather suggests that the author can still go back to it and make changes – that translation is still in progress.

The title was later used at various times by the publisher Einaudi, and it acquired a prestigious status: the other most prominent 'quaderni di traduzioni' in Italian literature are those of Sergio Solmi, Giorgio Caproni, Beppe Fenoglio and Edoardo Sanguineti. Other influential poets have published their 'quaderno' under a specific title, such as Sereni's *Il musicante di Saint Merry* (the title of a poem by Guillaume Apollinaire, the translation of which is featured in the volume).[31]

According to Blakesley, the characteristics of a 'quaderno di traduzioni' are that all the translations must be authored by a single poet, who also decides how to structure the book; that the collection does not feature original poems and it includes mostly (if not only) poetry; that the texts are translated from various languages and are put together not in order to achieve a reliable representation of a certain national literature or movement but rather because of the translator's interest and taste.[32] Robinson's volume perfectly fits this description. This shows that his interest in Italian poetry is not limited to an ambition to translate it into English and make it available to a new audience, but that he is also driven by the desire to belong to that same tradition. His status as

---

[29] Giuseppe Ungaretti, *Traduzioni* (Roma : Edizioni di Novissima, 1936).

[30] Giosuè Carducci, *Versioni da antichi e moderni* (Bologna: Zanichelli, 1940); Giovanni Pascoli, *Traduzioni e riduzioni* (Bologna: Zanichelli, 1913).

[31] Sergio Solmi, *Quaderno di traduzioni* (Torino: Einaudi, 1969); Giorgio Caproni, *Quaderno di traduzioni* (Torino: Einaudi, 1975); Beppe Fenoglio, *Quaderno di traduzioni* (Torino: Einaudi, 2000); Edoardo Sanguineti, *Quaderno di traduzioni* (Torino: Einaudi, 2006); Vittorio Sereni, *Il musicante di Saint Merry e altri versi tradotti* (Torino: Einaudi, 1981). Other examples are Luciano Erba's *Dei cristalli naturali: e altri versi tradotti (1950-1990)* (Milano: Guerini, 1991); Franco Fortini, *Il ladro di ciliege e altre versioni di poesia* (Torino: Einaudi, 1982); Giovanni Giudici, *Addio, proibito piangere e altri versi tradotti (1955-1980)* (Torino: Einaudi, 1982); Mario Luzi, *La cordigliera delle Ande e altri versi tradotti* (Torino: Einaudi, 1983).

[32] Blakesley, 'I Quaderni di traduzioni', 17.

prolific translator, and the way he approaches poetry and translation as closely related practices, show an understanding of the role of the European poet that is closer to that of the Italian sphere. Robinson thus transformed his long-standing activity as a translator into a concrete volume, inspired by the Italian poets he loves and has translated, for whom the pairing of composing and translating poetry is almost a given.

THE GREENER MEADOW

When *The Great Friend* was published, however, Robinson was not yet a renowned translator. An unusual collection with a precise model, it constitutes a strong declaration of poetics and intentions by someone still early in his career. After the Sereni volumes, the work that definitively established Robinson as a translator is the Erba collection, which he also considers his most positive translation experience, because of his relationship both with the author and the publisher. Robinson had started translating Erba by himself while working on the project for the Italian anthology in the early nineties, before meeting the Erbas and before the idea of *The Great Friend*. The surviving notebook of the time shows that he had already tackled more than twenty texts. These first attempts are very literal translations, maintaining the syntax and word order of the original: mostly intended to give a sense of the meaning of the poem, they lack the poetry and rhythm that subsequent versions will acquire. By 2001 he had completed, with the help of Perryman, a small section of twelve translations, with the intention of sending them to a journal. That did not happen, and four of them were later collected in *The Great Friend*: 'Without a Reply', 'Festival of Nations', 'When I Think of my Mother', and 'La Vida Es…'. All of this was done without knowing the poet himself. Later on, a connection was established thanks to Mairi MacInnes, who knew Erba and his wife personally, and put them in touch. Robinson got to work with Erba himself, building a solid relationship with the author. Around 2002-2003, there was an initial proposal to publish a small book with Arc press. This was never completed, but some translations were featured in *Modern Poetry in Translation* in 2004,[33] and eventually these various

---

[33] Poems by Luciano Erba trans. Peter Robinson, *Modern Poetry in Translation*, 3:1 (2004), 61-68.

initiatives led to the publication with Princeton University Press.[34]

The survival of the manuscript of the first sketched translations (pre-existing *The Great Friend*) and of three printed drafts for *The Greener Meadow* allows us to compare different versions of the poems and to observe their development closely, as well as the changes between the volumes themselves. The structure is relatively simple to understand, as the selected poems are organised chronologically, according to their original collections. The idea for the title came with the first of these printed drafts, substituting the previous neutral *Selected Poems* and *The Lesser Evil* (the title of Erba's fifth collection).[35] The process of rewriting is particularly long and intense: various drafts exist of every poem, and the final shape of the translation of *The Greener Meadow* is always very distant from the original sketch and often from the version published in *The Great Friend*. One poem that went through a particularly intense process of rewriting is 'A First-Degree Equation', a rendering commented on by Matthew Reynolds in *The Poetry of Translation*. There, Reynolds highlights Robinson's tendency strictly to adhere to the original text, which thus becomes 'a palimpsest of the foreign words and sensibility'. In his argument, 'Robinson's uncompromising phrases' challenge the readers' interpretation 'because English has been kept so close to Italian', and 'this verbal fidelity comes at the cost of pattern of sounds'. As Reynolds points out, Robinson's rendering of the initial lines of the poem does not replicate the original pattern of alliteration and internal rhyme, and the result he describes as 'flat' by comparison. However, this does not make Robinson's texts any less poetic, as his 'translations achieve the strangeness and complexity of poetry by interpreting as little as possible'.[36]

This poem is not featured in *The Great Friend*, and therefore its genesis will be discussed by comparing the original draft from the nineties' notebook to those of *The Greener Meadow*, and to the final printed text. The uncertainties and difficulties with this text are evident from the very beginning, and the handwritten draft already featured two subsequent and different translations of it (for the vast majority of

---

[34] Guernica Editions had already edited a small book of selected poems by Erba: Luciano Erba, *The Hippopotamus*, trans. Ann Snodgrass (Toronto: Guernica, 2003).
[35] Luciano Erba, *Il male minore* (Milano: Mondadori, 1960).
[36] Matthew Reynolds, *The Poetry of Translation: From Chaucer & Petrarch to Homer & Logue* (Oxford: Oxford University Press, 2011), 68-72.

the poems just one handwritten translation is present in the notebook). The title ('Un'equazione di primo grado') proved to be problematic for Robinson: variants for it include 'A Grade One Equation', 'A First Rate Equation' (handwritten copy), 'An Equation of the First Power' (first print draft), and finally the definitive 'A First-Degree Equation', introduced in the second print draft. This draft also presents the foreignising 'to leaf over pages of *temps perdu*' for 'sfogliare pagine del tempo perduto', privileging a Proustian interpretation of the line. But it is at the third print draft that Robinson attains a significant number of improvements, for instance by correcting the rendition of line 10: 'fiori affranti / dolcemente dai merci decollati' had been rendered with 'broken-hearted flowers / gently decapitated by the merchandise', a mistake caused by the ambiguity of the term *merci*. At this stage, Robinson corrects it into 'gently cut off by freight trains'. In addition, he reintroduces the pronoun 'you' a few lines before, thus creating a technical rhyme with '*perdu*'. In this case, by choosing a precise interpretation of the syntagm 'pagine del tempo perduto', Robinson has been able to create a new pattern of sound, unknown to the original, to characterise his translation. The various drafts of this poem also show Robinson's constant attention to the text and how he kept coming back to his translations (even those already published, in journals or in *The Great Friend*), reworking them until the very last moment, in a continuous effort to improve the results and with the aid of his growing knowledge of the Italian language. Some lexical choices are exemplary in this sense: to translate 'ci equipaggiavamo', Robinson went through 'to fit', 'to equip', and finally 'to kit out', a change in the third print draft, and chosen for the final translation. Similarly, he keeps rewriting other lines, such as 'cara provvista di ombra!', initially translated as 'dear foreseen shadow' (manuscript), then 'expensive purchased shade', and finally 'dear provisioned shade', a revision in the third print draft that gets closer to the original handwritten version and will be kept in *The Greener Meadow*. Other hesitancies involve, for instance, the word order of the first line, where Robinson tries both the option with the vocative 'Mercedes' at the beginning and at the end: finally, he will adhere to its position in the Italian text. In some other passages, he distances himself from the original and its vocabulary: in order to translate 'decollati', he initially resorts to 'decapitated', but will later (again, in the third print-out draft) change his mind and incline towards a more Anglo-Saxon diction: he suggests in the draft version 'taken off', and will opt in the final book for 'cut off'. The richness in changes of this third draft shows how Robinson, despite starting extremely closely to the original text, and staying so for a few rewritings, continuously re-assesses his choices and finds new ways to balance the Italian-ness of the text with more English options, in an attempt to create a text that can work independently in the target language, but without truncating its link to the original. Studying Robinson and Perryman's translations of Sereni, Michela Bandera has argued that, in their rendition, 'la vaghezza dello stile sereniano resta generalmente intatta' ('the mistiness of the Sereni style generally remains intact').[37] In *The Greener Meadow*, similar and opposite things happen at the same time: similar because Erba's style is preserved in English, the opposite because Erba's style is much more precise and detailed than Sereni's. By always keeping close to the Italian texts, Robinson is capable of rendering into English two very different kinds of poetry while preserving their specificity.

L'ATTACCAPANNI E ALTRE POESIE

Robinson's willingness to adhere to the Italian poetic tradition did not stop at the composition of a 'quaderno di traduzione' nor with translating two of the most important Italian poets of the second half of the twentieth century. He decided to take one step further by writing in the very language of the poets he loved and to become a part of the Italian poetry world by publishing his poems in that language. The story of Robinson's Italian self-translated collection, *L'attaccapanni e altre poesie*, is inextricably bound to the series of rape poems, to the Sereni translations and to the love story with his now wife Ornella Trevisan. While discussing how the collection was born, I will quote passages from the poems it features: *L'attaccapanni* is a distinctly autobiographical collection, which summarises a whole chapter of Robinson's relationship with Italy.

The earliest nucleus of what would one day form *L'attaccapanni* can be identified in the first Italian version of the eight rape poems which Robinson asked Tandello to translate. Further developments

---

[37] I am grateful to Michela Bandera, who has studied the Sereni translations and kindly shared her work with me: *Vittorio Sereni in inglese. Le traduzioni di Peter Robinson e Marcus Perryman,* MA thesis, Università degli Studi di Milano (2014-15), 58.

occurred after Sereni's death in 1983, when Perryman and Robinson went to Parma to revise their translations with the poet's daughter Maria Teresa. While there the following year, Robinson had the chance to see again an Italian woman, Ornella Trevisan, whom he had met in Cambridge when teaching English. '*Galeotto fu Sereni*', as many Italians would say, alluding to the *Inferno V* episode, as Robinson and Ornella fell further in love over working on Sereni versions.[38] In the poem 'Unfaithful Translations', the town of Parma, Ornella's home and the Mondadori offices at Segrate are linked by the common spectacle of fish swimming in a lake and the figures of Ornella and Sereni merge in the ending: 'your words / came offering in trust' might be referring to either of them, as they are both calling the poet, 'inviting me towards / myself'.[39]

Robinson wrote a poem to Ornella, 'an almost stranger / I must say goodbye to', and Perryman volunteered to translate it into Italian so that she could understand it. Thus, in 1984 'An Impossibility' was translated. As well as translating this poem, Perryman wrote an Italian prose piece, never published, entitled 'Autobiografia', as a form of introduction to Robinson's translated poems, whose number was starting to grow. The following year, something similar happened: Robinson wrote a poem, 'Aria di Parma', evoking a couple of Ornella's friends who were getting married, and dedicated, through its acrostic form, to Ornella herself.

Around 1988, when *This Other Life* was published, some handwritten revisions of Tandello's translations became the nucleus of a first book project entitled *Quest'altra vita* (literal translation of *This Other Life*), that also contained Perryman's 'Autobiografia' as well as some attempted translations by Robinson revised by Perryman, and a few translations by Perryman (from the rape series and of 'At Salò' and 'Leaving Parma'). These first translations had to deal with a necessary degree of reticence and ambiguity, as at that time Robinson was still married to his first wife. Poems such as 'Unfaithful Translations' and 'Towards Levanto', as Robinson stated, 'bring together the work of translating Sereni and the process of falling in love'.[40] At the same time, these two poems have the greater aim of redeeming Italy in his mind, as they 'are attempting

---

[38] Robinson himself uses this adjective in 'Vittorio Sereni nella vita di un poeta inglese', 351.
[39] *CP*, 122
[40] *TAP*, 89.

to bring together a renewed sense of possibility that I discovered by returning to Italy, by co-translating Sereni, and by meeting Ornella Trevisan'.[41] This positive feeling is, however, accompanied by a growing awareness of the unhappiness in his first marriage.

When Robinson moved to Japan, this marriage was slowly coming to an end and he was attempting to keep in touch with Ornella. 'Not Yet Out of the Wood' incarnates the struggle accompanying that complicated time of crucial decisions, economic – as he was 'financially embarrassed' – and personal. In this case, the self-translation into Italian brings new implications to understandings of the text. On the one hand, being 'out of the woods' is not an idiomatic expression in Italian, and thus the translated title, 'Non ancora fuori dalla selva', is unfamiliar to the Italian reader.[42] However, the words *wood* and *forest* present in the English version are both translated into Italian as *selva*, and *lost* is rendered not as *perso* but as *smarrito*. This configuration is distinctly familiar to every Italian reader because of the first line of the *Divine Comedy*. As Dante did, Robinson gets out of the wood – he moves to Japan – and this would influence his poetry more and more, as is testified in, for example, 'An Undetermined Heart' and 'Lost Objects', poems that illustrate how the change in Robinson's life was finally happening.

From the mid-1990s Robinson regularly spent the summer in Italy with Ornella and, subsequently, their two young daughters. This brought the Italian translations of his poems a step forward. In 1990 he gave a bilingual poetry reading in Volterra, at an event organised by the local poet Roberto Veracini and the artist Mark Brasington, and in 1992 one in Massa Marittima, at a summer school held there by the British Institute of Florence. For these readings, he and Ornella translated some more poems, including 'Unfaithful Translations', which was read at both events. In 1992 Robinson's collection *Entertaining Fates* was published, containing several poems set in Italy (first published in *More About the Weather*)[43] whose translations were read there too. Moreover, it is in the mid-nineties that 'Aria di Parma' was finally translated into Italian, so that the couple to whose wedding day it alluded could read it. It was there that the whole process accelerated: the first project of a

---

[41] *TAP*, 114.

[42] It can, however, be used as a metaphor, as Luzi's line, epigraph of Robinson's 'Clearing the Wood', proves ('ma fui certo che il bosco / non è senza via d'uscita'), *CP*, 171-72.

[43] Robinson, *More About the Weather* (London: Robert Jones, 1989).

collection of poems translated into Italian dates to just a few years later.

This collection was entitled *Nutrire i morti: Poesie scelte 1980–1995* and exists as an incomplete typescript of translations and a sketch of a contents page. It was the second attempt to create a book after *Quest'altra vita*, but these both remained private projects, as Robinson did not have a potential publisher in mind. By then, the poet was in a more stable situation, still living in Japan, but settled now with Ornella and their first child. Again, the summers spent in Italy led to significant developments. Robinson was more actively considering the possibility of a book of Italian poems, and in Parma he met Paolo Lagazzi, a friend and supporter of Attilio Bertolucci in contact with the publishing house Moretti&Vitali's poetry series. The agreement to go forward with a collection probably dates back to summer 2002, since the email correspondence between Robinson and Moretti&Vitali can be tracked to the autumn of that year. Marco Fazzini, an Italian academic and translator of British poets, also helped in the revision process. Despite some difficulties and disagreements, in the typical fashion of an author-editor-publisher triangle, the book was produced relatively quickly in spring 2004. The book launch took place on 16 March, at which Robinson gave a reading of his poems at the British Council in Milan in the presence of Luciano Erba, whom Robinson was then translating.

Italy in *L'attaccapanni e altre poesie*

While recounting how *L'attaccapanni e altre poesie* took shape, it has been natural to link the poems of the first sections of the collection to Robinson's biography. In this sense, these poems have a story to tell, Robinson's Italian *Bildungsroman*, starting with the establishing-shot of the first section, which ends on the 'blank drawing board' of 'How He Changes', where everything is yet to be written. Despite not being linked to Italy, the first section is required to set the frame for the rest. The second, third and fourth sections represent the core of the narration, dealing with the rape, Sereni and Ornella. The last part presents instead a distinct change and contains the culmination of the Italian love story: 'Variazioni di Via Sauro', a sequence of twenty-five short poems, is a heartfelt summary of all that had happened between Robinson and Ornella. The same section also starts to reflect on what is to come, including poems such as 'At la Villetta' (the municipal cemetery in Parma) and 'Parco Nord' (also in the town).

In these poems, as in the following ones of sections six and seven, Italy is at times evoked as a distant place (in 'Italian in Sendai', 'Winter Zoo Encounter' and 'Pasta-Making') and at times a setting ('Closure' and 'Italian Poplars' located in Parma, or 'Stranded' in Monterosso). This is Robinson's attempt to write about Italy itself and no longer as the setting for violence or love. Robinson does not fall into the trap of the touristic approach, just as he had not fallen into it when writing in and about Japan, as illustrated by John Roe in his essay on the poet's work.[44] His approach has proved to be rewarding, and it can be directly linked to the work featured in Robinson's latest collection, *Ravishing Europa*, which contains poems set on trains to Milan, in Monterosso again, in the Apennines, and looking at Italy's violated landscape. Robinson is Italian in the sense that he is trying to look at Italy just as it is, 'not prepossessing' ('Parco Nord'), with no fairy-tale of the South in mind to invite the interest of his audience. This is also true because Robinson does not write for an audience, but for individual readers, and asks them to be ready to confront the different: be it Italy, England or Japan. Robinson, as Miki Iwata stated, has a 'delicate sensitivity to the otherness behind the ordinary',[45] a sensitivity that always allows him to see things at a distance: he himself admits 'I *have* felt foreign everywhere – '('World Citizens').[46]

L'attaccapanni e altre poesie is a particularly significant collection in that it has no English equivalent. Robinson could have simply taken a previous English collection and translated it into Italian, but he decided instead to craft something new. The collection has been made with the Italian reader in mind, offering an explanation of why Robinson is writing in Italian, and at the same time a sample of what he can say about Italy. However, despite being targeted at the Italian market, there is little effort to conceal the inherent difference of the collection: in particular, its title sounds remote from the usual abstractness of Italian poetry collection titles – to which, for instance, *Nutrire i morti* would

---

[44] John Roe, 'The Refracted-Self: Japanese Experiences', in *The Salt Companion to Peter Robinson*, 175-92, 191.
[45] Miki Iwata, 'His Other Islands: Peter Robinson, Languages, Tradition', in *The Salt Companion to Peter Robinson*, 193-204, 196.
[46] *RE*, 28-29. The line is a self-allusion to the poem 'A Constitutional', *CP*, 261. Robinson does not feel fully British either: as he wrote in 'Your Other Country', 'I'm a tourist here myself', *CP*, 222.

have been significantly closer. Robinson is not striving to fit in: he chooses as a title *L'attaccapanni*, the poem ('Coat Hanger') that would appear to have the weakest link to Italy and to the collection's purpose. However, it is the most delicate reflection on loneliness in the collection and tactfully addresses the bodily pain felt when missing a distant lover. Despite not overtly lamenting this, Robinson is disclosing that the beloved is so present in his mind as to be glimpsed through the leaves of a tree, in an Ovidian metamorphosis. In this case, however, Daphne is not running away but revealing herself to the poet, as if to confirm the stability of her love, whose roots are unaltered by distance. The thought of the lover is so material and magnetic that it draws the attention of the poet back to itself, needing a physical incarnation despite absence: the lover momentarily becomes a tree and a brief bridge is created across the lovers' separation. In 'Coat Hanger', the cortex of the tree reminds him of the freckles of the beloved, with a similarity that was made famous in Italian poetry by Gabriele D'Annunzio's line 'Quasi fatta virente, par da scorza tu esca' in 'La pioggia del pineto'.[47] But this brief encounter is not enough, and the pain remains: the absence of the Italian lover – and of Europe – is felt in the poem as a phantom limb. With this title, Robinson is thus saying to the reader: I have missed your country as a part of myself.

THE ITALIAN LANGUAGE IN *L'ATTACCAPANNI E ALTRE POESIE*

Behind the autobiographical layer of the collection, Robinson addresses the language topic directly. *L'attaccapanni e altre poesie* testifies to his gaining intimacy with Italian, and indirectly retraces the steps for his long process of learning the language. In 'Towards Darkness', Italian is described as 'Bruised on my tongue, their rumorous / language, like an almost closed book': it does not yet belong to the poet, as it is 'their[s]', and he also sees it from a foreigner's perspective, defining it as 'rumorous'.[48] The adjective is a perfect example of Robinson's hidden belonging: while native English readers would mostly interpret it as 'full of rumour', the adjective is instead an Italianism, intended

---

[47] Gabriele D'Annunzio, 'La pioggia nel pineto', in *Alcyone*, ed. P. Gibellini (Milan: Mondadori, 1988), 83.
[48] *CP*, 97.

to mean 'noisy' (*rumoroso*).⁴⁹ In the same poem, he is also aware of his inability to master the Italian language and is almost afraid to hurt it, as if the language was 'bruised' by him, like he had been 'bruised' by others (and both are translated with *ammaccare*). This perception of a damaged language resurfaces in 'Variazioni di Via Sauro', where the communication between the lovers happens in 'the miscarried language we say', an imperfect tool that requires them to 'translate distances'. As William Empson wrote in 'Aubade', a poem also concerned with lovers speaking different languages: 'the language problem but you have to try'.⁵⁰ Once in Japan, as recounted in 'Italian in Sendai', Robinson and Ornella are both 'defenceless against nostalgias', 'knowing only too well / that a bottle of wine's not Italy / nor foreigner speaking your language, home': despite being an English teacher and thus able to stay constantly in touch with his mother tongue, Robinson has to face up to the fact that this cannot hide the cultural difference in Japan.⁵¹

This is particularly hard to deal with as Robinson is fully aware of the importance of language for happiness and a feeling of identity: in 'Winter Zoo Encounter' the Italian woman who has lost contact with her language and her people is an unnerving premonition of what he could become if he remained in Japan. Robinson is aware and afraid of the option, and conveys this with a reference to Italian culture, in the line 'another Florentine in exile'.

More than to Dante, this line refers to his friend and fellow poet Guido Cavalcanti, author of 'Perch'i' no spero di tornar giammai', in which he admits to having lost hope of returning home. Robinson finally moved back to the UK in 2007. Shortly after, in 2009, some of his poems ('For the Birds', 'To that Effect', 'Mi último adiós', 'Unwitting Epitaph', 'What Have You', 'Old Loves') were translated into Italian by Marco Sonzogni, and published in the *Journal of Italian Translation* IV.⁵² The poems had previously been printed in the collection *The Look of Goodbye*, which was also the first English collection to feature

---

⁴⁹ Both meanings are present in the OED, but the latter is archaic.
⁵⁰ William Empson, 'Aubade', *The Complete Poems*, ed. J. Haffenden (London: Penguin, 2001), 69.
⁵¹ *CP*, 201.
⁵² Peter Robinson, 'The Look of Goodbye: The Poetry of Peter Robinson', edited and translated by Marco Sonzogni, *Journal of Italian Translation IV* (II, 2009), 221-27. Available online at <http://userhome.brooklyn.cuny.edu/bonaffini/jit/>.

the poems in the last section of *L'attaccapanni*. Five years later, he published in *Quadernario* the Italian translation of another six poems from that same collection, rendered into Italian again with the help of his wife Ornella:[53] 'White Lines', 'The False Perspectives', 'Not Lost', 'Credit Rating', 'Silence Revisited', along with the prose poem 'Talking to Language' which had first appeared in *Untitled Deeds*. In this work, whose Italian title is 'Conversazione con lingua inglese' (specifying which language only becomes necessary in the bilingual context of the translation), the English language itself puts words in Robinson's mouth (and pen, we could add), as in 'Difficult Mornings' it had told him 'use me, yes, but use me well'.[54] The English version tells us how 'English itself' – a 'weary lover' – addresses Robinson, but in the Italian translation this has become an unspecified 'la lingua'.

Just as his translations of others remain close to the Italian text, his self-translations are first of all very close to the English, attempting to preserve its structure and recreate a rhythm that could work in Italian. Robinson is successful in giving his Italian poems a new orchestrated sound, arranging for the poem a suitable new acoustic economy. For instance, in 'Per Lavinia', the initial line features the alliteration 'da scempio e stupro', which creates a sound pattern that does not exist in the English (although echoing 'stared and strayed' and 'the shame she's not' of the English version) and forms a net with 'storta e snerva' at line eight and 'fissato e vagato e pianto' at line four. In 'Vite dopo', the Italian gains the assimilation of 'rinsavente o rossori', while in 'Alla villetta' the repetition in the line 'dal muro dei morti e stupirci o afferrarci' is added, while 'Chiusura' gains the stressed 'r' of the line 'Fisso attraverso finestre imbrattate'. Similarly, in the fourteenth part of 'Variazioni di Via Sauro' the repetition 'in being found again and try / again and try and try' is changed in order to be preserved into 'nell'essere / trovati ancora e tentare / ancora e ancor tentare', the successful ending of a strophe built on a crescendo of joy and emotion. One of the main differences of the translated style is the word order, as in the Italian versions Robinson quite often resorts to inversions that were not present in the English, and that can be fundamentally divided into two different groups. In some cases, Robinson is maintaining English word order into Italian, anticipating the adjective ('inside thin skin' > 'dentro sensibile pelle', 'Vacant Possession'), the possessive ('this respite's last light' > 'di questa tregua l'ultima luce',

---

[53] *Sei poesie* in *Quadernario: Almanacco di poesia*, I (2013).
[54] *CP*, 187.

'Stranded'), or the adverb ('the whole house helplessly resounds' > 'la casa intera disperatamente risuona', 'A Disturbed Night'; 'I still have desires' > 'che ancora ho desideri', 'Via Sauro Variations'). Elsewhere, he is echoing the tendencies of the so-called 'italiano poetico', postponing the subject (as in 'seagulls would rise' > 'si alzavano gabbiani', which is also moved to the end of the line, 'News Abroad'; 'beyond Milan the train curves' > 'oltre Milano curva il treno', 'Towards Darkness'; 'the cold exacts its price' > 'esige il suo prezzo il freddo', 'Via Sauro Variations'), the verb ('even if I've learnt it by heart' > 'anche se a memoria l'ho imparata', 'Italian in Sendai'; 'it was no dream' > 'sogno non era', 'Via Sauro Variations'; 'if she used her mother tongue' > 'se lei la lingua madre usava', 'Incontro invernale allo zoo') or the possessive ('our pasts' > 'i passati nostri', 'Via Sauro Variations').

Some of these cases are quite telling: in 'Curriculum Vitae', the syntagm 'a lack of love' is perfectly standard English, while the translation 'd'amore la mancanza' acquires with the inversion a higher lyrical value, summarizing the Italian poetic tradition in just one sentence. However, this is not always the case. When analysing the syntax of lines such as 'my father's and grandfathers' / wars played out' > 'di mio padre e dei miei nonni / le guerre allo stremo' ('Towards Darkness'), or 'some distant love's / skin can still be glimpsed' > 'di qualche amore lontano / la pelle si può intravedere' ('Coat Hanger'), it is clear that some constructions are preserved in order to prevent the differing syntax from altering the order of delivery in the English, and its syntactic ordering of attention. The poet is torn between the various options of translation: for instance, the draft of 'Italiana a Sendai' shows that Robinson, translating 'even if I've learnt it off by heart', hesitated between 'anche se l'ho imparata a memoria' and 'anche se a memoria l'ho imparata', the inverted form that will stay in the final version. This could be a trace influence of the Italian poets he has translated: Robinson recalls how he and Perryman had endless trouble in rendering Sereni's multiple inversions, which is particularly relevant as it illustrates how Robinson's long apprenticeship as a translator of Italian poetry shaped his Italian, and partially determined the style of his self-translations. The style of *L'attaccapanni* is a mirror of the anthology of Italian poets he never got to publish: all those translated poems are present in his style.

When considering the translation of a full poem, it is also possible to see how local choices come together in creating a new piece. In 'Traduzioni Infedeli', for instance, it is clear how the syntax of the translated version tries to render as closely as possible the structure of the English, with a few notable exceptions. At line four, 'almost too close to me' becomes 'a me quasi troppo vicino': the personal pronoun is moved to the beginning of the sentence according to Robinson's Italian predisposition for inversions and his fondness for their lyrical impact. In general, he tries to stay close to the English and only introduces small changes, such as the elimination of the verb in line twelve, for instance, or the alteration of the sentence structure in lines thirteen and fourteen, which successfully creates a plausible Italian expression where adhering too strictly to its English counterpart would have meant a loss in efficacy. With regard to the rendering of the sound of the poem, Robinson is lucky, as he has sometimes used English words whose sound is not so different in Italian: the alliterations of the line 'and I tried to touch those depths still without harm' is more or less easily carried in 'e tentai di toccare quelle profondità ancora senza ferita'. Moreover, like the fish he describes, the poet is also creating 'intersecting figures' within the collection: lines ten to twelve are quoted in 'Via Sauro Variations', combined with line six.

In this case, translations are unfaithful not only because Robinson was being unfaithful at the time, but primarily because of the mistakes foreign speakers unwittingly make. The unfaithful translations of the title are first of all those Sereni made addressing Robinson. By literally translating common Italian expressions such as "buon lavoro!" and "amichevolmente", he said something that was both wrong in English and different from what he meant. The poem thus tackles the problem of intentions and how words transform them (one of the main issues in the entire collection), ending on a positive note: those 'well-meant misunderstandings' did reach the poet in the end, implying that a translation does not have to be perfect (if such a thing exists) to be effective.

This reflection on what is the right distance to maintain when translating and what fidelity means in this context is also present in Robinson's statements and reflections on translation. On the back cover of *The Great Friend and Other Translated Poems*, we read that 'as the title underlines, these are not imitations or adaptations, but translations that remain faithful to their originals while [...] becoming English poems in their own right'. This is a statement that openly confronts Lowell, whose *Imitations* are, as Robinson acknowledged, 'a watershed – it divides the subsequent flow into rivers of imitators and anti-imitators'.⁵⁵ This created a divide among poet-translators: some, like Lowell, believe that it is impossible to preserve the poetry and the literal meaning at the same time (a contemporary example would be Don Paterson). To others, like Robinson, this is not necessarily true: 'la presunta impossibilità di tradurre poesia non è motivo sufficiente perché questo o quel testo non venga tradotto; semmai delimita la situazione linguistica entro cui la traduzione dev'essere fatta' ('the supposed impossibility of translating poetry is not sufficient reason why this or that text cannot be translated; rather it delimits the linguistic situation within which the translation has to be made').⁵⁶

In the preface to his *Imitations*, Lowell states that he has 'been reckless with literal meaning and laboured hard to get the tone'.⁵⁷ As Reynolds points out, in Lowell '"the tone" becomes "*a* tone" as the original aim of transference is trumped by the need to compose a poem that Lowell can hear in English'. In *The Poetry of Translation*, Reynolds chooses Robinson's translating style as an example of an anti-Lowell approach: 'Robinson's translation from Erba does less than is implied by the metaphor "translation is interpretation"'.⁵⁸ Rather than approaching a poem with a certain idea in mind, Robinson goes to the letter and sticks to it, keeping it as a constant guide. This, however, cannot prevent the creation of a certain degree of distance and difference between original and translation. He does admit that 'the process of translating a poem begins in every case with an infliction of damage', and when self-translating Robinson is experiencing a very peculiar case of self-damage and self-reparation. It is his own poem that he is decomposing, and it is his own poem that he has to see assembled in a different way in the new language – creating a parallel with the mistakes and errors of life, where Robinson also felt himself to be part of the harm and at the same time of the reparation. In self-translation, the necessary process of 'restor[ing] some of its original otherness' is not foreign to the poet, as he is both the original author and translator.⁵⁹ The self-translator thus has to see 'how such damage

---

⁵⁵ Robinson, *Poetry and Translation: The Art of the Impossible* (Liverpool: Liverpool University Press, 2010), 32, referring to Robert Lowell, *Imitations* (London: Faber and Faber, 1962).
⁵⁶ Robinson., 'Vittorio Sereni nella vita di un poeta inglese', 345.
⁵⁷ Lowell, iv.
⁵⁸ Reynolds, 65, 73.
⁵⁹ Robinson, *In the Circumstances*, 143.

could occur, and how it might be mitigated'.⁶⁰ It requires courage: it asks the poet to be ready to see what he had once written incarnated in a radically new shape. But Robinson is perfectly aware of this: 'there can be no union of the original with the translation. So they must be, at best, significantly different'.⁶¹ They are different because, in a way, their own authors are different: as Robinson explains, in self-translation 'you are yourself alive as you translate, though you are translating the results of a past creative moment'.⁶² In this situation, some poets choose to treat the self-translation of their work as a continuation of it: this is what, for instance, Joyce did with his Italian self-translation of *Anna Livia Plurabelle*, a text Robinson is familiar with and which provided the epigraph to his poem 'Animal Sendai'.⁶³ To Joyce, self-translation is a work in progress, where the text experiences new developments (for instance, in Italian, the experimentation with dialects).

Robinson's approach, however, is radically different. When translating himself, he tries to render the situation and thoughts of the past. There is no deliberate attempt to change it according to the poet's new mental state, but rather fidelity – faithfulness – to the past self. Robinson also described what being a faithful translator means when discussing Sereni's work: his translation of Pound's 'Villanelle' is faithful as 'it remains close to the disposition of meaningful shape in Pound's poem, while maintaining its own "lyrical effectiveness"'.

This is what Robinson also tries to do. When a stylistic feature is essential to the poem, like the acrostic form of 'Aria di Parma', he keeps it. Otherwise, he is ready to abandon what is not strictly necessary to create a new set of characteristics in the new language. Thus, faithfulness and loss are not related in Robinson's practice: linking them would restrict the concept of faithfulness in translation to a limiting evaluation of wrong and correct choices, while the translation should be received

---

⁶⁰ Robinson, *Poetry and Translation*, 169.
⁶¹ *TAP*, 88.
⁶² Robinson, *Poetry and Translation*, 66.
⁶³ In the short note 'Animal Sendai', written to explain the Joycean epigraph to his poem, Robinson recounts: 'in Italy one summer I found a trilingual copy of *Anna Livia Plurabelle*, which contained *en face* Joyce's text and Beckett's translation with, as footnote-style sub-text, an Italian rendition – and that's when and where I found the future epigraph, which chimed with my regular Sundays with our girls at the zoo, and re-prompted the idea of a poem and memories of an old failed draft', in 'Animal Sendai', *James Joyce Broadsheet*, 98 (2014), 3.

within a freer dynamic. The 'wrong' label belongs to a monoglot perspective, to a strict count of one-to-one equivalence, demanding exact correspondence. Instead, faithfulness is to be found in difference. As Robinson stated when commenting on his own self-translation of 'Aria di Parma', the goal is to 'try to get the translation to approximate, as closely as possible, to what the original poem says, while effecting a rhythmical equivalent for it in the entirely different sonic economy of the language into which it is being translated',[64] as he had managed in the examples discussed before. Despite the biographical context, and the Italian saying 'traduttore traditore', Robinson's translations, in this understanding, are not unfaithful at all.

As has been discussed, Robinson's path towards becoming an Italian poet started long ago, culminating in 2004 with the publication of the collection of self-translated poems *L'attaccapanni e altre poesie*. His practice can be read in the context of many significant works located between different national literatures, originating in the urge of some writers to express themselves in a language other than their own (as Conrad, Beckett or Kristóf did).

The Italian tradition is particularly rich in this sense. Historically, foreign writers have used Italian – writing directly in it or self-translating – in the Middle Ages (Raimbaut de Vaqueiras), during the Renaissance (Labé, Montaigne), the seventeenth and eighteenth centuries (Milton, Mozart, Voltaire) and later (Christina Rossetti, Joyce, and Pound).[65] Seen in this light, Robinson belongs to a long-established tradition of heteroglossia and his Italian collection is not a solitary experiment. He is an Italian poet because he has found his place in this diverse family and has contributed to its long history by publishing *L'attaccapanni e altre poesie*. At the same time, his role as mediator of contemporary Italian poetry in the UK and the US and his decision to carry to the Anglophone poetry market a characteristic Italian genre, that of the 'quaderno di traduzioni', define his Italian-ness in an ampler way. Robinson has not only operated from, with and within the Italian language, he has also been able to represent and transfer Italian culture abroad in a successful example of cultural dialogue and exchange. In a context in which many British authors approach Italy with many more

---

[64] Robinson, *Poetry and Translation*, 142, 168.
[65] For more on the topic of Italian heteroglossia, see Furio Brugnolo, *La lingua di cui si vanta Amore. Scrittori stranieri in lingua italiana dal Medioevo al Novecento* (Roma: Carocci, 2009).

or less hidden prejudices,[66] Robinson has instead kept interpretation to the minimum, getting to its substance.

---

[66] See for instance Kate Willman, 'Contemporary British Travel Writing on Italy and British Broadsheets: Tobias Jones, John Hooper and Tim Parks', *Modern Languages Open*, 8 (2018), 1-15.

Chapter 7
Dormiveglia and Values

Martin Dodsworth

1

Peter Robinson's poems present the world in specifically late twentieth-century, early twenty-first-century terms. Set in England, France, Germany, Holland, Italy and Japan, they reflect the new age of global travel and the culture of which it is part. They address such topics as, in 'On Contract',[1] the underlying ethic of our 'publish, that or perish, / bottom-line-at-any-cost regime', and they observe details such as 'the reminiscent / scents of air conditioners / on local railway trains' and the 'red-striped posts / (captured on your phone)' protecting a blossoming cherry-tree in Japan.[2] It is not by accident that so much of his critical work reads poems in the light of their historical moment; the title of his first collection of essays, *In the Circumstances* (1992), is suggestive of his view of himself as a poet of his own time and place.

He is not alone among contemporary British poets in depicting the world in frankly inelegant terms, but he does so in a way that allies his work, not with British predecessors so much as with certain Italian modernist poets. He has spoken of this on numerous occasions. In particular, he has translated, over many years, all the poems of Vittorio Sereni and much of his prose. The poem 'Towards Darkness'[3] is dedicated to Sereni, and he appears in a number of others.

It would be possible to cite specific instances of Sereni's influence on Robinson, but that is not the purpose of this chapter. Here, the emphasis is on the special place of Robinson's modernism in its British context. The poet's admiration for Sereni and affinity to him contribute importantly to this special quality and make Sereni an obvious point of reference. Eugenio Montale characterised Sereni in a review of his third book of poems, *Gli strumenti umani* (1965) as a poet who created:

---

[1] *CP*, 498.
[2] See 'Open Account' and 'The Question' in 'After all those years', *English*, 66.255 (2017), 372-74.
[3] *CP*, 97.

complex forms in which the significances are interwoven or superimpose themselves, as happens in that state of drowsiness which represents the life of the man of our times, reduced as he is to the condition of being the object of others and of himself.⁴

It is possible that Montale drew inspiration for this judgment from the knowledge that *Gli strumenti umani* was based on an unpublished collection, *Un lungo sonno* ('A Long Sleep'), which had won the Libera Stampa prize nine years earlier. In any case, *Gli strumenti umani* itself contains a long sequence 'Nel sonno' ('In Sleep') having to do with the end of the Second World War ('I don't like my times, I don't like them. / Italy will slumber with me'), as well as 'Un incubo' ('A Nightmare') and 'Un sogno' ('A Dream').⁵

Robinson's poetry of the historical moment is like Sereni's, especially when considered as viewed by Montale. He figures in his own poems as a 'man of our times', and their style is characterised as one of *dormiveglia* – correctly, but in this context unhappily, translated by Singh as 'drowsiness'. The word stands for a state of half-consciousness, of waking dream in which the self, reduced to a mere object, is incapable of action, although its passivity is neither willed nor complete. The opening of Robinson's poem 'From a Memory' shows what this means in practice:

> The cypresses disordered
> by stiff gusts, bedraggled strands
> flurried at her face beside me.
>
> Extenuating circumstances
> for my part towards him,
> I blame, then am uncomprehending.⁶

Here are interwoven or superimposed significances perceived by a speaker who is barely able to assume responsibility for what is happening

---

⁴ *Eugenio Montale: Selected Essays*, trans. G. Singh (Manchester: Carcanet, 1978), 92; Montale, *Il Secondo Mestiere: Prose 1920–1979*, 2 vols, ed. Giorgio Zampa (Milan: Mondadori,1996), Vol. 2,. 2,749.
⁵ *The Selected Poetry and Prose of Vittorio Sereni: A bilingual edition*, ed. and trans. Peter Robinson and Marcus Perryman, intr. Peter Robinson (Chicago, IL: University of Chicago Press, 2006), 35, 152-57,142-43, 166-67.
⁶ *CP*, 81.

to him: the disorder of the trees and the bedragglement of the hair seem to transfer themselves to the speaker's untidy, unsatisfactory attempt at summation. Ethical clarity dissolves into relativity in the teasingly modern state of half-consciousness described by Montale. In Keats's words 'Was it a vision, or a waking dream? ... Do I wake or sleep?' (*Dormiveglia*: between sleep and wakefulness.)

Robinson uses those last five words of Keats, along with Calderón's 'Life is a dream', as the epigraph to 'Waking Lives',[7] a fairly recent poem that ends: 'I'm / doubtful – still – we'll wake to find / nothing but the bottom line', where drowsiness is linked with the thought that the world he wakes to is a world in which, for other people, he and his companion are merely the objects reflected as figures on 'the bottom line'. The same words of Keats appear in an essay from the 1980s about Geoffrey Hill, where he discusses Hill's poem 'Loss and Gain':

> Is there a touch of self-delusion in the one who gains a vision of salvation, and, caught in Keats's quandary ('Was it a vision, or a waking dream? ... Do I wake or sleep?'), imagines that history may be atoned for?

He regards what he calls Hill's 'high agnosticism' sympathetically, his 'paradigm of language as debased and to be redeemed'; but he rejects the notion that redemption can be achieved – 'The scepticisms are not to be outstripped. Could a poem ever atone for history? Could it alone redeem the time?'

Robinson's point of view here is that of Montale's 'man of our times'. He admires Hill's 'vision of salvation' not only for its hopefulness (and 'Loss and Gain' is not in fact very positive about the chances of redemption), but also for including in it 'the exchanges of a discordant world'.[8] Robinson himself entertains no 'vision'; the effortful waking dream of his early poetry rehearses the world's discordances muffled in an all-encompassing *dormiveglia*. Action may be imperative, but it is undertaken amidst the entangled and entangling complications of this world, not another more harmonious one. In effect, this is

---

[7] *CP*, 497.
[8] 'Reading Geoffrey Hill', in *Geoffrey Hill: Essays on his Work*, ed. Peter Robinson (Milton Keynes: Open University Press, 1985), 211-12; this essay was expanded as 'Geoffrey Hill's Position' for *In the Circumstances: About Poems and Poets* (Oxford: Oxford University Press, 1992), 131-32.

what the lines from 'From a Memory' are about. In their 'unpoetic' quality (disorientating syntax, want of musical colouring, modern low mimetic vocabulary), they demonstrate that, rather than Hill, Sereni is Robinson's master. Montale, commenting on Sereni's association with an anti-poetry, describes him as a poet 'who finds the title of poet increasingly less justifiable'.[9] Robinson's eschewal of 'vision' smacks of the same discomfort.

However, neither for Sereni nor for Robinson does the suspicion of poetry amount to a rejection. Both think to some extent in terms of William Carlos Williams, whom Sereni admired and translated; certainly, Williams's discovery of the poetic in the conventionally unpoetic is implicit in both.

Sereni depicts a recognizably anonymous, featureless modern world and so does Robinson, for example, in 'the small hotel / on the edge of the industrial // quarter of town' of 'Autobiography'.[10] There is no hope of a transcendent redemption; the poem presents a world made unfamiliar by a consciousness that holds apart from it: 'a life intact and separate … Looking like we think we look, // other than what we look like'.

The places where things happen in Robinson's poems insist both on their own contemporaneity, on being all that there is, yet being inadequate as a supportive context for humanly responsible action. In the early poems, place is often present only in a hazy sort of way. This is not merely a representation of the alienation of mass society or of the urban planning that goes with it nor solely the consequence of subordination of place to what happens there; the prevailing haze signifies with what difficulty the way to responsible action can be found. The low-lit, waking-dream quality, characteristic of the early poetry, is associated with a degree of uncertainty about who is speaking in the poems and about whom they are spoken. The lines already quoted from 'From a Memory', for example, mention 'Extenuating circumstances / for my part towards him', but the reader is given no clue to 'his' identity. The third person is challengingly neutral, an expression of difficulty in seeing, on the one hand, and, on the other, in affirming the self. This poem, as we know from interviews with Robinson and from his novel *September in the Rain*, deals with a deeply distressing event in the poet's life; it can be reduced to certainty by using the other sources,

---

[9] Montale, *Selected Essays*, 94.
[10] *CP*, 39.

but its quality as a poem depends on such certainty's being withheld, as it is in the other poems in the group to which it belongs.[11]

In 'One of my Own', a poem not included in the *Collected Poems*, these lines figure:

> Beating the back of your head
> against a radiator, silently,
> 'Is this a translation
> or one of your own?'
> you'd asked, then called,
> 'Why can't your *you* be me?'[12]

There is an irony in the title, but the puzzle about what constitutes a person is real. It is the sort of thing that interests the (largely Anglo-American) philosophers who interest Robinson so much, and it suggests the affliction of being an object to others and also to yourself. In this state, *you* and *me* are very imperfectly distinguishable. Robinson uses a confusion of pronouns to evoke such a feeling. This is not only true of 'From a Memory', but also of other poems whose subject matter is not quite so painful. They use pronouns so as to express the existential uncertainty that lies beneath their pervasive *dormiveglia*. This anxiety is not confined to the speaker of the poems. It can be hard to say whether it lies more in the world perceived or in the perceiver's own self: 'Why can't your *you* be me?' This is what 'the exchanges of a discordant world' are like. As long as it lasts, the waking dream of *dormiveglia* presents discordant sensation that can only be defined, and so dissipated, on the advent of full consciousness. In Robinson's early poems, there is no such consciousness; action, context, and the will all evade definition, and their evasion is precisely observed.

2

'Early Territory',[13] in my view one of Robinson's best poems, illustrates both the pervasive quality of modern *dormiveglia* and the 'interwoven'

---

[11] *TAP,* 40-53. The poet himself thinks that 'From a Memory' 'suffers perhaps from being a stuttering start' to the sequence.
[12] *EF,* 44.
[13] *CP,* 86.

complexities that Montale associated with it.[14] The setting is a cemetery, apparently at the 'dead-end' of 'Belle View Terrace', a 'wilderness' where 'lupins in full bloom / stir between headstones'. Why the cemetery is a wilderness, where Belle View Terrace is, and what 'we' are doing there are all without explanation. The speaker of the poem is to some extent at home in this wilderness, although appearing uncertain about what is enacted there; the reader does not have even that degree of assurance. You would need to know a lot more about the headstones to give them any solidity of specification – eighteenth-, nineteenth- or twentieth-century? Limestone or granite? The headstones exist with as little sense of their substantial being as may be. Everything in the poem tends to the uncertain, particularly what is seen:

> Caught sight of, ground mist wafts
> after rainy spells across the Stray,
> or from allotments smoke drifts
> and Belle Vue Terrace is looking the same,
> though to us it conceivably was –
> its dead-end the rusty locked gate
> to this wilderness.

The emphasis on barely glimpsing in the awkward first line (awkward for many reasons but mainly because we are in the dark about who might be doing the catching sight) anticipates a feeling induced by the whole poem that neither the people in it nor its reader can fully understand what is going on. The awkwardness at the start is disconcerting, immediately putting the reader on the back foot, and it feeds into a sense of bafflement at its very end, as I hope to show. Passage through the poem is a passage through wafting mist. Even at its most explicit, the poem reminds the reader of what goes unsaid. We are told of 'rainy spells across the Stray', but what is 'the Stray'? Estuary, allotments, parkland, wasteland? The speaker, or the poet, does not care to say.

The place matters not for what it is but for what is associated with it, in the past and in the present:

> Shame-faced yet
> at self-deceiving explanations

---

[14] See *TAP*, 25, where Montale's essay, already cited, is quoted to explain Robinson's initial interest in Sereni.

> for motives others must have seen through,
> unforgiving, I conjure that time
> from the close afternoon, a stickiness
> even to the breeze that fans late
> blushes; lupins in full bloom
> stir between headstones and grasses
> pollinating.

The source of the speaker's shame is never revealed; the 'blushes' and 'self-deceiving explanations' hint at some sexual transgression, but because it is not brought into the light, we cannot know that this is so. Later on, we are told that 'short-cuts still twist through' the cemetery; the shame might not have been sexual at all, but merely the result of a child's taking a forbidden route home and lying about it. Such things can lodge themselves deep in the psyche, leaving a spreading stain in adult behaviour. In the light of 'Plain Money'[15] and the strict vicarage morality described there, such a reading is plausible. Perhaps, the 'others' (parents?) were 'unforgiving' of the shoddy explanations offered, perhaps the speaker is still unforgiving of the explanations or of the parents; the word hovers between past and present in its application, as does the indicator of time, 'yet', adding to the reader's sense of uncertainty. The instability of meaning in 'unforgiving' is paralleled in the 'late / blushes' that follow, which are either the speaker's or the lupins'; like 'unforgiving', 'late' changes application from one point of view to another, but in neither case can the reader seize *exactly* what is going on. An unspecific shame or guilt is diffused through the lines; although the sun shines, there is no brilliance of surface or clarity of view. Uneasiness is intrinsic to the verse – for example, in the remoteness of the one full rhyme 'gate' and 'late', six lines apart, with off-rhymes in-between: 'yet' and 'late', 'stickiness' and 'grasses'.

There is no sense that the speaker can afford an explanation of what is happening (or, rather, being undergone), although the end of the poem is full of a feeling that explanations are needed:

> Here, compounded
> by a cloudless false limit, strong
> sun exposes cool, perfidious

---

[15] *CP*, 77-78.

> tingling of my own skin; but, whereas
> short-cuts still twist through,
> now just you confront me, reckoning
> the years' uncalculated wrong.

The 'reckoning' that would constitute explanation does not emerge. As was the case with 'unforgiving', the word has no certain reference. It means 'rigorously totting up' (with a hint of accusation) or 'explaining' just as you choose to take it. It could be that 'you' are doing the reckoning in some recriminatory confrontation with the speaker, but, equally possibly, 'you' may be unaware of what is going on, and it is the speaker who is silently reckoning the years and, in the process, feeling confronted. 'Your' version of events may be that there is no confrontation, just a being-together there in the cemetery. The last line suggests that whoever makes the reckoning is likely to be wrong, since 'uncalculated' does not only mean 'yet to be calculated' but also 'not reckoned with (at all or at the time)', which, while not flatly denying responsibility, leaves it impossible now to assess what the extent of any responsibility might have been. The possibility, also present, that any 'wrong' could be the natural product of time passing rather than the consequence of culpable human behaviour brings little comfort. The discordant senses of 'reckoning' and 'uncalculated' mesh together in the suggestion of a world made unhomely, viewed in 'that state of drowsiness which represents the life of the man of our times'.

'Early Territory' conveys intense, complex feeling. What can be seen is managed so as to reinforce the reader's sense of the uncertainties compounded in the situation. The sky, for example, is depicted not as an infinite blue but as 'a cloudless false limit', the two adjectives resonating with the shame and implicit guilt at the heart of the poem, whilst 'limit' hints at the way in which the couple are trapped by those feelings. The reader is directed from the light of day to the shadowy space between speaker and confronting other. The uncertainties of meaning generated for the reader by the words of the poem have the effect of making possible only a tenuous link with the couple described, whose own uncertainties remain implicit. There is a striking want of any affirmative bond of human sympathy; but the poem is not an expression of hostility either. It is as though it were a theatrical presentation, having the eerie quality of a *tableau vivant*.

Robinson is not a didactic, but a dramatic poet. He is not concerned to promote any specific belief about the world or any specific course of action, but to dramatise the uncertainties that come from the human situation in the modern world as seen by Sereni and Montale. In 'Early Territory', an anguished situation is made worse by the unavailability of all but 'earthly reasons' for action:

> The vast, smutted mausoleum
> with its cypresses dilapidates.
> For earthly reasons, prolonging them,
> I'm wanting again to disinter
> a self mostly thought better dead.
> Disinterestedly looking for –
> you've not the least idea – someone
> absorbed in taking down particulars
> from mildewed, slant tombstones
> restores me, unnoticed, to the day's
> chance composition.

'Earthly reasons' for disinterring anything sound a bit ghoulish, and there is something ghoulish also about thinking a self 'better dead'. On the other hand, in the context of 'stickiness' in the breeze, 'lupins in bloom', 'grasses pollinating', the phrase also suggests the life of the present body rather than that of a corpse of some date, now revived. The speaker either does not know what the earthly reasons are or cannot articulate them. Presumably, it is they that are 'prolonged' by his wanting to disinter an old self but failing to do so. 'Wanting' has a provisional quality. The self to be disinterred is 'mostly thought better dead' – but by whom? The speaker may be referring to himself or may be dourly aware that this is the opinion of one or more other people – 'mostly'. It isn't clear that this self really *is* dead at all. The speaker composes himself by turning his attention away from thoughts of the past and associating himself with the day – that only has composition by 'chance'. 'Disinterestedly', meaning 'without reference to self-interest', is shaded into the popular and 'incorrect' sense 'uninterestedly', as though the speaker is indeed an object like any other for external forces to work upon. We are back again with 'the condition of being the object of others and of himself'.

As has been suggested, it does not follow that this condition is unaffected by what is presented. The poem presents intense feeling;

its syntactic obscurities and challenging ambiguities are a means of conveying this. But, in itself, and despite its use of the first person, the poem exemplifies the 'depersonalisation' of which Eliot writes in 'Tradition and the Individual Talent'. One may recall that Montale's early poems, as well as Sereni's, also have this quality and that Montale's admiration for Eliot, who had published 'Arsenio' in a translation by Mario Praz in *The Criterion*, only increased over the years. Robinson's poetry is more than the impressive fruit of his reading in twentieth-century Italian poetry; it sets up a vital relationship to modernist poetry in the English tradition.

3

Robinson's elected affinity with Sereni and Montale marks a determined difference in sensibility and poetic practice from poets in the English tradition deriving from Eliot, but it does not divorce him from it. The continuing dialogue with Geoffrey Hill in Robinson's criticism is testimony to this. Hill uses Eliot adversarially to define his own position as a critic and a poet; in his criticism, Robinson does something similar with Hill. In the poetry, he effectually uses practices derived from Sereni and Montale to turn the modernism of Eliot and Hill in a new direction. This is what is going on, for example, in the poem, I have just been looking at, 'Early Territory'.

Hill's poem 'The Turtle Dove' is just as ambivalent as 'Early Territory', but is a quite differently focused poem.[16] It describes another fraught relationship, but using the third person *he* and *she* (rather than the *I, you* and *we* of Robinson's poem). The effect is not only to distance the poet from the poem but also to make it one that focuses on its issues of gender. In 'Early Territory', we have to *assume* that the couple is man and woman, and the subject of their conflict is hidden from us. Robinson's silence in the poem, a variant on the silence about identity elsewhere, enlarges the range of possible reasons for, and kinds of, harm beyond the exclusively gendered. Hill's ambiguities, on the other hand, specifically focus on the erotic as painful and self-tormenting: 'She denied more love, yet her starved eyes caught // His, devouring, at times'. The compacted meanings of 'She denied more love' would

---

[16] Geoffrey Hill, *Broken Hierarchies: Poems 1952–2012*, ed. Kenneth Haynes (Oxford: Oxford University Press, 2013), 10.

require an Empson to be dealt with adequately. 'She refused to love or to be loved any more', 'she pretended that her love had not grown', 'she denied that his love *had* grown' – these are the major possibilities, defining a horrifically confining relationship between man and woman. Strongly stressed long lines, marshalled in quatrains, drive towards the line-end whilst the sense drives beyond it:

> Then, as one self-dared,
> She went to him, plied there; like a furious dove
> Bore down with visitations of such love
> As his lithe, fathoming heart absorbed and buried.

It is a superb achievement in its depiction of a conflicted love, possessing and consuming the couple involved and setting them apart from the rest of the world. Robinson's poem (characteristically, I think) goes the other way; 'the years' uncalculated wrong' folds whatever is wrong between the two people in his poem into the ample wrong of the world to which they belong. Hill's artistry shows in his particularities, an urge to define which, in his view of poetry, can still be fulfilled ('his lithe, fathoming heart'); Robinson's lies in a more inclusive view of things, in which particulars are subsumed in the general haze of *dormiveglia* – in his poems, the world is in half-shadow even in broad daylight.

In so far as 'The Turtle Dove' implies something about the world, in general, it is within a tradition of Christian thinking. The furious dove's visitations are an aspect of the mystery of God's love expressed in the pain and suffering of the world. The dove itself recalls Eliot's in 'Little Gidding':

> The dove descending breaks the air
> With flame of incandescent terror....
> Who then devised the torment? Love.
> Love is the unfamiliar Name
> Behind the hands that wove
> The intolerable shirt of flame.

The contrast between 'Early Territory' and 'The Turtle Dove', and the debt to 'Little Gidding' of 'The Turtle Dove', suggest a line of descent from Eliot to Hill to Robinson, representative of a change in modern British culture. Hill writes in a tradition to which *The Waste Land* belongs as well as *Four Quartets*. Notwithstanding dissatisfaction with Eliot, evident throughout the *Collected Critical Writings*, Hill never turned against *The Waste Land*. 'The Turtle Dove' has affinities with that poem and with 'Little Gidding'; its tormented couple would not be out of place in 'A Game of Chess'. 'Early Territory', set in a 'wilderness' where two people are locked in inexpressible struggle, also looks back to Eliot's poem. The cemetery's 'mildewed, slant tombstones' may recall 'the tumbled graves' in 'What the Thunder Said', and the invisibility of one person to another in Robinson's poem ('you've not the least idea…') is a version of the inability to communicate in Eliot ('Speak to me. Why do you never speak. Speak').

'Early Territory' presents, one could say, the world of *The Waste Land* sixty years on – a shrunken world in which the historical, religious, and literary context, which Eliot found indispensable to understanding and which Hill attempts to revise and reanimate throughout his work, has now lost its force. Robinson's uncomfortable scenes of city and country symbolise this shrinkage. In 'A Short History':

> the city's
> fringes, its vanished
> forestation, wrinkled asphalt:
> a drowsing land
> where grass can reach waist height
> on central reservations, sites
> of motor industries'
> loading bays no longer manned.[17]

In 'Scargill House':

> we had gone
> by a patch of mown green
> edged with grey cut stone
> where a chapel had once been,
> down an arbour of limes
> flanked by graveyard statues,
> defunct tombs, like our times
> and about as much use.[18]

---

[17] *CP*, 69.
[18] *CP*, 206.

The uncertainties of Robinson's poetry go with living in this landscape, in some fashion a *posthumous* landscape, certainly one of *dormiveglia*, in which signs of life are hard to find, and life itself, therefore, hard. Norms and standards of conduct, which are evoked by Eliot, and fought for in Hill, are not readily available; the situations in which action is required are themselves not easy to make out. Existence in such a waking dream or nightmare threatens the sense of moral priorities and of the self that tries to grasp them.

It is especially this that made Vittorio Sereni an exemplary predecessor for Robinson; both write a *secular* poetry. In both, the poetry is suffused by guilt and alienation but nevertheless focused on an attempt to make ethical sense of the personal life in a world where religion is marginal. Robinson admires Sereni's 'fidelity to reconsidered experience', registered in an 'evolving style' joining the 'technical' to the 'spiritual'; he shows 'how with sustained effort goodness can be born from error and self-betrayal'. Robinson commends Sereni for his search 'for what occasions in the life had meant, and for possibilities within them, unlived or to come';[19] there is a search of this kind in his own poetry. Its secular nature is realised in a moral tone composed at a distance from the concern with spiritual goodness in Eliot and Hill.

4

Peter Robinson's poetry, so intimately related to his own life, however, much distanced from it, grows and changes along with its author. Montale and Sereni, Hill and Eliot remain in the background, but the presence of an existential uncertainty in the earlier poetry gradually reduces over the years. The poet is still drawn to explicitly philosophical matters (as is the critic), but the emphasis in the poems is no longer on a half-lit omnipresent shame and guilt, but on the possibility of positive action in the straitened circumstances of modern life. The contrast is very great with the later poetry of Montale, which voices a life impatient with the mire in which it finds itself. He has nothing to compare with such a poem as Robinson's 'Der Philosophenweg',[20] which touchingly and directly affirms the bonds of affection that had proved so difficult earlier on. An aphorism from Lichtenberg serves as epigraph: 'There

---

[19] *The Selected Poetry and Prose of Vittorio Sereni*, 28 & 17.
[20] *CP*, 468-70.

exists no bridge that leads beyond our thoughts to the objects of them'.[21] The poem takes sides against its epigraph by acting as a bridge between the speaker and the unnamed person to whom it is sent. The aphorism, affirming some kind of idealist philosophy, brings to mind the charge of solipsism levelled at Robinson many years ago, a charge from which he has felt it necessary to defend himself.[22] The poem's title consequently has more meaning than first appears: most obviously, it refers to the path of that name above the Neckar in Heidelberg, where the memorials to Hölderlin and Eichendorff are to be found; less obviously, and with a touch of irony, it alludes to Robinson's own developing interest in a philosophy that is not solipsistic.

The poem begins with a very solid bridge, and goes on to others:

> Love's padlocks locked on *die alte Brücke*
> built from warm red sandstone
> I found, and walking out alone
> again along a Philosopher's Walk
>
> found wall menders, stonecrop, toadflax
> in leaf-viewing time, deep autumn,
> clouds hung under hilltops opposite
> and the misted distances.

This is straightforward when compared with 'Early Territory', where the speaker is qualified as 'Shame-faced' even before he appears in the poem. The 'misted distances' of 'Der Philosophenweg' do not get in the way as the 'ground mist' of the earlier poem did, and the perceiving self is not isolated in his thoughts – the wall menders, stonecrop, and other particulars crowd in upon him as a context that supports and counterbalances his reflections:

> No, not apart, but part of things,
> just like in any tourist town.
>
> [...]

---

[21] G. C. Lichtenberg, *Aphorisms*, trans. and intr. R. J. Hollingdale (London: Penguin, 1990), 196. This is an aphorism from Lichtenberg's final years, to be found in Notebook L.
[22] *TAP*, 22, 33-35.

>   bridges below me linking banks
>   as if thoughts and their objects

The world, in this poem, sustains: 'Europe, Europe looking after me / in its confusion of dialects, tongues ...' – Europe here even recalls a bit of Japan, 'Kyoto's *Tetsugakunomichi*', as the poem confidently stretches beyond the Eurocentric.

This poem might seem excessively polished in comparison with its predecessor, were it not for the tiny wobble in the speaker's point of view that confirms his vulnerable individuality. He sees a wealth of things,

>   But without that devil of a temptation
>   to get above yourself again
>   is how I would look down on them
>   and hear a stray cat's faint miaow
>
>   about its own states of affairs
>   between parked cars, descents of stairs,
>   from where I send this to you now,
>   send it with my thoughts.

The wobble is the lapse into the second person ('get above yourself'), followed by the return to first person in the next line. It suggests a division within the speaker that the reader would not have suspected. Its voicing in the use of pronouns looks back to past practice. Its associated uncertainty is present also in the wishfulness of 'how I *would* look down on them', as though the poet can't be sure even now that he is able to separate himself from an isolating tendency to pass judgement. The gesture is followed meaningfully by his allowing a stray cat 'its own states of affairs' without comment. The sentence is managed so as to move dreamily from looking down to hearing in such a way that the cat's cry is first of all something that happens into the poem by chance, something that the poet is not felt to will at all; any moral meaningfulness just hovers above the line, behind the words. Indeed, there is a doubt whether the cat is heard at all, since 'hear' may mean 'would hear', just as there is a doubt whether to 'look down' is an example of getting 'above *yourself*' or not. There is a suggestion of the old *dormiveglia* here, but the self is able to reassert itself in a move difficult to imagine in the earlier poems. Allowing the cat to have 'states of affairs' (rather than just the one) suggests that the speaker has returned to the benign pluralism of the rest of the poem; and by carrying on when you might have expected it to stop, the sentence turns attention away from any philosophizing to reveal that the poem is, something we had no means of knowing until this point, a letter or postcard whose words are all directed towards 'you'. In fact, the speaker only says that he is sending 'this … with my thoughts', suggesting that there is more *to* the poem than there is *in* the poem, complicating the relation of poem to epigraph since the thoughts are both part of the poem and not. They certainly seem to constitute a bridge, although we are not afforded a clear view of what is at the other end of it.

'Der Philosophenweg' is about being apart and not being apart, about substantial and insubstantial bridges, and about thoughts in the world and thoughts out of the world. 'Love's padlocks', with which the poem begins, are commonplace, a fashion that has spread in tourist places throughout the world in the last twenty years or so, but the love they symbolise is given a particularity in the poem that is not commonplace, especially by the title's characterisation of the poet-speaker as philosophic, with all the meaning that has in terms of Robinson's own writing, poetic and critical. There is no looking down on the padlocks. They are taken for what they are, with whatever retrospective irony, as enduring expressions of love in the moment. This is a revision of Montale's depressing notion of the modern world.

The love represented by the padlocks turns out to be incorporated in the poem itself, offered at last to the unnamed 'you' by the poet. As for him, if not above himself, he is at least a part of the world he so appreciatively describes. He is so much in the world that the thoughts that would once have separated him from it can now exist within it, without the need for us to be absolutely certain of what they are.

5

The 'sustained effort' which, according to Robinson, writing about Sereni, is needed for goodness to be 'born from error and self-betrayal' is present in 'Der Philosophenweg', but only just sufficiently effortful to convince. In 'Early Territory', on the other hand, the situation is so entangled that the speaker in its midst is barely able to show effort at all, other than that required to get through the day itself. The poem's 'earthly reasons' do not make it any easier to lead the good life than the reasons that might be drawn from religion, which are, significantly, *not* mentioned. The poem dramatises the perplexities and anguish of living by earthly reasons alone and ends in a way that can, and cannot, be read conclusively: 'now just you confront me'. Does 'just you' imply 'you alone, without power' or 'you in all your power'? Is 'confront' a neutral description or does it imply threatening opposition? The reader's uncertainty mirrors that of the speaker.

I have characterised the poetry as 'secular'. It is important to stress that the term does not entail an absolute separation from religion. For Robinson, a child of the vicarage, the question of living *well* has been important from the start. Religious and secular values are consequently bound together in his life-experience and his poetry. There is a consistent emphasis in both the poetry and the criticism on the need to make amends, which, in *In the Circumstances*,[23] is given a background in psychoanalysis, but which is not incompatible with the faith-based values of the poet's vicar-father. This mingling of secular and religious, strictly managed, allows a greater sense of being at ease in the world of the later poetry.

In 'Holy Dying',[24] the poet, staying with his mother, has to sleep in his parents' old room, where his father died. 'No ghost tried / to bring me word from an afterlife'; but 'to wake with no spectres in morning light … meant clearly he was well and truly gone / to live in us'. The father is gone and then not gone. It is in an entirely secular sense that he is not gone, but there is a hint of the ghostly all the same in the way that 'spectres', visitors from the afterlife (which is not secular), reaffirm themselves covertly five lines later: 'in us – *spectators* / of shadows on repainted bedroom walls, / relatively rested in the dawn' (emphasis added). 'Relatively' plays good-humouredly with a less than good night's rest earned in the course of being a good member of the family. If the father is truly living in us, he is also, we may presume, 'relatively rested'. Was his dying holy, as the poem's title says? The epigraph equivocates with yet another pun: 'you do not wholly die'. The puns in this later poem are different from the sort of thing we found in 'Early Territory' and its coevals by being self-possessed, even amused. The poem is moving in what it affirms, what it understands, and what it tolerantly accepts. As in 'Der Philosophenweg', it is comfortable with a

---

[23] See 'Envy, Gratitude and Translation' in that volume, 142-72 (sp. 145-46).
[24] *CP*, 419.

pluralism which was not available in the earlier poetry.

What was the heart of the house, his parents' bedroom, in 'Holy Dying', is now the room for guests. The poet is in the position of a guest in the parental home; he is, as it were, marginal to it. This marginality is part of what the poet has come to live with: 'I feel a sense of displacement practically all the time' he has said.[25] The displacement has been literal, in his long sojourn in Japan, but the sense of it must have predated that time; he has written about the ambiguous social standing of the vicar and his family, members of the community, yet apart from it, and its effect on him.[26] This connects with Sereni again – Robinson quotes the critic Giovanni Raboni's view that Sereni's importance as a poet, his 'centrality', depends on 'an initial marginality'.[27] Throughout Robinson's poetry also, from the neglected cemetery of the early poem to the 'Philosophenweg' above the city of Heidelberg, the marginal is central.

Besides Sereni, there is also an English poet whose concern with the marginal is important for Robinson. He is Roy Fisher, and his significance for Robinson is manifold, so much so that, really, nothing but another essay would do it justice. Robinson helped Fisher when he was putting together his last collected poems, *The Long and the Short of It* (2005), was responsible overall for getting out Fisher's *Slakki: New and Neglected Poems* (2016), and has edited Fisher's occasional prose as well as books of homage and criticism of the poet. This suggests deep affinity, as is the case, I believe, but in many ways the two poets are unlike. Fisher was more concerned with seeing clearly than with the representation of *dormiveglia*. The kind of poem he wanted to write would result in the reader's having 'perceptions re-arranged by reading it or having used it'. He disliked moralizing readings of poetry, which he considered evidence of a 'simplifying tendency ... people stop reading, people stop attending. [...] For my taste I moralise too much already'. If he wrote about the marginal, it was to promote a better seeing of the world as it was. In comparison with Sereni and Robinson, Fisher is scrupulous about keeping feeling to the minimum: 'I am chiefly interested in hauling words towards concreteness'; he is not so much concerned with 'being

---

[25] *TAP*, 84.

[26] See Peter Robinson (ed.), *Liverpool Accents: Seven Poets and a City*, (Liverpool: University of Liverpool Press, 1996).

[27] *The Selected Poetry and Prose of Vittorio Sereni*, 13.

the object of others and of himself'.[28] More often than not, Fisher writes himself out of the scene:

> The sight of Lucas's
> lamp factory on a summer night;
> a shift coming off about nine,
> pale light, dispersing,
> runnels of people chased,
> by pavements drying off
> quickly after them,
> away among the wrinkled brown houses
> where there are cracks for them, to go.[29]

These lines parallel the passage from Robinson's 'A Short History', quoted earlier, but whereas 'the city's / fringes' are there identified with 'a drowsing land', Fisher's half-lit scene is one of surprising animation, the quick dispersal of light in a clearly visible street scene.

Nevertheless, Fisher is clearly another poet interested in the marginal, showing how it could be used in an English context and, what is more, doing it in a very different way from Sereni. In both these aspects, he was important for Robinson, a poet who would never wish to be mistaken for a mere imitator. Fisher's difference from Sereni and from Robinson kept alive the possibilities for development in Robinson's poetry – kept him free. In this paradoxical fashion, Fisher may be seen as part-responsible for so un-Fisher-like a poem as 'Der Philosophenweg'. He must also have appealed to Robinson as another secular poet and one who was more explicit about it than Sereni, calling theology, for example, 'a hoax area' in *19 Poems and an Interview*. Robinson writes approvingly of Fisher that '[i]n the work of *A Furnace* and after, the poet has been quietly renegotiating for a secular culture'.[30] This is also the case with Robinson, who admires David Hume not only for his scepticism (which anticipates or justifies the poet's own uncertain experience of *dormiveglia*), but also for his hostility to organised religion and to 'canting assertion, moral bullying, and the

---

[28] All the Fisher quotations here come from Roy Fisher, *19 Poems and an Interview* (Pensnett, Staffs.: Grosseteste, 1975) 23, 16 & 20.
[29] 'For Realism': Roy Fisher, *The Long and the Short of It: Poems 1955–2005* (Tarset, Northumberland: Bloodaxe, 2005), 220.
[30] Peter Robinson, *Twentieth Century Poetry: Selves and Situations* (Oxford: Oxford University Press, 2005), 252, 259.

interests of caste and honour codes'.[31] If you contest 'the interests of caste and honour codes', you end up writing from the margins like Fisher and Robinson; but, given that the numbers are increasing all the time of those for whom you write, those marginalised within contemporary mass society, you end up after all in a 'central' position. Dissociated from organised religion, you can appropriate what seems good to you from general religious discourse (the 'spectres' and 'spectators' of 'Holy Dying', for instance), but still reject it as a whole.

One indication of marginalised centrality in Robinson's work is the way he uses his diction and syntax. Contrast him with Hill, whose diction, cemented in an overtly deliberated syntax, not only tends always to the elevated, but also exploits sudden swings to the demotic: in Robinson, diction is all on a level, and syntax often feels improvised. The effect is subdued and wanting in savour – it accommodates the vulgar, tasteless trade-name 'Lacrilube eye-gel' ('Convalescent Days') as easily as unrefreshed cliché ('all hell breaks loose', in 'On the Outskirts').[32] 'Spontaneously offered macaroni' is, for me, a particularly memorable example of demotic awkwardness, from 'Leaving Parma', a poem not included in the *Collected Poems*.[33] The phrase is right for the poem – but it is nevertheless inelegant and awkward. It is inelegant because it is such a mouthful, and it is awkward because highlighting spontaneity involves a hint of defensiveness, as if the poet wished to deny that he had given any encouragement in the matter of the macaroni, but, yet again, it is right because a certain tonelessness suits this writing from the margin. 'Be this as it may, we'd stopped too long / over spontaneously offered macaroni / and the wine talking'. The opening phrase of the sentence declines authority and is consistent not only with the phrase that I find awkward, but also with the spontaneity of the act described. Being authoritative is not what this poet is about, whether at the dead end of Belle View Terrace in 'Early Territory' or on the plane far above earth in 'The Cold':

> Somewhere over Sakhalin
> or with what was Port Arthur below,

---

[31] Peter Robinson, *Poetry, Poets, Readers: Making Things Happen* (Oxford: Oxford University Press, 2002), 96.
[32] *CP*, 181 & 195.
33 *TOL*, 67.

a pellucid azure on the wing-line
glinting above its wastes of snow.[34]

Not 'Port Arthur', but 'what was Port Arthur', because it is no longer called that. The periphrasis stresses literal and psychological distance; from this point of view, Sakhalin might just as well be Port Arthur as itself, and, anyway, what does 'Port Arthur' mean, either to the poet up there on the edge of the world or in itself to the reader at home? The choice of words is indicative of a general alienation from centres of power and value (and from the 'hoax area' of religion associated with it, although that is not what this poem is primarily about). 'The Cold' is about an old Russian woman who has just voted and is now being interviewed on television; she says, 'They promised us the future / … for seventy-odd years, but the future / I know now doesn't exist'. The ambiguity of 'now' (it can qualify either 'know' or 'doesn't exist') doesn't matter so much as the disillusionment that is signified either way: 'underneath runs the cold', and the old woman is left high and dry, or on the margin. The cold she feels is reflected in the colourless diction of the poem ('and through the poor headset I heard / a voice-over translation'). The poem's rhyming stanzas take the marginal figure of the woman, imperfectly perceived on board a plane on the edge of a land mass by a poet in transit and make her the subject of a poem in traditional form; they put the marginal figure at its centre. There is no New Testament sense, however, of the last being made first; the poem's abnegations are purely secular.

Asked by Jane Davies whether he had religious beliefs, the poet replied: 'Well, I'm a religious sort of person, but I don't think I have the kinds of beliefs you could put into very orthodox positions. […] I do think that having been brought up in religion it's very difficult not to have a religious turn of mind'.[35] This marks the limit to how useful it is to think of Robinson's poetry as 'secular'. It is that, but it is not concerned with promoting a secular *ideology*, any more than Fisher's or Sereni's. All three write a poetry that avoids moral bullying and concentrate on the effort to see goodness born out of error and self-betrayal. *Dormiveglia* in the modern world not only creates the conditions in which it is necessary for human beings to rely on their own resources, to avoid canting assertion and moral bullying, but it

---

[34] *CP*, 147.
[35] *TAP,* 83.

also frees the poet from any necessity to promote a secular certainty in opposition to the religious certainties of the past.

Keats's question at the end of 'Ode to a Nightingale', 'Do I wake or sleep?', should be taken in the sense of a sublime openness to possibility and that is what is also to be found in Robinson, for example (my last example), in an election-day travel poem, 'Sheffield to Reading', which is a kind of 'Not the Whitsun Weddings', and ends:

> The land's no-longer, its not-yet
> are shunted into sidings,
> still, at Didcot's railway museum,
>
> and they're, well, blurred by direction of travel
> to a politic body's dividing regret
> caught in an accelerated dream.[36]

The poem is not dated but does speak of an 'election' so it would be wrong to read it as a poem on the Brexit referendum, but it certainly fits, particularly that phrase 'a politic body's dividing regret'. Separation from the European Union feels more and more like the act of a sleepwalker, someone caught up in the waking dream of *dormiveglia*, and the poem evokes this quality strongly. 'The land's no-longer, its not-yet' wonderfully describes the exasperation that drove so many to vote to leave and the sorely tried hope that led almost as many to vote to remain. The 'accelerated dream' is not quite a nightmare that we are trapped in; the dream may be beneficent as dreams often are. The poem remains alert in its peculiar consciousness to the last moment, poised, ready for anything. Its speaker is not entirely 'the object of others and of himself'; the poem also intimates a subject capable of action, and I find this satisfying.

---

[36] *CP*, 491.

Chapter 8
Losing and Finding: Japanese Poetry

Andrew Houwen

In the early spring of 1950, an eighteen-year-old high-school student neatly wrote down in his notebook a six-line poem in pencil.[1] He titled it 'Kanashimi' ('Sadness'):

> Waves heard hereabouts in blue sky,
> a terrible something or other
> I seem to have mislaid.
>
> At a transparent station of the past,
> standing before a lost property man,
> I sense my sadness has increased.[2]

Recalled only to the vaguest outline of a memory ('a terrible something or other' that he seeks in 'the past'), the poem's speaker has not only lost something: he has almost lost the memory itself. Two years later, that eighteen-year-old student, Tanikawa Shuntarō, published his début collection, *Nijūoku kōnen no kodoku* (*Two Billion Years of Solitude*) to great critical acclaim, and is now undoubtedly post-war Japan's most popular poet.[3]

What many of the poems' speakers in *Two Billion Years of Solitude* seem to have lost and seek is a connection with others. In 'Kaze' ('The

---
[1] I am indebted to William I. Elliott and Kawamura Kazuo, Tanikawa Shuntarō's English translators, for explaining and showing some examples of Tanikawa's methods of composition at this time during an interview with them in Yokohama on 24 October 2013. Japanese names in this chapter appear with the surname first, in accordance with Japanese convention.
[2] Tanikawa Shuntarō, 'Sadness', trans. Peter Robinson and Horikawa Fumiko, unpublished typescript, n. d. [c. 1989]. The original is published in a bilingual edition as Tanikawa, 'Kanashimi' ('Sadness'), in *Nijūoku kōnen no kodoku*, trans. Elliott and Kawamura (Tokyo: Shūeisha, 2008), 26 (English), 36 (Japanese).
[3] Tanikawa, *Selected Poems*, trans. Elliott and Kawamura (Manchester: Carcanet, 2015), xi.

Wind'), its speaker walks in the 'white burning heat' in which 'the young clouds have flown away, / leaving only painful memories'.[4] He resolves, however, not to lapse into nostalgia for those memories, whatever they may be: 'I will stop being nostalgic about a small mythic age. / The only right thing at this moment / is that I am alone'. It is a connection with others that the speaker feels is lacking. This sense of isolation is also explored in the collection's title poem: although 'we all seek for one another' and the power of 'universal gravitation is the power of solitudes / pulling each other', the universe goes on expanding, pulling 'us' further apart.[5] In the context of Tanikawa's collection, then, the 'sadness' of 'Kanashimi' can be read as an unfulfilled longing for dialogue, though the poem on its own does not necessitate such a reading. Forms of reprieve for this longing in Tanikawa's oeuvre only began to appear in his next collection of the following year, *62 no sonnetto* ('62 Sonnets').

'Sadness' was among the first poems Robinson translated soon after he arrived in Japan in March 1989 to take up a lecturing position at Kyoto University, having moved there from Cambridge. In his first academic term, he met Horikawa Fumiko, then a fourth-year English Literature undergraduate student. Using a recent anthology of modern Japanese poetry, *Nihon no meishi* (*Great Japanese Poems*), Horikawa picked out ten poems to show Robinson – Shimazaki Tōson's 'Hatsu koi' ('First Love'), Murō Saisei's 'Kanashiki haru' ('Lonely Spring'), Ishigaki Rin's 'Shijimi' ('Clams'), Komatsu Ikuko's 'Niwa' ('The Garden'), Kiyooka Takayuki's 'Aozora' ('Blue Sky'), Ibaragi Noriko's 'Watashi ga ichiban kirei datta toki' ('When I was at My Most Beautiful'), Shiraishi Kazuko's 'Non-Stop', Tanikawa's 'Kanashimi' ('Sadness'), Shindō Ryōko's 'Chiisana hon no naka no e' ('Picture in a Tiny Book'), Aoki Harumi's 'Wani' ('Trap'), and Aida Chieko's 'Seibutsu' ('Still Life') – and marked particularly difficult phrases or passages in pencil.[6] Horikawa and Robinson then collaborated on translating these ten poems, with the former first providing more literal versions. An undated typescript of these survives and includes the English translation of Tanikawa's 'Kanashimi' discussed above.

---

[4] Tanikawa, 'Kaze' ('The Wind'), in *Nijūoku kōnen no kodoku*, 62 (English), 102 (Japanese).
[5] Tanikawa, 'Nijūoku kōnen no kodoku' ('Two Billion Light Years of Solitude'), in ibid., 44 (English), 72 (Japanese).
[6] Yamamoto Tarō (ed.), *Nihon no meishi* (Tokyo: Heibonsha, 1983), 2, 42, 228, 236-37, 242-43, 266-67, 312-13, 328, 340-41, 373 respectively.

The opening poems of Robinson's first collection written in Japan, *Lost and Found*, portray a similar sense of initial isolation to that of the speakers of *Two Billion Light-Years of Solitude*, which is of course understandable when first arriving in a new and very different culture such as Japan. 'The Rainy Season' opens with a sense of entrapment: the claustrophobic 'low cloud' forms 'a lid above blue roof-tiles'; and the perhaps easily overlooked choice of 'guard' to depict the 'umbrellas' in the 'entrance halls and café tills' anticipates the defensiveness of the ironically 'nervous calm' among the bus passengers.[7] Irony is equally felt in their 'close' features offering only 'distance in unrecognising eyes', and in the 'isolation' that 'brings home further losses': the sense of 'not being at home' is 'brought home' in Japan. It concludes:

> This is the life of double space:
> for some you seem too visible,
> an eyesore on the crowd's pure surface;
> for others, you're not there at all.[8]

This is the clearest irony of all: the speaker is treated as both different and indifferently. It is also possible, however, to find common ground between the poem's people. This is, after all, also a poem about the more widespread isolation of people from each other in urban spaces. Not only the use of 'you' above, but also the absence of an explicit 'I' allows for the isolation to be felt from multiple viewpoints within the poem: the 'unrecognising eyes' could be the speaker's as well as the other passengers', thus suggesting how they share their isolation.

This idea of being lost in the sense of 'misplaced', one of the 'losses' felt in 'The Rainy Season', is further explored in 'Lost Objects', whose theme most closely parallels the implications of the collection's title.[9] At first, the misplacement focuses on the Japanese custom of lost objects, such as a 'blue purse' or 'ring', being considerately placed 'on a wall, a window sill', awaiting their owner's return. From there, it shifts to the 'misplaced items' that 'interrupt skylines' such as 'Liberty with her torch upraised' or 'a Bavarian castle' (both of which are 'love hotels'). These have 'something missing', in the sense of being torn from their native contexts: they, too, are lost among the 'tiered expressway lanes'

---

[7] *LF*, 13.
[8] *LF*, 13.
[9] *CP*, 150-51.

of a modern Japanese cityscape. A broader sense of social unease is also implicit in the reference to love hotels: Japanese couples go there to escape the claustrophobia of cohabiting relatives. In the final stanza, the poem's final 'misplaced item' is found:

> Leaving a local station platform
> under white sky filled with heat,
> a memory, loved one, or poem
> has been left behind. But what?
> Wordless in front of the next
> lost property office's window
> you find yourself looking perplexed.[10]

This person not only cannot remember what he has lost as he stands in front of the 'lost property office's window', just as Tanikawa's speaker does in 'Sadness'; he finds, in his reflection, that he is himself another 'lost object', as Sumie Okada and Miki Iwata have also noted, misplaced and far from home.[11]

Several meanings of 'loss', then, are brought together in this stanza. That of 'memory' recalls the loss in 'Sadness', which in turn could be read as the 'poem' that has been 'left behind', alongside the allusion to Empson's 'Missing Dates'.[12] The sense of isolation from others is suggested by the possibly lost 'loved one', and further hinted at in the 'white sky filled with heat', a change from an earlier draft's 'blue sky' that brings to mind the 'lid' of 'low clouds' in 'The Rainy Season' as well as the 'white burning heat' of Tanikawa's 'The Wind'.[13] Through the addition of the reflection in the window, a further sense is given: the subject, in 'finding [him]self' in it as an object, experiences a loss of self-identity by momentarily seeing himself as another ('you'). Such an effect has been carefully created: previous drafts hesitated between

---

[10] *CP,* 151.
[11] Sumie Okada, *Western Writers in Japan* (Basingstoke: Macmillan, 1999), 140-41; Miki Iwata, 'His Other Islands: Peter Robinson, Languages, Traditions', in Adam Piette and Katy Price (eds), *The Salt Companion to Peter Robinson* (Cambridge: Salt, 2007), 193-204, 195.
[12] 'It is the poems you have lost, the ills / From missing dates at which the heart expires'. William Empson, 'Missing Dates', in *Collected Poems* (London: Chatto & Windus, 1962), 60.
[13] Robinson, 'Lost Objects', undated manuscript.

'you are looking perplexed', 'It's me looking perplexed', and 'Without you, looking perplexed'.[14] The temporary self-alienation created by the final version's 'you' allows us, however, to discover more about who we are. One of the ways in which Robinson could also be seen as enacting this kind of self-discovery in 'Lost Objects' is precisely by having seen himself as another – as the speaker of 'Sadness'.

In these first months of Robinson's stay in Japan, his closest Japanese companion was Horikawa. In 'At New Year', they commemorate the arrival of the new decade: 'Fumiko' suggests an 'early morning stroll' by the shore at Tsu, south of Kyoto on the Pacific coast.[15] The rising sun, however, reminds the speaker of the 'trickling gore / which made old aspirations stir, / dyed waves that lapped the shore'. These 'old aspirations' are commemorated at 'Yasukuni', a Shinto shrine where the spirits of the war dead are honoured.[16] It is the war, however, that offers common ground between the speaker on the one hand and Horikawa and her 'Christian grandma' on the other. The grandmother had been 'fifty years a widow':

> Half a life she's kept his shrine
> in the provincial seaside home.
> It had reminded me of mine.
> Here, I am made welcome.[17]

The family shrine, or *kamidana*, is in one sense analogous to Yasukuni in its honouring of a fallen soldier. Indeed, the promotion of *kamidana* ownership took place in the context of the rise of State Shinto before the war.[18] But, in this case, the speaker discovers a bond with her, emphasised through the poem's use of rhyme; moreover, the implied emphasis on 'am' indicates a feeling of being 'at home' that, by implicit contrast, is absent from his homeland.

Out of the translated poems on which Robinson and Horikawa initially collaborated, Ibaragi Noriko's 'When I was at My Most Beautiful' most inspired them to further investigate its poet's other work. Like

---

[14] Robinson, 'Lost Objects', undated manuscript and two undated typescripts.
[15] *LF,* 18-19.
[16] *LF,* 18.
[17] *LF,* 19.
[18] Helen Hardacre, *Shinto: A History* (Oxford: Oxford University Press, 2017), 419-20.

Tanikawa, Ibaragi was a member of the *Kai* ('Oar') group of poets, which she co-founded with Kawasaki Hiroshi in February 1953, also co-editing a poetry magazine of the same name, whose first issue appeared in May of that year.[19] Tanikawa was the third poet to join, and first appeared in their second issue the following July.[20] From the outset, Ibaragi's poetry often subverted conventional depictions of femininity. One of her first poems published in *Kai*, 'Musha shugyō' ('Warrior Training'), calls on the post-war generation to 'give your own flame to your five senses' and 'refuse the dream of wildfires': it stressed the importance of a defiant individuality that rejects being drawn into collective expressions of violence.[21] Of this poem, the critic Nakae Michitarō wrote that the poem did not appear as if it had been written by a woman because of its 'modern toughness', a quality he felt to be incompatible with femininity.[22] In the same issue as Nakae's article, however, Maki Yōko demanded that reviewers refrain from labelling poems as 'womanly' or 'unwomanly'.[23] Ibaragi was one of the first Japanese women poets to challenge such stereotypes.

The first Ibaragi poem that Horikawa and Robinson translated, 'When I was at My Most Beautiful', written in 1957, is a fitting example of this 'modern toughness'. Its speaker makes no bones about what she feels to be the war's stupidity:

> When I was at my most beautiful
> my homeland was overcome in war.
> Was there ever so foolish a thing?
> Blouse sleeves rolled, I stamped the humiliated town.[24]

In stark contrast with the fear of criticising the government before and during the war, when poets were even incarcerated for doing so,

---

[19] Ibaragi Noriko, 'Kai shōshi' ('A Brief History of *Kai*'), in *Koto no ha* ('Leaves of Speech') (Tokyo: Iwanami Shoten, 2010), 227-61.
[20] Tanikawa, 'E.K. ni' ('To E. K.'), *Kai*, no. 2 (July 1953), n. p.
[21] Ibaragi, 'Musha shugyō' ('Warrior Training'), *Kai*, no. 3 (September 1953), n. p. My translation.
[22] Nakae Michitarō, 'Ibaragi Noriko ron' ('On Ibaragi Noriko'), *Shigaku*, no. 10 (October 1955), 72-81, 75. My translation.
23 Maki Yōko', 'Sengo josei shijin ron' ('On Post-War Women's Poetry'), *Shigaku*, no. 10 (October 1955), 34-40, 37.
[24] Ibaragi, 'When I was at My Most Beautiful', in *When I was at My Most Beautiful and Other Poems* (Cambridge: Skate Press, 1992), 32-33, 32.

the speaker's directness is palpable. In Japanese, the explicit use of pronouns, particularly in poetry, is rarer than in English; Ibaragi's emphasis on the 'I' in the title, which is used as a refrain beginning each of the poem's eight quatrains, marks out her speaker's individuality. The Japanese for 'foolish' (*baka*) is even coarser, coming closer to the English 'stupid'. In Ibaragi's original, 'stamped' (*noshiaruita*) is perhaps nearer to something like 'boldly strode through', from the verbs *nosu*, 'to stretch' or 'to do something vigorously', and *aruku*, 'to walk'. In any case, the speaker refuses to be brought down with the bombed buildings around her: she is in the prime of her youth, her 'arms and legs, chestnut-hued, shin[ing]'.

She is forthright about the losses she encountered in the war, describing them bluntly and without ornament ('lots of people around me died'); yet her passion for life is, if anything, intensified by her experience of such losses. These serve to emphasise the pleasures of finding the 'sweet, exotic music' of 'jazz pour[ing] from the radio', which she 'devoured', a gesture of internationalist defiance against the pressure to conform to the time's fanatical nationalism.[25] Indeed, the anti-foreign sentiment was so intense in Japan during the war that in 1940 one of the most prominent avant-garde poets, Kitasono Katué, was forced to change his overly foreign-sounding poetry magazine title, *VOU*, to the Japanese *Shin gijutsu* ('New Technique') and to publish an editorial announcing that foreign loan-words and influences were banned. Another well-known surrealist poet, Takiguchi Shūzō, was even imprisoned for refusing to comply with such orders.[26] Listening to foreign jazz was thus an act of youthful rebellion against such fascistic policies.

Although she observes the many ways in which her youth was stunted by the 'foolish' war despite such illicit pleasures, having missed her 'chance to be well dressed' or receive 'tender gifts', for example, she ultimately chooses to focus instead on the possibilities open to her now that she has survived. The poem concludes:

> So I decided, if possible, I'd live a long life
> like that French artist grandpa Rouault

---

[25] Ibaragi, 33.
[26] See John Solt, *Shredding the Tapestry of Meaning: The Poetry and Poetics of Kitasono Katué* (Cambridge, MA: Harvard East Asian Monographs, 1999).

> who painted in old age outrageously fine pictures,
> wouldn't I?[27]

In these lines, there is none of the survivor guilt felt in poems such as Ayukawa Nobuo's 'Shinda otoko' ('The Dead Man') of 1946, in which its speaker laments the death of his fellow soldier, 'M.', and his own 'failure to die'.[28] The emptiness of the devastated towns becomes the freedom of the blank canvas on which to paint the life she wants. This freedom from the war's constraints is also suggested by the last line's formal variation on the expectation generated by the previous quatrains. In the Japanese, the final line simply reads *ne*, a particle inviting the speaker's agreement. Its friendly intimacy adds to this sense of liberation from formalities. If loss closes down some possibilities, then, new ones open in the space left behind; likewise, losses in the poem's translation can find redress through the new poem that grows in its place.

This image of new growth arising out of emptiness finds more detailed expression in another of Robinson and Horikawa's translations of Ibaragi, 'Invisible Postmen', a translation of 'Mienai haitatsufu', which was first published in January 1957.[29] Ibaragi recalled that the poem partly originated in childhood thoughts about what was sending the signals to make flowers bloom.[30] The poem imagines 'invisible postmen' that bring 'the news from root to root, / the heart of the season prone to pass away': that is, the forces driving the flowers' growth. These invisible processes are also at work in human societies: 'invisible postmen loyally running / are conveying to the people / the heart of ages prone to pass away'. Some such events, however, can mean that 'even they're at a loss, after wars or on scorched earth'. Out of such

---

[27] Ibaragi, 33.
[28] Ayukawa Nobuo, 'Shinda otoko' ('The Dead Man'), *Junsuishi*, no. 10 (January 1947), 20-21, 20. 'M.' refers to Ayukawa's friend, Morikawa Yoshinobu, with whom he co-founded the *Arechi* ('The Waste Land') magazine in March 1939. Morikawa died while serving in Burma in 1942. See Andrew Houwen, *Penguin's Post-War Japanese Poetry: Translation and Receptivity, 1964–1974* (PhD Thesis: University of Reading, 2015).
[29] Ibaragi, 29-30; Ibaragi, 'Mienai haitatsufu', *Shigaku* ('Poetry Studies') no. 1 (January 1957), 26-27.
[30] Ibaragi, 'Waga shi wo kataru' ('Talking About My Poetry'), in Nakamura Minoru et al. (eds), *Gendai no shi to shijin* ('Contemporary Poetry and Poets') (Tokyo: Yuhikaku, 1974), 202-3, 202.

devastation, however, a space is created. The poem concludes:

> feeding on emptiness, trying to flower,
> there are human blossoms too.[31]

The comparison between the invisible processes driving natural and human events is brought together in the image of the 'human blossoms'. It is through the 'emptiness' created by the war that new growth can emerge.

Such ways of loss finding redemption are similarly used in Robinson's own poetry of the time. 'A Classical Landscape', written in the spring of 1993, describes the 'necessary loss' that occurs with the passing of time and, in this case, of collapsing relationships. 'Watery eyes' gaze 'at hope's perspectives in time become regret'. The source of such regret is then more clearly outlined:

> Though peace had been declared between us
> there came no triumph or relief.[32]

Although there appears to be no sense of 'triumph or relief' for this particular relationship between speaker and addressee, the poem searches for an acceptance of the change through the Ovidian allusion to 'Baucis and Philemon', who 'have departed / or been altered to a pair of trees'; the allusion to the married couple who grow old together nonetheless forms a painful contrast with their predicament. The speaker's self-correction from 'departed' to 'altered' is key: rather than loss, change is the more appropriate metaphor, because each apparent 'loss' entails a discovery of something that takes its place. In the two lines following 'relief', which conclude the poem, the speaker himself is also figuratively metamorphosed into plant life, like Baucis and Philemon or, indeed, Ibaragi's 'human blossoms':

> Some shrubs were breaking into blossom;
> willows eased into leaf.

Despite the claim that no 'relief' came from the declared 'peace', a sense of new growth arising from the emptiness left behind by the

---

[31] Ibaragi, 29-30.
[32] *LF,* 72.

old relationship takes place; this contrast between unease and relief is emphasised by the rhyme of 'relief' and 'leaf'. The 'leaves' of *Lost and Found* similarly grow out of the losses undergone by its speakers, both pointing to and themselves enacting means of compensation.

'A Classical Landscape' was composed during one of Robinson's return journeys to Cambridge, when he and his first wife contemplated the possibility of divorce. It was in Cambridge, too, that he and Horikawa found a publisher for their translations of Ibaragi under the title *When I was at My Most Beautiful and Other Poems*. Horikawa had begun a relationship with John Constable, whom she married towards the end of 1991. Constable had set up the short-lived Skate Press at 5 St Peters Street, Cambridge. After conducting an illuminating interview with Ibaragi at her home in Tokyo on 30 June 1991, included in the collection, Robinson and Horikawa had the translations published with Constable's press the following year. Before this, however, Robinson had submitted them to Jacqueline Simms, the commissioning editor of Oxford University Press's Oxford Poets series. She rejected the submission of the Ibaragi poems, however. The reasons given for this rejection touch upon fundamental questions concerning notions of losing and finding in literary translation.

The letter, not dated but believed to have been written in 1991, suggested that Robinson and Horikawa's translations were not accepted because they appeared too near to literal translations; they were too odd and foreign to be easy to read. Robinson was asked to step freely away from the originals and remake the poems with his own voice as a British poet. This issue of fidelity in translation is touched on in his critical volume *In the Circumstances*: rather than the 'possessing and commanding' approach to translation typified by Robert Lowell's *Imitations* of 1962, which 'endangers a sense of the original and translator', he advocated 'respectful translation'. 'Through processes of work, study, and revision', it is possible to explore the 'partial equivalences and inevitable differences' between the source and receptor languages and so gain 'an increase in self-knowledge'.[33] In this way, Robinson anticipated Lawrence Venuti's criticism of 'domesticating' translations that 'invisibly inscribe foreign texts with the narcissistic experience of recognizing their own culture in a cultural other'.[34] A 'respectful translation' does not result in existing

---

[33] Robinson, *In the Circumstances: About Poems and Poets* (Oxford: Oxford University Press, 1992), 158.
[34] Lawrence Venuti, *The Translator's Invisibility: A History of Translation*, 2nd

ideas in the receiving culture about what makes good poetry being merely repeated and confirmed.

A telling example would be the close of 'Invisible Postmen' cited above. The two final lines in the Japanese read:

虚無を肥料に咲き出ようとする
人間たちの花々もあった

kyomu wo hiryō ni sakideyō to suru
ningentachi no hanabana mo atta[35]

I would interpret them as follows: 'there were (*atta* is the past tense of *aru*, 'to be') also (*mo*) human (*ningentachi* makes *ningen*, 'human', explicitly plural, though as an adjective in English modifying the following noun, it is necessarily changed to 'human') blossoms (*hanabana*, which can also mean 'flowers' and are also made plural) trying to break out (or 'about to break out', *sakideyō to suru*) with emptiness (*kyomu*) as fertiliser (*hiryō*)'. The last image in particular might strike an English translator as odd. It is rooted in the Buddhist notion, perhaps not as familiar to all Anglophone readers as it would be to Ibaragi's Japanese readership, that being and emptiness are opposite yet complementary entities that continually shape one another.[36]

A previous translation of Ibaragi's poem, translated by Kajima Shōzō and Lynn and Harry Guest and published by Penguin in *Post-War Japanese Poetry* in 1972, made significant alterations to these two lines to comply with the wishes of Penguin's commissioning editor at the time, Nikos Stangos, that the translators move away from the originals and avoid abstraction as much as possible. In their correspondence with Stangos, the translators particularly criticised these lines as overly abstract philosophy in need of greater clarity. The published version of the two closing lines reads:

---

edn (London: Routledge, 2008), 12.
[35] Ibaragi, 'Mienai haitatsufu', 27.
[36] Due to limits of space, this is necessarily a somewhat oversimplified explanation of the notion. An expression of it relatively well-known in East Asia is the *Hannya shingyō* or 'Heart Sutra'. See Tanahashi Kazuaki (ed.), *The Heart Sutra: A Comprehensive Guide to the Classic of Mahayana Buddhism* (London: Shambhala, 2014).

> I can see new flowers about to bloom
> rooted in the past.[37]

Although 'the past' is no less an abstraction than 'emptiness', the translation replaces the image of the 'human flowers' fertilised with 'emptiness' likely to be more unfamiliar to English readers with the omission of 'human' and the more conventional English phrase, 'rooted in the past'. This translation arguably remains faithful to the original's sense, because the 'new flowers' are, in the poem's context, already implicitly human too, and their rootedness in the past similarly suggests the contrast between the war's devastation and the new growth that appears in its place. Nevertheless, their version demonstrates the difficulties translators encounter in trying to negotiate between responsibilities to their source and receiving cultures.

Robinson and Horikawa's translation, likewise, cannot simply be categorised as either 'literal' or 'domesticating'. Horikawa helped Robinson with an alphabet Japanese text of the poem; together, they then proceeded to discuss the meanings of individual words and phrases. In the earliest extant manuscript draft, for example, 'kyomu' is given as 'emptiness', 'hiryō' as 'fertiliser' and 'nutrients', and 'ningentachi no hanabana' as 'human beings' flowers'. Out of this literal transcription, however, Robinson and Horikawa experiment with phrases that give a sense of poetic musicality in English. The first attempt at this reads:

> blossom
> feeding on emptiness trying to ~~flourish~~
> there are also human beings' flowers.
> ~~flowers of human beings~~[38]

In the final, published version, 'human beings' flowers' is changed to 'human blossoms', not only because converting 'human' to an adjective more accurately gives the sense of the original, but because the removal of the extra foot results in two sonorous four-stress lines.

Through such processes of 'work, study, and revision', then, they

---

[37] Ibaragi, 'Invisible Messengers', in Kajima Shōzō, Lynn Guest and Harry Guest (eds), *Post-War Japanese Poetry* (Harmondsworth: Penguin, 1972), 104-5, 105.

[38] Ibaragi, 'Invisible Postmen', tr. Robinson and Horikawa, undated manuscript, n. p.

achieve a remarkably successful balancing of fidelities to the source and receiving languages. Moreover, by arguably incorporating part of the sense of these lines in 'A Classical Landscape', Robinson also achieves an increase in self-knowledge rather than merely imposing previously received ideas.

Both Robinson and Horikawa's and Kajima and the Guests' translations of 'Mienai haitatsufu' demonstrate how good translators seek, in different ways, to balance fidelities to the source and receiving languages. As Robinson has more recently suggested in *Poetry & Translation: The Art of the Impossible*, fidelity implies difference.[39] His notion of fidelity is based on a belief in the need for ethical responsibility, as Andrew Fitzsimons has also pointed out: translators 'have a nexus of responsibilities because they are entrusted with the conveying into other languages of qualities and values from other people's writings'.[40] Neither the translator nor the original writer should be invisible. Umberto Eco similarly contends that translations should entail a 'negotiation' between the demands of source text, translator and receiving culture instead of a one-way appropriation.[41] The lack of such negotiation results either in the redundancy of complete fidelity to the source or that of complete fidelity to the receiving culture, even if either were possible. It is in its very hybridity that translation can offer something new and invigorating to be gained for both the source text and the receiving culture. While Robinson and Horikawa's translations of Ibaragi offer a commendable example of such practice, Oxford University Press's rejection of them exemplifies how the view of translation as one-way appropriation remained dominant in the world of British poetry at that time.

Despite this setback and Robinson's move to Sendai in March 1991 to take up a lecturing position at Tōhoku University, which meant that he and Horikawa were no longer in touch as frequently, the interest in Japanese poetry continued. At around the same time as their drafts of

---

[39] 'These terms ['fidelity and accuracy'] require that there is an acknowledged gap between the original and its translation. You can only be faithful to someone or something when you have acknowledged both its integrity and the need for that to be cherished and protected'. Robinson, *Poetry & Translation: The Art of the Impossible* (Liverpool: Liverpool University Press, 2010), 43.
[40] Ibid., 132. Andrew Fitzsimons, '"The Great Friend": Peter Robinson and Translation', in *The Salt Companion to Peter Robinson*, 151-63, 152.
[41] Umberto Eco, *Mouse or Rat? Translation as Negotiation* (London: Weidenfeld & Nicolson, 2003), 6.

translations from ten modern Japanese poets, they had collaborated on English versions of one hokku, four haiku, one senryū and one waka.[42] Two haiku are highlighted in pencil as ones they found particularly thought-provoking or amenable to translation. One of these is by Kawahigashi Hekigodō, a disciple of Masaoka Shiki, the nineteenth-century reformer and reviver of traditional Japanese poetic forms:

> Cold Spring:
> over the ricefield,
> a rootless cloud.[43]

An explanatory note is appended to each of these translations: in this case, 'the author comments on his life and career as a poet'.[44] During these years, Robinson must have particularly felt like a 'rootless cloud' as well as a 'lost object', having moved from Cambridge to Kyoto and then Sendai, while also experiencing considerable upheavals in his personal life, as 'A Classical Landscape' indicates. Robinson's poems frequently reference weather to indicate weathers of the mind, with the 'lid' of 'low clouds' in 'The Rainy Season' and the 'white sky filled with heat' in 'Lost Objects', for example, respectively suggesting the speaker's sense of entrapment and distress.

In the autumn of 1992, the poet Charles Tomlinson came to visit the north of Japan.[45] Tomlinson, Robinson and two other members of the department there, Suzuki Zenzō and Saitō Yasushi, travelled to Ryūshakuji, the Buddhist temple which served as the location for a famous hokku by Bashō. This hokku, and their visit to this temple, was the occasion for Robinson's poem 'Deep North' as well as Tomlinson's

---

[42] Before Masaoka Shiki's reforms of traditional Japanese poetic forms, the term *haiku* was hardly ever used; the famous poets Matsuo Bashō and Yosa Buson wrote what were then called *hokku* (lit. 'starting verse'), the opening three sections (usually given in English as lines) of a linked-verse sequence. Similarly, during Shiki's time, the term *tanka* (lit. 'short song') for a five-section poem, first used in the eighth century, was revived, replacing what had until then usually been termed an *uta* (lit. 'song') or *waka* (lit. 'Japanese song').

[43] Kawahigashi Hekigodō, untitled haiku, tr. Robinson and Horikawa, undated typescript, n. p.

[44] Ibid., n. p.

[45] The autumn of 1992, according to the poet's recollection. Personal correspondence with Robinson, 29 March 2017. The 'ten years' after Vittorio Sereni's death mentioned later in the poem also suggests 1992.

'Yamadera', the fourth part of his poem-sequence 'Zipangu'.[46] The hokku is given as the epigraph for Robinson's poem:

> What silence
> penetrating rock
> the voice of the cicada[47]

Bashō visited Ryūshakuji on his travels in the north of Japan between the spring and autumn of 1689, an account of which formed his haibun *Oku no hosomichi*.[48] Before the hokku appears, Bashō describes the situation: 'In Yamagata there is a mountain temple called Ryūshakuji [...] It is an especially quiet place'. Before the sun set, 'all the temple doors were closed'; his 'heart' was 'satisfied' by the 'tranquillity' of the 'beautiful scene', he writes, before giving the hokku.[49]

In Bashō's Japanese, the 'silence' ('shizukasa') is clearly separated from the rest of the hokku by the *kireji*, or 'cutting-word', *ya* ('shizukasa ya'), which splits it into two contrasted parts. An earlier version has 'yamadera ya' ('mountain temple') for the first part.[50] As with his famous 'frog' hokku composed three years before this journey, Bashō first wrote the second part before deciding on a suitable contrast. The addition of 'silence' instead of 'mountain temple' creates an opposition between the noise made by the cicadas on the one hand and the silence of the closed temple doors and the graves of the dead on the other.

Indeed, the 'closed doors' arguably figure in Bashō's choice of character for 'silence', 閑: its etymology is a representation of a bolted stable door. An additional juxtaposition thus suggests itself: the barrier of the closed doors and the penetration of the rock by the cicadas' noise.

---

[46] Robinson's return visit ten years later is commemorated in 'Silence Revisited', *CP*, 290-91.
[47] *CP*, 169-70.
[48] How to translate the title is discussed in Tomlinson's poem: the 'deep north' is suggested to be a possible 'mistranslation' of *Oku*, and 'journey to the interior' as a more appropriate rendering, with its double sense of a journey to Japan's interior and to the poet's own heart. However, as Eiichi Hara has kindly pointed out to me, the 'deep north' is also a perfectly acceptable translation of *Oku*. Charles Tomlinson, 'Yamadera', in *Selected Poems* (Oxford: Oxford University Press, 1997), 212-14 (212).
[49] Matsuo Bashō, *Oku no hosomichi*, ed. Ogata Tsutomu (Tokyo: Kadokawa Shoten, 2001), 278. My translation.
[50] Bashō, 281.

Robinson's version, however, creates an ambiguity about the reference of 'penetrating rock': the subject of the action could be either the silence or the voice of the cicada, thereby enriching the effect of the hokku's middle section. The rock, like the hokku itself, is thus permeated by both the life of the voices and the deathly silence that surrounds them. The translation is likewise permeated both by the original's death and the life that springs from it.

'Deep North' opens with a question about the hokku that Robinson and Tomlinson discussed, namely, 'were there one or more voices / in his cicada verses'? Suzuki's answer – '"They're plural," you'd reply' – carries a secondary meaning within Robinson's poem: they are plural because the voice of the cicada applies to the voices of the poem itself and their similar mortality. Indeed, this becomes the poem's major preoccupation. Robinson draws on the association between the cicadas' brief lives and the 'wood stakes at Yamadera', 'memorials' for the dead. What the speaker 'supposed' was 'a noise of gunfire' in the valley seen below from the 'viewing platform' reminds him of 'someone / dead ten years, but no less hurt / at warfare and war's echoes'.[51] The noise was 'just a birdscarer's report', the 'shot on shot / from a whole army / of automatic scarecrows', as Tomlinson's poem has it.[52] That 'someone' is the Italian poet Vittorio Sereni, who was imprisoned in a P.O.W. camp in Algeria during the Second World War and died in 1983. Inspired by Bashō's hokku, Robinson thus uncovers a new emblem of mortality in Ryūshakuji's view over the landscape.

The theme of loss in relation to Japanese poetry persists in Robinson's next collection written during his residence in Japan, *About Time Too*, published four years after *Lost and Found*. 'After Bansui' refers to a poem written in traditional alternating lines of seven and five syllables in 1898 by the Sendai poet Tsuchii Bansui, 'Kōjō no tsuki'.[53] It was translated in Geoffrey Bownas and Anthony Thwaite's popular anthology, *The Penguin Book of Japanese Verse*, as 'Moonlight over the Ruined Castle' in 1964, which is where Robinson found it.[54] The

---

[51] *CP,* 169-70.

[52] Tomlinson, 'Yamadera', 213.

[53] 'Syllables' is used here for the sake of convenience to translate the Japanese *mora*, which is often, though far from always, equivalent to an English syllable (*n*, for example, is counted as one *mora*).

[54] Tsuchii Bansui, 'Moonlight over the Ruined Castle', in Geoffrey Bownas and Anthony Thwaite (trans. and eds.), *The Penguin Book of Japanese Verse*

poem's castle is based, according to the poet himself, on visits to the castle ruins of Aizuwakamatsu and Sendai, both destroyed in the Bōshin War of 1867–68.[55] Whichever castle is intended, the poem laments its ruin, making it stand for the wider humiliation of the unequal treaties forced on Japan before the Meiji period. The 'moonlight' over the castle in the spring 'flashing on row on row / Of planted swords: that light – where is it now?' the poem asks, before concluding with the question, 'Is it to copy them now, brighter yet, / Over the ruined castle the midnight moon?'[56] The moonlight thus comes to represent Japan's martial strength. It is a deeply nationalistic poem written at a time when Japanese militarism was brimming with confidence following Japan's recent victory in the Sino-Japanese War of 1894–95.

'After Bansui' explores the ultimate result of such militarism in the Second World War, thus giving the title's 'After' its double sense. It traces the images Bansui uses to forge his ode to military glory. The 'late-flowered cherries' staining the 'grey pavement' in the opening section, for example, echo the 'flower-viewing banquets' held in the castle at the height of its power. As 'After Bansui' later observes, the 'pink stain' reminds us what 'that fleeting blossom meant': that is, the bloodshed of the soldiers' deaths in defence of their shōgun defending Aizuwakamatsu Castle in the Bōshin War against the Imperial Meiji forces, as well as that of Japanese soldiers in the Second World War. The 'grass stalks' that 'pierce crazed asphalt' likewise recall how in the original poem 'only the laurel is left behind' over the ruined castle.[57] This reference, however, also makes clear Bansui's debt to the Chinese poet Dù Fǔ's 'Chūn Wàng' ('Spring Prospects'), in which 'nations are broken; mountains and rivers remain / and grass and trees grow over the castle in spring'.[58] The irony

---

(Harmondsworth: Penguin, 1964), 177-78.
[55] Ishii Masamitsu, *Tsuchii Bansui, Jōnetsu no shijin: sono hito and sakuhin* ('Tsuchii Basui, Poet of Passions: His Life and Work') (Sendai: Tōhoku Shuppan, 1953), 6.
[56] Bansui, 'Moonlight over the Ruined Castle', 177-178.
[57] *CP,* 189-191.
[58] Dù Fǔ, 'Chūn Wàng', in Ráo Zōngyí (ed.), *Táng shī sān bǎi shōu* ('Three Hundred Tang Poems') (Hong Kong: Zhōnghúa Shūjú, 2012), 159. My translation. Another of Bashō's famous hokku in *Oku no hosomichi* is similarly inspired by this poem (which Bashō directly quotes beforehand): 'Summer grasses – all that remains of warriors' dreams'. My translation. This hokku was written on the occasion of Bashō visiting Hiraizumi, now in Iwate

is thus revealed that Bansui's poem is inspired by the culture of the very country Japan had just defeated. The speaker of 'After Bansui' concludes: 'Bansui, you're their local poet, not mine'.[59] 'Their' in this case refers not simply to residents of Sendai or the Japanese, but rather to those who adhere to the kind of militarism that Bansui's poem glorified.

Another aftermath of the Sino-Japanese War can be traced in a haiku that serves as a prompt for 'The Last Resort', in Robinson's final collection written in Japan, *The Look of Goodbye*.[60] According to the note given in the back of that collection, the poem was inspired by 'Yosa Buson's haiku which I read in French: "Pour celui qui part / pour celui qui reste – / deux automnes"'.[61] This translation appears in Corinne Atlan and Zéno Bianu's *Haiku: Anthologie du poème court japonais*.[62] Their anthology does indeed attribute the work to Buson; the 'haiku' was not in fact written by Buson at all, however, but by Masaoka Shiki. The source of this error stems from its misattribution by the post-war populariser of haiku in English, R. H. Blyth. That this error has persisted for so long exposes the degree to which many later translators have merely adapted Blyth's version instead of checking for an original. In this case, though, Robinson himself is not the translator and has every right to respond to the French translation as an autonomous work. The discovery of Shiki's authorship is discussed here because it enriches the relationship between the haiku and the poems it inspired. Shiki wrote it shortly after returning in 1895 from the Sino-Japanese War, which he had hoped to witness as a war correspondent for the newspaper *Nippon*. His departure was delayed for a month, during which time it had already ended (on 30 March), but he sailed to China anyway. On the return journey in May, he suffered a recurrence of his tuberculosis.

After remaining in hospital for two months, he stayed with his school-friend, the then barely known Natsume Sōseki, in their home town of Matsuyama for a further two months during his recovery.[63] On

---

Prefecture, on 29 June 1689, some two weeks before reaching Ryūshakuji. Bashō, *Oku no hosomichi*, 239 ff.

[59] *CP*, 191.
[60] *CP*, 303.
[61] *TLG*, 136. I would interpret this version as: 'For the one who goes, for the one who stays – two autumns'.
[62] Corinne Atlan and Zéno Bianu (eds.), *Haiku: Anthologie du poème court japonais* (Paris: Gallimard, 2002), 119.
[63] Wada Katsushi (ed.), *Shiki no isshō* ('Shiki's Life') (Nagaizumi: Zōshinkai,

19 October 1895, he departed again for Tokyo, writing the following haiku for the occasion:

> Taking leave of Soseki
>
> For me who am going
> for you who are staying
> two autumns[64]

The French translation omits the use of the first- and second-person pronouns (*ware* and *nare*) used in the original's first and second sections respectively. The 'me' is Shiki going back to Tokyo; the 'you' is Sōseki, who is staying in Matsuyama. The subsequent divergence of their fates gives a retrospective poignancy to the haiku, especially Shiki's 'going': while Sōseki's fame as arguably the most revered novelist of modern Japan still lay ahead of him, Shiki's condition continually worsened until, already bed-ridden and in constant pain for some years, he passed away in 1902.

'The Last Resort' similarly thematises divergences of fate. It was written in the aftermath of Adrian Poole and Margaret de Vaux's visit to Japan in the early autumn of 2003. After their departure, the annual department visit to a hot springs resort took place, but due to over-bookings elsewhere they went to a more run-down venue:

> For the ones who go and those about to stay,
> two autumns: they're turning decay
> in another of the spa towns money forgot
> to contradictory signs and tokens –
> like ripened apples or purple potatoes,
> dropped leaves borne down-river, for ever
> alighting to drift where the ducks sun themselves.[65]

Those facing the choice whether to go or stay are, in the first of its two sections, the 'proprietors', who in fact probably had no choice but 'to walk away'. In the second section, however, the speaker reflects on someone

---

2003), 370-77.
[64] Masaoka Shiki, *Kushū* ('Haiku Collection'), ed. Takahama Kyoshi (Tokyo: Iwanami Shoten, 1993), 155. My translation.
[65] *CP,* 303.

'bitten by mosquitoes / at a terraced vantage point', wondering if that person has made the right choice to stay, perhaps not just at the resort but in Japan. Different roads that could have been taken are reflected on:

> they're fretful about what, not leaving, they'll miss
> and grieve for younger selves, ones
> long squandered on a promise,
> and gaze at those hotels like scuttled battleships.[66]

Faced with where he finds himself due to the series of decisions made in the course of a lifetime, the speaker ponders on all those places where he is not because of them, and what has been lost by not being elsewhere. This feeling is then exacerbated by the death in Sendai of a close family friend at the time, Lisetta Yoshimochi, who also thus experienced, like Shiki, a different autumn.[67] Both staying and leaving result in losses. To focus only on what is lost, however, is itself a choice; the inevitability of such loss, whichever way one turns, can only be countered by also considering at the same time what has been found; the latter is only made possible by the loss of something else.

This view is apparent in another poem on which 'The Last Resort' looks back. 'The Views from a Bridge', in *Lost and Found*, anticipates Robinson's later discovery of the Shiki haiku, as well as Horikawa's own tragic suicide in the autumn of 1999, which is explored over the same ground in 'All Around' and other poems in *Ghost Characters* (2006).[68] Its speaker looks down the steep drop by Yagiyama Bridge in Sendai, 'where suicides go':

> Today, when ochres, umbers, russets, crimsons,
> ripe oranges, yellow rust, almost maroons
> of leaves had made a plenitude, police
> stopped and climbed to see how someone else
> had not found it so.[69]

---

[66] *CP*, 303.
[67] This is expanded upon in 'Nowhere in Particular', 'Frost Shadow' and 'Mortuary Passport', *CP*, 303-5, 307-8.
[68] See 'All Around' and the following sequence of poems in *CP*, 254-60.
[69] *CP*, 161.

The meaning of 'views from a bridge' thus shifts to a further sense: someone else had experienced a different autumn and had not seen those autumn leaves in the way the speaker did, if at all. When the speaker of 'All Around' later reflects on Horikawa's death while walking through the same scenery, he wonders 'why hawks, why gusted leaves, / why stones and skies were not enough' for his addressee who took her own life.[70]

Loss, then, is in some sense subjective. Though it may prove difficult to find at times, out of any loss comes a space for something to grow, such as Ibaragi's 'human blossoms' out of the war's devastation, the brief song of Bashō's cicadas, or, indeed, the 'plenitude' of the leaves that emerged from Robinson's encounter with Japan. Thus, when weighing up the losses and discoveries of the eighteen years that he spent there, one can in any case say that he took the road less travelled by – and that it has made all the difference.

---

[70] *CP*, 255.

Chapter 9
Topophilia in Tohoku

Miki Iwata

Before going back to his country of birth in 2007, Peter Robinson spent eighteen years in Kyoto and Sendai, Japan. His poetry during this long period working in a foreign country – especially in the 14 years as a visiting professor at Tohoku University in Sendai (1991–2005) – understandably demonstrates many curious examples of cultural conflict, although in *Talk about Poetry* the poet has professed that he feels 'a sense of displacement practically all the time'.[1] Displacement, of course, is such a complex phenomenological experience that you can feel it in your hometown, or indeed any other place to which you are supposed to belong. Nevertheless, as Robinson's earliest poem composed in and about Japan, 'A Dedication', implies, geographic remoteness in his poems can function as an index for discrepancy in feelings. In the piece, the poet's unfamiliarity with Japan makes him humorously mistake firemen's helmets for those of samurai warriors and headlamps of cars for glowworms' lights – stereotypical images of the ancient Japanese capital. As the repetition of the interjection 'no' in the second and third stanzas suggests, he enjoys these consciously noted mistakes.[2]

However, such apparently naïf misconstruals are actually priming water for the revelation of more serious and complex misunderstandings between the poet and his first wife in the UK. In the fourth stanza, the gap between them is materialised in the echo and delay of their voices during an international phone call, and the poet describes this baffling miscommunication as: 'I approach to distance'. The word 'distance' is ambiguous enough to be interpreted as either a noun or a verb. While in the noun case the poet simply says that he tries to close the distance, the verbal usage betrays a more painful meaning by the connotation: 'I approach only to widen the distance'. The second meaning might sound pessimistic, somehow reminiscent of the ever-receding water in Tartarus that tormented Tantalus. However, the poet's everyday and slightly deflating life experiences described in the first three stanzas

---

[1] *TAP,* 84.
[2] *CP,* 145.

(some of those are already mentioned above), invite the reader to respond otherwise. Paradoxically, the commonplaceness of Kyoto and its humorous effects in the poem help the poet settle in the ancient capital and understand it as it is now. The misunderstandings here are a way to understand not only an estranged partner, but also a place that is still strange. Thus, 'A Dedication' ends not without a hope, as the poet launches 'words of explanation [...] on the air'.[3]

As Yi-Fu Tuan, the pioneer of humanistic geography, has pointed out, place is an emotionally bounded area towards which an individual or group, like it or not, bear a spiritual relationship. The term he adopts for this relationship is 'topophilia'. We should note that it includes 'all the human being's affective ties with the material environment', and is not confined to favourable or positive feelings.[4] Robinson's poems written in Japan illustrate how topophilia works in a poet's mind and, at the same time, how human psychology and experience establish the sense of place. In this chapter, I will look at some of Robinson's poems about the Tohoku (north-eastern) region of Japan, a district far stranger than Kyoto for the average British visitor, and examine what kind of interrelationship there is between the poet and the place. While Tohoku functions as a catalyst for the poet to express the existential sense of alienation (confessed to be more or less inevitable wherever he may be), his poems also give Tohoku an authentic shape and cast it as not a 'flatscape', a monotonous landscape lacking uniqueness, which is in reality the fate of many regional cities and tourist sites in modern Japan.[5] The interaction is rendered even richer by Robinson's typical penchant for intertexual references to both Japanese and Western literature. Furthermore, Robinson's poems about Tohoku, written from a stranger's point of view, help liberate the region from the stereotypes formed from accumulated textual images regarding it and

---

[3] *CP,* 145.
[4] Yi-Fu Tuan, *Topophilia: A Study of Environmental Perception, Attitudes, and Values* (Englewood Cliffs: Prentice-Hall, 1974), 93.
[5] I borrow the idea of 'flatscape' in contrast to the 'authenticity' of a place from Edward Relph, *Place and Placelessness* (London: Pion, 1976), 79-121. However, Relph explains that the word 'flatscape' is not his coinage but that of C. Norberg-Schulz. The more important concept in Relph's book is 'placelessness', by which he means 'a weakening of the identity of places to the point where they not only look alike but feel alike and offer the same bland possibilities for experience' (90).

draw up a new topography of Tohoku, which cannot be expected to emerge without the transcultural exchanges exercised in these poems.

'The Yellow Tank' and the Poetics of Neighbourhood Ordinariness

At first glance, it might appear odd that the first poem to be discussed in this section is 'The Yellow Tank', which descants upon, not a beautiful landscape in the Tohoku region, but a rusty water tank on the rooftop of an apartment block built solely for non-Japanese teachers employed by Tohoku University. For most people, a bright yellow water tank 'stained with rain smears and some rust' would be an eyesore rather than an inspiration and, indeed, the poet in the first stanza feels it chafing as it blocks a view from the window: 'you could think this yellow tank / a punch in the eye or personal affront'. Soon, though, the poem begins seeking for a way to come to terms with the tank, and in the second stanza compares it to 'a beach resort accessory / or ready-made in an art museum', likening the ladder attached to it to 'croziers' or 'philosophers' scare-marks'. These interpretational concessions to the tank by the poet lead to a new relationship between them. In the third stanza, it begins (or so the poet begins to think) to harmonise with the environment – 'against the hillside's heaving pines / the yellow tank is all repose'. Finally, in the fourth stanza, the poem introduces the secret of reconciliation: 'as with a disaffected child, / photograph, make fusses of it'.[6]

The phrase indirectly refers to the photographs of the tank taken by his friend Diethard Leopold, to whom, with his wife Waltraud, the poem is dedicated. According to Robinson, Leopold took many pictures of his apartment in Yagiyama when he, his wife and their twin children lived there. He would then project these slides on the white wall of their flat's dining room.[7] Robinson's memorable experience of enjoying the yellow tank images on the wall, while the real tank lurked outside their window, gave him a new perspective on it.

The double defamiliarisation of the tank, first achieved by slides and, then, by the poem itself, transforms an unremarkable, concrete

---

[6] *CP*, 159.
[7] Robinson's self-elaboration on 'The Yellow Tank' at a reading called 'Tohoku: Two Voices in English' held on 26 May 2017, at Books Kinokuniya, Tokyo.

apartment block into a *locus poeticus*. We might see this as attempting to reverse the process of dehistoricisation that the Yagiyama district suffered in the late nineteenth and early twentieth centuries. Yagiyama is a hillside residential district to the south west of Sendai city centre. Before the Meiji Restoration in 1868, it was called Koeji-yama, which literally means 'a border-crossing mountain', as it was situated on the other side of a gorge behind the castle of the local feudal clan, the Date family. Since the whole mountain was their private game park as well as a natural fortress to protect the castle from enemy attack, common people were not allowed to set foot on it during the Edo period.

After the Date clan, which remained loyal to the Tokugawa Shogunate, had lost the civil war (1868–69) against the new Meiji government, Koeji-yama was seized by the new government and redistributed to former samurai, who had lost their status and role, by way of compensation. As a natural result of joint ownership among some 800 people, the hill was left unattended and rapidly fell into decay. Local celebrities, the Yagi family, who grieved over the decline of Koeji-yama, attempted over two generations to purchase the whole area, and Kyubei Yagi (1865–1940) completed the project in 1924. From that time on, Koeji-yama was renamed 'Yagiyama' after him. Yagi constructed Yagiyama Bridge, which appears in a number of Robinson's poems,[8] and Yagiyama Ball Park (now Yagiyama Zoo, which figures in two others)[9] at his own expense, but then donated them to the City of Sendai for public use. Thus, the once venerable hills, with a historical proper name related to a feudal family that dates back to the 13th century, was redeveloped into a normal modern residential district, whose history is mostly unknown even to its residents. Considering the lines from 'After Bansui', in which the poet at the castle site meditates on the civil war – 'Now when the emperor was restored /

---

[8] Robinson's poems about Yagiyama Bridge include 'The Views from a Bridge' (*CP,* 161), 'All Around' (*CP,* 254-5), and 'Calm Autumn' (*CP,* 295-6). These poems, together with 'The Yellow Tank', form a good example of a co-textual cluster about Yagiyama (the term 'co-textuality' will be discussed later in this section).

[9] Yagiyama Zoo provides a scene for two poems by Robinson, 'Animal Sendai' (*CP,* 240-1) and 'Winter Zoo Encounter' (*CP,* 241-2). In both poems, the issues of language and communication are foregrounded by way of allusions to James Joyce and Randall Jarrell.

these trees were on the losing side'[10] – we can see that Robinson was quite conscious of the history of the district. In 'The Yellow Tank', on the other hand, Yagiyama's flatscape gains a humorous aura of place by the poetic transformation of a nondescript object of modern life in contrast to the way Koeji-yama lost its history and, accordingly, its earlier sense of place.

You cannot retrieve what is lost during the natural passage of time. Yet the poem shows that a different way of looking at things can create a new emotional attachment even to the now blank-looking landscape, and this is exactly what poetry achieves – or, perhaps, only poetry can achieve. For instance, in 'Anecdote of the Jar' (1923) by Wallace Stevens, the speaker begins the poem with the sentence, 'I placed a jar in Tennessee'. Then, without any explanation of causality, the poem reports that 'It made the slovenly wilderness'. Once this happens, there is no stopping the topographical change: 'The wilderness rose up to it, / And sprawled round, no longer wild'.[11] George Steiner interprets the poem as Stevens's declaration of art's metamorphosing power. A jar put on a hill in Tennessee is taken to represent artworks in general and, according to Steiner, 'The aesthetic proposition is unambiguous: [...] the work of art re-organises, sets ordinance upon the surrounding chaos'.[12] In a way somewhat similar to Stevens's deliberately simple, folk-tale style, Robinson uses casual words to transform a mass-produced apartment with a rusty water tank into a site of artistic interest.

Importantly, you should take time to develop this kind of emotionally charged meaning. 'For My Daughter', a poem addressed to Robinson's elder child, provides a good example of how time plays a role in the transformation of the yellow tank into a modern *genius loci* of Yagiyama. Here, the daughter joyfully laughs at a crow perching on the yellow tank, which is described as follows: 'Below the blackness of that bird, / once more appears our yellow / water tank'. While it is clear that the possessive pronoun 'our' is used to suggest their established familiarity with the tank, the verb 'appears' might sound a little unusual, since the tank must always have been there, neither appearing nor disappearing. Of course, this is not something the tank is doing, but a psychological reaction to it from the poet's side. By

---

[10] *CP,* 189-191.
[11] Wallace Stevens, *The Palm at the End of the Mind: Selected Poems and a Play,* ed. Holly Stevens (New York: Vintage, 1990), 46.
[12] George Steiner, *On Difficulty and Other Essays* (Oxford: OUP, 1978), 39.

then, the yellow tank, once offensive to the eye, has become so natural that it is virtually invisible to him. However, this does not particularly imply that the tank has lost its significance. This time it is his daughter who is inspired by the tank, and her laughter prompts him to compare the tank capped with its winter covering to 'an ice cream tub of snow'. Appreciating the girl's joy, the poem's final two lines invite her, and the reader, to 'laugh again / at these ordinary arrangements of things'.[13]

In 'Re-thinking Textuality in Literary Studies Today' (2010), Peter Barry proposes a new concept, 'co-textuality', to be distinguished from the familiar 'intertextuality': 'Co-textuality at its most basic can be exemplified by a "composite" literary form such as the sonnet sequence'. Reading such a co-textual cluster is, Barry argues, useful for 'the identification of a "reservoir" of running motifs which provide the material for all of them, along with a comparative analysis of the different permutations and deployment of elements from the "reservoir" which occur in each of the component pieces'.[14] In this sense, 'The Yellow Tank' and 'For My Daughter' form a good example of co-textuality. The two poems, read together, provide the reader with a new sense of the poetic spirit of a place, which was developed through his (as well as his family's) days in Yagiyama, together with other poems about their family life there such as 'Coat Hanger', 'Occasional Sunset' and 'Pasta-Making'.[15] Ironically enough, Tohoku University decided to abandon this apartment in 2007, the same year that Robinson returned to the UK, and the once residential site is now just an empty lot without a trace of the yellow tank; Robinson alludes to this change in his short story 'From the Stacks' in *Foreigners, Drunks and Babies* (2013). Nevertheless, the image of the tank remains in the poem and with the reader. Like the sonnet-maker declaring the power of his lines to defy all-devouring death in Shakespeare's Sonnet 18 – 'So long lives this, and this gives life to thee' – these poems by Robinson keep the tank alive as an evocation of what was once his everyday life in Yagiyama.[16]

---

[13] *CP,* 208.
[14] Peter Barry, 'Re-thinking Textuality in Literary Studies Today', *Literature Compass*, 7/11 (2010), 999-1008, 1000-01.
[15] *CP,* 227, 264, 266 respectively.
[16] William Shakespeare, *The Sonnets and A Lover's Complaint,* ed. John Kerrigan (London: Penguin, 1995), 85.

Interpreting Bashō in Yamadera

While cherishing the ordinariness of a normal residential area, Robinson's poems are often drawn to places of note in Tohoku too, though the poet's interest is as much in the intertextual exchanges with Japanese literary works about the place as in the scenic beauty itself. Here, his great predecessor as a travelling poet in Tohoku is the haiku master of the Edo period, Matsuo Bashō (1644–94).[17] In this section, I will look at Robinson's two poems that quote Bashō as an epigraph, that is, 'Deep North' and 'Silence Revisited'. Born in Iga Province (famous for the Iga ninja community) as the son of a lower-samurai-class family, Bashō entered the service of the Todo family at the age of 19 and learned haiku from the heir-apparent of the family, Todo Yoshitada. After Todo's death, however, he moved to Edo, giving up his career as a samurai, and established himself as a full-time poet and haiku teacher.

In his later years, he set out on a journey to Tohoku with his disciple, Kawai Sora, a journey that came to fruition in his best-known work, most famously translated as *The Narrow Road to the Deep North* (1689). Among the haiku in this volume, one which is often taken as his best is 'What silence / penetrating rock / the voice of the cicada' [閑さや岩にしみいる蝉の声], a haiku composed when he visited Risshakuji Temple in Yamagata, commonly known by the name of Yamadera (a mountain temple).[18] Jin'ichi Konishi much admires the haiku, saying that 'the whole mountain composed of rocks [...] is silent, and the silence is strengthened by the single voice of the cicada. When the voice becomes at its clearest [...] it is not a cicada's voice any more [...] and the mountain itself melts into the greater silence of this voice and no voice – the highest level of the mind a haiku can describe'.[19] Considering that Zen Buddhism provided the ideological

---

[17] According to customary notation, I write the names of Japanese historical literary figures in the surname then first name order, while other Japanese names (including my own) are written in the same style as English names.

[18] I am quoting Peter Robinson's translation here. See *CP*, 169 & 290. In *The Penguin Book of Japanese Verse: From the Earliest Times to the Present*, ed. and trans. Geoffrey Bownas and Anthony Thwaite (London: Penguin, 1998), the same work is translated as: 'Silent and still: then / Even sinking into rocks, / The cicada's screech' (106).

[19] Jin'ichi Konishi, *The World of Haiku* (1952; Tokyo: Kodansha, 1995) [小

background for Bashō's haiku, and of haiku in general after him, until the modernizing movement of Masaoka Shiki (1867–1902), Konishi's explication is neither extraordinary nor transcendental, but typical and characteristic of Japanese haiku criticism.

Since the haiku and its interpretation have become so pervasive, it is really difficult for modern Japanese people to think about Yamadera without them. What Edward W. Said called 'a textual attitude' in *Orientalism* (1978) is perfectly true of Yamadera, by which he meant 'a common human failing to prefer the schematic authority of a text to the disorientations of direct encounters with the human' – a failing so many European orientalists in the nineteenth century displayed.[20] After the fame of Bashō, Yamadera has always been expected to offer both the voice of the cicada and a Zen silence and, in turn, the temple itself has advertised its association with the famous haiku poet, gladly internalizing the qualities that the haiku represents. In short, Bashō, a traveller from Central Japan, and the accumulation of related texts have long defined the topography of Yamadera.

By contrast, in 'Deep North', Robinson, free from the Japanese literary tradition, reinterprets the intertextual proposition in collaboration with Zenzo Suzuki, the then head professor at the department of English literature at Tohoku University, who is addressed as 'you' throughout the poem. As a person born and bred in Tohoku, Suzuki is described as being resistant to the mainstream interpretations of Bashō and his haiku. For instance, Suzuki's 'half-serious theory / that Bashō was a government spy' succeeds in transforming the supreme haiku master into a lightly humorous figure (it is a popular but unreliable view of Bashō, based on his 'ninja' place of birth). More importantly, in defiance of Konishi's assertive comment about 'the single voice of the cicada', the poet reports Suzuki saying, 'They're plural'. This difference mainly comes from their interpretational attitudes, textual or empirical. The mainstream critics attach importance to the fact that the haiku by Bashō alludes to classic Chinese verses, including the works of Shi Hanshan [釈寒山] (dates unknown) and Wan Ji [王籍] (dates unknown). While these preceding texts provoke critics to regard the chirp of the cicada as a single voice, the down-to-earth experiences of the place would never lead the reader to that explanation, as there are always numberless cicadas in Yamadera

---

西甚一『俳句の世界』、講談社], 141. The English translation from the Japanese original is mine.

[20] Edward Said, *Orientalism* (1978; Harmondsworth: Penguin, 1995), 93.

in summer – ones that never cease chirping.

And yet, while Suzuki resists the orthodox reading of the haiku in the poem, he also offers a series of guidebook interpretations for the things seen in Yamadera such as 'memorials for their dead' on which posthumous Buddhist names are inscribed 'to fend off terror / at death'. Though he is trying to proffer inspiration for poetry out of kindness to their mutual guests, the poet Charles Tomlinson and his wife Brenda, Robinson as the other poet present inwardly declines the given afflatus, thinking in the final stanza that 'But I would be obliged to wait, / let sound sink into stone'. Interestingly, the poem concludes with a misunderstanding – the poet's confusing 'just a bird-scarer's report' with 'A noise of gunfire' that conveys the thoughts of the dead (a confusion that also appears in Tomlinson's poem 'Yamadera').[21] As already seen in 'A Dedication', misunderstandings in Robinson's poems often function as the first step towards poetic defamiliarisation. Whereas the poet merely reports the ready-made textual attitude about Yamadera, the association of a sound (gunfire) with the thoughts of the dead insinuates that the lyricism in the final stanza is in fact motivated by Bashō's haiku and Suzuki's explanations about wooden memorials for the dead. Thus, 'Deep North', borrowing its title from the most familiar translation of Bashō's work, dexterously plays with the preceding texts about Yamadera, and attempts to sketch its topography from a slightly different perspective.

Barry's idea of 'co-textuality' is useful here too. The counterpart piece that forms a pair with 'Deep North' is 'Silence Revisited', in which the poet visits Yamadera once again after many years. In this poem, Robinson defamiliarises his own experience in the past and 'Deep North' as well. This time, what is first introduced in the poem are the touristy elements of Yamadera for he has gone there by car with his family – 'the gauntlet of parking attendants, / present vendors, signs / any tourist trap wants' – only after which can the poet enter the long mountainous approach to the temple. The poet does not seem so conscious of the literature-charged image of the place (in clear contrast to the opening lines of 'Deep North', where the poet is making his version of the English translation of Bashō's haiku), and neatly evokes the way to the inner temple with a knowing eye – 'a cliff-front / with

---

[21] *CP, 169*. Charles Tomlinson, 'Yamadera', in *Selected Poems* (Oxford: Oxford University Press, 1997), 212-14, 212.

pauses and vertigo / at breath-taking stone steps, outcrops, viewing platforms / precarious on narrow high ledges'.[22]

He already knows about the climbing experience, which gives him a feeling of security in this landscape; hence the verse form can be compacted and phrases abbreviated. It is true that Robinson generally prefers free verse to more traditional metrical verse and, therefore, it might not be wise to put too much emphasis on formal issues. However, given his sensitivity to their contributions to meaning in his criticism, it is unlikely that the poem's form is arrived at without considerable reflection. For the lines in 'Silence Revisited' have distinctly unstable numbers of syllables, as if visually imitating the steep, zig-zag approach to Yamadera. Suspended between the senses of security and insecurity, the poet in the second stanza looks down to the valley from the platform, only to find that 'there was mist across valleys this time / all seen without alien / sensations of years ago'. This is an ingenious turn of phrase to express the twisted sensation of the experience. The fact that the 'alien' landscape that he expected is blurred by the misty weather is in itself an unexpected surprise.

The overwriting of the landscape in his memory awakens other memories associated with the previous visit, but everything now seems anticlimactically lacking in dramatic qualities. At the time of the first visit, Robinson was presumably experiencing the onset of the symptoms that would require brain surgery as well as the worsening relations of his first marriage; he subsequently remarried and became a parent. He now looks down on the same landscape 'with no ten years' bickering, sulks or resentments, / tit-for-tats, cries…'. He proceeds: 'In the silence, I was wondering where they had gone' – a sentence which gives an impression that the troubles have naturally solved themselves over the course of time rather than being settled by human efforts. Even the silence is bereft of the intertextual connotations of the voice of the cicada. The season mentioned in the poem is 'early May', when it is too early for cicadas to come out of the ground.

In the simple silence without the cicada song, the poet discovers a new aspect to the topography of Yamadera. In the beginning of the third and final stanza, 'Here again, the eyes have it', the past tense changes into the historic present, as it does in the first line of the second stanza ('From here I look down…'). In both cases, passages

---

[22] *CP*, 290.

written in the present tense convey the poet's mild surprise at finding unexpected scenery from a known standpoint and, though it is in a sense disappointing, he affirms and appreciates it. The sentence 'the eyes have it' is a pun on 'the ayes have it' (the affirmative votes win), a set phrase used in parliamentary sessions. Assessing both the landscape in his mind and the other in front of his eyes, he gives the decision firmly in favour of what he is looking at now.

At the same time, however, the poet does not refuse the rich literary connotations with which the place is charged. In the final three lines, the new serenity which he has found is described again in relation to the haiku by Bashō – 'as if sounds had all been absorbed into rock' – and, more importantly, he concludes the poem by saying that 'it seemed that what the landscape wanted / was only for us to rise above it'. From the grammatical context, the final word 'it' may refer to his perverse temptation 'to pick a quarrel' with the scene's tranquillity, but the word can include, in a broader sense, the life-difficulty in general.[23] 'It' can also refer to the landscape: rising above it, the poet aims to rise above aggression or problematic desires. Thus, for the poet, it is not his own determination, but 'the landscape' that encourages him to get over this human predicament. At the core of the whole process of the reassessment of the place and himself are the triangular interactions between the place itself, the preceding literary texts about it and the poet's inner self. While a new topography of Yamagata less dependent on Bashō emerges from the companion pieces, the refreshed Yamadera in turn gives the poet a new idea about himself and his past memories.

When it comes to the other nationally noted site in Tohoku, Matsushima, Miyagi, Robinson's freedom is all the more conspicuous because Bashō himself was caught up in its accumulated textual significations. Matsushima is a historical place famed in the classical Japanese poetry anthology, the Goshūi Wakashū [*Later Collection of Gleanings of Japanese Poems*; 後拾遺和歌集], commissioned by Emperor Shirakawa in 1075. In *The Narrow Road to the Deep North*, Bashō describes the scenery of Matsushima Bay (a great many small islands with pine trees on them) with a collection of clichés – 'Matshushima is the best landscape in the country of Fuso [a poetic denomination of Japan, derived from the legendary Chinese divine tree under the sea], not second to Dotei [洞庭] and Seiko [西湖]'

---

[23] *CP*, 290.

(my translation).²⁴ While Bashō parallels Matsushima with two famous lakes in China, which he had never seen, he makes no haiku there and, instead, quotes a poem about the place by his disciple, Sora. According to Sora, his master told him that 'when I face an unparalleled beauty, I become too possessed to find words for it' (my translation), though modern scholars have identified Bashō's draft haiku about Matsushima, one which he later attempted to discard.²⁵

Along with 'High Time', a poem set in Tsukihama, Higashi-Matsushima, and 'Equivocal Isle',²⁶ which evokes the scenery at Oku-Matsushima, 'From the World' provides a good example of Robinson's nonchalant approach to the famous island-filled bay, in contrast to Bashō's curiously muted diction. Here, what the poet first notices amidst the supposedly matchless scenery of Matsushima is its eyesore – 'Now, their mothballed power station / underneath a cloudy sky'. Nonetheless, the poem finally accepts this disturbing element in the historical bay as one of the possible tales that the place can subsume. From this point of view, 'the moth-balled power station' is in fact 'setting off the beauty of their beauty spot' , as if the power station were a modern beauty patch on the face of the old bay.²⁷ The contemporary British poet succeeds in revealing a Matsushima that could never have been guessed at by those who well knew the literary tradition of the place, including Bashō himself.

Memory and Topography in 'Last Resort'

In the previous sections, I have examined what new kind of *genii loci* Robinson's poems call up from his neighbourhood or from a too well-known site of interest. However, as Adrian Poole points out, this is not the typical setting for Robinson's poetry. Poole argues that 'Peter Robinson's poetry asks what it means to lose your sense of direction or not to have one in the first place. "For the minute there's nowhere to go," he writes (*SP*, 31). This might be a relief no less than a predicament. Having

---

²⁴ Matsuo Bashō, *The Narrow Road to the Deep North*, ed. Yasuo Hagiwara (Tokyo: Iwanami Bunko, 1979), 36. [芭蕉『おくのほそ道』萩原恭男校注、岩波文庫]
²⁵ Bashō, notes, 38 and 79.
²⁶ *CP,* 289, 258.
²⁷ *CP,* 301.

nowhere to go can mean freedom from movement, purpose, urgency, sequence, story, for the time being.'[28] Poems about Japan like 'Lost Objects', in which the poet sees a parallel between himself (a foreigner in Japan) and a lost object which is waiting to find 'some means of coming home', indeed reflect this sense of being on the road without any fixed destination. In the final section, I would like to examine a poem about a run-down spa resort which seems, in the poet's eyes, nobody's terminus.

In 'The Last Resort', Robinson explores the possible topography of a tourist destination which is not really any tourist's favourite destination any more.[29] Here again, the intertextuality plays an important part, with even more peculiar allusions than in the two poems about Yamadera, in the sense that they go some way beyond what the poet is conscious of. 'The Last Resort' was occasioned by an annual study trip by the department of English literature at Tohoku University. They would normally visit a spa town in Miyagi or Yamagata equipped with a training centre dormitory, but, in this particular year, the department's assistant could not book any of the department's usual haunts and, as her last resort, chose a once-prosperous spa town near her hometown, namely, Iizaka, Fukushima. Although Iizaka Spa is one of the oldest spa resorts in Tohoku, dating back even to the mythical age (legend reports that Prince Yamatotakeru, younger brother to Amaterasu the Sun Goddess, cured his injuries in this spa) and visited by Bashō on his journey to the 'Deep North', the town had declined to a hollow shadow of its former self, having failed to update to meet tourists' demands, when Robinson and his colleagues and students came there.

The poem's unique point of view is already introduced in its opening two lines where, rather than meditating on a visitor's sentiments, the poet imagines the different fates between those who left the town for better fortunes and those who remained – 'For the ones who go and those about to stay, / two autumns'. The apparently fragmental sentence is based on Shiki's haiku, 'For me, who must go, / and you remaining behind / two different autumns' [行く我にとゞまる汝に秋二つ].[30] When Robinson composed the poem, curiously, he

---

[28] Adrian Poole, 'Robinson's Roads', in *The Salt Companion to Peter Robinson*, ed. Adam Piette and Katy Price (Cambridge: Salt, 2007), 26-35, 26.
[29] *CP*, 303.
[30] I am quoting Peter Robinson's translation of the verse here. See Robinson, *Approach to Distance: Selected Poems from Japan* (Tokyo and London: Isobar, 2017), 111.

thought that he had borrowed it from a haiku poet of the Edo period, Yosa Buson (1716–83), adapting it from a book of French translations that he had consulted.[31] However, his unwitting borrowing from Shiki to evoke Iizaka is in fact particularly appropriate, for Shiki functions as a hub around which the 'Deep North' literary traditions and the theme of journeys without destinations are interlaced with each other.

To understand the possibly rich context that can connect Shiki with 'The Last Resort', we have to note the historical background of the above-quoted haiku as well as of Shiki's own version of a 'narrow road to the deep north'. As regards the haiku, Shiki composed it on 19 October 1895 in Matsuyama, on parting from his friend, Natsume Sōseki (1867–1916), the future novelist famous for *I Am a Cat* (1905) and *Sanshirō* (1908). According to Shizuo Miyasaka, the real subtlety of the haiku is far beyond the contrivance of separating the season into two, as if they were material objects. In fact, there is a complicated chiastic relationship between the two cities implied in the haiku, Matsuyama and Tokyo. While Matsuyama is Shiki's birthplace, Sōseki was born and bred in Tokyo. They first met each other at University Preparatory School in 1887 and both of them proceeded to Tokyo Imperial University (now the University of Tokyo), but then their career paths became intertwined when Sōseki began to work as a middle school teacher in Matsuyama, while Shiki stayed in Tokyo to devote himself to haiku. At the time the above-quoted haiku was made, the haiku poet had spent about two months in his hometown partly to aid his convalescence from tuberculosis (which later developed into spinal caries). With this background, the undertone of 'me, who must go, / and you remaining behind' is charged with cross-implications – 'me, who must go to your hometown, leaving my own / and you who must remain in my hometown, far away from yours'.[32] Both of them are, at the same time, associated with and alienated from their respective places of life. Robinson, without really knowing it, picked up a perfect text to enrich the vacillating sense of belonging described in 'The Last Resort'. This is especially so when we note that, as Andrew Houwen

---

[31] See Robinson's note to the poem in *TLG*, 136. Andrew Houwen's chapter in this volume refers to Reginald Horace Blyth (1898–1964) as the original source of the misidentification.

[32] See Shizuo Miyasaka's comments on the haiku. *The Dictionary of Haiku: Commentaries and Interpretations*, ed. Isao Ogata, (Tokyo: Kasama Shoin, 2000), 334. [尾形仂編『俳句の解釈と鑑賞事典』、笠間書院]

explains in his chapter in this volume, the poet thought of Adrian Poole and Margaret De Vaux as those who leave (after an academic visit to Japan), as compared to himself who remains without hope, at that point, of returning to his country.

Shiki's literary link with Iizaka does not stop here. Two years before the separation from Sōseki (more correctly, between 19 July and 20 August 1893), Shiki made a tour around Tohoku, following in the footsteps of Bashō. His travel log appeared serially in *Nippon* (a daily newspaper which was published between 1889–1914), with the title of 'A Travel Diary Which Knows No Destination' [はて知らずの記].[33] While skipping Yamadera, he stayed at Iizaka from 26 to 28 July and made a haiku about a waterfall which poured into River Surikami: 'O coolness / A waterfall gushes out / Through the gap between the hotels' [涼しさや瀧ほとばしる家のあひ] (my translation). Partly because he was already showing symptoms of tuberculosis, he suffered much from the heat of the summer and rejoiced at finding coolness in anything during the tour. By contrast with this image of early summer freshness, however, here is what Robinson in 'The Last Resort' finds by and on the same river: 'contradictory signs and tokens – / like ripened apples or purple potatoes, / dropped leaves borne down-river, for ever / alighting to drift'. To the poet's eye, autumnal fruition symbolised in agricultural crops is paired with the image of death and uncertainty represented in dead leaves floating without any ultimate goal. The 'two autumns' in this poem, then, refer not only to those who left and those who remained, but also to the fullness and the hollowness of the season as it permeated through this almost deserted spa resort.

---

[33] Shiki's travel journal has been sometimes translated as 'A Journey Without an End', interpreting the word 'hate' [はて] as 'an end' rather than 'a destination'. However, this appears inaccurate, if not wrong, when we look at Shiki's own elaboration on the title in the first instalment of the serial publication. After wondering where to go since it is impossible to see all the places the great haiku master visited, Shiki gives up the idea of drawing up an itinerary at all, and persuades himself with the rhetorical question: 'How many travellers have ever decided their final destination when they made a floating travel in this floating world?' (the translation is mine). See Shiki Masaoka, 'A Travel Diary Which Knows No Destination', *The Travel Writings in the Meiji Period*, ed. Kiyoto Fukuda (Tokyo: Chikuma Shobo, 1974) [福田清人編『明治紀行文學集』、筑摩書房], 72-90, 72.

The double-sidedness of the landscape leads to the poet's 'gaze at deserted bed- and bath-rooms / of bankrupted hotels' ('gaze at' is used as a verb phrase in the original). It would obviously be too opportunistic as well as far-fetched to draw attention to the fortuitous suggestion of what subsequently occurred in Fukushima, where the issues of the devastation of traditional communities became so problematic after the nuclear plant accident in 2011 (in fact, although both are in Fukushima, the Fukushima Daiichi Nuclear Plant lies about 100 km away from Iizaka). And yet the poem reminds us of the fact that the 'nimby' nuclear plant policy of the Japanese government led to the building of many nuclear plants in already decayed provinces remote enough from Tokyo, persuading local people to feel that they had to rely on nuclear plants to revitalise the regional economy.

As one of these economically ruined historical villages, Iizaka makes the poet suppose that 'once upon a time, there were stories to tell'. These are not stories he knows, but the desolation paradoxically evokes some untold stories – at the time when he visited Iizaka, the above-mentioned assistant who booked the hotel was self-deprecating about the town, and even the literary waterfall about which Shiki composed the haiku was totally obscured by untended, overgrown trees – so that nobody knew for sure where it really was.[34] With its unique literary as well as historical significance lost not only to tourists 'who go' staying only one night, but also to 'the ones who must endure this season's / boredoms, its nervous collapse', the spa resort appears as just one of the declining regional communities all over Japan. Unable to take pride in their town, those who are bound to it are, the poet imagines, pining away as they keep watch over the progressive decay, but cannot turn their eyes from it either.[35]

---

[34] The local newspaper, *Fukushima Min'yu* (27 June 2016), reports that the waterfall at issue was rediscovered and, after the necessary lumbering of trees around it, once again exposed to the public view in June 2016. See http://www.minyu-net.com/tourist/naka/FM20160627-087477.php (an article in Japanese).

[35] This is one possible interpretation: the poem can be read with a complex doubled sense throughout. The poet can be regarded either as a visitor (to Iizaka), among 'the ones who go', or as a resident (in Japan), as among 'those about to stay', in contrast to his compatriot Adrian Poole. See Houwen's chapter in this volume for the latter interpretation of this poem.

In the final line of the poem, as if they were soldiers in a lost battle, they 'gaze at those hotels like scuttled battleships'.[36] It is noteworthy that the same verb phrase 'gaze at' is used here once again to conclude the poem. Though the viewpoint of a tourist (the poet) and the residents must be different from each other, they may still have something in common in the act of gazing, and cooperate to record the new, composite topography of Iizaka, which, subsuming the historical imagery of the place, offers the sense of 'here and now'.

In order to summarise poetry's creative power to cause a new poetic place to emerge, I would like to refer to Wallace Stevens again. J. Hillis Miller, reading 'The Idea of Order at Key West', pays attention to its setting in which an impersonal narrator describes a woman who 'sang beyond the genius of the sea'.[37] Her song is apparently neither dedicated to nor inspired by the sea, as 'she was the maker of the song she sang. / The ever-hooded, tragic-gestured sea / Was merely a place by which she walked to sing'. Notwithstanding, line 17 is abruptly followed by a mysterious question, '*Whose* spirit is this?' (my italic). For Hillis Miller, this question is essential to understanding the aim of Stevens's poem: 'That spirit was not there before the song, neither as the genius of the sea nor as the poet's own preexisting self. Nevertheless, it absorbs both the seascape and the poet's consciousness into a new totalizing construct presided over by a new *genius loci*. This construct Stevens calls a "world".'[38] The true subject of the poem, then, is far from the seascape off the island of Key West in Florida: the power of poetry that generates a new world.

Notwithstanding Hillis Miller's profound reading of the poem based on a Heideggerian sense of place, his conclusion might make the reader misleadingly suppose that the actual location has little importance in Stevens's poem. On the contrary, Key West is a literary resort island loved by many American poets and novelists such as Robert Frost (1874–1963) and Ernest Hemingway (1899–1961), among whom Stevens himself is included. The literary undercurrents with which the place is charged are an indispensable impulse for the poem to give birth to a new world, even if they never emerge on the surface. Likewise, in his poems written about Yamadera and Iizaka, Robinson absorbs the historical contexts of the places and amalgamates and transforms them into a new domain, a poetic locus.

---

[36] *CP*, 303.
[37] Stevens, 97.
[38] J. Hillis Miller, *Topographies* (Stanford: Stanford UP, 1995), 275.

At a panel discussion on 'Space and Spatiality in Theory', held at the Annual Meeting of the Association of American Geographers, Washington, DC, April 2010, answering a question from the organisers, 'Is a theory of space and spatiality in general possible?', Yi-Fu Tuan pointed out that, were there one, we would have now had 'a common vocabulary and a common set of goals'. Instead, he argues, if a theorist should construct a framework that can appeal to many, 'its power lies not, as the theorist himself may believe, in its compelling logic, but rather in its hidden metaphors – its poetry'.[39] Peter Robinson's poems written during his days in Tohoku wonderfully answer to this appeal by the human geographer of topophilia.

---

[39] 'Space and Spatiality in Theory', *Dialogues in Human Geography*, 2/1, (2012), 3-22, 13. This is an edited transcript of the panel discussion.

Chapter 10
'Understanding relations':
An Anglo-American Reading

Alison Stone

In March 1962, the British poet Roy Fisher sent a letter to his friend and fellow poet Gael Turnbull, addressing observations made by critics about the apparent Americanness of his work. Fisher wrote: 'I really must read this *Paterson* which everyone says I mimic,'[1] referring of course to the long poem by the American doctor-poet, William Carlos Williams.

It is perhaps more than coincidental – especially given the documented relations between Roy Fisher and Peter Robinson – that such words denying an American influence may as well have been Robinson's; upon the publication of *This Other Life*, his second collection of poetry, in 1988, Robinson received a note from his undergraduate tutor, the writer Nicole Ward Jouve, remarking the 'American influence' in his work.[2] Much as Fisher had been, Robinson was puzzled by such a compliment, having not considered American poetry a prominent influence at that time.

My chapter will therefore address this question – that is, what it is about Robinson's work that can potentially be construed as emanating from an American influence, because I believe such a discussion brings into greater focus some of the key intricacies of Robinson's poetic. Chief among these are what the poet has described as the effort required to '[understand] relations'[3] and also a necessary grounding in experience as the prerequisite to a poetic sensitively attuned both to the world and to others. While it is not my intention here to make a claim for Peter Robinson as an inherently transatlantic poet, I want to use some ideas from American modernist poetry and poetics as a useful framework through which to interpret his work. While Robinson's poetry is not always – at least at first glance – formally analogous to much of the Anglo-American poetry he professes to admire, there is a great deal in his

---
[1] 19th March 1962. Acc.12554/1. National Library of Scotland, Edinburgh.
[2] Personal communication, 10th March 2018.
[3] *TAP,* 119.

attention to language, respect for 'things' and his belief in poetry's ability to make things happen,[4] that can be illuminated by such a reading.

As Peter Robinson's influences are so wide-ranging and internationally diverse, it is difficult to tie his oeuvre confidently to single poets, poems and traditions (and to do so would be to do his work a disservice), as Robinson himself acknowledges: 'I could go on mentioning poets I've felt affinities with for a long time, and the list probably wouldn't add up to any single tradition'.[5] The *Salt Companion to Peter Robinson* (2007) contained a number of essays examining Robinson's travels and the effect of Japanese and Italian languages and spaces in particular.[6] Given Robinson's biography, tracing intersections with Italian and Japanese poetry are more immediately obvious international readings to make than considering his work in relation to an American tradition. In this respect, he has confessed to a somewhat unchronological encounter with American poetry: he had bought and read selections of Ezra Pound's and Robert Lowell's poems while still at school, and studied Eliot in sixth form; at university he added an awareness of Marianne Moore's syllabics and William Carlos Williams's poetry of 'no ideas but in things', then was directed to the late modernist Anglo-American influencers including Louis Zukofsky, Charles Olson, Ed Dorn, Robert Creeley and, a little later, John Ashbery and Frank O'Hara, before progressing backwards once more to Elizabeth Bishop, then, via others, to Walt Whitman and Emily Dickinson.[7] This is likely reflective of Robinson's undergraduate years at York and graduate ones at Cambridge, in which he encountered a number of writers such as J. H. Prynne, Andrew Crozier and Elaine Feinstein – all of whom were influenced by American modernism – and he also helped edit seven issues of *Perfect Bound* magazine.[8] A younger contemporary of these Cambridge poets, it appears that the 'inescapable

---

[4] That poetry can or cannot 'make things happen' is a contention that Robinson takes up in his 2002 critical work, *Poetry, Poets, Readers: Making Things Happen* (Oxford: OUP, 2002). It of course refers to the famous lines in Auden's poem 'In Memory of W. B. Yeats'.
[5] *TAP*, 24.
[6] Adam Piette and Katy Price (eds.), *The Salt Companion to Peter Robinson* (Cambridge: Salt, 2007). See especially John Roe 'The Refracted Self', 175-192, and Miki Iwata 'His Other Islands', 193-204.
[7] Personal communication, 10th March and 20th September 2018.
[8] See also Piette and Price, 'Peter Robinson's Tokens of Affection', 3-4, in the *Salt Companion*.

and belated novelty of much foundational modernism' that Andrew Crozier described,[9] did have an influence on Robinson's work too. This less evident international convergence has been insufficiently explored, and on first impressions there appears little about Robinson's work that might associate him with the likes of, for instance, Olson, Zukofsky or Williams; unlike these poets, Robinson's work instead is often underpinned by autobiography (though Roy Fisher was quick to identify the complexities inherent within this particular characteristic),[10] first-person pronouns, comprehensible punctuation and sentence structure, as well as a great importance placed on the sense of locale and time. However, in the words of prolific poet-critic Donald Davie, national characteristics in poetry are often to be found at a level 'more profound than technique alone',[11] and in a number of Robinson's comments in interviews a startlingly American influence can be uncovered. For instance, talking about the relation of modernism to his own work in an early interview, Robinson expressed an affinity with

> ...a line of non-metropolitan, northern and north-midlands poets that would include Basil Bunting, Roy Fisher, Charles Tomlinson and Donald Davie ... What those poets have in common is some relation to the Poundian line of modernism, a commitment to the world as recalcitrant and 'other' than the perceiver.[12]

Robinson's comments draw attention to a perceived split in modernist poetry along Eliotic (commonly thought of as more European) and Poundian delineations. The intricacies of this split are too extensive to be unravelled in the course of this essay,[13] but it suffices to say that this

---

[9] Andrew Crozier, *An Andrew Crozier Reader*, ed. Ian Brinton (Manchester: Carcanet, 2012), 17.
[10] See Roy Fisher, 'Preface', *Salt Companion*, 22.
[11] Donald Davie has suggested that conventional punctuation is a key difference between English and American poetries, as it implies the acknowledgement of an audience. See his essay 'The English and American in *Briggflatts*', *P.N. Review*, 5.1 (1978) 17-20.
[12] *TAP*, 40-41.
[13] For a useful account, see John Xiros Cooper, 'T. S. Eliot and American Poetry' in Mark Richardson (ed.) *The Cambridge Companion to American Poets* (Cambridge: CUP, 2015), 245-257.

was a binary felt by a number of modernist-influenced, post-war British poets, including those at Cambridge and those 'northern and north-midlands' poets whom Robinson names above,[14] for all of whom Pound and also William Carlos Williams were important influences. Yet it is the declared affinity with a mind-set where the world is 'recalcitrant and other' that is of most interest here in regards to an Anglo-American reading; it marks Robinson's commitment to a poetic of direct and lived experience, where objects and occasions are painstakingly observed and reflected upon but not impregnated with additional afflatus or ego-derived significations. Such a 'commitment' – Robinson's own, morally charged word – bears a substantial relation to American modernism.

This imperative is particularly evident in Robinson's early work, and a number of poems from *Overdrawn Account* display a keen, almost documentary-like perception of objects and places. 'Some Hope' is an especially strong example, as here in the first stanza:

> A salmoning cloud
>   that moves against the deepening blue
> and at this moment, poised
>   between the towers of the two flat-blocks,
> points up their clean, prestigious weight.
> The light at this unstable hour
> appeases the township's stone of its harshness.
> Back-to-backs are burnished gold.
> The day's work has drained you. Relax now.
> Obsessive, precise eyes
>   lose their focus.
>   Edges warm
> and habit does accommodate.[15]

Here, 'eyes' acts to affirm the separateness of perceiver and observed – in this case an un-named, post-industrial landscape. The poem as a whole

---

[14] Andrew Crozier is a poet who has been overt about his allegiance to a 'Poundian line'. As late as 1987, when Crozier wrote the introduction to the anthology *A Various Art,* he pointed to 'an interest in a particular aspect of post-war American poetry and the tradition that lay behind it – not that of Pound and Eliot but that of Pound and Williams'. In *Thrills and Frills: Selected Prose*, ed. Ian Brinton (Bristol: Shearsman, 2013), 50-52.
[15] *CP*, 33.

contains five such references to the eye, and is acutely concerned with alterations registered through vision. In particular, the eyes in 'Some Hope' are attuned to contrasts between distinct and indistinct, and what is seen for the first time and what is 'accommodate[d]' by habit: 'Obsessive, precise eyes / lose their focus. / Edges warm'; 'there's nothing the tired eye / will not integrate'. One can certainly draw likenesses here with the multiple imperatives to attention that are a common feature in the 'Poundian line of modernism', especially Williams's 'intensity of perception', Zukofsky's focus on seeing and communicating 'particulars' and even Heidegger (an important influence for both George Oppen and Tomlinson), who emphasises seeing 'in the widest sense of seeing' and apprehending 'what is present'.[16]

For Robinson then, such demonstration of careful and conscious observation is evidence both of the poet's care for his subject matter and also an acknowledgement of the world as 'recalcitrant other'. Indeed, a line from the second section of 'Some Hope' – 'What goes away / is only your attention' – clearly affirms a world which is 'other' and exists irrespective of the poet's gaze. Yet in spite of the separateness of landscape and observing eye, the poem's last section ends with an enticement to the onlooker:

> Down from the moor's arterial road
> the valley floors are crammed close
> with a curve of roof slate, necklace of millstone.
>
> Spongy, glistening, terrace house frontage
> suffers a distant eye's interest
> in the hardening of arteries, the heart.
>
> You are small, old relatives
> with no personal marks of recognition,
> swivel drawn, careful features

---

[16] William Carlos Williams, *Collected Poems II 1939-1962*, ed. Christopher MacGowan (Manchester: Carcanet, 200), 54; Louis Zukofsky, 'An Objective', *Prepositions + The Collected Critical Essays*, ed. Mark Scroggins (Wesleyan: University of Wesleyan Press, 2001), 16; Martin Heidegger, *Poetry, Language, Thought*, tr. Albert Hofstadter (New York: Harper Colophon Books, 1975), 59. Robinson has also taken inspiration from Heidegger's essay 'On the Origin of the Work of Art' in his 2014 poem 'Sein und Zeit' (*CP*, 467).

> going off in whichever way – a population
> whose heart is worn like stone.
>
> Some hope cleaves as moss and grass
> cling to a sheer face, cracking the stone
> to flakes of raucous laughter,
> an access for some eye to work.[17]

Here, a bodily connection is formed between landscape and observer, where arteries (the arterial road) 'harden' and the houses suffer a lack of 'interest' as well as suffering from it. In doing so, Robinson confirms that there is a personal, even emotional investment in such attention, in spite of the world's separateness: 'whose heart is worn like stone' – the verb 'worn' suggesting that the heart is both donned and abraded. Robinson reaffirms his interest in relations through another subtle play on the word 'cleave' in the final stanza; hope 'cleaves' as it binds together communities (through the moss and grass simile), yet stone can be 'cleaved' – that is, broken – into many pieces. Again, the poet is keen to emphasise the variations that can be uncovered through such careful observation, and the final line is yet another confirmation of this: 'access for some eye to work' points first, using the analogy of hairline fractures in stone, to the care needed on the poet's part to truly 'gain access' and prise apart the intricacies of existence – the use of the word 'work' signalling that this is an ongoing and active process. Certainly, 'Some Hope' is early evidence of Robinson's sense of poetic responsibility and of poetry not just as descriptive embellishment or documentary recall but as a serious cognitive undertaking.

I want to return briefly to this idea of work for the eye in a moment, but in order to think further how such perceptual and perceptive effort relates Robinson's work to American modernism, we can turn to his poem 'Coat Hanger',[18] which draws directly from William Carlos Williams's 'Red Wheelbarrow'. In this poem (which I shall not quote in full here),[19] the definitive 'so much depends' of Williams's poem has been replaced with the more speculative and contingent 'and so much

---

[17] *CP*, 35.
[18] *CP*, 227-8.
[19] This poem has been addressed a number of times in the *Salt Companion* in more detail than I shall do here. See Roy Fisher's 'Preface' (25) and 'Peter Robinson's Tokens of Affection' (13-14).

else that could depend', a shift that posits the poem as less doggedly attached to 'things', and more concerned with the relations that those things enact. Robinson has elaborated on this poem in an interview:

> [The poem] seeks to replace obsession with objects by attachment to people, or to achieve attachment to people by working through obsession. If you think of the poems as objects too, then there's your trajectory towards the sponsorship of understanding relations.[20]

Certainly, Peter Robinson has a number of poems in which objects appear, initially at least, to take centre stage. A prominent example is 'Take Care of Things', another poem which comes early in Robinson's body of work:

> The window box's marigolds,
> beneath them, the frame,
>
> and also wrought-iron rails
> with cherry trees in blossom are
>
> inert, but your green carboy
> distorts them in uneven glass.
>
> Light globules on the brass
> hanging basket shimmer. Look,
>
> a heart-shaped bread plant leaf
> is unravelling itself,
>
> and now the settled appliances
> shift under her regard –
>
> drawer-sided toaster, kettle.
> For him they are hard, still;
>
> but, to her, certain utensils
> not as she found them.

---

[20] *TAP*, 119.

> I've not touched a thing.
> You confront the changes.
>
> You say, 'Again I have to
> put everything away.'[21]

There is much in 'Take Care of Things' – the gradual unravelling of detail, the line-per-object arrangement that signals the focus afforded each new observation – that brings to mind the opening of Williams's similarly early poem, 'Good Night':

> In brilliant gas light
> I turn the kitchen spigot
> and watch the water plash
> into the clean white sink.
> On the grooved drain-board
> to one side is
> a glass filled with parsley –
> crisped green.
>   Waiting
> for the water to freshen –
> I glance at the spotless floor – :
> a pair of rubber sandals lie side by side
> under the wall-table
> all is in order for the night.[22]

While attention to the objects in both poems and the employment of proper nouns is similar, Robinson proves himself '[more than] a poet of domesticity'[23] in that his objects have no special quality in themselves, but rather are situating lacunae in which the attachment to people gathers and takes shape. In 'Take Care of Things', much about the characters of the 'you' and the 'I' are revealed in their contrasting regard and nonchalance towards the placement of these objects; it is the first-

---

[21] *CP*, 46.
[22] William Carlos Williams, *Collected Poems I 1909–1939*, eds. A. Walton Litz and Christopher MacGowan (Manchester: Carcanet, 2000), 85-6.
[23] Peter Riley, 'Peter Robinson: Six New Poems: An Introductory Note', *Fortnightly Review*, 3 June 2013, <http://fortnightlyreview.co.uk/2013/06/poems-peter robinson/>. Web. 8th July 2018.

person pronouns which catalyse the shift in focus in the ninth and tenth couplets, from objects to human relationships.

In another poem, also from *Overdrawn Account,* Robinson makes this relationship between objects and people even more overt: 'Their Inventory', inspired by American Modernist Wallace Stevens's poem 'Theory', takes Stevens's statement 'I am what is around me'[24] as its central premise for exploring relations:

> An electric clock
> to wake us, mornings: we own one.
>   I click
> the alarm down when you're gone.
>   You have
> a table mirror, cleansing cream
>   to save
> your look, where the fear and blame
>   are traced.
> Unlike that picture, as I say,
>   your face
> is getting better every day.
>   This place
> resembles you and me too well:
>   armchairs,
> you like upholstery material,
>   earthenware;
> I am closer to the window sill.
>   Your ring
> was not to promise relations,
>   but things
> invite formal properties, loved ones.
>   Our set
> is portable and switched on when
>   you get
> back from work, feel strained
>   with care
> and regard for others' ease.
>   Then here

---

[24] Wallace Stevens, *Collected Poems.* (London: Faber & Faber, 2006), 75.

> be careless and diverted, please.[25]

This poem is far more people-centred than its list-like arrangement would initially suggest. The interspersion of verbs – particularly possessive verbs ('you have', 'we own', and the second-person possessive 'your') – posits the items as intrinsically related to their human owners, taking on significance according to their use rather than their material properties alone. In this sense, the objects themselves are not the subject of 'obsession', but rather components in a larger and more emotive relationship. Indeed, the shifting of a number of these verbs and personal and demonstrative pronouns to the right-hand margin visually indicates these phrases as connections, on which the correspondence between person and inanimate object rests. Such connection is further enhanced through sound; not only are the transformative right-hand phrases almost all a uniform two syllables, but they are frequently full rhymes ('place / face', 'ring / thing') and often contain assonance ('save / traced').

Between the final four lines, the anticipated full rhyme of 'care' with 'there' becomes instead the slant rhyme of 'care' and 'here'. This is a change which both increases the objects' proximity to the speaker and makes the space appear more close-at-hand, and also, in deferring the final full rhyme to 'ease' and 'please', gives a sense of the completeness that comes with familiarity and comfort in one's surroundings.

'Their Inventory' is quite an atypical typographical arrangement for a Robinson poem, and its epigraph from an American, twentieth-century poet belies the fact that there is a much earlier source for the poem's form: 'His Grange, or Private Wealth', by English poet Robert Herrick:

> Though clock,
> To tell how night draws hence, I've none,
> A cock
> I have to sing how day draws on.
> I have
> A maid, my Prew, by good luck sent
> To save
> That little Fates me gave or lent.
> A hen

---

[25] *CP*, 45.

> I keep, which creeking day by day,
>   Tells when
> She goes her long white egg to lay.
>   A goose
> I have, which, with a jealous ear
>   Lets loose
> Her tongue, to tell that danger's near
>   A lamb
> I keep (tame) with my morsels fed,
>   Whose dam
> An orphan left him (lately dead).
>   A cat
> I keep that plays about my house
>   Grown fat
> With eating many a miching mouse.
>   To these
> A Tracy I do keep whereby
>   I please
> The more my rural privacy;
>   Which are
> But toys to give my heart some ease;
>   Where care
> None is, slight things do lightly please.[26]

Robinson's near-pastiche version even shares some of Herrick's rhymes – most notably the final pairing of 'ease' with 'please' and the use of the word 'care'. Read alongside Herrick's, it is clear that Robinson's poem is *not* merely an 'inventory', and in fact includes a great deal of personal and emotive detail; it is an overt and conscious fitting together of different 'parts' in order to bring the relations between people and their surroundings – or possessions – into relief. Thinking about Robinson's poems concerning objects from an Anglo-American standpoint then, we are perhaps inevitably drawn to Williams's mantra of 'no ideas but in things'. Yet, while Robinson is clearly a poet deeply concerned with experience and 'things' observed, 'Their Inventory' actually displays a real ambivalence towards material possessions, as a number of lines from the poem show: 'Unlike that picture, as I say, /

---

[26] Robert Herrick, 'His Grange, or Private Wealth', www.luminarium.org/sevenlit/herrick/grange.htm. Web. 30th September 2018.

your face / is getting better every day'; 'things invite formal properties, loved ones.' Therefore, though 'Their Inventory' proceeds via things, it in fact questions objects' ability to both encompass the nature of relations and to bestow happiness (or 'ease' in both poems). It is Herrick's poem, therefore, that reads more like an inventory, a matter supported by the title, which points to the transactional nature of possessions: 'His Grange, *or Private Wealth*' (my emphasis). However, it seems that Herrick too is aware of the fleeting value of material things compared to human relations; his animals are 'but toys', and simply 'slight things [which] do lightly please', the lilting rhyme of 'slight' and 'light' emphasising such possessions' ultimate frivolity.

Such an acute attention to the detail of everyday life and everyday objects, as well as connections informed by sound, is an impetus that continues in Robinson's later work. Yet this in itself, as Robinson states in the aforementioned interview, is just one aspect of the potential of his poems to work towards 'understand[ing] relations'. The second – 'think[ing] of poems as objects too' – is a statement which bears a strong relation to the Poundian line of modernism, and most particularly to American Objectivism. In this way, the one-time Objectivist George Oppen defined the purpose of this group of 1930s poets, correcting misconceptions: 'There's been tremendous misunderstanding. People assume it [Objectivism] means the psychologically objective in attitude. It actually means the objectification of the poem, the making an object of the poem'.[27] Oppen's words refute the facile assumption that the Objectivists were 'objective' in attitude and would seem to fit well with Robinson's stated aims to write poetry where the world is acknowledged and respected as 'other', yet is still the subject of deeply personal reflection and investment. Indeed, for the Objectivist poet, it is the act of making the 'object' of the poem that confirms the connection with and care for the poem's subject matter.

That Robinson had formulated this thought – that is, he has thought of his poems concerning objects to also *be* objects – is another aspect which connects him to the Anglo-American credentials of Basil Bunting, Charles Tomlinson, Donald Davie and again Roy Fisher. Fisher, examining Robinson's use of personal pronouns in the 'Preface' to the *Salt Companion,* is astute in realising this connection:

---

[27] George Oppen, 'George Oppen.' Interview with L. S. Dembo. 'The Objectivist Poet: Four Interviews.' Spec. issue of *Contemporary Literature* 10.2 (1969). JSTOR. 159-177. Web. 3rd September 2018.

> [Robinson] appears to treat the 'I' 'you' and 'we' in as lapidary a fashion as the carefully layered words of his observations of scenery, weather and situations. Treating the pronouns in this way means they have to be given the stability and respect accorded to things; and a reader is steered away from over-dramatic reactions by this fastidiousness of the author. He doesn't psychologise much: and when he does venture in to analysis of motives or emotions it's only by way of the briefest of excursions, securely supported by the structure of the poem.[28]

The word 'lapidary' relates Robinson's work to an interest in poetry writing as analogous with handicrafts and labour, again identifiable in much Poundian and Objectivist modernism. To give a few brief examples, there is Bunting's chiselling stonemason in *Briggflatts*; Zukofsky's likening of poetry writing to cabinetmaking;[29] the 'butted together' quality of Oppen's (a carpenter by trade) poems which Tomlinson praised.[30] In fact, it would seem that Robinson displays this impetus early, when he writes at the end of 'Some Hope' of the eye 'work[ing]' the landscape, a verb that contrasts the 'lack of work' and the 'worn economy' evident in the dilapidated warehouses and chimneys that are observed.[31] Such a concern marks Robinson's writing as more than straightforwardly autobiographical or metaphorical – another point Fisher is keen to stress in his preface – and affirms poetry as a 'serious undertaking' bearing a direct relation to the world and requiring substantial effort and work to accomplish.[32]

This twinned belief in the solidity of words and their potential to bring oneself into closer relation with the world is evident in the short poem 'True Blank'. Appearing in *The Returning Sky*, it is prefaced by the words of philosopher Bernard Williams: 'no way in which... the

---

[28] *Salt Companion*, 21.
[29] Zukofsky, 17.
[30] Charles Tomlinson, 'Introduction', *Poems of George Oppen (1908–1984)*. ed. Charles Tomlinson (Newcastle: Cloud, 1990), 8-13, 10.
[31] *CP*, 35.
[32] Perhaps there is a parallel to be drawn here with Crozier's first impressions of American modernism: 'the Americans suggested, through the very narrow representation of their work afforded to me in London and Cambridge at the time, that being a poet was in some way a full time, serious activity' (*Crozier Reader*, 17).

understanding / of life can get ahead of life itself.'

> 1
> The world outside had lost its story.
> A wintry grey-ness covered all.
> As if the drear was a lack of fiction,
> some were staring into screens
> for menus, for alternative
> likely stories they could live
> the blank hours and no-places by.
> Painfully early, it was Easter –
> an Easter without resurrection
> of greenery or sky.
>
> 2
> The world outside had lost its story.
> Hanging over shrubberies
> of what had flashed off diamond brickwork,
> plastic bag ghosts caught on trees
> flapped inside quotation marks;
> but words between us, like a self-styled
> understanding, a projection,
> found you able to re-found
> the look of things on a lack of fiction,
> being reconciled.[33]

The two ten-line stanzas (which are numbered, a feature evident in many of the poems in *The Returning Sky*) sit equally as separate, discrete perspectives or as two versions of a similar course of events set side by side. Robinson's notably pared down vocabulary and use of repetition indeed gives the impression of a lapidary, examining or polishing each word and making minor alterations in order to achieve varying effects from the same materials. The lexis here too is direct and matter-of-fact – 'a wintry grey-ness covered all' – and contains a large number of nouns, evidencing the poet's care not to 'get ahead' of words themselves and their significations too. Most striking here, however, is the alteration between regular metrical forms and more free-flowing stresses and assonance: the

---

[33] *CP,* 380-1.

first seven lines of the first stanza are mostly in tetrameter, predominantly iambic rather than trochaic (five lines as opposed to two), and both stanzas end on a short line. This shift from regular to irregular is most clear in the second half of stanza two, where the poem assumes a personal address in which 'words' themselves are considered as both an 'understanding' and a 'projection', interfacing 'between' the unnamed 'us' of the poem. 'True Blank', then, appears eager to display its own artifice, to highlight words and their arrangements as the consciously chosen construction of the poet, capable of simultaneously conveying 'fiction', but also 'understanding'. These strong sonic patterns enhance the material qualities of the poem's language and arrangement, positing it as an object in its own right. This is reinforced by the homonymic repetition of 'found' in the third from last line – 'found you able to re-found' – whereby the second can be taken equally to mean the craftsman-like melting and remoulding of metal, but also as its other, literary definition: 'formed by taking a piece of non-poetic text and reinterpreting its structure metrically' (*OED*). In this way, Robinson appears to be demonstrating how work which is 'founded' on a 'lack of fiction', and is true to direct experience, is apt material for poetic re-moulding.

In 'True Blank' we can see Robinson's acute concern for the specifics of experience and his interest in the 'thingly' quality of words and poetic construction working in tandem. Robinson has spoken on a number of occasions of the central importance of experience to his poetic approach:

> A desire to make high claims for what a poem can do, however virtuous in intention, miscarries if art is freed from correlating its independent powers with the circumscribed conditions of experience. Poems will not be 'a profound recognition of the existences of other beings' if so freed.[34]

Such a statement confirms the worldliness of Robinson's poetic; it is concerned with the happenings of the world at large, rather than seeking to synthesise observed phenomena with the workings of the poet's own mind. In this way, Robinson's poetry demonstrates its fascination with the changing conditions of experience, where correlation or contrast are equally valid. If we combine then Robinson's dedication to experience

---

[34] Robinson, *In The Circumstances: About Poems & Poets* (Oxford: Clarendon Press, 1992), 10.

with his aforementioned figuring of the poem as object, and objects themselves as a means of forming 'attachments to people', there is much that can be found in common with American, late-modernist poetry. In particular, some of Oppen's comments on the relations between things, ourselves and others come to mind; there is the memorable first line from *Of Being Numerous* – 'There are things / we live among "and to see them / Is to know ourselves"' – and also the epigraph (taken from Jacques Maritain) to *The Materials:* 'we awake in the same moment to ourselves and to things'.[35] For Oppen, a recognition of 'otherness' – whether inanimate objects or other beings – is crucially tied to an understanding of ourselves. 'Awakening' and 'knowing' are words that speak with conviction about the important role poetry has to play in enacting relations. This is a view with which Robinson would surely concur:

> Art can make things happen... which is why I have not been urging you to believe that poetry *'can'* or *'must'* make things happen, but, rather, inviting you to take part in how it *does*.[36]

For this poet, the implicitly participatory nature of poetry – between poets, readers, selves and others – is also a happening in itself, and evidence of a dedication to 'understanding relations' via a careful but active working-through. Robinson does indeed not 'make high claims for what a poem can do', but his insistence both on experience as a grounding force and that the 'recognition of the existences of other beings' is profound posits poetry as a medium capable of bringing about a more vital and meaningful relationship with the world and with others. These are extrapolations which ally Robinson's ethic closely with Anglo-American and Objectivist idioms, which are constantly at pains to present poetry writing as an expression of contact with the world and others, 'the act of being / More than oneself'.[37]

In order to consider how Peter Robinson's poems are at once both personal, but also figure poetry-writing as concerned with the world at large, I wish to turn to a very recent poem which concerns itself with a singular object. 'Empty Vase' once more highlights the subtle

---

[35] George Oppen, *New Collected Poems,* ed. Michael Davidson (New York: New Directions, 2008), 163, 38.
[36] Robinson, *Poetry, Poets, Readers: Making Things Happen,* (Oxford: OUP, 2002), 187.
[37] Oppen, *New Collected,* 159.

distinction between a 'no ideas but in things' mentality and an approach where things appear prominently, but in fact play only a supporting role in the conceptual and emotional workings of the poem. Things and 'stuff' are indeed evidence of a grounding in experience, yet the possession *of* or attention *to* things is, in itself, not something to be lauded and worthy of poetic consideration – rather, it is in the way that these objects serve as markers for relations that makes their use interesting. The 'Empty Vase' itself is one such marker:

> 1
> That empty vase in a front window bay,
> vase with blue willow-pattern lines,
> it's missing a birth- or a Valentine's day
> for us to have our rare designs
> upon its inner emptiness, that vase
> come from a junk, no, a charity shop
> where I'll have paid a tiny sum
> on a nondescript autumn afternoon
> to take its vacancy away.
>
> 2
> Though forgotten in such emptiness
> long winters long, still, it serves to say
> of all the infinite times or places
> in which two might have moved and loved,
> oh no, you didn't miss each other,
> for here it was we coincided –
> communicating through these times of ours,
> and like that vase were a momentary stay
> waiting for its complements of flowers.[38]

'Empty Vase' is an intimate poem containing many first-person pronouns, yet it still speaks to the wider realm of human relationships and the moments and spaces that these occupy. The vase itself stands as an empty vessel full of potential, both awaiting its 'complements' of flowers but also ready to receive the 'rare designs' of the people that purchased it at a charity shop (certainly another example of a poem that

---

[38] *RE*, 88.

'replaces obsession with objects with attachment to people'). It seems that taking away the 'vacancy' of the vase is somewhat analogous with the writing of a poem, in which carefully chosen words occupy the vacancy of a blank page in direct response to the occasions and experiences of life. The harmoniousness of regular rhyme at the start of the poem and the continued assonance throughout also suggest a cohesion between the vessel and its contents. It becomes clear as the poem progresses that while 'Empty Vase' is rooted in everyday, personal experiences, it is also in contact with wider, social significances, of which human relationships and the passage of time are marked by a number of public occasions (Valentine's Day, a birth). In this way, there are a number of things that 'coincide' within the vase: the figures of the partners themselves, their personal feelings and public routines. Furthermore, to coincide involves two, distinctly separate entities. Even in this poem of romantic union then, the speaker embraces the necessity of 'otherness' in order to meditate truly on the nature of relations. Indeed, Robinson is not the only British poet to display such an interest in otherness, and the words of Brian John writing about Charles Tomlinson (one of Robinson's named 'non-metropolitan, northern' poets, and variously influenced by American modernism) could equally be applied to Robinson's work: '[an] acknowledgement of the otherness of things, whether people or world ... is central to civility and true relationship'.[39] In such active coinciding then, 'mov[ing]' and 'lov[ing]' is juxtaposed with the singular, stationary object of the vase, which acts as a vessel for 'momentary stay(s)'. Robinson therefore uses the inconspicuous, unexceptional 'thinglyness' of a bargain vase in order to bring the details, routines and changes of a long-term relationship into clearer relief.

'Empty Vase' is a poem that displays what Roy Fisher has identified as a somewhat discreet style, devoid of 'eye-catching idiosyncrasies' and 'convenient grab-handles', yet nevertheless full of subtle complexities that reveal themselves under scrutiny. Though Robinson's body of work contains a huge amount of variety, 'Empty Vase' *is* typical of a Peter Robinson poem in that the clarity and simplicity of its language and subject matter reveal new perspectives and new relations at each re-reading. As I began this chapter by noting, Robinson's poems are not immediately synonymous with American modernism, as they infrequently display the unconventional lineation and paratactic

---

[39] Brian John, *The World as Event: The Poetry of Charles Tomlinson* (Montreal: McGill-Queen's UP, 1989), 95.

word arrangements that characterise a good deal of the work of the Objectivists and the Poundian modernists. It is not in form or technique, but rather in poetic conviction that we find an approach analogous with these American poets: Robinson's empirical interest in ordinary objects, his dedication to keeping his poems 'grounded' in experience, his contemplation of writing as a craft-like activity, and his determination to acknowledge that which is 'other', all speak to the aims and idioms of American modernism. Additionally, and even more importantly, there is the conviction emanating from Robinson's body of work that writing poetry is an absolutely essential activity, indicated by Robinson's aforementioned comments about how poetry '*does* [make things happen]'. Once more, Roy Fisher seems accurately to encompass the energy of Robinson's work when he says that the poems express the 'urgencies of new creations'.[40] While such an urge to create cannot, of course, be claimed exclusively for any one category, style or nationality of poetry, there is much in Objectivist poetics and Poundian modernism that speaks for poetry writing as an absolute necessity, as the life-blood of a connection between individual and world.[41] There is a seriousness in the Objectivist poet's undertaking, and Robinson's poetry too, at times, seems full of obligation: to the accuracy of events, the authenticity of emotions, and to the efficacy of words; all this is evident in the sensitivity and attunement to relations that his poems display. It is perhaps in the appreciation of this attitude, rather than via line-by-line comparisons of technique alone, that we can find elucidating affinities between Peter Robinson and American poetry which speak to the heart of this British poet's achievements.

---

[40] *Salt Companion*, 22-23.

[41] For instance, George Oppen has spoken in an interview of poetry as being synonymous with 'an act of conscience, of feeling that one was worth something or other', and how poetic exploration is a vital part of 'know[ing] what the world [is]'. George and Mary Oppen, 'Poetry and Politics: A Conversation with George and Mary Oppen', interview with Burton Hatlen and Tom Mandel, ed. Burton Hatlen, *George Oppen: Man and Poet*, 23-50 (25).

Chapter 11
Objects in the World

James Peake

1

Peter Robinson's first novel, *September in the Rain*, was published in that month of 2016 by Holland House Books. While the novel is not the first volume of prose fiction that Peter Robinson has published,[1] it is the most significant to date, both in its potential to affect perceptions of how the writer's still-growing *oeuvre* is orientated as well as in the achievement it represents. For many and various reasons – medical, ethical, geographical and aesthetic – the composition of the novel was a protracted process. No less than forty years separate the composition of its earliest extant sections and its eventual publication. *September in the Rain* is a novel impossible to discuss without touching on some of the freely available biographical facts informing its narrative and while such considerations fall well outside the scope of a brief introductory chapter looking at Robinson in the guise of prose fiction writer, the fact of its remarkably lengthy composition does endorse extra-literary considerations which complicated that process and, paradoxically, sustained it. *September in the Rain* is identifiably a first novel insofar as it takes impetus from the author's life. It is less typical of a first novel in arriving at a stage in a literary career when its author is internationally established in other forms.

In aphoristic mode Robinson has written: 'The very thing that prompts you to start a piece of writing may be just what you'll have to leave behind to finish it.'[2] The thought has a distant relative in T. S. Eliot's 'East Coker'[3] and it likewise occupies that temporal and procedural space between the artist who begins a work and the one

---

[1] *FDB*: the earliest story it collects, and therefore the first of his prose fiction to see publication, is 'Music Lessons', written in 1981–2.
[2] *STS*, 46.
[3]   '…one has only learnt to get the better of words
    For the thing one no longer has to say, or the way in which
    One is no longer disposed to say it.'
'East Coker' V. 5-7: *The Complete Poems and Plays of T. S. Eliot* (London; Faber and Faber; 1969), 202.

who completes it. I give precedence to the workmanlike aspect of this aphorism (and let retreat any more impertinent psychological interpretation) by admitting that after a certain organisational moment a structure must be sufficiently strong without the scaffolding. And yet an outside-in metaphor doesn't allow for the existence of the sequence of poems which constitute Part II of Robinson's 1988 collection, *This Other Life*. This untitled sequence of eight poems addresses some of the same events as the novel and in relation to which the novel can be viewed as an opening out. I touch later on certain details which survive the repositioning in prose of shared episodes. Read again from the vantage of the prose work, these poems release more of their meaning and show quite how compressed some of that overlapping material was by the lyricist compared to the novelist. It's possible now to view the sequence as somewhat cryptic, not only as a result of economy but also the ethical impetus to treat trauma more indirectly than directly. The poems were written between 1979 and 1985 and the poet has said of them: 'eight short poems in seven years, between four and ten years after the fact'.[4] It will be necessary to explain shortly the import of the 'fact' in question and its relation to the novel's plot.

Robinson's work on the novel was of course not constant throughout the forty years and this time is divisible into roughly five stages which I've included as an Appendix, based closely on the author's own recollections. I'll discuss the relationship of Robinson's prose to the public facts of his biography, then, as well as that of the novel to Robinson's other published prose fiction, namely the short stories collected as *Foreigners, Drunks and Babies* and 2019's *The Constitutionals: A Fiction*. I'll also sketch out a possible understanding of how the fiction relates to the poetry, of which there is so much more and for which Robinson is inevitably far better known. It has been possible to a degree to identify some potentially characterizing trends in the imaginative prose already and to notice how certain preoccupations and techniques make these fictional works so recognisably products of Robinson's hand. And considering the deeply personal nature of the first novel and its long and difficult struggle to find final form artistically and commercially, the project may even come to be seen in hindsight as a kind of self-imposed obstacle, the removal or supersession of which will enable more energy for other forms of writing. Where the poet's fiction might ultimately reside within the *oeuvre* is

---

[4] Peter Robinson, 'Through Frosted Glass', interview by Ian Sansom, first published *Oxford Poetry* (1994), reprinted *TAP*, 22.

something about which I can only speculate, and I have tried to resist any attempt to fix Robinson's prose fiction identity in anticipation of its being modified in the future.

2

'We were going to Italy in September'. So the narrator of *September in the Rain*, Richard English, explains innocuously enough near the start of the novel. But he is addressing someone in particular, Mary Young, and by the end of the novel the reader will understand the harrowing resonance of this simple statement in both their lives, but especially hers. The book is an account of a love triangle told by Richard (his surname will prove significant and I'll return to it), who is the common vertex. The three of them – Alice completes the trio – are at the start of their adult lives. They try out ideas and careers. They experiment with love.

When we meet him, Richard is working at the National Hospital for Nervous Diseases in Queen Square, London (now the National Hospital for Neurology and Neurosurgery), reading and saving what money he can ahead of a planned trip to Europe. He is excited and challenged by both of these intelligent and emotionally resilient women, but, to all of their costs, they fail to resolve their entanglement soon enough. The central event of the novel is a grave crime against Mary, a sexual assault in a car which Richard is forced to witness at gunpoint. For reasons Richard will examine repeatedly and remorsefully[5] they were hitchhiking and were picked up by the soon-to-be perpetrator of the attack.

Anyone already familiar with Robinson's own biography will know that the novel has some relationship to a real past. A very similar incident took place over forty years ago in Italy, at night, in a car, during a rainstorm, a crime Robinson was forced to witness at gunpoint.

> Time and space distanced me from the material of the novel, and made it possible, slowly and not surely, to create its almost entirely fictional frame, to distance, in varying degrees, the characters from their originals, to close definitively the book of life in some respects so as to open it again as a novel, and, most of all, to give me time to write and rewrite every sentence in it.[6]

---

[5] *STR*, 249-250; 263.
[6] Peter Robinson, personal communication, 9th July 2016.

This scrupulosity has been an intrinsic part of the undertaking and where all of Robinson's output is marked by care (he is never slapdash) the novel's complex responsibilities to living persons[7] and a conspicuous belief in literary conscience have intensified in this work to an uncommon degree:

> I always thought that the thing that would justify the book had to be the way it was written – nevertheless, it has been a long hard climb to get it to sing throughout in the way I hope it more or less does.[8]

The decision to move the narrative into the second person, to address directly the woman against whom the violent act was perpetrated, was a late but significant shift. While the level of access this affords a reader to privately addressed material can be unsettling the novel is understated in tone, and set against this enforced intimacy is a refusal to dramatise or trumpet its shock. To pitch *September in the Rain* to 'you' is also an attempt to bypass the accretions of naming (there is much to be said about names and naming in Robinson's fiction) as well as refreshing the relationship of speaker and addressee with the use of the most unencumbered form of address that exists.

> ... [R]ecasting of the entire narrative as like a lyric poem addressed to Mary in the second person ... was my best shot at resolving the problem about the narrator's feelings towards the main female character, which (aside from the late-written Chapter 20) could not be done by 'telling' them, as we put it in creative writing classes, but could perhaps be 'shown' by means of the ambivalent intimacy effected in the shift to the second person.[9]

The prose moved closer to the work of the poet as a result. However, if it brought the novel to eventual completion, it would also open it up to a particular kind of criticism (one potential by-product of Robinsonian

---

[7] The disclaimers to both of *September in the Rain* and *Foreigners, Drunks and Babies* are more comprehensive than is usual and are recommended to the interested reader. I return to this issue and quote them below.
[8] Peter Robinson, personal communication, 9th July 2016.
[9] Ibid.

technique I'll look at again in the light of criticisms of his poetry, particularly as it has been examined by William Wootten). Discomfort and doubt about the lack of distance between life and creative analysis are not without precedent in Robinson's poetic career or irrelevance to the poet's work in prose. It's a condition of the novel's aesthetic success then that it be willfully resistant to, and profoundly engaged with, the unexamined treatment of biographical experience.

A significant part of Robinson's poetic terrain is what might be termed the 'interstitial', by which I mean those spaces created by the presence of more than a single sentient agency, as well as processes of attraction and repulsion between recorder and recorded, shifts in feeling which require an interlocutor (whether mute or otherwise). He is justly admired as the articulator of these omnipresent[10] and unstable zones. In interview he has confirmed that the 'kinds of poem that take place *between people* are ones I'm particularly drawn to'[11] (my italics). A Robinsonian lyric might be considered a visitation of sorts, a scene into which the reader is, as it were, insinuated. The poems I have in mind are (recalling the Italian origin of the term) stanzaic frames inside which narrator and/or interlocutor are not always named or explicitly relativised the one to the other. His meticulous craftsmanship and preference for plain language is, as I read it, a self-corrective (in terms of balance) to the deeply personal material that provokes his imagination. But the novel – this one specifically but even perhaps any full-length linear narrative work – does not allow for such techniques. Suggestive games with anonymity or meta-narrative would not be appropriate in a novel so concerned with individuals as *September in the Rain*. Of his poems he has said: 'If the reader cannot tell who I'm talking to or why, as someone recently complained, then suffice to say that I don't think the reader needs to know. Readers are free to disagree.'[12] Robinson the novelist however is forced to declare his characters more than this version of Robinson the poet. It would be interesting to know if the novelist would wish to soften the poet's statement in this regard and reconsider a reader's 'need to know' more generously. To my ear the comment I've quoted has a ring of defensiveness, presumably as a

---

[10] A potential irony in the cases for and against Robinson's alleged solipsism is that the spaces so described, and which his imagination finds congenial, do not exist for a consciousness in isolation.
[11] *TAP*, 21.
[12] *TAP*, 23.

response to certain hostile criticism regarding the nature of his poetic project. The phrase comes from the world of intelligence-gathering (or at least its popular portrayal) and however useful it might seem, its very applicability is a source of mistrust.

At a formal level and even before the novel was finished, completion of the poetic sequence was not sufficient for the poet:

> I also had the haunted feeling that the real relations in this material could not be explored in lyric poems, not least because I couldn't get more narrative into them than was there inscribed or implied in their occasions.[13]

The novel is far from satisfactorily taken either as a bowing to readerly appetite for both more (and more intense) fictionalised biographical detail, or as the mere provision of facts only partially unpacked previously. It resists these polarities and must therefore occupy another, harder to define, space.

3

Of the volume in which the Italian poems appear, Marcus Perryman challenged Robinson directly: 'you don't seem like the sort of poet who likes to distinguish between them [life and art]. The otherness of other life [sic] is both others and writing, I take it.'[14] Robinson responds: 'You take it right ... the problems and paradoxes with ... interrelations between art and life have led me to back off, a little more recently.' While this can't be taken as assent to the first of Perryman's statements it doesn't quite constitute dissent either.

Whether fiction should make open use of biographical material, or whether it should, preferably (and somehow) be derived from somewhere further away than the near at hand, many critics consider it should be at least more heavily disguised. Timothy Harris is a critic who has notoriously denounced Robinson the poet for 'a self-absorption amounting almost, if not in fact to, solipsism'.[15] The

---

[13] Peter Robinson, personal communication, 9th July 2016.
[14] 'The Torque in Poetic Talk', interview by Marcus Perryman, first published *The Animist* (1998), collected in *TAP*, 32.
[15] *TAP*, 33.

charge was sufficiently serious for the poet to respond in an interview: 'Timothy Harris's phrase [...] might be aiming at, but failing to hit through the ad hominem, a complexity of lyric poetry, and perhaps of art more generally'.[16] In this sense at least the 1998 interviewee was already equipped, if necessary,[17] to defend the future novelist. He had also provided readers with one of the pillars of his own aesthetic.

The risk to any author of fiction of the seemingly actual is that it will invite adverse personal judgments. For one thing readers will be forced to consider their own beliefs about the function and remit of fiction as well as the nature of its relationship (if any) with the life. As I've inevitably already touched on, these issues in respect of Robinson's poetic work have not gone unchallenged or unnoticed. And yet the apology (in the original sense) for this aesthetic is made explicit time and again in poems, interviews and fiction. The most eloquent defence might be the novel itself, the fact of its existence. I'd go further and suggest that something the long form allows us to witness in Robinson's sensibility is that such committed attention at the level of restless interpersonal change encodes within itself (predicated as it is on an ideal of even-handedness) the very concerns that the more hostile critics have raised as their own discoveries. The novelist is all too aware that the conspicuous use of material very close to the printed life – it's notable how many of the interviews collected in *Talk About Poetry* tackle the Italian events in depth and with no evasion – inevitably risks *ad hominem* criticism. And yet the work exists and continues to be produced.

This particular line of criticism is more instructive when it is less severe than Harris and encompasses a more fulsome poetic context than simply misattributing to this most dialogical poet the belief that only he is real. To overstate as Harris has done is also to overlook the innate seriousness in the act of bringing so much attention to bear, repeatedly, on biographical material of so traumatic a nature.

William Wootten identifies a telltale moment for Robinson the critic in an essay about Geoffrey Hill, a moment of such applicability to Robinson's own work it is as if he is giving up something close to his

---

[16] *TAP,* 32.
[17] In fact reviews of the novel have been sympathetic. Among the more valuable to those interested in the source of the novel is Ian Brinton, 29th August 2016, *Tears in the Fence* blog in which Ovidian allusion (and Dantean comparison) is elucidated. https://tearsinthefence.com/2016/08/29/september-in-the-rain-by-peter-robinson-holland-house-books/

own method:[18]

> There are poets now, and [Donald] Davie is among them, who seek to compose a transition between public and private. The poet adopts an intimate tone where integrity of voice can be sustained, while remaining aware that the poem is intended to be overheard by people other than those to whom it is addressed.[19]

As Wootten persuasively explains:

> It is a way of writing which risks breaching confidence with the addressee or making a transition between the public and private realm which fails to take into account all the reasons why something was private in the first place – particularly so in Robinson's case as his addressees are almost always easily identifiable. It also risks alienating the reader either by turning him into an uneasy eavesdropper, or by making him feel excluded from the intimacies he overhears.[20]

Might the novel exist as a counter to these accusations? It is undeniably a risk of the kind Wootten describes but might it not therefore be the subject of praise rather than derision? Or does its existence merely compound these problems? For a critic such as Stephen Romer in a review preemptively entitled 'Intimate Intrusions', the first response can be an earned attention from the reader rather than blanket dismissal:

> But the word 'confessional' is inappropriate here [in relation to discussing *This Other Life*], it has too many associations that attach it negatively to a certain self-indulgence. The active moral sense that informs these poems preserves them from this laxness.[21]

---

[18] William Wootten, 'Time to Heal", Cambridge Quarterly, Sept, 2002, Vol.31 (3), 282-292.
[19] Peter Robinson, *In the Circumstances: About Poems and Poets* (Oxford; OUP; 1992), 107-108, quoted by Wootten.
[20] Wootten, ibid.
[21] Stephen Romer, 'Intimate Intrusions', *Times Literary Supplement*, issue 4455, August 19th 1988, 915.

Furthermore the distinction between what is or should remain public or private is further complicated by having nothing like a fixed boundary. On the contrary the distinction demonstrably shifts and has certainly done so since the mid-1970s. If we even fleetingly reference, for example, disclosures on social media platforms which older generations would deem shameful or shocking, then the Britain into which this novel is published is a very different one to the country in which its characters were young. Nevertheless readers of the novel may feel (*à la* Wootten) that they are being asked to eavesdrop on what can be read as an extended and confessional missive to a woman wronged by more than one man (since the novel examines the narrator's own initial and continuing emotional failings).

4

I've described the rape as the central event of the novel and yet structurally the immediate aftermath of the crime is where the novel opens. This is a second late but major change in the final compositional stage in addition to the move to the second person I've already discussed.[22] The scene was previously at the approximate centre of the text where it operated as a fulcrum. The writing in this episode is of a different intensity and while I'm aware of one reader reacting negatively to an uncharacteristic chapter opening the book ahead of the novel's settling into its predominant and less heightened mode,[23] it can also be understood as a deliberate jarring, one that serves to energise the novel's progress by providing a sort of narrative First Cause. It performs the basic function of equipping us as readers with the knowledge we require to understand and to become concerned about the events following. In a novel so bound up with the consequences of trauma it's fitting to place the aftermath here, at the beginning, to introduce us to the night beneath which all else in the book depends, and to which every character, event and detail must establish a relationship if it is to be understood. Encountering the aftermath before the characters do also means the Italian events operate as an as-yet-unrealised blight

---

[22] See Appendix A.
[23] The objection was made to the author privately, but can be characterised as a suspicion of false pretences, this section operating at a higher dramatic pressure than the rest of the novel.

on their innocence when we meet them (and so better delineates that innocence as something brief in the experiencing). This change has also given a more definite edge to Richard's portrayal, one that may tempt readers to be less sympathetic to him, but one that will give an ongoing resonance to Mary's admission that she's glad she's the innocent one (though to so differentiate is not the same as locating guilt specifically elsewhere).[24] Richard's passivity is remarked upon by others in the novel (the exasperated lovers, the fond sister), but the re-structural gesture allows a contrapuntal pressure because we know of the dark events towards which his reasonable hopes, lack of romantic assertion and temping work are taking him. Our sympathy is stirred rather than begged. Near the end of the book, but close to its core, Richard and Mary are reunited after time apart. They had found each other's presence to be increasingly problematic and had separated, and on seeing her again Richard writes: 'Alone with you again, I felt your unfamiliarity like an accusation.'[25]

5

The title story from the collection, *Foreigners, Drunks and Babies*, orbits around the suicide by hanging of a student, Aiko Mori. Although Aiko was married and there was no sexual dimension to her relationship with the narrator, he falsely admits to his wife amorous feelings for the woman while she was alive. Unable to fully explain the suicide in their midst, his wife and colleagues make the narrator's silence the focus of their unease. By admitting to feelings that never were the narrator addresses their – and his own – grief and confusion. In other words, he uses fiction, the paradoxical power of untruth, as a means to access the consolation of its opposite, to give explanatory shape to experience, to communicate that experience and (in the poet's already-quoted phrase) 'leave it behind'. This is an interpretation which readily lends itself to *September in the Rain* and might prove (subject to my previous disclaimer) to be Robinson's ultimate fictional disposition.

Conferring the status of title story on 'Foreigners, Drunks and Babies' is a mark of authorial confidence, recognition that this is a successful story. It's also one that bears a characteristic of the available

---

[24] *STR*, 229.
[25] *STR*, 142.

fiction. A preoccupation with names and the processes and meaning of naming is there, the academic life viewed from (professionally) within and (sardonically) without, as well as the subject of Japan. Aiko Mori's own name is an oxymoron, literally 'love-child'/'death', a sort of morbid bridge between east and west. In an earlier draft of Robinson's second novel, *The Constitutionals,* Aiko has a nominal echo in one Frank Mort, a fellow student of the 'Robinson' narrator described as having 'an enviably meaningful name'. *The Constitutionals* is preoccupied with the 'meaningful name', specifically Robinson and its fortunes in the world and in literature. The book follows the narrator from youth in the north of England to study at York and then working on a far side of the planet (though not named, the identity of Japan is clear enough). The pursuit of reputation and the recognition of the ugliness of the pursuit is a concern too in *The Constitutionals,* where Robinson's narrator is afflicted by 'nominal aphasia', a rare and outwardly levelling condition which is itself a statement on hierarchies:

> ...[I]t feels like a horrid punishment for the desire possessing me in youth to be somebody, to make a name for myself, as it were, as so many have before, and so many after, too. In fact, it [the nominal aphasia] may be...judgment upon it, or a dreadful psychological side effects of that youthful desire to be a name.[26]

Frank Mort is also the coiner of another nickname for the narrator, Hyacinth. The narrator only understands the significance of this name much later, having read Henry James's *The Princess Casamassima*:

> he was able to say, very gravely and quietly, 'Mr. Robinson has shot himself through the heart. He must have done it while you were fetching the milk.'

The would-be political assassin and ultimate suicide, Hyacinth Robinson, is a bastard with social aspirations. At the end of the novel he decides to kill himself rather than his appointed victim. To point out that Hyacinth Robinson is a bookbinder would be a happy comparison, but one too far beyond (we assume) Frank Mort's knowledge and one

---

[26] *TC*, 5

intended for readers familiar with the James novel. What is there, then, to envy in Frank's name? It would seem to be the proximity of candour and death. Or, more precisely, the perception of the accuracy of Frank's name, the rightness of its fit considered by one who does not feel that same rightness in his own name. But the fictional Robinson is also proud. Instead of simply dismissing the insult he attempts to refashion it into something more agreeable, a confirmation of his values:

> But was it my seemingly inappropriately proud poverty, or my relentless cultural ambition, or innocent flirting with political radicalism that Frank had had in mind? Doubtless, it was all these and more besides.[27]

The novel is the weaving and meandering of a Robinson around Reading in space and time. It takes it bearings from Defoe's novel, as well as an infatuation with the Patrick Keiller trilogy of films, *London* (1994), *Robinson in Space* (1997) and *Robinson in Ruins* (2010), which the narrator has rented and returns at the fiction's opening. He has encountered films which are made up of archive footage, riddled with literary allusions and with an invisible Robinson hooping allusion and place together. Their concerns are many but include utility and change in the social, political and architectural spheres. Again, albeit in a more ironised mode than *September in the Rain*, the narrator of *The Constitutionals* shares or even co-opts many facts of the author's biography, including a childhood in the north of England, a period as a student at York, time in an 'economic migrant phase' on a distant and very different island to this one and an ambivalent return to the country of his birth. He is accompanied by a beloved Friday and two 'piratical' daughters. The narrator weaves association and digression from a series of *idées fixes*, including the commercial success of psychogeography and its extra-literary (possibly magical) claims to influence in the world.

The risk for the author is that readers should conflate the ironised and refracted text as somehow confessional or directly autobiographical. It is a variation of the problematics of reception I've touched on and which have attended Robinson's career.

By his own token this Robinson is 'a marginalised individual' who 'sets out to avert global catastrophe'. He is 'hoping to trigger the

---

[27] The revised text of this paragraph is in *TC,* 82.

end of neoliberalism by going for a walk.' The comedy is enjoyable and welcome, and the projects of certain artists who have risen to prominence are both admired and ribbed. There is a fixation with bringing out the almost countless literary associations of Reading – from the better known of Oscar Wilde and Thomas Hardy to the lesser of Eugenio Montale or Paul Muldoon – and somewhere close to the heart of the enterprise is the self-diagnosed revolutionary act:

> ... let's face it, to attempt to overthrow the officially anarchised system of neo-liberal economics by taking the very model of its own '*homo economicus*' for a walk through that triptych of films [Patrick Keiller's 'Robinson' trilogy] had about it the air of a picaresque experiment, of what had been called even in 1719 '*the Quixotism of R. Crusoe*'. You might well say the same of me – writing this protracted homage to that masterpiece [*Robinson Crusoe*] in the form of a fictional autobiography.

Across the published prose fiction then, there is a preoccupation with naming, specifically the way in which names can confer value and arise by involuntary association. What is arguably our most intimate verbal relationship – ourselves and our own names – is usually established without our conscious assent and sometimes (the significance of teasing or mockery in certain of the stories) despite protestation. Most names are 'shared' insofar as they are not unique (itself a kind of embarrassment) but some names are more shared than others and that ubiquity can apply pressure to the sense of an exclusive or discreet self.[28] Other possessors of a name in the world are reminders of simultaneity, or even of our having so many forebears and namesakes as to erode the notion of personal exceptionalism. Consider the short story 'From the Stacks'. Here the narrator, Charles, adopts a knowing stance towards his fellow academics even as he gleefully participates in some form or other of 'high' intellectual pursuit. He is separated from his fellows by mere dint of taking advantage of the otherwise ignored professional privilege of access to the basement library, a curiously high-tech arrangement of button-operated 'concertina' shelves. In a copy of Thomas Lovell Beddoes's *Complete Poems* he finds a letter to an unknown 'Charles' from one 'Marian'.

---

[28] See also 'A Murder Mystery' in *FDB*, 123-133.

Bored and isolated (there is frequent reference to himself and his colleagues as 'aliens'), the stray letter provides the narrator with an arbitrary purpose, which is to reunite it with either or both author and recipient from the 1920s. 'I checked again on a full list of foreigners who had held this post, it turned out only one of them was christened Charles and – you might think it a strange coincidence – he had the same surname too (though it's quite a common or garden one that there could quite easily have been two of us)'. The surname is later made explicit at the grave-side ('Smith'), but the, as it were, double infraction represented a double namesake is also enough of a preoccupation that would resurface in another short story, the satirical 'A Mystery Murder'.

Here the shade of Agatha Christie is drolly invoked and a group of critics assemble for a conference. The violence is literary, and invitees other than the narrator are to be 'writers and critics whom I had either abused out of earshot or else in print. Some of them had stabbed me in the face in articles, columns, or reviews…'. The narrator wonders why he'd even accept such an invitation and while he finds reasons of his own ('Mortally wounded *amour propre*, most likely.'), the deeper joke is the tyranny of professional necessity. This narrator is attuned to the presence of hierarchy and the professional jostling and vying for position within it. It becomes the opportunity for the narrator to complain of a celebrity novelist:

> "God, I could kill him", "Why?" […] "Because he's gone and taken my name in vain!" "Oh, calm down, we all of us have a more famous crime writer with just the same handle," said the perpetual writer-in-residence.[29]

Robinson himself does in reality have a famous crime writer namesake. In the age of Amazon's dominance of the book market and when discoverability is an almost existential challenge to any cultural product (a search engine being unable to assign value or discriminate in the way a literary critic does), the strength of the narrator's irritation will likely be recognised by a thousand authors labouring under the indignity of being the less-famous owner of their own name.

---

[29] 'A Murder Mystery', *FDB*, 129.

6

It's not unknown for a poet to take the opportunity of their *Collected Poems* to revise certain poems. The Italian sequence, subsequent to the 'definitive' drop down to seven poems,[30] has also been altered at the level of the line between its original publication and its appearance in that volume in 2017.[31]

The poem 'A Trial' – dropped from the sequence as it appeared in the *Selected Poems* and excluded again from the *Collected Poems* – is, by virtue of its specificity, not a companion to the others in the aforementioned Italian sequence. While the decision to remove it is therefore sound, the lyric itself is a strong poem and worthy of republication.

Nevertheless Robinson has said: 'It ['A Trial'] reads to me like a note for the trial chapter of *September in the Rain* – which I wrote about five years later.'[32]

Late in the novel Richard and Mary receive a summons to Italy. The man the Italian authorities think responsible is to be tried, one Cesare Moretti. While he is named as the defendant (and his guilt is confirmed by Mary's recognition of him), neither Richard nor Mary will ever learn of the sentence. They decide to leave before the trial's conclusion and Richard later admits that, despite his own later and frequent visits to Italy, he never takes the opportunity to find out. Their coming to the tribunal is therefore an ending of sorts, albeit not a conventional one. While Mary might conceivably have found out once the couple have separated and not passed that information on, the reader is guided to suppose that neither possess the answer and probably neither ever will.

---

[30] Peter Robinson, personal communication, 9th July 2016.
[31] The revisions are largely restricted to punctuation, and include the substitution of hyphens and insertion of commas. Certain other changes in 'From a Memory' become the more questionable – 'sharp gusts', for example, become 'stiff gusts', 'until you half-forget them' becomes a more impatient and less drowsy 'until you just forget them', and 'the part raised shutter' become 'a part raised shutter', perhaps to bring in a lightness, a half-upwardness which 'the' does not quite allow. In 'For Lavinia', the most stern and arguably most affecting of the sequence – three dots are included and made to infer the criminal event itself. To describe 'For Lavinia' as the most successful of the sequence brings with it further complications of an aestheticising drift, the paradox of a decorous aesthetics being used to both examine the crime and make that crime more available for examination.
[32] 'Occasion to Revise or Think Again', *TAP*, 44.

This is a final shared intimacy, an untroubled ignorance which both postpones further pain and amplifies it.

Certain eidetic details survive from poem to prose rendering. The 'yellowed marble walls' of the poem become 'a blank yellow marble wall', but elsewhere the prose reads like a decompressed and more comprehensible rendering of the identical scene.[33]

In a Dickensian moment of accidental perception Richard is challenged by a guard as soon as he enters the Tribunale: "'You English?" he [the guard] asked "What do you want?"'[34] The guard has of course identified him quite by accident or, if not wholly by accident, with more accuracy than one might expect from a judgment made (we must assume) on clothes and bearing and nothing other than superficial signifiers of nationality.

Mary is summoned and while Richard is left waiting outside the courtroom a man asks him a question. He replies to the man in Italian – the language of the initiating question – that he does not understand what he is being asked. The poem records the exchange:

> One of them asked was I your husband.
> – No, il fidanzato della ragazza,
> as he would explain.

Against a background of relatively scant detail the 'he' of this lyric is a little perplexing. In a short poem what detail there is is to be heeded closely and yet we're only really referred back to 'he' being 'one of them', an otherwise undistinguished foreigner (the national difference being more pronounced in the case of the novel). Yet the more fulsome treatment in the novel shows not only that the exchange is an important one for Richard and his sense of his and Mary's relationship but also, at a basic level, the longer version gives the reader more confidence to comprehend *why* it is an important exchange:

---

[33] The encounter outside the courtroom with the accused's wife is given as follows in the poem: 'But in the lobby, where everyone waited/until the accused had been brought in chains,/his lame wife was haranguing us.' In the prose this becomes: 'From the little crowd outside the court, there came a small, poorly dressed woman, walking with a limp towards the defendant being led into the courtroom. She was shouting something at him [the defendant] [...] Then this must be his wife. The accused had a wife who was lame.'
[34] *STR*, 189

'You are the – married with the – girl there inside?'
The man hadn't asked it aggressively at all. No, rather he was asking me an all-too-pertinent question about what relation there might be between us. But I would hardly have known how to explain in English, so shook my head in a vain attempt to deflect the man's curiosity.

Richard's scrupulosity, his misplaced desire to give a wholly precise answer where a curt platitude would suffice, takes him deeper into the nominative complexities between himself and Mary:

Not that it made me your fiancé, of course, but what else could be said that wouldn't require fluent Italian and far more perspective, far more perspective altogether?

And so it seems not too much of a leap to regard the treatment of this same scene in prose as an attempt to enable that 'far more perspective'. The second time the man asks in English Richard gives wordless confirmation:

'Un amico'
The man appeared surprised. 'Ah, il fidanzato?"
I made no reply.
'Fiancé?' he asked, pronouncing the word accurately in French.
I hesitated, racking my brains for what else could I say, then nodded. 'Ah sì, il fidanzato della ragazza,' the man said, and seemed satisfied.

An external agency requires a certain interpretation of their relationship for reasons of its own and decides they're engaged. Richard goes on to note that the couple had talked about marriage, but would only consider it if prompted by pregnancy. The man's questioning of Richard takes in three languages before he is satisfied with the answer he'd assumed at the outset. English or otherwise, societal pressure to conform – or perhaps confirm – expectations is ever-present regardless of language and the degree of honesty with which the question is met.

As the poet himself has reflected, '…the autobiographicality [of the poetic sequence in *This Other Life*] was a means to an end: it might have been that what mattered was that this was *my* life or *me* saying it, but time had made this a life among others and someone happening to say it.'³⁵

7

The novel attends only as closely as the plot requires to legal process, but nevertheless it is concerned to tell us about the expenses to which a witness is entitled and to which there is also brief reference in the corresponding poem.³⁶

> I glanced down at the papers on my lap to check again the expenses that we could claim after the trial. 'Mrs. Young, Mary Jane'… and it suddenly struck me that the girl who lay not far away, evenly breathing now in the low double bed had been addressed by the Italian Government as if she were, in fact, a married woman.³⁷

A letter of 2ⁿᵈ January 1979 from Italian Embassy, London N1 is addressed to Mrs. Young, Mary Jane. It reads:

> '…you will be paid: a) cost 2ⁿᵈ class return rail ticket; b) lire 1.400 (about one pound) for each day of the journey; c) lire
>
> 2.500 (about Lsd. 1.70) for each day you are required to stay there.'

The prosecution will attempt to establish whether there was money exchanged, a fact which would obviously radically alter the nature of the event as well as Mary's status, a dramatic veer from victimhood to complicity. If the significance of money is purely transactional and the value that which the consensus assigns to it, we can position it as usefully analogous to the names we use to describe people and the relationship of one person to another. The poetic treatment of the trial also references 'expenses', another detail that thrives to have the space

---

[35] Peter Robinson, *TAP*, 32.
[36] As typified by the title of his early collection, *Overdrawn Account* (1980), money and its transactional and symbolic operations is another preoccupation in Robinson's work.
[37] *STR*, 187

and air of prose treatment and which otherwise requires a knowledge of that entitlement previously: '…relieved, then given our expenses,/we'd step down into clear January air'.[38]

> The accused man's lawyer stood up and spoke to the president of the court. The president, in turn, said a phrase to the young translator.
> 'Did you… from this man… receive at all any payment?'[39]

What transpires in the courtroom itself must be shared at a later time between the pair and as the addressee of the novel Mary will be receiving her own retelling of her own experience retold. The section is worth quoting at length:

> 'Did they ask you if we were given any payment?'
>
> 'Presumably he couldn't claim he didn't do it once we appeared,' you said, 'so he changed his defence to a payment in kind – or something like that.' 'Perhaps he went away to change his plea … or his line of defence.' 'Maybe,' you said. 'But I don't really want to talk about it anymore.'[40]
> […]
> You didn't want to talk about it. There and then, in the hope that time would do its work, we enveloped ourselves in the silence of what was meant to be forgetting. […] our September in the rain and trial at the court of Milan were locked inside as if forever. I couldn't take responsibility for the damage caused, for there was no one there to acknowledge the gesture; I couldn't distinguish that gesture from being actually responsible for the hurt, when all the time trying to act as if nothing had happened. The flashes of memory and inexplicable blanks tangled up inside me, like the thin brown tape snagging out of a snarled cassette. They formed a knot of shame and guilt for something that, I now begin to see, had been done to me too. They left me, as it seemed back then, with nothing more to say.[41]

---

[38] *TOL*, 28.
[39] *STR*, 197.
[40] *STR*, 202.
[41] *STR*, 202.

For this reader these lines are akin to a foundational statement. They articulate the reason for the composition of this novel. The material's ultimate arrival into full-length fictional form can be profitably regarded as a forty-year movement away from silence and lack of self-forgiveness engendered by the crime. While the sequence of poems highlights rather than delineates this, both are formal attempts to end the silence this passage frames. If the poetic gesture was not premature as such then it certainly was not definitive.

8

Towards the end of *September in the Rain* Richard has written to the Galleria Nazionale with a request to see a specific work, 'La Lattante' by Cletofonte Preti. Preti, we are told, was born in 1842 and lived in Reggio Emilia, near Parma. Richard is immediately impressed by the painting and begins to speculate that it might make 'a suitable subject for one of the later sections of my long-meditated book'. His trained eye bores into the picture and he is drawn to the pentimenti and the loss of a small piece of paint, the absence of which lets the canvas be seen. He is writing, he will explain to the Soperintendente, a book provisionally entitled *Genre Painters of Nineteenth-Century Italy*.[42]

> When she [Marta Serra, the *Soperintendente della Galleria Nazionale* who has responded to Richard's request to see a work] reciprocated with a polite enquiry, I decided to tell her there was no Mrs English – without going into the business of how you hadn't changed your name after we got married. Marta couldn't, unfortunately, miss the faintly hapless note in which I referred to you, and graciously she let the topic drop.

It seems increasingly that one of the driving forces behind this novel is the desire to do the opposite, to not 'let the topic drop'. Here Robinson

---

[42] The novel was launched with a series of four readings in 2016: London (Lutyens & Rubinstein, Kensington Park Road, 1st September 2016), Cambridge (Heffer's Bookshop, Trinity Street, 6th September), Oxford (Albion Beatnik Bookstore, 8th September) and Reading (Waterstones, Broad Street; 10th September). During the London launch Robinson quipped that this book was, to the best of his knowledge, still awaiting an author.

is picking up on a commonplace of adult interaction, that for reasons of time, politesse, notions of courtesy or professionalism, or other concerns entirely, emotional complexity is often avoided when it is sensed. The novel is not a corrective to such occurrences, which are often well enough meant, but it is a refusal to remain silent. It is, as I've already proposed by extrapolating from Wootten, a risk, or raid, on silence.[43]

Marta and Richard cross the Piazza della Pace towards La Pilotta. The building was bombed by the Americans during the Second World War and since then the city council has never quite decided what to do with it.

> Divided, I thought, like most of Italian history – all the other Septembers of confusion and betrayal, when the country was yoked together by violence.

It is a reminder of the malevolence – although admittedly not specific to Italy – which the translations from Sereni in part had attempted to counter:

> The rape ... took place on a road somewhere between Milan and the Northern Italian Lakes, where Sereni was born. Working on him helped to transform a nightmarish sense of Italy into something much more benevolent.[44]

When Richard meets his sister – in buoyant and forthright mood since she is planning to have a baby – Richard drifts off mid-conversation. She chides him.

> 'On your metaphysical worthlessness trip again?' she asked rather sharply. 'Want to talk about it, you old spirit broker?'
> 'Water under the bridge...'
> 'Whatever it is,' she said, 'best let it go.'
> It was just the phrase you had used those years before.

Richard uses this as a prompt for deeper reflection.

---

[43] 'And so each venture/Is a new beginning, a raid on the inarticulate...' 'East Coker' V. 9: *The Complete Poems and Plays of T. S. Eliot*, 202.
[44] 'Through Frosted Glass', *TAP*, 25.

> It's perfectly true that, like Italy during the Civil War [or La Pilotta a few pages previously] we [he and Mary] were yoked together by violence. The links between us forged by that night's events had quickly made my involvement with Alice seem as if glimpsed in a department store mirror ... it was as if the only way either of us could get away from that violence was by getting away from each other; as if our relationship was to violence itself and not the other person.[45]
> [...]
> 'And how is Mary?' my sister asked.
> 'Getting on with her life,' I said, repeating the set phrase for dealing with the question of your continuing existence.

Again, the acknowledgement of the 'set' phrase contributes to Richard's suspicion of social cliché, acknowledging its usefulness, but also its obstacle to examination and eventual explanation.

> When it all appeared to be recovered from, when there was no longer the need, or apparent need, to work on it, to make amends and live up to them, then suddenly it seemed there was no longer any reason for us to stay together.[46]

The amount of time and thought the novel required is indeed testament to the centrality of those events to the poet's life and imagination. And to portray the poems as pure autobiography is reductive, a failure to account for their evident formal discipline and the decision to treat the material using the indirections of literary presentation not once but twice. While the poetic centrality and obvious importance of the Italian sequence is reinforced by its promotion on the blurb of *Collected Poems*, I would argue this reductionist view would introduce a corollary error. Locating the novel as the expression in prose of an imaginative centre is one I've articulated in order to avoid. The *oeuvre* is too varied and copious to reduce to the extrapolation of a single event. To make it so is akin to a journalistic temptation, a prompt by the extrinsic details currently available rather than an analysis of the nascent prose writer – a temptation that might give ground to an interpretation in which the Italian events become a point of finite density around which all of the

---
[45] *STR*, 263-264.
[46] *STR*, 264.

imaginative work is then required to assemble.

The prose is continuous terrain to the poetry, but also allows a different writer to show through. The attention, the noticing, the concern to give subtlety something of its infinite due, all of these are present, but the need to move the narrative along, the space one needs to fill to justify the novel form, have brought out different abilities. I would caution against this easy conclusion when Robinson's attention to fiction is crescent. By publishing further works of fiction such *The Constitutionals* he is not only assisting readers in a broader contextualisation of *September in the Rain*, but also allowing his sensibility to experiment with long-form techniques and away from not only what may be that sensibility's methods as established in the lyric mode, but also the uniquely difficult and overshadowing event with which he has engaged with the utmost seriousness for so long.

September in the Rain is, as I've said, written carefully enough as to approximate if not constitute a moral act. While carefulness alone cannot be said to seek anything so lofty as redress, or even full understanding, the faith in the mediation of literary form implied will allow the making available to the moral consensus of unspeakable (and perhaps otherwise unspoken) crimes, and the violence to which innocent people are forced to submit as well as the urgency of the search for meaning in the aftermath of such violence.

> I suppose that writing poems about something like this [the Italian events], which couldn't be talked about at the time, suggests the need to give an experience its due, to give its implications and consequences form and, in a sense, reality: to make them objects in the world.[47]

Which we can extrapolate to include the novel, which enacts this schema on a larger more comprehensive scale. It also allows a reading of the novel which casts it as an act of gratitude, belated only as much as it wasn't fully possible before, for reasons which are partly technical and partly outside the scope of a brief essay.

[The rape] took place when we were both twenty-two years old,

---

[47] 'Occasion to Revise or Think Again', Peter Robinson interview by Marcus Perryman, first published in *The Cortland Review* (1998), collected in *TAP*, 47.

so that practically everything I've written has been shadowed by that far-off event. By enduring what she did, she probably saved both our lives.[48]

As with Robinson the poet, then, of crucial importance are the ways in which literary form mediates the material of the raw stuff of life. In novelist as in poet there is the same self-knowledge and slow digestion of happenings, as well as characteristic attention to the emotional and physical interstitial between intimate agencies. So while the facts of the characters' biography overlap with some of those volunteered elsewhere, there is also necessary divergence – of career, character, name – as arguably crucial for being as slight at times as wide, and most crucially of all the bringing to bear of a searing literary conscience.

Tellingly, however, the prose writer has made full use of the 'customary'[49] disclaimer both in the publication of his stories and first novel:

> ...each character in it [*September in the Rain*] is a composite drawing upon several individuals and the author's imagination. Place and time have been adapted to suit the shape of the book, and with the exception of a few public figures, any resemblance to persons living or dead is coincidental. The opinions expressed are those of the characters and should not be taken for ones held by the writer.[50]

The invitation to assume we as readers can tell the factual shining through the fictional is one we are being warned against making. And yet the obvious care with which the novelist has attended to what is so often a throwaway gesture (such a disclaimer would not, for the sake of argument, dissuade a determined media lawyer) might lead some to

---

[48] 'Through Frosted Glass', collected in *TAP*, 22.
[49] The disclaimer to *FDB*.
[50] The author's disclaimer on the imprint page of *September in the Rain*. The same concern that the fictional nature of the text following be properly understood is there also in *Foreigners, Drunks and Babies*: 'And by way of customary disavowal, let me echo the epigraph to 'Foreigners, Drunks and Babies': "There are no such people."' We turn to that epigraph and find there, Oscar Wilde, 'The Decay of Lying' (1891): 'In fact the whole of Japan is an invention. There is no such country, there are no such people.'

suggest otherwise, and that he does, in fact, protest too much.

The prose of *September in the Rain* and the short stories (I exempt *The Constitutionals* on the grounds that it is a more distinct engagement with narrative art, as confirmed by its published sub-title, 'A Fiction') is defined by the planes of, on the one level, the known and outward facts of the poet's biography and, on another, the fictional treatment of certain of those facts. These two planes work together like a camera lens which, within self-appointed limits and in varieties of concord, bring the material into focus at will. It's not always possible to tell the autobiography from the fiction – inevitably – but as a general rule it seems one is not allowed to come to prominence without authorial attention to the proximity of the other. To stretch the metaphor a little further, I would suggest this interplay is a form of self-correction, a means by which the prose is kept decorous, even-tempered and comprehensible within a self-composed boundary of mnemonic and ethical-aesthetic investigation.

Appendix

The five main compositional stages of September in the Rain. *The timeline reproduced herein takes its detail (chronological and compositional) from a three-page document written by Robinson in July 2016 in response to questions put to him by me about the novel for the purposes of drawing up an author profile (unpublished) and in anticipation of a 'Q & A' session which would follow a reading from the novel at the Albion Beatnik bookshop in Oxford on 8th September 2016.*

1976

The first passages are written – two attempted prose poems about the taxidermy fish on the toilet cistern (Chapter 3, 63) and the faulty shower in the Brussels hotel room (Chapter 9, 139-40). A description of the dinner with friends is also attempted (Chapter 18, 218-21). This writing occurs at 'about the same time' as the three Dutch poems in *Overdrawn Account* (1980) – 'Ear to the Night', 'Finding the Range', and 'Autobiography'. Also attempted is at least one poem about visiting the Kröller-Müller Museum, material that eventually went into Chapter 8.

1979
Writes poems about the central Italian events which became the eight that appeared in *This Other Life* (1988) and, 'definitively as seven', in *Selected Poems* (2003). Of the excluded poem, 'A Trial', Robinson records that he thought it necessary for the 'story' of the sequence, but was never satisfied by it. While awaiting an occasion to reprint these poems 'A Trial' exists in a prose poem version. There is a further poem, never published, about waiting for a day in the Belgium hotel room (Chapter 9).

1985–1986
'The impetus to start writing a draft of the novel ... occurred in September 1985, when I was left for a few days, during his working hours, in Marcus Perryman's flat in Verona and wrote a sketch of the romantic episode in Hampstead (Chapter 3).' This was immediately after Robinson had written 'Aria di Parma'. A version of the novel (minus its final chapters) is written in the third person over the next two years, the main character being called Tom. What is now the opening prologue, '20 September 1975', is written over Easter 1986 and 'this must have been the second main chapter I attempted, because I thought that if I couldn't do that one, then I wouldn't be able to write the book at all.' A single typescript is then circulated and the author remembers Alison Rimmer, a manager and fiction buyer at Heffer's Bookshop, thinking it worth attempting the novel in the first person in order to get 'closer' to the events and the emotions relating to them.

1989–1990
The second of the first-person versions of the novel is revised and typed into an early computer owned by Robert Jones, the publisher of Robinson's volumes *More About the Weather* (1989) and *Leaf-Viewing* (1992), and goes with the author to Kyoto in 1989. Later that year it is submitted to a literary agent, Dieter Klein. One provisional plan is to try and place the novel with Robinson's third book of poems, perhaps as a two-book deal with the fiction. The agent's ill health brings this effort to a close and Klein writes to Robinson to say that he thinks the events in the fiction just did not have the shape to become a novel: 'I think it was something to do with the central event making the narrative curve break in half, so that the story couldn't properly grow.' Work resumes on the novel in 1990 when Robinson is spending a second year in Kyoto, living near Ryoanji temple. He gives the characters their current names, cuts

various passages of back-story for the three main figures, and shapes it to include allusions to the song that now provides its title. This comes from a poem of Vittorio Sereni's called 'In una casa vuota' ('In an Empty House'), which remembers the Munich Crisis in September 1938 and alludes to the song. Sereni had cited its English title in a magazine printing, and then changed it to 'settembre sotto la pioggia'. This version of the novel is submitted to certain agents and publishers.

2003–2015
A busy personal life (including diagnosis and treatment for a brain tumour, as well as remarriage and fatherhood) delays work on the novel. It is when Robinson is in almost daily contact with Marcus Perryman in Verona – entering the final stages of publishing their Vittorio Sereni translations with Chicago, as well as embarking on two online interviews that appeared in magazines and *Talk About Poetry* (2006) – that Perryman agrees to respond to sections of the novel if Robinson revises them. 'I recall Marcus saying that even if I couldn't publish it, I should at least try to get it right. The 1990 version ended at p. 240 with the words "It was time to let it go" – the reflective return to their university town in Chapter 18. This was enlarged with further reflection, and the last three chapters (Chapter 20 then at the beginning) were written to round it out and off definitively, and to answer various criticisms it had received over the years, going right back to the problem about the fractured curve of its narrative, the problem of getting close enough to the events, feelings and the reflections on them, as well as the narrator's muffled responses to Mary.' Richard's life trajectory is also removed further from its author's, the final visit to Milan and Parma being the 'nearest thing' to completely fictional events in the book. It is submitted to a handful of agents and a publisher, as well as being read by further friends and acquaintances. The poet Kate Behrens responds with misgivings about the treatment of the central female character and final stages of revision occur between about 2013 and 2015, these in response primarily to Kate Behrens's feelings about the treatment of the central female character. The prologue chapter is shifted to the beginning and the text divided into two numbered parts, and, 'most dramatic of all, I think, the recasting of the entire narrative as like a lyric poem addressed to Mary in the second person. This was my best shot at resolving the problem about the narrator's feelings towards the main female character, which (aside from the late-written Chapter 20) could

not be done by "telling" them, as we put it in creative writing classes, but could perhaps be "shown" by means of the ambivalent intimacy effected in the shift to the second person. That shift also required a close revision of all the detail, because the pronominal adjustment enabled some kinds of comments, reflections, and descriptions, but disabled others.' Finally, Robert Peett, in discussion with the author, re-chapters the novel into twenty-one-chapters-plus-prologue (Robinson's final version being about ten equal-length chunks), and they finish it with a light-touch line edit.

Chapter 12
Bringing It All Back Home

Peter Carpenter

1

Peter Robinson's *The Constitutionals* is a 'fiction' that is intensely engaging, moving and intelligent; the poet's adopted local habitation, the town of Reading, is at its centre, and the informing preoccupations of the piece are 'psychogeographic' in nature. The author, via many analogues and sources, including Defoe's novel, the 'Robinson' films of Patrick Keiller, and a triggered memory of a childhood nickname, embarks upon a series of walks. These are intended, as the pun in the title suggests, as a necessary restorative process, to both an ailing 'self' and a body politic in crisis: microcosm and macrocosm are fused. The example of Defoe's novel, 'to convert the misfortunes of life into a source of strength to resist them',[1] may be said to be felt in the heroic persistence of all Robinson's work. The following twenty-two staging posts have at their centre both method and subject matter: how Peter Robinson alludes to 'home' and how he finds homes for his allusions, principally in the *English Nettles* collection, published by Two Rivers Press in 2010.

2

Robinson's trademark principled and stoic doggedness is realised in language that confronts and embodies the warp and weft of the everyday: the 'weariness, the fever and the fret', as Keats has it: life's prosaic dilemmas, delights and tragedies. Life is the matter of his art: every day, as Elvis Costello has it, he writes the book. His mock-heroic attempt in *The Constitutionals*, as he wryly puts it, to 'change the world and institute an honest politics', is simultaneously one of self-acknowledgement: 'the recognition of your sickness in the symptoms you're setting out to treat'.[2] Such a moral complexity informs the tones,

---

[1] *TC*, 274.
[2] *TC*, 275.

diction and concerns of Robinson's work across the genres (aphorisms, critical essays, fiction and, of course, the major body of poetry). This is what first attracted me to the work and was where I came in.

3

The textures and methods of Robinson's work invite close reading and re-reading akin to the tracing and re-tracing of a journey: such a re-visiting of old haunts, a process akin to the liberating associative flow of walking. Robinson sets out such an agenda in *The Sound Sense of Poetry*: 'the regular pattern is not heard simultaneously behind an irregular variation; rather, tension is produced by comparing and contrasting in memory temporally distinct verbal experiences of themes and variation. To hear and experience the rhythm you have to read the poem out loud (or attentively listen to it being read), monitoring while you do what you are hearing and feeling in body-and-mind. Rhythm is experienced as muscular, aural and conceptual'.[3] In *The Constitutionals* there is an attempt through writing down 'the trace' of walks to counter the crises and pulls of neo-liberalism, with its 'economic imperatives … at your throat'. The aim thereby is to preserve a sense of community. Such a precarious rearguard action seeks to maintain a continuity with 'what passes for community' in people and literature. This is felt in Robinson's writing in many ways, but one of the chosen focal points for this piece is Robinson's link to the community of writers, artists and thinkers in his use of allusion: allusions to words, ideas, rhythms and images. Such a process calls to mind Heaney's coinage of 'cultural depth charges', informed itself by what Eliot termed the 'auditory imagination'. Towards the very end of *The Constitutionals* there is an admission, via Robinson's narratorial 'construct': 'it has not proved possible in every case to ascertain exactly from whom the author has been borrowing, whose words and which texts he has cited in every case'. Further to this: 'Others are embedded, allusion-fashion, in the texture of his prose, whether consciously of not there is no way of knowing'.[4] The power and range of such 'embeddings' may be felt throughout his work. Just as Hamlet seems to be a character who speaks in quotations, so Robinson is a poet whose language invites any reader to explore a community of writing via these embedded allusions and

---

[3] Robinson, *The Sound Sense of Poetry* (Cambridge: CUP, 2018), 40.
[4] *TC*, 290.

citations. Finding a home for such allusions cannot be disseuered from Robinson's recurrent exploration of what 'home' signifies in life and art or finding allusions for home. Iain Sinclair's blurb for *The Constitutionals* is another way into the rest of Robinson's writing: 'Here the solitary poet walks with his invisible peers, ventriloquizing the grateful dead.'

4

Mikhail Bakhtin's essay from 1937, 'Forms of Time and of the Chronotope in the Novel', is often in the back of my mind when I read Robinson's poetry. Bakhtin's 'chronotope' (the etymology is 'time-space') refers to 'the intrinsic connectedness of temporal and spatial relationships that are artistically expressed in literature'. The term is borrowed from mathematics, introduced as part of Einstein's Theory of Relativity, according to Bakhtin, 'almost as a metaphor (almost, but not entirely). What counts for us is the fact that it expresses the inseparability of space and time (time as the fourth dimension of space) … In the literary artistic chronotope, spatial and temporal indicators are fused into one carefully thought-out, concrete whole. Time, as it were, thickens, takes on flesh, becomes artistically visible; likewise, space becomes charged and responsive to the movements of time, plot and history. This intersection of axes and fusion of indicators characterises the artistic chronotope.'[5] Bakhtin's notion acknowledges Wordsworth's 'spots of time' ('pre-eminent' in their 'vivifying virtue') from *The Prelude*, and pre-figures T. S. Eliot's exploration of the intersections of time and space in 'Little Gidding', where history is felt as 'a pattern / Of timeless moments'.

5

In several ways *The Constitutionals* picks up where the collection *English Nettles* leaves off. This sequence of twenty-two poems has itself been subsequently 're-settled' into *The Returning Sky* and *Collected Poems 1976–2016*, both from Shearsman. Its point of departure is Robinson's repatriation, his move from Japan to the town of Reading in 2007.

---

[5] 'Forms of Time and of the Chronotrope in the Novel: Notes towards a Historical Poetic', in Mikhail Bakhtin and Michael Holquist, *The Dialogic Imagination: Four Essays* (Austin, TX: University of Texas Press, 1981), 84-258.

English Nettles arrived in its initial Two Rivers incarnation, complete with notes and the luminous and illuminating illustrations by Sally Castle.[6] A close look at some of these poems might allow discussion of how Robinson alludes to home and finds homes for his allusions. This is linked to his abiding enquiries in poetry and critical writing: the potential for poetry to 'make things happen' in the world; art and its hopes to act as a reparative force; and the fusion of epistemological and ontological concerns in the 'sound sense' of poems.

6

The 'melancholy peregrinations', as Iain Sinclair has it, of *The Constitutionals* take in territory already visited for readers of *English Nettles*: this includes Reading Goal, Cemetery Junction, Whiteknights Park, Robinson's own address in Addington Road. Along with the territory come the 'charged and responsive' echo chambers of 'time, plot and history' as Bakhtin has it: thus Arthur Rimbaud, Oscar Wilde, Alexander Pope *et al.* become part of the mix. Robinson's move back to Britain from Japan coincides with the global financial crisis, specifically the period following the failure of Northern Rock in September 2007. The poems are thus local and global, bringing to the town of Reading, Robinson's new place of residence, the intimations of events, figures and places that have come back with the returning self. Doctor Johnson's assessment of Pope's particular genius in *The Rape of the Lock* is applicable to Robinson: 'In this work are exhibited, in a very high degree, the two most engaging powers of an author. New things are made familiar, and familiar things are made new' (*The Lives of the Most Eminent English Poets*, 1781).

7

So Reading is a place 'charged and responsive to the movements of time, plot and history' where time takes 'on flesh'. The setting is a place that resembles 'home' enough to make Robinson feel 'at home'; added to this is the disorientation of entering a country that is alienating and

---

[6] Peter Robinson, *English Nettles and Other Poems* (Reading: Two Rives Press, 2010).

'foreign' to your family. Let's start with the opening of 'Like a Foreign Country',[7] the sixth poem in the sequence:

> That much would have to be explained:
> how cloud-roofs at dawn
> were burned off by a July sun
> and showers washed out washing day,
> how identity theft protection
> or laundry would get done
> when there was a tax disc to display.

The near rhymes ('dawn', 'sun', the more distant, 'protection', then 'done'), the weather and its paradoxical lingo ('washed out washing day'), the perfectly judged enjambment that allows pause in the flow, and then the remote fat chance chime of 'explained' and ' display' that puts its arms round the stanza: all evoke the tentativeness of such an 'explanation'.

With it we have the ironies of the coinage 'identity theft protection' and its wonderful coincidence with the heart of the matter: identity itself. The conflicting pulls, the mixed-up confusion if you like, of hopes for the future, urgent practical needs and a hinterland of anxieties flicker through the poem's sound systems as new patterns in adapting or acclimatising to a new environment are established.

8

The fragility of 'identity' in the face of economic uncertainty and the re-education required by an experience akin to what Piaget terms 'the stranger experience' are thus evoked with tenderness and irony. This is an 'insider' account allowing itself some element of detachment. Explanations are required by one and all; subtle 're-definitions' as experience and 'meaning' are weighed up. Robinson gives an account of his poetic practice in one of his aphorisms, number 73, collected in *Spirits of the Stair*. 'In best cases, poems claim less and deliver more: their descriptions are by definition limited in scope, are a seeing from the inside, and are impacted with experience, emotion and idea. If poems arrive late and confused on the scene, they have, again in best cases, more staying power because they are more thoroughly embedded in the culture and occasion to which they

---

[7] *CP*, 343-4.

belong.'⁸ In this poem and sequence readers experience such a 'seeing from the inside': all connotations of 'moving' are felt. From a 'daughter's school report' being used as a yardstick of feeling ('me too, I'm happy as can be / expected, coping well / with moving ... in a foreign country') to the need to explain a new take on the weather: the 'cloud-roofs at dawn' that would be 'burned off by a July sun'.

9

The last of the poem's four stanzas opens with this line: 'Days gone, terraces, terra incognita'. The glide from 'terraces' in and then away from the underlying homophone 'terror' into another language, Latin, and that which needs to be translated, the 'terra incognita' or unknown land, is beautifully managed. A land reached that isn't really a home; precarious hope from a daughter's report: T. S. Eliot's 'Marina' mutters away in the back of my mind: 'What seas what shore ... what images return/ O my daughter'.⁹ Having read and settled the poem's interconnections and sound patterns I realised that the second stanza (which concerns the resolve to get to grips with a forsaken garden plot, an overgrown lawn) had another embedded allusion to home: 'where blades of whitened grass / hid creatures still alive / beneath their mossy stone / or in a creosoted shed /with ivy bursting through its boards – / still lives of paint and so on.' The throwaway tone ('and so on' with its lovely rhyme chance) and a painter's eye for the particular ('blades of whitened grass') draw the reader in and allow breath to be drawn for consideration. 'Still alive' is the pun rustling in the grass of artistic possibilities held in 'still lives'. The eyed chance for artistic creativity is fused with the held connotations of 'still': 'enduring', 'unmoving' and 'calm'.

10

Keep going through the sequence from this poem sixth in, to the twentieth poem, 'Gasometers',¹⁰ and you become aware of longer and

---

⁸ *STS*, 21.
9 T.S. Eliot, *Collected Poems 1909–1962* (London: Faber & Faber, 1963), 115-6.
¹⁰ *CP*, 367-8.

deeper patterns. The last line of this poem ('still here, still alive') is an affirmative declaration from a dream-like sequence that emerges from the past ('the summer, say, of '75') with a 'fugitive touch', a figure who emerges from the crowd 'with a kiss'. This is in itself a play or turn on the epigraph from Raymond Roussel's 'La Vue' ('Le souvenir vivace et latent d'un été / Déjà mort, déjà loin de moi') which, when translated in the notes by Robinson, goes like this: 'The lively and latent memory of a summer/ Already dead, already far from me'. So here Robinson's poem finds new life and hope via the phantom figure, moving in translation from 'already dead, already far from me' to something living and enduring ('here ... alive'), conjuring up that fragment from Keats ('This living hand, now warm and capable / Of earnest grasping ...'), a poem concerned with a willed spectral haunting. The whole poem turns us back to Eliot's 'Marina' again ('let me / Resign my life for this life, / my speech for that unspoken, / The awakened, lips parted, the hope, the new ships') and then invites the reader to re-visit the last stanza of 'Like a Foreign Country': 'for time had taken its advantage / over us, the gained / and lost perspectives realigned'. Here there are further memories of Eliot again, this time *East Coker* (Part V) where the struggle to create something new ('a raid on the inarticulate / With shabby equipment always deteriorating') moves towards the urge 'the fight to recover what has been lost / And found and lost again and again' and then the resignation of 'But perhaps neither gain nor loss. / For us, there is only the trying. The rest is not our business.'[11]

11

The play of words in 'gain ... loss ... business' also links microcosm and macrocosm; Robinson returns to Britain in 2007, aware of the hollowness of 'global' economies, a chronicler of the collapse of Northern Rock (see 'Ode to Debt' with the title's wonderful pun on 'owed')[12] and the 'nationalisation' of the banks in the 'crash'. Both these poems, and indeed the whole sequence, are about the hopes and fears for the survival of love (paternal, familial and 'universal') that should be shown to all.

---

[11] Eliot, 203.
[12] *CP*, 346.

12

Let's go back. In the second stanza of 'Like a Foreign Country' the narrator investigates what is hidden in 'blades of whitened grass'. He finds 'creatures still alive / beneath their mossy stone', their own natural habitats, to be respected, marvelled at and protected. So Robinson uncovers respect for all creatures (as with Dickens' Joe Gargery in *Great Expectations* and his expression of common humanity towards Magwitch the convict, a 'poor, miserable fellow-creature').

13

It is here that Robinson embeds Wordsworth's Lucy poem ('She Dwelt Among the Untrodden Ways'), a poem that cherishes and thereby perpetuates the memory of someone otherwise forgotten, marginalised, overlooked:

> She dwelt among the untrodden ways
> Beside the springs of Dove,
> A Maid whom there were none to praise
> And very few to love:
>
> A violet by a mossy stone
> Half hidden from the eye!
> Fair as a star, when only one
> Is shining in the sky.
>
> She lived unknown, and few could know
> When Lucy ceased to be;
> But she is in her grave, and, oh,
> The difference to me!

Robinson transforms place, habitat and versions of the pastoral: the 'blades of whitened grass' for the 'springs of Dove'; the 'violet' as metaphor for the dead figure in Wordsworth's poems 'half-hidden from the eye' to the very much 'alive': 'creatures ... beneath their mossy stone'. Robinson's skill makes all the difference to us in finding such a new home for this allusion. 'Like seeing the world through a mosquito net, the artist creates an overall harmony by making innumerable minute distinctions': an application of this aphorism (number 134 from *Spirits of the Stair*)[13] to Robinson's own writing is clear enough, and the choice of image ('the mosquito net') chimes with this poem's attention to detail and, by extension, care for the 'creatures' of our world. Through his tiny adjustments, his 'minute distinctions' in this allusion, he draws us to heed a life in the shade of a lost love.

14

A few broader strokes. These poems look backwards and forwards, in time and place, and, like all of Robinson's poems treat readers with respect. There are contexts to explore: the fresh exploration of a place resonant in association, the lead up to the global financial crisis from 2007 and its attendant tremors, and the long and deep memories of the language and rhythms we encounter, all of which alert us in glimpses and nuance to preoccupations explored in the literary heritage that Robinson's own writing furthers and echoes. The notion of the poems as 'echo chambers' is too crude, and two of Roy Fisher's distinctions come to mind when we consider the reader's experience. The first is his notion of 'absorbed metaphor' in Robinson's writing, that may be profitably linked to Bakhtin's notion of the chronotope: 'the device that, grammatically, lies hidden, absorbing the qualities of, say, a mood into itself and dispensing them back into the poem without a click of cleverness or the hint of the bottomless school satchel'.[14]

15

It brings to mind Basil Bunting's advice: 'Never Explain'. We will be shown, not told, and the absorption is a quality that moves towards a union or integration of the world as experienced, observed, travelled through, with the poet's craft. Second, Fisher warns against a 'simple chronological reading' of the poems: 'Individual poems have individual lives, individual musical qualities'. Thus a reader new to Robinson's

---

[13] *STS*, 32.
[14] Roy Fisher, 'Preface', in Adam Piette and Katy Price (eds.), *The Salt Companion to Peter Robinson* (Cambridge: Salt, 2007), 24.

poetry starting with *English Nettles* might subsequently find, as I have tried briefly to show, earlier and later poems that are companion pieces, dwelling-places neighbourly in concerns and tones. Robinson's intricate and delicate 'patterns' – the play of what abides and what is lost – also brings a more complex and profound examination of how and what we recall, as we fare forward, half-looking over our shoulder.

16

Take one word: 'returning'. It is going to find its way into the title of the collection that will 're-house' the twenty-two poems of *English Nettles*. These poems are about 'returning' to England. It is used as an adjective in the title of the collection (and the title poem which has as its point of departure the disappearance of trees, principally 'neighbour fir trees' which 'succumb to saws' and thus give more 'blue / to populate') but flickers as a present participle verb.[15] One of Robinson's great skills in his composition of poems is to allow the living reverberation of words, in the contexts of the surrounding words and the sounds of them in the individual poem, and then in mind of what the word brings in its different voicings and associations beyond the poem and at particular junctures in history. 'Returning' might thus turn the reader to such contexts: for example, a return match, a return ticket, tax returns, an electoral return, the profit in financial yield of a business, returning a compliment or a library book, the expression 'many happy returns', an architectural return or change in direction.

Such connotations are allowed consideration alongside the sense of 'recurrence' or coming or going back. Robinson's poems are perpetually providing the reader with cultural returns via such 'enrichment'; they invite an openness and attentiveness as we embark on our travels: '… the return of weather / like a further dice throw' ('165 King's Road').[16]

17

Around the time of the writing of these poems I interviewed Robinson for *Poetry Ireland Review*, a piece later collected as 'A Tourist in Your

---
[15] *CP*, 375-6.
[16] *CP*, 340.

Other Country' in *Talk about Poetry*.[17] We started up with a question about 'displacement': 'I might then be writing to register more forcefully to myself the presence of what is present, and to realise concretely the sensed presence of things absent, and then to accommodate both to each other. So I would imagine that the rhythms and the evocations and the occasioned speech in the poems are aiming at achieving some kind of realisation and integration of these disparate materials.'

18

This seems especially apposite with 'Huntley & Palmers',[18] the first poem in *English Nettles*, where the site of the old biscuit factory is appraised. In this poem 'the sensed presence of things absent' in the 'rhythms and the evocations and the occasioned speech' is realised. The 'integration' of what's there, present, here and now, and what is sensed, apprehended, as a 'presence', with all its ghostly familiarity, is beautifully done. The poem starts a trail that invites the reader simultaneously backwards and forwards temporally and topographically.

The notes in this edition[19] also gently nudge us back to one of Robinson's most important earlier poems, '472 Claremont Road' (originally the first poem in *Anaglypta* published by The Many Press in 1985, subsequently appearing in *This Other Life*).[20] As the opening poem, 'Huntley & Palmers' simultaneously leads us forwards into the rest of the collection.

The poem takes the texture of biscuit as its 'objective correlative'; Robinson works out a downbeat play on the Proustian 'madeleine moment' in which the sensory experience unlocks an involuntary memory. The poem opens with the sight of a preservation act: the 'preserved office-building' of the biscuit factory, which is, according to Robinson's notes, the trigger. This in turn recalls the previous poem's imagery of the 'brick or plaster' under the wallpaper (the anaglypta) that 'like digestive biscuit / crumbled under packaging'. That's one way the cookie crumbles. It is no surprise that Robinson's concerns with the nature of 'home' should lead to 'embedded' allusions to his own

---

[17] *TAP*, 84-92.
[18] *CP*, 339.
[19] *English Nettles*, 54.
[20] *TOL*, 20; *CP*, 74.

childhood home. The concerns of '472 Claremont Road' are prefaced in its epigraph ('Poetry "is capable of saving us," he says; it is like saying that the wall-paper will save us when the walls have crumbled'). This epigraph is from T. S. Eliot: this source is acknowledged in *Anaglypta*, hidden from the reader in *This Other Life*, but re-emerges from the shadows in the *Collected Poems*. I. A. Richards is the 'he', and Eliot is taking issue with Richards's *Science and Poetry* ('Literature, Science, Dogma' (1927)). The debate it leads the reader back to is a central one for Robinson, with several attendant questions. What is the relation between language and objects, words and the world? Does poetry have the power or potential to 'make things happen'? The hope that poetry is a way of happening that can have an impact on the reader, 'contributing to some material change, small or large, in the history of man'[21] is an abiding one.

The first stanza of 'Huntley and Palmers' goes like this:

> Then that tightening in the chest
> and tear-duct, like a taste
> of whatever it might be,
> comes with the looked-at brick façade
> seen on a canal bank walk
> but in so much perspective,
> with the strollers' voices
> heard as if by alien ears
> (ones too full of other views,
> views, reverses and reversals)
> as if from somewhere else.

There are so many memories of other poems and texts here that they resemble sub-lettings in this new-build. The memory of '472 Claremont Road' begins on the edge of utterance and naming: in that poem the 'brick or plaster' is registered as just beyond naming ('whatever the thing was'); here we have 'like a taste / of whatever it might be' which allows for the echo of the vernacular 'like the taste of things to come'. Here are a few other flickerings that inform the 'taste' or 'textures' of the poem: Robinson's 'the looked-at brick façade' allows in T. S. Eliot's trip in the summer of 1934 to the uninhabited shell of 'Burnt Norton', a 'third rate manor house' built on 'the site of an older one

---

[21] Robinson, *Poetry, Poets, Readers Making Things Happen* (Oxford: OUP, 2002), 28.

which had been destroyed by fire' (as he put it in a letter to Hermann Peschmann in September, 1945). It is here in the rose garden that there is 'unheard music' which is 'hidden in the shrubbery' and roses that 'Had the look of flowers that are looked at' (*Burnt Norton*, ll. 27-30).[22] So encased within Robinson's 'shell' there is another one; and within Eliot's 'unheard music' there is Keats' 'Heard melodies are sweet, but those unheard / are sweeter' from 'Ode on a Grecian Urn' (ll. 11-12).[23] Not to be taken any further here, but I also detect Ted Hughes' stir-crazy creature 'The Jaguar' and the nearby caged parrots in Regent's Park Zoo, that strut and shriek to attract the 'stroller with the nut'.[24] More substantially present is the Old Testament story of Ruth's grief and resilience. Here the homesick Moabite is condensed into 'heard as if by alien ears', to expand upon re-reading Keats's version of her from "Ode to a Nightingale': 'Perhaps the self-same song that found a path / Through the sad heart of Ruth, when, sick for home, / She stood in tears amid the alien corn' (ll. 65-68).[25]

19

An interview with John Kerrigan entitled 'Back Now' (collected in the tremendous online journal *Blackbox Manifold*, Issue 9)[26] is an essential read and extremely elucidatory with this poem and sequence in mind. Here are two instances of Robinson's responses: 'So the poems aren't straightforward reports on experience, but interpretations of sometimes multiple happenings, angled to build a poem, in which the subject to whom the incidents occur might be the least important issue' and 'Proust-fashion, again, one effect of returning to Britain may be that the thematic materials of the poems became even more layered and condensed, because everything around seemed to be yelling its implications. Quite ordinary things could seem loaded with possible meaning.'

---

[22] Eliot, 176.
[23] John Keats, *The Complete Poems* (London: Penguin, 1973), 344-5.
[24] Ted Hughes, *Collected Poems* (London: Faber & Faber, 2003), 19.
[25] Keats, 346-7.
[26] *Blackbox Manifold*, 9, web: http://www.manifold.group.shef.ac.uk/issue9/index9.html

20

This reader finds in subject matter and textures much from Bob Dylan's songs in Robinson's poetry. Lines from 'Tangled Up in Blue' ('But all the while I was alone / The past was close behind')[27] are there when I read *English Nettles*; his 'lifelong obsession' with the work of Bob Dylan is perhaps felt most keenly in his elegy for David Mather, 'Like the Living End', one of his finest works. This piece was originally the title poem for a chapbook published by Worple Press in 2013, before it was gathered into the collection *Buried Music*.[28] Robinson revisits the hiding places of his power and has it thus as he traverses a golf course: 'Uncanny in both senses, / life histories among neglect / at such dilapidations / old stones that cannot be deciphered / have grown forgetful now, / as if those years had never happened'. We are again with Eliot's *Four Quartets* but also, via 'Uncanny in both senses', with a source in Freud's 1919 essay, 'Das Unheimliche'. The translated root is pertinent if we want to take up Robinson's 'both senses'; Freud has it that 'the uncanny' is that category of the frightening which 'leads back to what is known of old and long familiar'. (Rooted in the term is 'heim', German for 'home', this is a source for the Old English 'ham', the root for our 'home'.) So, not so much a fear of the unknown, but a sense of something both simultaneously strange and familiar. 'Coincidences'[29] is another poem that plays on this sensation, a poem that starts with a coincidental meeting with the poet Tim Dooley on the Tube: 'Uncanny that we should be travelling home / in the one compartment underground'. Here is a poet who takes what he can gather from coincidence and allows his readers to take what they can as they take a seat in the same compartment.

21

Ravishing Europa is a collection from Peter Robinson that had the publication day of March 29th, 2019. I write this article before October 31st, 2019. We at Worple tried to 'reach out' by offering copies of the

---

[27] Bob Dylan, 'Tangled Up in Blue', *Blood on the Tracks* (Columbia Records, 1975).
[28] *CP*, 411-416.
[29] *CP*, 407.

collection to protesters camped outside Westminster at College Green. This experiment divided opinion. Here is the final poem, part 15, from the sequence 'European Epitaphs'.[30] We think it especially fine. The world is full of home; this is for us a kind of home from home:

England in 2019

> Even as the hollyhocks will still grow tall,
> lattice-work fencing need to be replaced,
> bottle banks choke, the rose petals fall
> across walls double-edged graffiti has defaced,
> still the people's will will have been done
> and dusted, somehow, rain, it will still rain
> from storm-clouds upon our fainting country,
> sun pick out brick courses, into the bargain.
> From a muddy spring, the mud will invite them,
> rulers, managing interminable wars,
> to reverse engineer a continental system –
> spiting faces, beggaring the neighbours…
> Then, as deficits mount, some phantom may
> burst to illumine our chilly, real day.

22

I leave you with an image of the poet walking, considering an old haunt, in 'The Walk Out', a poem also recalling just such a constitutional that we took together not long after his return to England and its nettles:

> The very last of October and blackberries
> still there, edible, past barbed wire coiling
> from fence-posts in diminishing concentrics
> and it's cumulus that's built up its case
> over an old haunt, the beach at Walberswick.
> We are left to imagine it – the tide angling
> into gradations of pebbles, staggered groynes.
> Verticals in flat-lands play such funny tricks

---

[30] *RE*, 81.

> so let's keep our heads down, take in bracken,
> its fish-spine patterns, ivy over flint, hacked-at
> nettles spring-green, resurgent, a sign for 'loose
> recyclables only'. On this 'characteristic' open
> heath we might catch silver-studded blue butterflies,
> and, later on, there's the strong chance of stargazing.

This poem of mine was first published as part of a tribute to Peter on the occasion of his sixtieth birthday.[31] I have been reading and studying his poems since we first met in Cambridge back in 1978. It all started with the stapled chapbook *The Benefit Forms* from The Lobby Press. The body of his work, now to be found in his *Collected Poems*, and in subsequent collections, constitutes one of the major achievements in contemporary poetry.

His poems continue to surprise and delight. Every day he writes the book.

---

[31] *Blackbox Manifold*, 9, web: http://www.manifold.group.shef.ac.uk/issue9/PeterCarpenterPR9.html

Peter Robinson: A Bibliography

Derek Slade

In compiling this bibliography, I have had a huge amount of assistance from Peter Robinson, who not only patiently answered numerous questions but provided a great deal of the information contained within the bibliography. Sincere thanks to Peter. I also benefited from the Bibliography 1976–2006 included in *The Salt Companion to Peter Robinson* ed. Adam Piette and Katy Price (Cambridge: Salt Publishing, 2007). I must also thank Tom Phillips for his support and editorial advice. Jane Commane, Belinda Cooke, Tim Dooley, Tony Frazer and Todd Swift responded helpfully to requests for information. Finally, I wish to thank my wife Mary for her support and encouragement.

I wish to dedicate this bibliography to the memory of Roy Fisher, great friend and eloquent supporter of Peter Robinson.

1. BOOKS

a. Poetry

The Benefit Forms (Cambridge: Lobby Press, 1978)
Going Out to Vote (London: Many Press, 1978)
A Part of Rosemary Laxton (Cambridge: No Publisher, 1979)
Overdrawn Account (London: Many Press, 1980)
Anaglypta (London: Many Press, 1985)
This Other Life (Manchester: Carcanet Press, 1988)
More about the Weather (Cambridge: Robert Jones, 1989)
Entertaining Fates (Manchester: Carcanet Press, 1992)
Leaf-viewing (London: Robert Jones, 1992)
Lost and Found (Manchester: Carcanet Press, 1997)
Via Sauro Variations (Providence, Rhode Island: Ridgeback Press, 1999)
Anywhere You Like (Sendai: Pine Wave Press, 2000)
About Time Too (Manchester: Carcanet Press, 2001)
Selected Poems 1976–2001 (Manchester: Carcanet Press, 2003) [hereafter *SP*]
Ghost Characters (Nottingham: Shoestring Press, 2006)
There are Avenues (Bristol: Brodie Press, 2006)
The Look of Goodbye: Poems 2001–2006 (Exeter: Shearsman Books, 2008)

Ekphrastic Marriage (Reading: Pine Wave Press, 2009) with artworks by Andrew McDonald
English Nettles and Other Poems (Reading: Two Rivers Press, 2010) illustrated by Sally Castle
The Returning Sky (Bristol: Shearsman Books, 2012)
Like the Living End (Tonbridge, Kent: Worple Press, 2013)
Buried Music (Bristol: Shearsman Books, 2015)
An Epithalamium (Reading: Pine Wave Press, 2016)
Collected Poems 1976–2016 (Bristol: Shearsman Books, 2017) [hereafter *CP*]
Ravishing Europa (Tonbridge, Kent: Worple Press, 2019)
Bonjour Mr Inshaw: Poems by Peter Robinson / Paintings by David Inshaw (Reading: Two Rivers Press, 2019).

b. Prose Poems, Aphorisms and Fiction

Untitled Deeds (Cambridge: Salt Publishing, 2004). This volume contains sequenced aphorisms, observations and two sequences of prose poems, 'The Draft Will' and 'Side Effects' (both subsequently published in *The Draft Will* – see below)
Spirits of the Stair: Selected Aphorisms (Exeter: Shearsman Books, 2009)
'A Mystery Murder': short story in *The London Magazine*, October–November 2011
Foreigners, Drunks and Babies: Eleven Stories (Reading: Two Rivers Press, 2013)
The Draft Will (Tokyo: Isobar Press, 2015). This volume contains two sequences of prose poems, 'Side Effects' and 'The Draft Will', plus 'From the Life', seven memoir-pieces
September in the Rain: A Novel (Newbury: Holland House Books, 2016)
'A Seaside Funeral': short story in *The London Magazine*, June–July 2018
The Constitutionals: A Fiction (Reading: Two Rivers Press, 2019)

c. Criticism

In the Circumstances: About Poems and Poets (Oxford: Oxford University Press, 1992)
Poetry, Poets, Readers: Making Things Happen (Oxford: Oxford University Press, 2002)
Twentieth Century Poetry: Selves and Situations (Oxford: Oxford University Press, 2005)
Poetry & Translation: The Art of the Impossible (Liverpool: Liverpool University Press, 2010)
The Sound Sense of Poetry (Cambridge: Cambridge University Press, 2018)

Poetry & Money: A Speculation (Liverpool: Liverpool University Press, 2020)
The Personal Art: Essays, Reviews & Memoirs (Bristol: Shearsman Books, 2021)

d. Interviews

Talk about Poetry: Conversations on the Art, Peter Robinson (Exeter: Shearsman, 2007). Contains 11 interviews with PR. The interviewers are: Ted Slade, Ian Sansom, Marcus Perryman, Nate Dorward, Jane Davies, Peter Carpenter, Katy Price, Adam Piette, Alex Pestell and Tom Phillips. (See also Section 5.)

e. Translations

Six Poems by Ungaretti (Verona: Plain Wrapper, 1981) with Marcus Perryman.
The Disease of the Elm and Other Poems, Vittorio Sereni (London: Many Press, 1983) with Marcus Perryman.
Selected Poems of Vittorio Sereni (London: Anvil Press, 1990) with Marcus Perryman.
When I was at My Most Beautiful and Other Poems by Noriko Ibaragi (Cambridge: Skate Press, 1992) with Fumiko Horikawa.
The Great Friend and Other Translated Poems (Tonbridge, Kent: Worple, 2002).
Selected Poetry and Prose of Vittorio Sereni: A Bilingual Edition (Chicago, IL: Chicago University Press, 2006) with Marcus Perryman (hardback) and (Chicago UP, 2013) (paperback).
The Greener Meadow: Selected Poems of Luciano Erba (Princeton, NJ: Princeton University Press, 2006).
Poems by Antonia Pozzi (Richmond, Surrey: One World Classics, 2011). Reissued (Richmond, Surrey: Alma Classics, 2015).

f. As Editor

(i) Books
With All the Views: Collected Poems of Adrian Stokes (Manchester: Carcanet Press, 1981; Redding Ridge, CT: Black Swan Books, 1981).
Geoffrey Hill: Essays on his Work (Milton Keynes and Philadelphia: Open University Press, 1985).
Liverpool Accents: Seven Poets and a City (Liverpool: Liverpool University Press, 1996).
Enlightened Groves: Essays in Honour of Professor Zenzo Suzuki (Tokyo: Shohakusha, 1996) with Eiichi Hara and Hiroshi Ozawa.

The Thing About Roy Fisher: Critical Studies (Liverpool: Liverpool University Press, 2000) with John Kerrigan.
News for the Ear: A Homage to Roy Fisher (Exeter: Stride, 2000) with Robert Sheppard.
A Choice of British Poetry (Tokyo: Seitousha, 2003) with Shoichiro Sakurai.
Mairi MacInnes: A Tribute (Nottingham: Shoestring Press, 2005).
An Unofficial Roy Fisher (Exeter: Shearsman Books, 2010).
Complete Poetry, Translations & Selected Prose of Bernard Spencer (Bloodaxe Books: 2011).
Reading Poetry: An Anthology (Reading: Two Rivers Press, 2011).
A Mutual Friend: Poems for Charles Dickens (Reading: Two Rivers Press with the English Association, 2012)
Bernard Spencer: Essays on his Poetry & Life (Bristol: Shearsman Books, 2012).
The Oxford Handbook of Contemporary British and Irish Poetry (Oxford: Oxford University Press, 2013; paperback 2016).
The Arts of Peace: An Anthology of Poetry (Reading: Two Rivers Press, 2014) with Adrian Blamires.
An Easily Bewildered Child: Occasional Prose 1963–2013, Roy Fisher (Bristol: Shearsman Books, 2014).
Thomas Hardy, Places and Other Poems, chosen and with an afterword by Peter Robinson (Reading: Two Rivers Press, 2014).
Memoirs of Caravaggio, F.T. Prince (Perdika Press, 2015).
The Rilke of Ruth Speirs: New Poems, Duino Elegies, Sonnets to Orpheus, and Others (Reading: Two Rivers Press, 2015) with John Pilling.
Henry James Poems: A Keepsake of Samples (The British Library, 2016).
Slakki, Roy Fisher (Hexham: Bloodaxe Books, 2016).
Stanley Spencer Poems: An Anthology (Reading: Two Rivers Press, 2017) with Jane Draycott and Carolyn Leder.
A Furnace, Roy Fisher (Chicago, IL: Flood Editions, 2018). With Introduction, A Note on the Text and Notes by PR.
The Citizen and the Making of 'City', Roy Fisher, ed. Peter Robinson. (Hexham: Bloodaxe Books, 2022). With Introduction and critical apparatus by PR.

(ii) **Magazines**
Perfect Bound, 1976–1979, 7 issues, published in Cambridge. Issues 1-2 co-edited with Bill Bennett; issues 3-5 co-edited with Aidan Semmens; issues 6-7 co-edited with Richard Hammersley. [For PR's reflections on *Perfect Bound*, plus reproductions of the cover images for each issue, see 'Nate Dorward talks to Peter Robinson – The Life of a Little Magazine: *Perfect Bound* 1976–1979' (ref. Section E above). See also Aidan Semmens, 'A Perfect Bound from Cambridge into the poetic life', http://www.manifold.group.shef.ac.uk/issue9/AidanSemmensPR9.html.]

Numbers, 1986-1990, 6 issues, published in Cambridge. Co-edited with John Alexander, Alison Rimmer and Clive Wilmer.

2. Essays and Articles

a. Contributions to Books

Pound's Artists: Ezra Pound and the Visual Arts in London, Paris and Italy, ed. D. Humfries (London: Tate Gallery Publications, 1985). 'Ezra Pound and Italian Art'. 121-176.

Poets of Great Britain and Ireland since 1960, ed. Vincent B. Sherry, Jr. (Detroit, MI: Gale Research, 1985). 'Jeremy Hooker'.

Politics and the Rhetoric of Study: Perspectives on Anglo-Irish Poetry, ed. Tjebbe A. Westendorp and Jane Mallinson (Amsterdam: Rodopi, 1995). 'Muldoon's Humour'.

International Aspects of Irish Literature, ed. Toshi Furomoto et al. (Gerrard's Cross: Colin Smythe, 1996). 'Joyce's Lyric Poetry'.

Enlightened Groves: Essays in Honour of Professor Zenzo Suzuki, ed. Eiichi Hara et al. (Tokyo: Shohakusha, 1996). 'Innocence, Sincerity and Bodies in *The Rape of the Lock*'.

Making Connections: A Festschrift for Matt Simpson, ed. Angela Topping (Exeter: Stride Publications, 1996). '"Come Home to Myself": Matt Simpson's Poetry'.

Dante's Modern Afterlife, ed. Nick Havely (Basingstoke: Macmillan, 1996). '"Una Fitta di Rimorsa": Dante in Sereni'.

The View from Kyoto: Essays on Twentieth-Century Poetry, ed. Shoichiro Sakurai (Kyoto: Rinsen, 1998). 'Elizabeth Bishop's One Art'. This essay also appears in *Twentieth Century Poetry: Selves and Situations*.

The Thing About Roy Fisher, ed. John Kerrigan and PR (Liverpool: Liverpool University Press, 2000). 'Introduction' (1-15) and Chapter 11 'Last Things' (275-311). 'Last Things' also appears in *Twentieth Century Poetry: Selves and Situations*.

Poetry and the Sense of Panic: Critical Essays on Elizabeth Bishop and John Ashbery, ed. Lionel Kelly (Amsterdam and Atlanta: 2000). 'The Bliss of What?' This essay also appears in *Twentieth Century Poetry: Selves and Situations*.

News for the Ear: A Homage to Roy Fisher, ed. Robert Sheppard and PR (Exeter: Stride Publications, 2000). 'Invitation' (co-written with Robert Sheppard) (7) and 'In A Tight Corner' (66-68).

Elizabeth Bishop: Poet of the Periphery, ed. Linda Anderson and Jo Shapcott (Newcastle: Bloodaxe Books, 2002). 'Pretended Acts: "The Shampoo"'.

Literature and Translation 12, Translation and Modernism special issue, ed. Adam Piette (Edinburgh: Edinburgh University Press, 2003). 'Translating Sereni'.

W.S. Graham: Speaking Towards You, ed. Hester Jones and Ralph Pite (Liverpool: Liverpool University Press, 2004). 'Dependence in the Poetry of W.S. Graham'. This essay also appears in *Twentieth Century Poetry: Selves and Situations.*

The Oxford Handbook of British and Irish War Poetry, ed. Tim Kendall (Oxford: Oxford University Press, 2007). Chapter 26: '"Down in the Terraces between the Targets": Civilians'.

Some Versions of Empson: Essays on his Writing, ed. Matt Bevis (Oxford: Oxford University Press, 2007). 'C. Hatakeyama and W.E.'. 60-83.

Inspirations and Technique: Ancient to Modern Views on Beauty and Art, ed. John Roe and Michele Stanco (Zurich: Peter Lang, 2007). 'Wittgenstein's Aesthetics and Revision'. 261-276.

An Unofficial Roy Fisher, ed. PR (Exeter: Shearsman Books, 2010). 'Preface' (5-6) and 'Collected and Recollected' (142-160).

The Salt Companion to John Tranter, ed. Rod Mengham (Salt Publishing, 2010). 'John Tranter and Tradition'.

Ford Madox Ford: Modernist Magazines and Editing, ed. J. Harding (Amsterdam and New York: Rodopi, 2010). '"Written at least as well as Prose": Ford, Pound, and Poetry'. 99-114.

The Salt Companion to John Matthias, ed. J.F. Doerr (Salt Publishing, 2011). 'John Matthias: Speaking Personally'. 64-85.

The Edinburgh Companion to Twentieth-Century British and American War Literature, ed. A. Piette and M. Rawlinson (Edinburgh: Edinburgh University Press, 2012). '" That Fighting was a Long Way Off": Desert and Jungle War Poems'. 448-455.

The Oxford Handbook of Victorian Poetry, ed. M. Bevis (Oxford: Oxford University Press, 2013). 'The Poetry of Modern Life: On the Pavement'. 254-272.

Contemporary Political Poetry in Britain and Ireland, ed. U. Klawitter and C.-U. Viol. Anglistik & Englischunterricht Series. (Heidelberg: Universitätsverslag Winter, 2013.) 'Conflicts in Form: The Politics of Roy Fisher's "City"'. 95-116.

Thomas Hardy in Context, ed. P. Mallett (Cambridge: Cambridge University Press, 2013). 'Hardy's Poets as his Critics'. 99-109.

The Oxford Handbook of Contemporary British and Irish Poetry (Oxford: Oxford University Press, 2013; paperback 2016). Introduction: 'The Limits and Openness of the Contemporary', 1-17. Ch. 34, '"There Again": Composition, Revision, and Repair', 676-93. Ch.38, 'Contemporary Poetry and Value', 727-48.

Poetry and Geography: Space and Place in Post-War Poetry, ed. N. Alexander and D. Cooper (Liverpool: Liverpool University Press, 2013). 'Roy Fisher's Spatial Prepositions and Other Little Words'. 204-216.

The Oxford Handbook of Shakespeare's Poetry, ed. J. Post (Oxford: Oxford University Press, 2013). 'Shakespeare's Loose Ends and the Contemporary Poet'. 599-617.

An Easily Bewildered Child: Occasional Prose 1963–2013, Roy Fisher, ed. PR (Bristol: Shearsman Books, 2014). 'Introduction'. 9-13.

Thomas Hardy, Places and Other Poems, ed. PR (Reading: Two Rivers Press, 2014). 'Afterword'.

Don Paterson: Contemporary Critical Essays, ed. N. Pollard (Edinburgh: Edinburgh University Press, 2014). 'Punching Yourself in the Face: Don Paterson and his Readers'. 131-144.

Edward Lear and the Play of Poetry, ed. Matthew Bevis and James Williams (Oxford: Oxford University Press, 2016). 'Edward Lear: Celebrity Chef'.

Reading F. T. Prince: Liverpool English Texts and Studies 67, ed. Will May (Liverpool: Liverpool University Press, 2017). 'Truth and Style'. 51-76.

The Shakespearean World, ed. J. L. Levenson and R. Ormsby (London: Routledge, 2017). 'The Subject of "Shakespeares Sonnets" and Afterlife in Lyric Poetry'. 263-280.

British Prose Poetry: The Poems Without Lines, ed. Jane Monson (Cham, Switzerland: Palgrave Macmillan, 2018). 'Roy Fisher's Musicians'. 299-315.

A Furnace, 2nd edition, Roy Fisher, ed. PR. (Chicago, IL: Flood Editions, 2018). Introduction and additional Notes by PR.

Reading Dylan Thomas, ed. E. Allan (Edinburgh: Edinburgh University Press, 2018). 'Dylan Thomas: "on out of sound"'. 71-88.

The Oxford Handbook of Eighteenth-Century Satire, ed. P. Bullard (Oxford: Oxford University Press, 2019). Ch. 37, 'The Edge of Satire: Post-Mortem and Other Effects'. 628-644.

Aphoristic Modernity: 1880 to the Present, ed. K. Boyiopoulos and M. Shallcross (Leiden: Brill, 2019). 'Aphoristic Gaps and Theories of the Image'. 21-36.

Modernism & Non-Translation, ed. J. Harding and J. Nash (Oxford: Oxford University Press, 2019). '"I like the Spanish title": *William Carlos Williams's Al Que Quiere!*'. 86-103.

b. Contributions to Journals

Joe Soap's Canoe 1, 1978. 'A Note on Pierre Reverdy'.

PN Review 15, 7:1, September–October 1980. 'On an Unpublished Poem by Adrian Stokes'.

English 31:141, Autumn 1982. 'In Another's Words: Thomas Hardy's Poetry'.

The Fiction Magazine, 2:2, 1983. 'Franco Fortini in Cambridge'.
The Many Review 1, 1983. 'In Dreams begin Responsibilities: The Poems of Tim Dooley'.
Sitting Fires 2, 1983. 'A Note on Vittorio Sereni'.
PN Review 32, 9:6, 1983. 'Vittorio Sereni (27 July 1913-10 February 1983)'.
The Cambridge Review 106:2287, 1985. 'Is Poetry a Performing Art?'.
PN Review 46, 12:2, November–December 1985. 'Ezra Pound's Broad Analogies': an essay relating to the Kettle's Yard exhibition (June–August 1985) *Pound's Artists*.
Numbers 2, 1987. 'Editorial'.
The Sunday Telegraph, 25th October 1987. 'Josef Brodsky: Nobel's Poet'.
Bulletin of the Society for Italian Studies 21, 1988. [With Emmanuela Tandello] 'Two Italian Poets in London'.
Numbers 4, 1988. 'Editorial'.
Review of English Literature [Kyoto] 58, 1989. 'Charles Tomlinson in the Golfo dei Poeti'. A revised version of this essay also appears in *Twentieth Century Poetry: Selves and Situations*.
The Sunday Correspondent, 10th December 1989. 'The Triumphant Homecoming of Japan's Rising Son'.
Review of English Literature [Kyoto] 59, 1990. 'Philip Larkin: Here and There'. Available at: https://repository.kulib.kyoto-u.ac.jp/dspace/bitstream/2433/135236/1/ebk00059_001b.pdf.
Review of English Literature [Kyoto] 60, 1990. 'Dependence in the Poetry of W. S. Graham'. This essay also appears in *Twentieth Century Poetry: Selves and Situations* and also, revised, in *W. S. Graham: Speaking Towards You*, ed. Hester Jones and Ralph Pite (Liverpool: Liverpool University Press, 2004).
Review of English Literature [Kyoto] 61, 1991. 'Talking Yourself to Death: *The Rape of Lucrece*'.
Poetica [Kyoto] 36, 1992. 'Contracts and Prophets'.
Shiron [Sendai] 31, 1992. 'Not a Villanelle: Ezra Pound's Psychological Hour'. This essay also appears in *Twentieth Century Poetry: Selves and Situations*.
PN Review 88, 19:2, November–December 1992. '"As Wallpaper Peels from A Wall": Words and Things for Donald Davie', 'Donald Davie at 70: A Celebration'.
Scripsi 9:1, 1993. 'The Rape of Dolly Haze: on Rorty on Nabokov'.
Perversions 1:3, 1994. 'Elizabeth Bishop's One Art'. This essay also appears in *Twentieth Century Poetry: Selves and Situations*.
PN Review 99, 21:1, September–October 1994. John Ashbery in Britain: A Supplement. 'As My Way Is: John Ashbery's Gift'.
Durham University Journal Supplement, 1995. *Sharp Study and Long Toil: Basil Bunting Special Issue* ed. Richard Caddel. 'Bunting's Ballads'. This

essay also appears (as 'Basil Bunting's Emigrant Ballads') in *Twentieth Century Poetry: Selves and Situations*.
PN Review 108, 22:4, March–April 1996. 'A Personal Art'.
Modern Poetry in Translation, New Series 9, 1996. '"How Distant We've Become": Syntax and Apostrophe in Fortini and Sereni'.
Shiron [Sendai] 35, 1996. 'Muldoon's Humour'. This is a longer version of the essay in *Politics and the Rhetoric of Poetry*, 1995 (see section 3a above).
PN Review 119, 24:3, January-February 1998. 'Montale and the Muse'.
Shiron [Sendai] 38, 1999. 'Matters of Fact and Questions of Value'.
The Cambridge Quarterly 29:3, 2000. 'Making Things Happen'.
The Gig 4-5, *The Poetry of Peter Riley*, November 1999–March 2000. 'On Untitled Sequence'. 62-76.
English 49:193, 2000. 'Allen Curnow Travels'. This essay also appears in *Twentieth Century Poetry: Selves and Situations*.
PN Review 135, 27:1, September–October 2000. 'Attilio Bertolucci 1911–2000'.
PN Review 139, 27:5, May–June 2001. 'End of Harm: Douglas Oliver'.
PN Review 140, 27:6, July–August 2001. 'Donald Davie and "The Exam of Future Life"'.
Essays in Criticism 51:3, July 2001. 'Pretended Speech Acts in Shakespeare's Sonnets'.
Samizdat 9, 2002. 'John Matthias's Dedication'.
Shiron [Sendai] 40, 2002. 'MacNeice, Munich and Self-Sufficiency'. This essay also appears in *Twentieth Century Poetry: Selves and Situations*.
The Cambridge Quarterly 31:2, 2002. '"Absolute Circumstance": Mairi MacInnes'. A revised version of this essay also appears in *Twentieth Century Poetry: Selves and Situations*.
The Gig 13-14, *Removed for Further Study: The Poetry of Tom Raworth* May 2003. 'Tom Raworth and the Pop Art Explosion'. 49-72. This essay also appears in *Twentieth Century Poetry: Selves and Situations*.
Times Literary Supplement 5233, 18th July 2003. 'Very Shrinking Behaviour: William Empson's Poetic Collaboration with Chiyoko Hatakeyama'.
Translation and Literature 12:1, 2003. 'Translating Sereni: Two Poems and a Discussion', with Marcus Perryman.
Metre 14, Summer 2003. 'Thom Gunn's Sense of the Movement'.
Modern Poetry in Translation 3:1, 2004. 'Luciano Erba'. Available at: http://www.poetrymagazines.org.uk/magazine/record.asp?id=16720.
Yearbook of Miyagi Gakuin for 2003, July 2004. 'Chiyoko Hatakeyama's Correspondence with William Empson'.
Modern Poetry in Translation series 3:1, July 2004. 'The Poetry of Luciano Erba'.

Poetry Review 94:2, Summer 2004. '"A Changed Other Person": W.S. Graham's *New Collected Poems*'.
Poetry Ireland Review 80, September 2004. 'Vittorio Sereni's Escape from Capture'.
The Dickens Fellowship Japan Chapter Journal 27, October 2004. '"This Fiction of an Occupation": Mr Boffin's Encounter with Blight'.
PN Review 160, 31:2, November–December 2004. 'C. Hatakeyama [Trans. W.E.]'.
Shiron [Sendai] 42, 2004. '"A Blank to Me": Thomas Hardy and the Loss of Meaning'.
Agenda (Australian Issue) 41:1-2, July 2005. 'John Tranter and Tradition'. 155-161. This essay also appears in *The Salt Companion to John Tranter* ed. Rod Mengham (Cambridge: Salt Publishing, 2006).
Agenda (American Issue) 41:3-4, December 2005. 'Translation and Self-Accusation: Vittorio Sereni's "momento psicologico"'. 125-134.
English Literature Review 49 [Kyoto], 2005. 'The Sound Sense of Poetry: Reading Techniques'. Available at: http://repo.kyoto- wu.ac.jp/dspace/bitstream/11173/654/1/0020_049_003.pdf.
Adrian Stokes, 1902–1972. 'Stokes – the Poet'. Available at: http://www.pstokes.demon.co.uk/ads5/prpi.htm.
Poetica 64 [Tokyo], 2006. 'Wallace Stevens and British Poets in the 1950s'.
Essays in Criticism 57:2, 2007. 'Captain Benwick's Reading'. 147-170.
Agenda 42:3-4, 2007 (special issue 'A Reconsideration of Rainer Maria Rilke'). 'Rilke, Thou Art Translated'. 153-163.
Publishing History 62, 2008. 'Twists in the Plotting: Bernard Spencer's Second Book of Poems'. 81-102.
English Association Newsletter, Spring 2008. 'Teaching English Literature in Japan'.
The Bridge 32, Winter 2008. 'Telling Tales and Showing Signs': on Bob Dylan's *Tell the Signs* CDs.
The Cambridge Quarterly 38:3, 2009. '"Readings will Grow Erratic" in Philip Larkin's "Deceptions"'. 277-305.
Agenda 44:4, 2009. 'Bernard Spencer (1909–1962): A Centenary Supplement', edited with an introduction by PR. 234-262.
Catalogue of the Bernard Spencer Collection at the University of Reading, ed. Verity Hunt (Reading, University of Reading, 2009). 'Bernard Spencer at Reading'. 11-19.
The London Magazine, 2009. 'Bernard Spencer in "The London Magazine"'. 66-72.
English 58:223, 2009. 'Bernard Spencer's "Boat Poem"'. 318-339.
The Reader 36, 2009. 'Poet on His Work: Behind "Otterspool Prom"'. 49-53.
Eyewear blog, 3rd July 2009. 'Bob Dylan: Back in the Rain'. Available at: http://toddswift.blogspot.co.uk/2009/07/guest-review-robinson-on-dylan.html.

Poetry London 64, Autumn 2009. 'Old Incurables': essay on Ian Hamilton. 25-27.
Times Literary Supplement, 3rd September 2010. 'In the Lombard Line': appreciation of Luciano Erba.
The London Magazine, June/July 2010. '"Anything But Gentle": Henry Moore Revisited'.
The Bow-Wow Shop 6, 2010. 'Bernard Spencer: "The Wind-Blown Island of Mykonos" and "Questions Asked of a Poet"'.
Essays in Criticism 60:2, 2010. 'Christina Rossetti's Promises'. 148-167.
The London Magazine, 2010–2011 (December-January). 'An Uncollected Poem and the "Madrid Journal" by Bernard Spencer'.
Poetry Wales 47:2, Autumn 2011. 'John James and *The White Stones* 71: Music, Rhyme, and Home'.
World Literature Today 85, 2011. 'Six Translated Italian Poems: The Many Voices of Italian Literature'.
Poetry Review 102:2, Summer 2012. 'Beyond Dictionaries: Vahni Capildeo and Etymology'.
The Cambridge Quarterly 44:4, 2015. 'Sex, Lies and Poetry: The Ballad of Reading Gaol'. 299-320.
The Guardian, 11th August 2015. 'Lee Harwood: Obituary'. Available at: https://www.theguardian.com/books/2015/aug/11/lee-harwood.
Literary Imagination 17:3, November 2015. '"Battles Long Ago": J.H. Prynne and "The Solitary Reaper"'.
The Poetry Society, 2016. Tribute to Geoffrey Hill. Available at: http://poetrysociety.org.uk/news/geoffrey-hill-1932-2016/.
Raceme 5, Autumn 2016. 'Giorgio Bassani, 1916-2001'. 97-100.
The High Window, 6th December 2016. '"He Examines the Nightingale's Code": Bob Dylan, Poetry, and Literature by Peter Robinson'. Available at: https://thehighwindowpress.com/2016/12/06/he-examines-the-nightingales-code-bob-dylan-poetry-and-literature-by-peter-robinson/.
Brexit and the Democratic Intellect, symposium held at Durham University, 13th–14th January 2017. PR read a paper, 'Respecting a Decision: The Experts, the People, and the Politicians'. A revised version of this paper is available at: https://readdurhamenglish.files.wordpress.com/2017/05/brexit_complete_ver-1-3.pdf.
Blackbox Manifold 18, Summer 2017. 'When Tom Raworth Died'. Available at: http://www.manifold.group.shef.ac.uk/issue18/TR-PeterRobinsonBM18.html.
Raceme 6, 2018. 'Charles Tomlinson in the Deep North'. 92-101.

3. Translations

a. In Anthologies

A Choice of Twentieth-Century French Verse ed. S. Romer (London: Faber and Faber, 2002). Contains 'On Ten Fingers' by Pierre Reverdy.

The Faber Book of 20th Century Italian Poems ed. J. McKendrick (London: Faber and Faber, 2004). Contains poems by Saba, Ungaretti, Sereni, Fortini, Erba *et al*.

Corno Inglese: An Anthology of Eugenio Montale's Poetry in English Translation ed. Marco Sonzogni (Novi Ligure: Edizioni Joker, 2009). Contains 'Scissors, don't cut that face …'.

The FSG Book of Twentieth-Century Italian Poetry: An Anthology ed. Geoffrey Brock (New York: Farrar, Straus & Giroux, 2012). Contains 'After the News' by Giorgio Caproni; '*from* Algerian Diary', 'Saba' and 'A Dream' by Vittorio Sereni [with Marcus Perryman]; 'Salute to Rome' by Giorgio Bassani; 'My Forties' and 'The Metaphysical Tramdriver' by Luciano Erba; and 'March in Rue Mouffetard' by Maria Luisa Spaziani.

Those Who from Afar Look Like Flies: An Anthology of Italian Poetry from Pasolini to the Present, Tome 1, 1956–1975, ed. Luigi Ballerini and Beppe Cavatorta (Toronto: University of Toronto Press, 2017). Contains 'Book of Hours' and 'Hippograms and Metahippograms of the Painter Giovanola' by Luciano Erba.

b. In Journals

Poetry and Audience 23, 1977. 'Mao-Tcha', 'The Name of the Wings', 'On Ten Fingers' by Pierre Reverdy.

Saturday Morning 4, 1977. 'Sombre', 'Century' by Pierre Reverdy.

Granta 76, 1977. 'The Man and the Weather', 'The Walls of Towns', 'O.' by Pierre Reverdy.

The Wolly of Swot 1, September 1977. 'The Valley's Turning', '4 & 9', 'The Name of the Wings', 'The Noise of Wings', 'The Man and Night', 'The Far Away Voice', 'His Contemporary Life', 'The Blue Corner of the Sky', 'Footpath' by Pierre Reverdy.

Perfect Bound 6, 1978. 'Guesthouse', 'Curfew', 'Poem', 'Man's Memory' by Pierre Reverdy.

Joe Soap's Canoe 1, 1978. 'In the Field', 'Beyond', 'On the Threshold' by Pierre Reverdy.

Green Lines 2, 1978. 'The Red Head' by Pierre Reverdy.

Alembic 8, Spring 1979. 'The Shadow of the Wall', 'Silence', 'Street', 'Point', 'Behind the Station', 'Space at the End of the Corridor', 'Cinema', 'Drama' by Pierre Reverdy.

Argo 1:2, 1979. 'See-saw' by Pierre Reverdy.

Molly Bloom 1, 1980. [With Marcus Perryman] 'September', 'Passing On', 'Saba' by Vittorio Sereni.

Stonechat 1, 1980. [With Marcus Perryman] 'Chiaroscuro' by Giuseppe Ungaretti.

The Fiction Magazine 2:2, 1983. [With Marcus Perryman] 'To the Gods of Morning', 'One September Evening', 'In a Florence Street', 'Genre Theory', 'Sixth Recitative' by Franco Fortini.

Argo 5:1, 1983. [With Marcus Perryman] 'City of Night', 'Italian in Greece' by Vittorio Sereni.

PN Review 32, 9:6 1983. [With Marcus Perryman] 'Algerian Diary' by Vittorio Sereni.

Poetry Ireland Newsletter: Poetry Ireland Translations 7, 1983. [With Marcus Perryman] 'Haze' by Vittorio Sereni.

Sitting Fires 2, 1983. [With Marcus Perryman] 'Soldiers in Urbino', 'Balcony', 'Belgrade', 'Saba', 'In Sleep', 'Your Memory in Me' by Vittorio Sereni.

New Directions in Poetry and Prose 47 (ed. J. Laughlin, P. Glassgold and E. Harper (New York: New Directions, 1983). [With Marcus Perryman] 'Works in Progress', 'Revival', 'Interior', 'Festival', 'Niccolo', 'The Disease of the Elm', 'In Ascent', 'In Parma with A.B.', 'Autostrada della Cisa', 'Rimbaud' by Vittorio Sereni.

Grosseteste Review 15, 1984. [With Marcus Perryman] 'Glenn' by Maurizio Cucchi.

The Many Review 2, 1984. [With Marcus Perryman] ' "Poet, drive out of me the memory": A review of Sereni's *Stella Variabile (1981)*' by Maurizio Cucchi.

Argo 6:2, 1985. [With Marcus Perryman] 'Expulsion Order' by Franco Fortini.

PN Review 46, 12:2, 1985 (Cambridge Poetry Festival Special Issue). [With Marcus Perryman] 'In Parma with A.B.' by Vittorio Sereni.

Numbers 1, 1986. [With Marcus Perryman] 'Twenty-six' by Vittorio Sereni.

The London Magazine 27:1-2, 1987. [With Marcus Perryman] 'Soldiers in Urbino', 'He knows nothing any more, is borne up on wings', 'Appointment at an Unusual Hour', 'Autostrada della Cisa' by Vittorio Sereni.

Numbers 3, 1987. [With Marcus Perryman] 'How the world has narrowed…', 'Of your timid cat…', 'Note on Poussin', 'The Promise', 'Reading a Poem', 'Genre Theory', 'The Goodnight', 'The Near Abolition of Nature', 'The Animal' by Franco Fortini and 'Niccolò' by Vittorio Sereni.

Numbers 4, 1988. [With Christine Tweddle] 'At the Chevrolet's wheel on the road to Sintra', 'A cross on the tobacconist's door', 'Tripe in the Oporto style', 'Dactylography', 'They didn't have any electricity there' by Álvaro de Campos [Fernando Pessoa].

Bulletin of the Society for Italian Studies 21, 1988. [With Marcus Perryman] 'Saba' by Franco Fortini. [With Emmanuela Tandello] 'Sea of need, Cassandra…' by Amelia Rosselli.

Poetry Tokyo 4, 1991. [With Fumiko Horikawa] 'Smoking Lesson', 'Flowers of Time' by Yoko Isaka.

Testo a Fronte 9, 1993. 'Luino-Luvino' by Vittorio Sereni.

Scripsi 9:2, 1994. [With Marcus Perryman] 'Interview with a Suicide' by Vittorio Sereni.

Modern Poetry in Translation new series 5, 1994. [With Marcus Perryman] 'It Will Be the Boredom', 'Image' by Vittorio Sereni; 'Woman', 'My Poems' by Umberto Saba.

Modern Poetry in Translation new series 8, 1995. 'Motets' by Eugenio Montale.

Modern Poetry in Translation new series 9, 1996. 'Someone is still…', 'The little bushes…', 'I'm in the room…', 'And so one March morning…', 'In the night…', 'Saba', 'This Line', 'Upon this stone…', 'It's not the light switch…', 'If another time…' by Franco Fortini.

The London Magazine 36, 5-6, 1996. [With Marcus Perryman] 'Port Stanley like Traponi', 'It will be the boredom', 'In the True Year Zero', from 'Fragments of a Defeat', by Vittorio Sereni.

Poetry Kanto 13, 1997. [With Marcus Perryman] 'The Great Friend' by Vittorio Sereni.

New Grains 2, 1998. [With Marcus Perryman] 'The Reunited', 'Summer in the Po Valley' by Vittorio Sereni.

Jacket 20, 2002. 'Poem' by Pierre Reverdy.

Wandering Dog, December 2002. 'Graphology of a Goodbye', 'A Visit to Caleppio', 'Implosion', 'The Metaphysical Tramdriver', by Luciano Erba.

Poetry Ireland Review 77, November 2003. 'When I was at My Most Beautiful' by Noriko Ibaragi.

Literature and Translation 12, Translation and Modernism Special Issue ed. A. Piette (Edinburgh: Edinburgh University Press, 2003). 'A Holiday Place' (1) and 'Translating Char' by Vittorio Sereni.

Modern Poetry in Translation Series 3:1, c.2004. Eleven poems by Luciano Erba: 'La Grande Jeanne', 'Tabula Rasa?', 'The Mirage', 'Book of Hours', 'The Young Couples', 'New Methods of Doctor K', 'Without Compass', 'The Circus Hypothesis', from 'Railway Suite', 'Black Angels', 'I Would Like to Enter History'.

Kawauchi Review 3, March 2004. 'Note' by Pierre Reverdy, 'After Shakespeare' by Rolf Dieter Brinkmann, 'Cinema Leaves' by Rafael Alcides, and 16 others.

Poetry Ireland Review 80, September 2004. 'Soldiers in Urbino', 'Terrace', 'Belgrade', 'Il Piatto Piange', from 'Holland', 'Earthly Pantomime', from 'A Holiday Place', and 'Self Portrait' by Vittorio Sereni.

Times Literary Supplement 5294, 17th September 2004. 'The Goodbyes' by Luciano Erba.

Agenda, Translation Issue, 2005. 'A First Degree Equation' by Luciano Erba and 'A Holiday Place' (6) by Vittorio Sereni.
Fire 25, 2005. 'La Grande Jeanne', 'Closing a Trunk Once More', 'I Live Thirty Metres from the Ground', 'End of the Holidays', 'One of the Things', by Luciano Erba.
Writing: A Literary Review, January 2005. 'Toronto Saturday Night' by Vittorio Sereni and 'Far Beyond the Frozen Seas' by Luciano Erba.
Jacket 29, April 2006. Twelve poems from *Remi in barca* [Shipping the Oars], Luciano Erba. Available at: http://jacketmagazine.com/29/erba.html.
Times Literary Supplement, 11th May, 2007. 'Travellers' by Luciano Erba.
Fire 29 & 30, Spring 2008. 'Eight Poems from the German' by Goethe, Heine, Rilke, Bachmann and Brinkmann.
The Maritime Museum, Liverpool, 2nd July 2008. Performance of 'Arandora' by Marcello Fois, translated with Ornella Trevisan, the text for an Oratorio by Fabrizio Festa.
Poetry Ireland 95, October 2008. 'Travellers' and 'The Apple' by Luciano Erba.
Annals of the University of Craiova 32:1-2, 2010. Three uncollected poems by Luciano Erba.
World Literature Today 85:4, July–Aug 2011. Poems by Fernanda Romagnoli, Luciano Erba, Maria Luisa Spaziani, Pier Luigi Bacchini, Patrizia Cavalli, and Valerio Magrelli.
Nuovi Argomenti blog, 20th January 2014. 'Vittorio Sereni, trent'anni dopo' ['Vittorio Sereni, Thirty Years Later'], by Gabriella Sica. Available at: http://www.nuoviargomenti.net/poesie/vittorio-sereni-trentanni-dopo/.
ReadingItaly blog, 28th January 2014. 'Reading at Basle' by Fabio Pusterla and '*from* Sweet Fairytale' by Maurizio Cucchi. Available at: https://readingitaly.wordpress.com/2014/01/28/translation-academia/.
The High Window 1, 1st March 2016. 'Trieste' by Umberto Saba, 'Little Ode to Rome' by Attilio Bertolucci, and 'Autumn Evening' by Giovanna Bemporad. Available at: https://thehighwindowpress.com/2016/03/01/italian-poetry/.
The High Window 3, 1st September 2016. 'The House by the Sea' by Maurizio Cucchi, 'Towards the "Ideal Republic" (Vico)' by Luciano Erba and 'Conjugal' by Fernanda Romagnoli. Available at: https://thehighwindowpress.com/category/translation/.
Raceme 5, Autumn 2016. Giorgio Bassani, 'Nine Poems Presented in a Postscript': the poems translated are 'Towards Ferrara', 'Evening at Porto Reno', 'Idyll', 'Angelus', 'Dawn on the Panes', 'Villa Glori', and 'Te Luci Ante' nos. 5, 7 and 13. 100-107.
The High Window, 10th September 2017. Three poems by Ibaragi Noriko: 'When I Was at My Most Beautiful', 'Your Own Sensitivity at Least', 'Garden at Night'. Available at: https://thehighwindowpress.com/2017/09/10/japanese-poetry/.

Modern Poetry in Translation, 'Dream Colours' 2020, no. 1. Two poems by Noriko Ibaragi, translated by PR and Andrew Houwen.

4. Memoirs

Hertforde Poets Journal 20, 1981. 'Revising a "Temporary Poem"'.
The Independent, 7th February 1990. 'Westward Ho: Kyoto Diary'.
Liverpool Accents: Seven Poets and a City, ed. PR (Liverpool: Liverpool University Press, 1996). 'Liverpool… of All Places'. Also published in *The Draft Will* (see section 1b above).
News for the Ear: A Homage to Roy Fisher, ed. PR and Robert Sheppard (Exeter: Stride Publications, 2000). 'In a Tight Corner'. 66-68. Also published in *The Draft Will* (see section 1b above).
Japan Experiences: Fifty Years, One Hundred Views, ed. Hugh Cortazzi (London: Japan Library Press, 2001). 'Lost and Found'. Also published in *The Draft Will* (see section 1b above).
The Reader 13, 2003. 'Becoming a Reader'. Also published in *The Draft Will* (see section 1b above).
English 58:221, 2009. 'Fellows' Poetry Prize 2008'. 112-15.
Prac Crit 6, March 2016. 'Deep Note': on 'Sein und Zeit' (including a reproduction of a notebook draft of this poem). Available at: http://www.praccrit.com/essays/sein-und-zeit- deep-note-by-peter-robinson/.
English after Brexit: English Association Issues in English 11, ed. Adrian Barlow (Leicester: The English Association, 2016). 'Balkan Diary'. 35-46.
Folia Linguistica et Literraria 15: *Writing Places: The Conceptualisation and Representation of Space, Location and Environment in Literature* (Niksic: University of Montenegro Press, 2016). 'At Home from Home: A Poet's Experience of Country and Migration'. 13-28.
Axon Capsule 4 (Special Issue), April 2019. 'Four Lyric Occasions': essays on four recent poems, 'Ravishing Europa', 'The Truth in New York', Diplomatic Memo' and 'La Considération du Retour'. Available at: https://www.axonjournal.com.au/four-lyric-occasions.
Liverpool University Press blog, 18th September 2020. 'Poetry, Money & Me'. PR considers the beginnings of his study that led up to *Poetry & Money: A Speculation* (Liverpool University Press, 2020). Available at: https://liverpooluniversitypress.blog/2020/09/18/poetry-money-me/.

5. Interviews

a. As Interviewer
Granta 76, June 1977. 'Peter Robinson Talks to Roy Fisher'.

Mairi MacInnes: A Tribute, ed. PR (Nottingham: Shoestring Press, 2005). 'Mairi MacInnes in Conversation'.

Interviews Through Time and Selected Prose, Roy Fisher (Kentisbeare, Exeter: Shearsman Books, 2000). This includes the *Granta* interview listed above, plus '"They Are All Gone Into the World": Roy Fisher in Conversation with Peter Robinson', previously unpublished. Both interviews are included in the revised second edition of the book, *Interviews Through Time: Roy Fisher*, ed. Tony Frazer (Bristol: Shearsman Books, 2013).

b. As Interviewee
[See Section 1 (d) above for details of *Talk about Poetry*, a collection of interviews with PR.]

Radio Cambridgeshire, and the BBC World Service, Spring 1988.

Oxford Poetry, 1994. 'Through Frosted Glass: An Interview with Peter Robinson by Ian Sansom'. Date of interview not given. Available at http://www.oxfordpoetry.co.uk/interviews.php?int=viii1_peterrobinson.

BBC Radio 3, February 1994. Interview with Tim Dee.

The Richmond Review, 1999. '"Making Something of Life": Peter Robinson Talks to Michael Bradshaw'.

The Animist, 1999. '"There has to be Torque in Poetic Talk": Peter Robinson in Conversation with Marcus Perryman'.

The Cortland Review, June 1999. '"Occasion to Revise or Think Again": Peter Robinson interviewed by Marcus Perryman'. Interview conducted March–April 1999. Available at: http://www.cortlandreview.com/features/99/06/.

The Poetry Kit, 1999. 'The Poetry Kit interviews Peter Robinson'. The interviewer is Ted Slade. The online publication is dated 1999; actual date of interview not given. Available at: http://www.poetrykit.org/iv/robinson.htm.

The Reader 8, 2001. 'The Reader Talks to Peter Robinson'. The interviewer is Jane Davis.

Jacket 20, December 2002. 'Nate Dorward talks to Peter Robinson – The Life of a Little Magazine: *Perfect Bound*, 1976–1979'. Interview conducted via email, September-November 2001. Available at: http://jacketmagazine.com/20/pbi.html.

Salt 17:1, 2003. 'A Sense of Process: Kate Price talking to Peter Robinson'

Tears in the Fence 36, Autumn 2003. 'Peter Robinson Talks with Adam Piette'.

BBC Radio Merseyside, March 2003. On Angela Heslop's 'Artwaves'.

Jacket 25, March 2004. '*Al Que Quiere!* "If Not, Not": Peter Robinson in Conversation with Steve Clark'. Available at: http://jacketmagazine.com/25/rob-clark.html.

Poetry Ireland Review 78, 2004. '"A Tourist in Your Other Country": Peter Robinson in Conversation with Peter Carpenter'. Available at: http://www.poetryireland.ie/publications/poetry-ireland-review/online-archive/view/interview-with-peter-robinson.

BBC Radio 3, 27 March 2004. Interviewed on Ian Macmillan's *The Verb* programme.

La Gazetta di Parma, 1st September 2005. 'La Poesie Delle Cose'; the interviewer is Lisa Opici.

Signals Magazine 2, October 2005. 'Peter Robinson Talks to Alex Pestell'.

Venue, February 2006. 'Peter Robinson Talks to Tom Phillips'.

The Guardian, 30th September 2008. 'Awards bring translators out of "darkened rooms"': an account by Alison Flood of an award-giving ceremony on 29th September 2008 at which PR received an award for *The Greener Meadow*. Includes brief interview with PR.

Agenda, online c.2009. 'Peter Robinson in Conversation with Belinda Cooke'. http://www.agendapoetry.co.uk/documents/Robinson-Cook-Interview.pdf

The Use of English 60, Summer 2009. '"What Sorts of Poetry Were You Reading?" A Conversation with Peter Robinson'. The interviewer is Ian Brinton. 215-223.

Annals of the University of Craiova, 32:1-2, 2010. 'Translating Luciano Erba: a Conversation with Peter Robinson'. 195-204. The interviewer is Lorenza Gastaldo.

Interview conducted via Facebook, May–June 2012, concerning PR's poem 'Another Twilight'. The interviewer is Pegatha Hughes.

Blackbox Manifold 9, December 2012. 'Back Now: John Kerrigan Interviews Peter Robinson'. The interview was conducted August–September 2012. Available at: http://www.manifold.group.shef.ac.uk/issue9/JohnKerriganPR9.html.

The North 50, 2013. 'In Conversation: Helen Mort talks to Peter Robinson'. 77-81.

Reading Italy (Italian Studies Postgraduate Forum, University of Reading). 'Translating Italy: A Conversation with Peter Robinson', posted 28th January 2014. The interviewer is Stefano Bragato. Available at: https://readingitaly.wordpress.com/2014/01/28/-academia/.

Ramuri 6, 2015 [Romania]. The interviewer is Sabina Marcu, who translated the interview into Romanian for this publication. The interview was conducted on 2 November 2014.

Journal of Poetics Research. 'Peter Robinson in Conversation with James Peake'. The interview was conducted in 2015. Available at: http://poeticsresearch.com/article/peter-robinson-and-james-peake-in-conversation/.

'Trauma, Memory and Creativity: A Conversation between Kate Behrens and Peter Robinson'. Unpublished. Made available for a University of Warwick MOOC, 'Literature and Mental Health: Reading for Wellbeing', run by Jonathan Bate and Paula Byrne. The interview took place in June 2015.

The Poetry School, c. 2015. 'Pub Chats: Two Rivers Press'. Interviewer not identified. Available at: https://poetryschool.com/interviews/pub-chats-two-rivers-press/.

Limerick Leader, 12th November 2017. 'Peter Robinson: Internationally Renowned Poet and Novelist Who Spoke in Limerick Recently'. This is a set of responses by PR to questions by John Rainsford, though the questions have not been included. Available at: http://www.limerickleader.ie/news/the-arts-interview/281231/peter-robinson.html.

Fortnightly Review, February 2019. 'Poetry written in Britain's "long moment"', an exchange (via email) between Tim Dooley and PR, conducted between September and December 2018. Available at: http://fortnightlyreview.co.uk/2019/02/britains-long-moment/.

6. Reviews and Letters

Perfect Bound 1, 1976. 'Veronica Forrest-Thomson: *On the Periphery*'. Available as part of *Jacket* magazine, http://jacketmagazine.com/20/pbs.html#sotp.

Perfect Bound 2, Winter 1976–77. 'Roy Fisher's "Body Sensations"': on *Roy Fisher, 19 Poems and an Interview*.

Perfect Bound 4, 1978. '*Marxism for Infants* by Denise Riley'.

The Cambridge Review 100:2244, 1978. 'Stations of the Cross': on *In the Stopping Train* and *The Poet in the Imaginary Museum*, Donald Davie.

Perfect Bound 5, 1978. 'Thomas A. Clark: Poet as Herbalist'.

Granta 77, May 1978. 'Dada and Surrealism Reviewed'.

Broadsheet, 10th–23rd October 1979. 'Sad Café' [as Jack Hughes].

Broadsheet, 24th–30th October 1979. 'Making It' [as Jack Hughes].

Broadsheet, 31st October–7th November 1979. 'Intimate Studies' [as Jack Hughes].

Broadsheet 8, 13th November 1979. 'Peter Robinson Reviews': on *Programme Notes* by Adam Clarke-Williams and *True Adventures on the A10* by A.T. Tribble.

Broadsheet, 14th–20th November 1979. 'Still Life' [as Jack Hughes].

Broadsheet, 21st–27th November 1979. 'At a Loss' [as Jack Hughes].

Broadsheet, 28th November–4th December 1979. 'Jenny's Face' [as Jack Hughes].

Broadsheet, 5th–11th December 1979. 'Woe' [as Jack Hughes].

Broadsheet, 16th–22nd January 1980. 'The Witches of Ensor' [as Jack Hughes].

Broadsheet, 23rd–29th January 1980. 'Drawing the Customers' [as Jack Hughes].
Broadsheet, 30th January–5th February 1980. 'Mental Furniture' [as Jack Hughes].
Broadsheet, 6th–12th February 1980. 'Small Prospects' [as Jack Hughes].
Broadsheet, 13th–18th February 1980. 'In Difficulties' [as Jack Hughes].
Broadsheet, 20th–26th February 1980. 'Some Figuring Out' [as Jack Hughes].
Broadsheet, 27th February–2nd March 1980. 'Blessed Clever' [as Jack Hughes].
Broadsheet, 5th–12th March 1980. 'O.K.' [as Jack Hughes].
PN Review 12, 6:4, March–April 1980. '2 or 3 Things about Roy Fisher': on *The Thing about Joe Sullivan* by Roy Fisher.
The Cambridge Review 101:2255, 1980. 'David Arkell, *Looking for Laforgue: An Informal Biography*'.
Grosseteste Review 13, 1980–81. 'Liberties in Context': on *Poems 1955–1980* by Roy Fisher.
Essays in Criticism, 32:4, October 1982. 'Fatal Twists': on *Collected Poems of Bernard Spencer*.
PN Review 29, 9:3, January–February 1982. 'Essential Marginalia': on *Poetry of Place* and *A View from the Source* by Jeremy Hooker.
Aquarius 13:14, 1982. 'A Dream of Maps by Matthew Sweeney'.
English 32:142, Spring 1983. 'Seeing the World': on *These the Companions* by Donald Davie. Available at: http://thirdworld.nl/seeing-the-world.
PN Review 31, 9:5, May–June 1983. 'Muscular Christianity and Verse': on *Dissentient Voice* by Donald Davie.
Argo 4:3, 1983. 'Extending the Occasions for Poetry': on *Poems of Thirty Years* by Edwin Morgan.
English 32:144, Autumn 1983. 'Standing by Moving': on *The Mystery of the Charity of Charles Péguy* by Geoffrey Hill. Available at: http://thirdworld.nl/standing-by-moving.
Grosseteste Review 15, 1983–84. 'A Book of John Welch': on *Out Walking* by John Welch.
English 33:146, Summer 1984. 'Difficult Situations': on *The Lords of Limit* by Geoffrey Hill.
Argo 5:5, 1984. 'Time and Again': on *Collected Poems 1971–1983* by Donald Davie.
English 34:150, Autumn 1985. 'Family Affairs': on *Using Biography* by William Empson.
London Review of Books, 8:3, 20th February 1986. 'Received Accents': on *Collected Poems*, Charles Tomlinson; *Selected and New Poems: 1939–84*, J.C. Hall; *Burning the Knife: New and Selected Poems*, Robin Magowan; *Englishmen: A Poem*, Christopher Hope; *Selected Poems: 1954–1982*, John Fuller; *Writing Home*, Hugo Williams.

The London Magazine, 27:1-2, April–May 1987. 'A Thread of Faith': on *Tutte le Poesie* by Vittorio Sereni.
Poetry Durham 22, 1989. 'Gaps': on books by Maura Dooley, Michael Donaghy, Adam Thorpe, Jo Shapcott.
English 39:165, 1990. 'Shorter Measures': on *Andromache* trans. Douglas Dunn.
Studies in English Literature [Tokyo], English Number, 1990. 'Attuning the Facts': on *The Music of What Happens* by Helen Vendler and *Poetry and Possibility* by Michael Edwards.
PN Review 73, 16:5, May–June 1990. 'Real Criticism': on *The Printed Voice of Victorian Poetry* by Eric Griffiths.
PN Review 74, 16:6, July–August 1990. 'Private Faces, Public Places': on *Antaeus: Journals, Notebooks and Diaries* [Issue 61 of *Antaeus*].
PN Review 77, 17:3, January–February 1991. 'Genuine Risks': on *Collected Poems* by Donald Davie.
Printed Matter 16:2, 1992. 'An Asocial Art': on *Prospect into Breath: Interviews with* North and South Writers.
Studies in English Literature, English Number, 1993. 'Behind the Lines': on *The Enemy's Country* by Geoffrey Hill.
PN Review 93, 20:1, September–October 1993. 'Delivered up to Fiction': on *Collected Poems 1935–1952* by F.T. Prince.
PN Review 94, 20:2, November–December 1993. 'Remedies for Depression' (letter in response to a review by T.J.G. Harris of *Entertaining Fates*).
Modern Poetry in Translation new series 5, 1994. On Attilio Bertolucci, *Selected Poems*, trans. Charles Tomlinson.
Perversions 1:3, 1994. 'Brazen Leech': on *Juvenilia* by W.H. Auden.
PN Review 102, 21:4, March–April 1995. 'Comprehending It': on *Collected Poems* by Norman Nicholson.
Modern Poetry in Translation, New Series, 8, 1995. 'Giacomo Leopardi, *The Canti*', trans. J.G. Nichols.
Perversions 5, 1995. '*Patrick White: Letters* ed. David Marr'.
Times Literary Supplement 4868, 19th July 1996. 'The Music of Milan': on *Poesie* by Vittorio Sereni and *Scritture Private* ed. Zeno Birolli.
Essays in English Romanticism 21, 1997. 'Poetry and Knowledge': on *Centre and Circumference* ed. Kenkichi Kamjima et al.
The Cambridge Quarterly 26:3, 1997. 'Toiling in a Pitch': on *Canaan* by Geoffrey Hill.
Notre Dame Review 8, Summer 1999. '*The Triumph of Love* by Geoffrey Hill'.
The Cambridge Quarterly 28:4, 1999. 'What's the Big Idea?': on Jorie Graham and Charles Simic.
PN Review 126, 25:4, March–April 1999. 'Counting the Beats' (letter). Available at: http://www.pnreview.co.uk/cgi-bin/scribe?item_id=343.

Studies in English Literature [Tokyo], English Number 42, 2001. 'Denis Donoghue, *The Practice of Reading*'.

Jacket 16, 2002. 'Distances, Losses, Links': on *Collected Poems* and *Doubtful Sounds* by Bill Manhire. Available at: http://jacketmagazine.com/16/nz-robi-manh.html.

Metre 11, 2002. 'Allen Curnow: "The Mixture's Moment"'.

The Guardian Review, 15th June 2002. 'When Crusoe was Homesick': on *Collected Poems* by Donald Davie. Available at: https://www.theguardian.com/books/2002/jun/15/featuresreviews.guardianreview20.

Notre Dame Review 14, Summer 2002. 'Early Retirement': on *Landscape with Chainsaw* by James Lasdun.

The Reader 11, 2002. 'The Reader Reviews': on *Clearances: A Memoir* by Mairi MacInnes.

The Gig 12, 2002. 'Caddel's Favourites': on *Magpie Words: Selected Poems* by Richard Caddel.

Tears in the Fence 34, Spring 2003. 'Laugh, Damn You!': on *The Orchards of Syon* by Geoffrey Hill.

Sewanee Review 66:2, Spring 2003. 'Taking the Low Road': on *Clearances* by Mairi MacInnes.

The Guardian, 22nd February 2003. 'Small Change': on *A World Perhaps: New and Selected Poems* by John Lucas and *The Whitworth Gun* by John Whitworth. Available at: https://www.theguardian.com/books/2003/feb/22/featuresreviews.guardianreview14.

The Guardian, 19th April 2003. 'Survivor's Art': on *From a Diary of Non-Events* by Michael Hamburger; *A Puzzling Harvest: Collected Poems 1955–2000* by Harry Guest; *Under the Breath* and *One Another* by Peter Dale; *New and Selected Poems* by A. Alvarez; and *The Return of the Cranes* by John Heath-Stubbs. Available at: https://www.theguardian.com/books/2003/apr/19/featuresreviews.guardianreview12.

Times Literary Supplement, 13th June 2003. 'Painters of the Forth Bridge': on *The Light Trap*, John Burnside; *Madame Fifi's Farewell and Other Poems*, Gerry Cambridge; *The Tip of My Tongue*, Robert Crawford; *The Big Bumper Book of Troy*, W. N. Herbert.

Times Literary Supplement 5229, 20th June 2003. 'A Friendly Exchange': on *The Way You Say the World: A Celebration for Anne Stevenson* ed. John Lucas and Matt Simpson, and *A Report from the Border* by Anne Stevenson.

Times Literary Supplement 5243, 26th September 2003. 'In Human Camouflage': on *For and After* by Christopher Reid.

Times Literary Supplement 5247, 24th October, 2003. 'Ice Cream with Empson' (letter).

Notre Dame Review 17, Winter 2004. 'Robinson's Reply': on four books by and about Weldon Kees. Available at: http://www3.nd.edu/~ndr/issues/ndr17/Peter%20Robinson/ROBIN~UU.PDF.

Agenda 40:1-3 (Triple Irish issue), May 2004. 'Loving his Food': on *God in France: A Paris Sequence 1994–1998* by Harry Clifton, 431-5; 'So Good So Far': on *Between Here and There* by Sinéad Morrissey, 448-52.
Times Literary Supplement 5304, 26th November 2004. 'In the Reader's Hands': on *Collected Poems* by Lee Harwood.
Poetry Review 94:4, Winter 2004–5. 'Have a Care': on *The Faber Book of 20th-Century Italian Poems*, ed. Jamie McKendrick.
PN Review 161, 31:3, January–February 2005. 'Have You No Homes?': on *Under the Influence* by Bill Manhire.
PN Review 163, 31:5, May–June 2005. 'Deaths of the Poets': on *The Columbia Anthology of Modern Korean Poetry*, ed. David R. McCann.
Poetry Ireland Review 83, Summer 2005. 'The Way We Die Now': on *New and Selected Poems* by Dennis O'Driscoll.
Times Literary Supplement 5340, 5th August 2005. 'Sleeves of Europe': on *Selected Poems* and *Nonetheless* by Peter Sirr.
PN Review 166, 32:2, November–December 2005. 'Smacks at Auden': on *Randall Jarrell on W.H. Auden*, ed. Stephen Burt.
Notre Dame Review 22, Summer 2006. On *The Triumph of Love* by Geoffrey Hill. Available at: http://www3.nd.edu/~ndr/issues/ndr8/reviews/love.html
Notre Dame Review 22, Summer 2006. 'Keeping It Strange': on *The Long and the Short of It* by Roy Fisher. Available at: http://www3.nd.edu/~ndr/issues/ndr22/Peter%20Robinson/Robinson-review.pdf.
Poetry Ireland Review 85, 2006. 'The Spaces Between': on *Door in the Mountain: New and Collected Poems 1965–2003* by Jean Valentine.
Poetry Ireland Review 86, 2006. 'Romantics and Foreigners': on *Collected Poems* and *A Living Language* by David Constantine.
Studies in English Literature [Tokyo], English Number 47, March 2006: '*Differentials* and *The Vienna Complex* by Marjorie Perloff'.
Essays in English Romanticism 29-30, 2006. 'Post-Conceptual Triste': on *Voyages of Conception* ed. Eiji Hayashi.
Poetry Ireland Review 88, Autumn 2006. 'Here Comes (Almost) Everybody': on *The Bloodaxe Book of Poetry Quotations*, ed. Dennis O'Driscoll.
Jacket 34, 2007. 'No Apologies and No Prizes': on *The Collected Poems of Ted Berrigan*, ed. Alice Notley. Available at: http://jacketmagazine.com/34/robinson-berrigan.shtml.
Poetry Ireland Review 89, April 2007. 'Grace Abounding': on *Collected Poems* by Gael Turnbull.
Poetry Ireland Review 90, 2007. 'Insider Trading': on books from the Worple Press by Iain Sinclair, Beverly Brie Bahic and Elizabeth Cook.
Notre Dame Review 24, Summer/Fall 2007. 'Exact as Horror': on *Edgar Allan Poe and the Juke-Box: Uncollected Poems, Drafts, and Fragments*

by Elizabeth Bishop, ed. Alice Quinn. Available at: http://www3.nd.edu/~ndr/issues/ndr24/Peter%20Robinson/Robinson-review.pdf.

The Dark Horse 22, 2008. 'An English Belli': on *Sonnets* by Giuseppe Gioacchino Belli, trans. Mike Stocks.

Poetry Ireland Review 94, 2008. 'Showing and Telling': on books by Eamon Grennan and Ciaran Berry.

Times Literary Supplement, 14th March 2008. 'Naked for the Master': on *Selected Poems* by W.S. Merwin.

Cambridge Quarterly 37:3, September 2008. 'A Proper Caution': on *The Art of Eloquence: Byron, Dickens, Tennyson, Joyce* by Matthew Bevis.

Poetry London 60, Summer 2008. 'Authenticity and Grace': on books by Janet Frame, Bernard O'Donoghue and Alison Brackenbury. 36-39.

Poetry London 62, Spring 2009. 'Love Translated': on books by Matthew Mead and John Welch. 32-34.

Poetry Ireland Review 97, Spring 2009. 'Borrowed Armour': on *Collected Poems* by Ciaran Carson.

The Bridge, Summer 2009. 'Ringing the Changes': on *Together Through Life* by Bob Dylan.

Poetry London 64, Autumn 2009. 'Old Incurables': on *Collected Poems* by Ian Hamilton.

The London Magazine, August–September 2010. 'Quiet Regrets': on *White Egrets* by Derek Walcott.

Times Literary Supplement, 1st July 2011. 'Lovers' Quarrels': on *The Essential Petrarch*, ed. and trans. Peter Hainsworth.

Translation and Literature 20:2, 2011. On *Valerio Magrelli: Vanishing Points*, trans. Jamie McKendrick.

Notre Dame Review 32, Summer/Fall 2011. 'Magrelli's Winter Journey': on *Valerio Magrelli: Vanishing Points*, trans. Jamie McKendrick. Available at http://ndreview.nd.edu/assets/47782/robinson_review.pdf.

The London Magazine, December 2011–January 2012. On *Great Works* by Tom Lubbock.

Poetry Wales 47:3, Winter 2011/2012. On *In Romsey Town* by John James.

Translation and Literature 22:1, March 2013. On *A Tongue Not Mine: Beckett and Translation* by Sinéad Mooney.

Times Literary Supplement, 4th October 2013. 'Through the Windscreen': on *Through the Looking-Glass: Landscapes of Desire in the Poetry of Vittorio Sereni* by Francesca Southerden.

Poetry London 78, Summer 2014. 'Returning an Echo': on *Echo's Grove* by Derek Mahon. Available at: http://poetrylondon.co.uk/returning-an-echo/.

Poetry Salzburg Review 28, Autumn 2015. On *Itself* by Rae Armantrout.

The Journal of the Sylvia Townsend Warner Society 2015, 2016, ed. Peter Swaab. On *Threads: The Delicate Life of John Craske* by Julia Blackburn. 68-72.

Poetry London 86, Spring 2017. 'We'll Enamel Him!': on *The Poems of Basil Bunting*, ed. Don Share.
Dublin Review of Books, 117, February 2020. 'Questions of Balance': on *The Painter on his Bike* by Enda Wyley. Available at: http://www.drb.ie/essays/questions-of-balance?

7. Radio Broadcasts

BBC Radio Three, 1979. 'New Voices'.
BBC Radio Three, 26th June 1983. 'The Associations of War: *The Dry Salvages*'. (Repeated 7th January 1985.)
BBC Radio Four, c. 1983–4 and 1986: at least two appearances on *Kaleidoscope* reviewing Roy Fuller's memoirs, and Bob Dylan's *Knock Out Loaded*.
BBC Radio Three, 14th December 1989. 'Poetry Now': PR read from *This Other Life* plus new work.
BBC Radio Three, February 1994. PR read a selection of poems from *Leaf-viewing*.
BBC Radio Three, c. spring 2005. *The Verb*. PR reading some aphorisms from *Untitled Deeds* and discussing them with W. N. Herbert.
BBC Radio Four, 30th August 2007. Interviewed for 'Son of a Preacher Man', presenter Darcus Howe. (Repeated 11th August 2008).
BBC Radio Three, December 2007. *The Verb*, presenter Ian McMillan. PR read 'English Abroad' and 'Not Lost'.
BBC Radio Three, April 2008. *The Verb*, presenter Ian McMillan. Discussing loan words in Japanese.
BBC Radio Berkshire, 15th November 2019. Bill Buckley in conversation with PR about writing poetry and the composition of *Bonjour Mr Inshaw*.

8. Recorded Readings

a. Sound Files

Archive of the Now. Recording made on 19 July 2005. PR reads 'Above the Falls', 'Apropos of Nothing', 'Aria di Parma', 'By the Way', 'Closure', 'Coat Hanger', 'Convalescent Days', 'Electric Storm', 'Equivocal Isle', 'In the Twilight', 'Leaving Sapporo', 'Marking Time', 'Out of Circulation', 'Pasta-Making', 'Point of View', 'Something to Declare', 'Talking to Language', 'The Sky's Event', 'The Yellow Tank', 'Unpopular Song' and 'Untitled'. Available at http://www.archiveofthenow.org/authors/?i=81.
Also: some recordings from the Cambridge Poetry Festival Radio programmes are held in the National Sound Archive at the British Library.

b. Videos and Clips

Poetry reading at the University of Notre Dame London Centre, 14 June 2011. PR reads 'Westwood Dusk', 'At the Institute: After Charles Sheeler', 'Enigmas of Departure', 'Abroad Thoughts: For Bill Manhire', 'Northumberland Avenue', 'Doctrines of Unripe Times', 'Lawrie Park Avenue by Camille Pissarro 1871' and 'Next to Nothing'. Available at https://www.youtube.com/watch?v=jNw8ZbnUl0U.

Bernard Spencer: Mystery Poet. PR contributes to a research seminar at the Institute of English Studies, 11 October 2012. Available at https://www.youtube.com/watch?v=_NZYqPxObAo.

Festival of the Future City: Poets, Writers and the City. Bristol, 19th November 2015. PR introduces and reads 'Bristol Voluntaries'. Available at: http://www.ideasfestival.co.uk/events/poets-writers-and-the-city/ (go to 38:00).

'A Woman a Poem a Picture', read by PR. Available on YouTube at: https://www.youtube.com/watch?v=_l-2lBuaubc.

'After the Visit', read by PR. Available on YouTube at: https://www.youtube.com/watch?v=mBurODJg43o.

'Haunting Landscapes', read by PR. Available on YouTube at: https://www.youtube.com/watch?v=4LQrKJVb7x8.

9. Paintings and Drawings

Anywhere You Like, Peter Robinson (Sendai: Pine Wave Press, 2000). Cover: untitled painting.

The Look of Goodbye: Poems 2001–2006, Peter Robinson (Exeter: Shearsman Books, 2008). Cover: unfinished painting (1991–92) of Yagiyama, Sendai.

The Returning Sky, Peter Robinson (Bristol: Shearsman Books, 2012). Cover: painting, 'The Clothes Chair' (1982–3).

Like the Living End, Peter Robinson (Tonbridge: Worple Press, 2013). Cover: untitled painting.

Buried Music, Peter Robinson (Bristol: Shearsman Books, 2015). Cover: painting, 'Neighbour's Window Fico Rosso'.

Collected Poems 1976–2016, (Bristol: Shearsman Books, 2017) Cover: detail from 'Self-Portrait with Lampshade' (1981).

See the interview with James Peake (2015), ref. section 5b above, for some reflections by PR about using his paintings as covers for his books.

10. In Translation

a. Books

After Chardin: Selected Poems translated by Takao Furukawa (Okayama: Shimyakusha, 1996).

80 poeti per gli ottant'anni di Luciano Erba, ed. Silvio Ramat (Milan: Interlinear, 2003). 'Italian Poplars', with translation as 'Pioppi italiani' by PR and Ornella Trevisan

L'Attaccapanni e altre Poesie, a bilingual edition with Italian translations by PR and Ornella Trevisan (Milan: Moretti and Vitali, 2004).

Dialogue: Tadashi Toyama in Search of a Vessel for the Soul (Tokyo: Itto-Hensheshitsu, November 2003). 'Unwitting Epitaph', with Japanese translation by Tomoku Kurumada.

Approach to Distance: Selected Poems from Japan, a bilingual edition with Japanese translations by Miki Iwata (Tokyo: Isobar Press, 2017).

Voces del extremo: Antología 2012–2016, compiled Antonio Orihuela (Madrid: Amarcord ediciones, 2017). 'Plaza de las Monjas', with translation into Spanish.

b. Journals

Clarin: Revista de Nueva Literatura 54, November-December 2004. 'Domestic Ghost', 'Corner Store', 'Dandelion Clocks', and 'What Lies Sleeping', with Spanish translations by Jaime Thonney Prunnell.

Neue Rundschau 119:2, September 2008. 'Mortuary Passport', as 'Leichenpass' in a German translation by Jan Volker Röhnert.

Journal of Italian Translation 4:2, Fall 2009. A selection of poems from *The Look of Goodbye* plus translations into Italian by Marco Sonzogni: 'For the Birds' ('Per gli uccelli'), 'To that Effect' ('A qualcosa del genere'), 'Mi ultimo adiós' ('Mi ultimo adiós'), 'Unwitting Epitaph' ('Un epitaffio involontario'), 'What Have You' ('E quant'altro'), 'Old Loves' ('Antichi amori').

Escombros con hoguera, blog entry for 16th August 2016. 'Oda a la deuda': translation into Spanish of 'Ode to Debt' by Conrado Santamaria Bastida and Amalia García Fuertes. Available at: http://escombroscon hoguera.blogspot.co.uk/search?updated-max=2016-08-18T09:04:00-07:00&max-results=12.

En sentido figurado (Special issue), 2017. 'From "Ringstead Poems"' translated into Spanish by Gerard Moreno Ferrer.

Contemporanul: Ideea Europeană [Romania], Anul XXVIII, 6:783, June 2017. 'An Air', 'Difficult Morning', 'Exchange Values', 'A Homage', 'How He Changes', 'Autobiography', and 'For Lavinia' translated into Romanian by Roxana Ghiţă and Oana Băluică şi Radu Grigoriou.

Literaturen Vestnik (*Literary Newspaper*) [Bulgaria], 35, 1st–7th November 2017. 'Balkan Trilogy' translated into Bulgarian by Alexander Shurbanov.

E-sushtnost [Bulgaria], 9 December 2018. 'Belonging', 'Post-Truth', 'The Prospects' translated into Bulgarian by Dimana Ivanova.

Free Poetry Society [Bulgaria], 2018. '23 January 1980', 'Your Other Country', 'Still Life Portraits', 'Talking to Language', 'On the Electricity' translated into Bulgarian by Bozhil Hristov. Available at: http://freepoetrysociety.com/articles/peter-robinson-stihove.

Sovremennost (Modernity) [North Macedonia], 74:1, 2019. '23 January 1980', 'Your Other Country', 'Still Life Portraits', 'Talking to Language', 'On the Electricity' translated into Macedonian by Mitko Gogov.

Sovremeni Diyalozi (Contemporary Dialogue), [North Macedonia] 7:7, 2019. 'Return to Sendai' and 'Though Spring is Here' translated into Macedonian by Silvana Heshkovska.

11. On Peter Robinson

Palantir 10, 1978. Review by Yann Lovelock of *The Benefit Forms* and *Going Out to Vote*.

Aquarius, 1978. Review by Tim Dooley of *The Benefit Forms* and *Going Out to Vote*.

Lobby Press Newsletter, 1980. Review by Andrew Tibble of *Overdrawn Account*.

Molly Bloom 1, November 1980. Review by Adam Clarke-Williams of *Overdrawn Account*.

Hertforde Poets Journal 19, 1981. Review by Julian Le Saux of *Overdrawn Account*. 17-20.

Delta 62, 1981. Review by David Holloway of *Overdrawn Account*.

Thames Poetry, 1982. 'Shorter Notices': brief review of *Overdrawn Account* by the editor.

PN Review 27, 9:1, 1982. 'A Place of Birth': review by Paul Carter of *With All the Views: Collected Poems of Adrian Stokes*, ed. PR.

Times Literary Supplement 4126, 30th April 1982. 'From the Manifest to the Therapeutic': review by Donald Davie of *With All the Views: Collected Poems of Adrian Stokes*, ed. PR.

The Many Review 1, Spring 1983. 'A Balance Sheet': review of by John Turner of *Overdrawn Account*.

Siting Fires 1, 1983. Review by James Lasdun of *Overdrawn Account*.

The Guardian, 18th April 1983. 'Cambridge's Greek Affair': review by Peter Levi of *The Disease of the Elm and Other Poems* by Vittorio Sereni, trans. PR.

PN Review 35, 10:3, January-February 1984. 'The Benefit of Doubt': review by Eric Griffiths of *Overdrawn Account*.

London Review of Books 7:6, 4th April 1985. 'The Case for Geoffrey Hill'. Review by Tom Paulin of *Geoffrey Hill: Essays on his Work*, ed. PR. [See also the extended correspondence following this review.]

English 34:149, 1985. 'Difficult Friend': review by David Atkinson of *Geoffrey Hill: Essays on his Work*, ed. PR.

Times Higher Education Supplement, 5th April 1985. 'Of the First Rank': review of *Geoffrey Hill: Essays on his Work*, ed. PR.
London Review of Books 7:16, 19th September 1985. 'Pound and the Perfect Lady': review by Donald Davie of *Pound's Artists*.
Arts Review 1985. 'Remembering Ezra Pound': review by Frederick Tomlin of *Pound's Artists*.
British Book News, June 1985. Short notice of *Geoffrey Hill: Essays on his Work*, ed. PR.
The Year's Work in English Studies 66, 1985. Short notice of *Geoffrey Hill: Essays on his Work*, ed. PR.
Times Literary Supplement, 4th April 1986. 'Geoffrey Hill: refined, furious – and great?': review by Alastair Fowler of *Geoffrey Hill: Essays on his Work*, ed. PR.
The Anglo-Welsh Review, c. 1986. Review by David Annwn of *Geoffrey Hill: Essays on his Work*, ed. PR.
The Spectator, c. 1986. 'Rattling Chains': review by Richard Jacobs of *Geoffrey Hill: Essays on his Work*, ed. PR.
Argo, 1986. Review by Tim Dooley of *Anaglypta*.
Iron, 1986. Review by John Lees of *Anaglypta*.
Acumen, 1986. Review by Yann Lovelock of *Anaglypta*.
Cambridge Quarterly 15:3, 1986. 'Geoffrey Hill, His Critics and His Criticism': review by David Gervais of *Geoffrey Hill: Essays on his Work*, ed. PR.
Critical Quarterly 28:3, Autumn 1986. 'Modern Perplexity': review by Andrew Swarbrick of *Geoffrey Hill: Essays on his Work*, ed. PR.
The Spectator, 17th January 1987. 'The True Undertaking': review by P. J. Kavanagh of *'Twenty-Six'*, Vittorio Sereni trans. PR.
The Salisbury Review, April 1987. 'Hill's Lost Kingdoms': review by Richard Cronin of *Geoffrey Hill: Essays on his Work*, ed. PR.
Financial Times, 20th February 1988. Review by Rachel Billington of *This Other Life*.
The Guardian, 13th May 1988. Review by Martin Dodsworth of *This Other Life*.
Times Literary Supplement, 19th August 1988. Review by Stephen Romer of *This Other Life*.
London Review of Books 10:18, 13th October 1988. John Kerrigan, 'Travellers': includes review of *This Other Life*. 15-17.
PN Review 64, 15:2, November–December 1988. 'Observing the Properties': review by Andrew Shelley of *This Other Life*.
Cambridge Review, December 1988. Review by John Mole of *This Other Life*.
Sunday Telegraph, 4th December 1988. 'Books of the Year': includes a review by Eric Griffiths [as Rhodesia Wackett] of *This Other Life*.

Poetry Wales 24:3, Winter 1988–89. Review by Tom Phillips of *This Other Life*.
Poetry Review 79:2, September 1989. Review by Keith Jebb of *This Other Life*.
Times Literary Supplement, October 1989. 'Amid the Blankness': review by Giles Foden of *More About the Weather*.
Many Review 6, January 1990. 'Places Not Our Own': review by Tom Phillips of *This Other Life*.
The Literary Review, Spring 1990. 'Some Enemies of Suburbanism': review by Adam Thorpe of *Selected Poems of Vittorio Sereni*, trans. Marcus Perryman and PR.
The Independent, 19th May 1990. 'A Ghost with One Foot in the War': review by Charles Tomlinson of *Selected Poems of Vittorio Sereni*, trans. Marcus Perryman and PR.
Poetry Review 80:2, Summer 1990. 'Raccomandazioni': review by Jamie McKendrick of *Selected Poems of Vittorio Sereni*, trans. Marcus Perryman and PR.
Times Literary Supplement, 14th December 1990. 'A Monologue Overheard': review by Clive Wilmer of *Selected Poems of Vittorio Sereni* trans. Marcus Perryman and PR.
PN Review 77, 17:3, January–February 1991. 'Negative Capabilities': review by John Pilling of *Selected Poems of Vittorio Sereni* trans. Marcus Perryman and PR.
Times Literary Supplement, 1992. 'The Behaviour of Poems': review by Mark Wormald of *In the Circumstances: About Poems and Poets*.
Testo a Fronte 8, 1992. Review by Eduardo Zuccato of *Selected Poems of Vittorio Sereni* trans. Marcus Perryman and PR.
Leaf-Viewing by PR, 1992 (see Section A): contains an essay on PR by Peter Swaab.
London Review of Books 14:11, 11th June 1992. 'Jokes': review by Donald Davie of *In the Circumstances: About Poems and Poets*. 18-19.
The Guardian, 11th June 1992. 'Back to Baggy Monsters': review by Terry Eagleton of *In the Circumstances: About Poems and Poets*.
English 41:171, 1992. Review by Andrew Michael Roberts of *In the Circumstances: About Poems and Poets*.
London Review of Books 14:19, 8th October 1992. Nicolas Tredell, 'Love in the Ruins': includes review of *Leaf-Viewing*. 17-18.
Angel Exhaust 8, Autumn 1992. 'Introduction: Two Tribes' by Andrew Duncan contains a brief comment on PR. 3.
The Cambridge Review 113:2319, December 1992. Review by Ralph Pite of *In the Circumstances: About Poems and Poets*.
The Cambridge Guide to Literature in English, ed. Ian Ousby. Cambridge: Cambridge University Press, 1993. Alison Blair-Underwood: 'Robinson, Peter 1953– '.

PN Review 93, 20:1, September-October 1993. '"Once only, Till the End of the World'": review by T. J. G. Harris of *Entertaining Fates*.
Modern Languages Review 89:4, 1994. Review of *In the Circumstances: About Poems and Poets*.
PN Review 99, 21:1, September–October 1994. 'John Ashbery in Conversation: with David Herd'. Ashbery refers to PR in a list of English poets he reads.
Review of English Studies 46:183, 1995. Review by Peter McDonald of *In the Circumstances: About Poems and Poets*.
The Oxford Companion to Twentieth-Century Poetry, ed. Jenny Stringer (Oxford: Oxford University Press, 1996.) 'Peter Robinson', 576.
Liverpool Echo, 13th July 1996. 'Poetry with an Accent Exceedingly Rare': review by Peter Grant of *Liverpool Accents: Seven Poets and a City*, ed. PR.
Liverpool Daily Post, 13th July 1996. 'Homesick exile's tribute to Liverpool poets': unsigned review of *Liverpool Accents: Seven Poets and a City*, ed. PR.
The Big Issue, c.29th July 1996. 'Liverpool Accents': review by Neil Jones of *Liverpool Accents: Seven Poets and a City*, ed. PR.
Times Literary Supplement 4879, 4th October 1996. 'Short Notices' by KJ includes a brief review of *Liverpool Accents: Seven Poets and a City*, ed. PR.
Schreibkunst in und aus Großbritannien [literature festival publicity material], Wien, 20–22 October 1996. Peter Waterhouse, 'Peter Robinson'.
The London Magazine, December–January 1996–97. 'Bricolage and Outrage': review by Michael O'Neill of *Liverpool Accents: Seven Poets and a City*, ed. PR.
The Argotist 3, 1996. Review by Angela Topping of *Liverpool Accents: Seven Poets and a City*, ed. PR.
Essays in English Romanticism [Tokyo], 1997. Review by Lawrence L. Hanson of *Enlightened Groves*, ed. Eiichi Hara, Hiroshi Ozawa and PR.
The Sunday Times, 1st June 1997. 'Wandering Minstrels': review by Alan Brownjohn of *Lost and Found*.
Stand 38:3, Summer 1997. Review by John Saunders of *Liverpool Accents: Seven Poets and a City*, ed. PR.
College Green, December 1997. 'Recommended Reading': review by David Wheatley of *Lost and Found*.
Tears in the Fence 21, 1998. 'Reclaimed Lands': review by Peter Carpenter of *Lost and Found*.
Shearsman 36, 1998. Editorial comment by Tony Frazer on *Lost and Found*.
Times Literary Supplement, 4th September 1998. 'Reading the Signs': review by Peter Swaab of *Lost and Found*.

Journal of Eighteenth-Century Studies 22:1, March 1999. Review of *Enlightened Groves*, ed. Eiichi Hara, Hiroshi Ozawa and PR.

Invisible Forms: A Guide to Literary Curiosities, Kevin Jackson (London: Picador, 1999). Refs. to PR 75, 174.

PN Review 126, 25:4, March–April 1999. 'Marred in a Way You Recognize': review by James Keery of *Lost and Found*. Available at: http://www.carcanet.co.uk/cgi- bin/scribe?showdoc=342;doctype=review.

Western Writers in Japan, Sumie Okada. Basingstoke and New York: Palgrave MacMillan, 1999. Chapter 11, 139-144, contains 'Peter Robinson: A Sense of being Misplaced'. See also 13, 87-89.

The Critical Quarterly 28:4, 1999. '"The Hard Lyric": Re-registering Liverpool Poetry': review by Peter Barry of *Liverpool Accents: Seven Poets and a City*, ed. PR.

Ambit 158, Autumn 1999. Review by Carole Baldock of *Liverpool Accents: Seven Poets and a City*, ed. PR.

Jacket 12, July 2000. Review by Nate Dorward of *The Thing About Roy Fisher*, ed. John Kerrigan and PR and *News for the Ear*, ed. PR and Robert Sheppard.

PN Review 136, 27:2, 2000. 'The Fisher Thing': review by William Wootten of *The Thing About Roy Fisher*, ed. John Kerrigan and PR, 57-58.

Raw Edge 11, Autumn/Winter 2000. Review by David Hart of *News for the Ear*, ed. PR and Robert Sheppard, 27.

Poetry Review 9:4, Winter 2000–2001. 'Barnadine's Reply': review by John Goodby of *The Thing About Roy Fisher*, ed. John Kerrigan and PR, and *News for the Ear*, ed. PR and Robert Sheppard, 67-70.

Cambridge Quarterly 30:2, 2001. 'Poetry and Pragmatism: New Things About Roy Fisher': review by Ralph Ingelbein of *The Thing About Roy Fisher*, ed. John Kerrigan and PR, and *News for the Ear*, ed. PR and Robert Sheppard, 175-179.

City Life, 2nd May 2001. 'Catching a Glimpse': review by Ra Page of *About Time Too*. 81.

PN Review 141, 28:1, September–October 2001. 'Trompe L'oreille': review by James Sutherland-Smith of *About Time Too*.

The Reader 9, October 2001. 'The Practice of Poetry: Rhyme'. Adam Piette, discussion of 'An Air' [published in *Ghost Characters*]. 41-3.

Times Literary Supplement, 19th October 2001. 'Poetry – Books in Brief': includes review by Jules Smith of *About Time Too*.

Thumbscrew 19, Autumn 2001. 'De-anglicizing England': review by Arthur Aughey of *The Thing About Roy Fisher*, ed. John Kerrigan and PR, and *News for the Ear*, ed. PR and Robert Sheppard, 41-44.

Notes and Queries (new series) 48:4, December 2001. Commentary by Kelvin Corcoran on *The Thing About Roy Fisher*, ed. John Kerrigan and PR, 459-60.

Notre Dame Review 11, Winter 2001. 'Maps to Roy Fisher': review by Devin Johnston of *The Thing About Roy Fisher*, ed. John Kerrigan and PR, and *News for the Ear*, ed. PR and Robert Sheppard, 173-9.
Metre 11, Winter 2001-2. 'Out of Time': review by Jonathan Ellis of *About Time Too*. 23-5.
The Cambridge Quarterly 31:3, 2002. Review by William Wootten of *About Time Too*. 282-92.
Review of English Studies 53:3, 2002. Review by Stan Smith of *The Thing About Roy Fisher*, ed. John Kerrigan and PR, 466-7.
The Modern Language Review 97:2, 2002. Review by Julian Cowley of *The Thing About Roy Fisher*, ed. John Kerrigan and PR, and *News for the Ear*, ed. PR and Robert Sheppard, 409-410.
9 West Road: A Newsletter of the Faculty of English 1, c.2002. 'Legenda': review by Kevin Jackson of *The Thing About Roy Fisher*, ed. John Kerrigan and PR.
Poetry Book Society Bulletin, Spring 2002. 'Douglas Dunn writes…': on *The Great Friend and other Translated Poems*. 22. Available at: http://www.worplepress.com/the-great- friend-by-peter-robinson/.
The Reader 10, April 2002. '*The Reader* Reviews': review by Kate Price of *About Time Too*.
Acumen 43, May 2002. 'Poetry Comment': review by Glyn Pursglove of *About Time Too* and *The Great Friend and other Translated Poems*. 122-3.
Times Literary Supplement 5176, 14th June 2002. 'Poems that Growl in Zoos': review by Peter MacDonald of *Poetry, Poets, Readers: Making Things Happen*.
English 51, Summer 2002. 'The Editorial Commentary' by Peter Barry contains an extended discussion of *The Thing About Roy Fisher*, ed. John Kerrigan and PR. 185-192.
Cambridge Review 31:3, Autumn 2002. 'Time to Heal': review by William Wootten of *About Time Too*.
Poetry Review 92:3, Autumn 2002. 'A Walk Through the Woods': review by John Redmond of *About Time Too*. 109-10.
The Frogmore Papers 60, Autumn 2002. Review by Catherine Smith of *The Great Friend and other Translated Poems*.
Poetry Review 92:4, Winter 2002. 'Out of the World': review by Andrea Brady of *Poetry, Poets, Readers: Making Things Happen*. 96-99.
PQR 18, 2002. 'Beyond Modesty': review by Keith Jebb of *News for the Ear*, ed. PR and Robert Sheppard. 9.
Critical Survey 15:1, 2003. Review by Hugh Underhill of *The Great Friend*.
A Choice of British Poetry, ed. Paul Hullah, Peter Robinson and Shoichiro Sakurai (Tokyo: Seitousha Press, 2003). Paul Hullah: commentary on 'For Lavinia', 'Leaving Saporo' and 'Pasta-Making', plus a profile of PR.
City Life, March 2003. Review by Steven Waling of *SP*. 63.

Venue, April 2003. Review by Tom Phillips of *SP*.
The Times, 12 April 2003. Review of *SP*.
Times Literary Supplement, 1st August 2003. 'Home for Memories': review by Jules Smith of *SP*.
Shearsman 55, Summer 2003. Review by Tony Frazer of *SP*.
The Use of English 54:3, Summer 2003. Review by Nigel Wheale of *SP*.
The Japan Times, 20th October 2003. Review by David Burleigh of *SP*. Available at: http://www.japantimes.co.jp/culture/2003/10/19/books/book-reviews/out-of-the-ordinary-2/#.V9FtVKNTFLM.
Notre Dame Review 15, Winter 2003. 'True Colors': review by Peter Carpenter of *About Time Too*. 162-5.
Modern Language Review 99:1, January 2004. Review by Alan Munton of *Poetry, Poets, Readers: Making Things Happen*.
Shearsman 59, June 2004. Review by John Couth of *Untitled Deeds*.
Gazzetta di Parma, 1st September 2004. Review by Giuseppe Marchetti of *L'Attaccapanni e altre poesie*.
Modern Philology 102:2, November 2004. Review by Stephen Burt of *Poetry, Poets, Readers: Making Things Happen*. 294-299.
Orbis 131, Winter 2004. Review by Andy Brown of *Untitled Deeds*.
Poetry Review 94:4, Winter 2004–5. 'All Forms Filled In': review by Patrick McGuinness of *SP* and *Untitled Deeds*.
The Use of English 56:2, Spring 2005. Review by Peter Carpenter of *Untitled Deeds*. Available at: http://www2.le.ac.uk/offices/english-association/schools/teaching- poetry/poetry-portal-1/reviews-1/uereviews#untitled-deeds-by-peter.
Studies in English Literature (Tokyo), March 2005. Review by Steve Clark of *Poetry, Poets, Readers: Making Things Happen*.
Poetry Ireland Review 82, March 2005. Denis O'Driscoll, 'Pickings and Choosings', cites *Untitled Deeds*, 115, 117.
Modern Philology 102:4, May 2005. Review by Stephen Burt of *Poetry, Poets, Readers: Making Things Happen*.
The Use of English 57:1, Autumn 2005. Review by Nigel Wheale of *Twentieth Century Poetry: Selves and Situations*. Available at: http://www2.le.ac.uk/offices/english-association/schools/teaching-poetry/poetry-portal-1/reviews-1/uereviews#twentieth-century- poetry-selves.
Times Literary Supplement, 11th November 2005. 'Good Words, Bad World': review by Angela Leighton of *Twentieth-Century Poetry: Selves and Situations*.
Critical Survey, December 2005. Review by Kathryn Daszkiewicz of *Mairi MacInnes: A Tribute*, ed. PR.
Shearsman, 2006. Review by Belinda Cooke of *There are Avenues*. *The North* 40, 2006. Review by Belinda Cooke of *Ghost Characters*.

Stride Magazine, 2006. 'Sniffing the Air': review by Martin Caseley of *Ghost Characters*.

Essays in Criticism 56:2, April 2006. 'Limits as Power': review by Emily Taylor Merriman of *Twentieth Century Poetry: Selves and Situations*. 209-17.

Forum for Modern Language Studies 42:3, July 2006. Review of *Twentieth Century Poetry: Selves and Situations*. 326-7.

New Hope International Review (n.d., c. 2007). Review by Susan Woollard of *Talk About Poetry: Conversations on the Art*. Available at: http://www.geraldengland.co.uk/revs/bs267.htm.

Year's Work in English Studies 86, 2007. Review by John Brannigan of *Twentieth Century Poetry: Selves and Situations*. 869.

The Salt Companion to Peter Robinson, ed. Adam Piette and Katy Price (Cambridge: Salt Publishing, 2007). Contents: *Introduction* by Adam Piette and Katy Price; *Preface* by Roy Fisher; essays by Adrian Poole, Paul Hullah, Eric Griffiths, Steve Clark, David Pascoe, Jane Davis, Adam Piette, Andrew Fitzsimons, Ralph Pite, John Roe, Miki Iwata, Neil Corcoran, Katy Price, and David Taylor, plus 'Peter Robinson: A Bibliography 1976–2006'.

Writing Liverpool, ed. Deryn Rees-Jones and Michael Murphy (Liverpool: Liverpool University Press, 2007). Peter Barry, ch.18, '"Out of transformations": Liverpool Poetry in the 21st Century'.

Modern Poetry in Translation Series 3:7, 2007. Review by Belinda Cooke of Luciano Erba, *The Greener Meadow: Selected Poems* trans. PR, and Vittorio Sereni, *Selected Poetry and Prose* ed. and trans. Marcus Perryman and PR.

Stride Magazine, 2007. 'Three Turns of Tulle': review by Raymond Humfreys of *The Greener Meadow: Selected Poems of Luciano Erba*, trans. PR.

Modern Language Review 102, 2007. Review by Philip Tew of *Twentieth-Century Poetry: Selves and Situations*. 218-219.

PN Review 175, 33:5, May-June 2007. 'Not Wanting': review by Maria-Daniella Dick of *Selected Poetry and Prose of Vittorio Sereni*, ed. and trans. Marcus Perryman and PR.

The Use of English 58:3, Summer 2007. Review by Nigel Wheale of *Talk About Poetry*. Available at: http://www2.le.ac.uk/offices/english-association/schools/teaching-poetry/poetry-portal-1/reviews-1/uereviews#twentieth-century-poetry-selves. This issue also includes a review by Belinda Cooke of *The Salt Companion to Peter Robinson*.

Sisif 25-26, 2008. Review by Catalin Ghita of *SP* and *The Look of Goodbye* [in Romanian].

Times Literary Supplement, 4th January 2008. Peter Hainsworth, 'Longings and Loathings': includes review of *Selected Poetry and Prose of Vittorio Sereni*, ed. and trans. Marcus Perryman and PR.

Jacket 35, Early 2008. 'Drawing a Line': review by Ben Hickman of *The Look of Goodbye*. Available at: http://jacketmagazine.com/35/r-robinson-rb-hickman.shtml.

The Warwick Review, 2:1, March 2008. Charlotte Newman, review of *The Look of Goodbye*.

The Yale Review 96:2, March 2008. Review by John Taylor of *Selected Poetry and Prose of Vittorio Sereni* and *The Greener Meadow: Selected Poems of Luciano Erba*, trans. PR. 152-73.

Stride Magazine, 2008. 'Pasts, Presents and Futures', Matt Simpson: includes review of *The Look of Goodbye*.

Eyewear blog, 21st April 2008. Review by Tom Phillips of *The Look of Goodbye* and *The Greener Meadow: Selected Poems of Luciano Erba*, trans. PR. Available at: http://toddswift.blogspot.co.uk/2008/04/guest-review-phillips-on-robinson.html.

Poetry London 60, Summer 2008. 'Travelling without Leaving': review by Martyn Crucefix of *The Look of Goodbye*.

Anglia – Zeitschrift für Englische Philologie 126:1, July 2008. Review by Rainer Emig of *Twentieth-Century Poetry: Selves and Situations*. 176-77.

Agenda 43:4/44:1, Summer-Autumn 2008. 'A Felicity of its Own': review by Belinda Cooke of *The Look of Goodbye*.

Times Literary Supplement 5504, 26th September 2008. Review by Adrian Tahourdin of *The Greener Meadow: Selected Poems of Luciano Erba*, trans. PR. 29.

The Guardian, 30th September 2008. 'Awards bring translators out of "darkened rooms"': an account by Alison Flood of an award-giving ceremony on 29th September 2008 at which PR received an award for *The Greener Meadow: Selected Poems of Luciano Erba*, trans. PR. Includes brief interview with PR.

Modern Philology 106:2, November 2008. Review by Gareth Reeves of *Twentieth-Century Poetry: Selves and Situations*. 363-366.

Georgiasam (David Wheatley's blog), 29th September 2009. 'To the Paparazzi of the Soul': includes comments on *Spirits of the Stair*. Available at: http://georgiasam.blogspot.co.uk/2009/09/to-paparazzi-of-soul.html.

All Aphorisms, All the Time (James Geary's blog), 7th October 2009. 'Aphorisms by Peter Robinson': review of *Spirits of the Stair*. Available at: http://www.jamesgeary.com/blog/aphorisms-by-peter-robinson/.

The Cat Flap blog, 29th October 2009. 'The Metaphysical Tramdriver': review by Peter Sirr of *The Greener Meadow: Selected Poems of Luciano Erba*, trans. PR. This review first appeared in *Poetry Ireland Review* 80. Available at: http://petersirr.blogspot.co.uk/2009/10/metaphysical-tramdriver-reading-luciano.html.

Contemporary Poetry: Poets and Poets Since 1990, Ian Brinton (Cambridge: Cambridge University Press, 2009). Refs. to PR on 6-7, 23-4, 30, 33, 115.

Eyewear blog, 12th January 2010. 'Guest Review: Phillips on Robinson': review by Tom Phillips of *Spirits of the Stair*. Available at: http://toddswift.blogspot.co.uk/2010/01/guest-review-tom-phillips-on-spirits-of.html.

The Manchester Review, July 2010. Review by Ian Pople of *An Unofficial Roy Fisher*, ed. PR. Available at http://www.themanchesterreview.co.uk/?p=945.

The Use of English 62:1, Autumn 2010. Review by Belinda Cooke of *Spirits of the Stair*. Available at: http://www2.le.ac.uk/offices/english-association/schools/teaching-poetry/poetry-portal-1/reviews-1/uereviews#spirits-of-the-stair.

Times Literary Supplement, no. 5617, Friday 26th November 2010, 8. 'Hyphenated Footpaths': review by Stephen Burt of *An Unofficial Roy Fisher*, ed. PR.

The North 46, 2010. Review by Belinda Cooke of *English Nettles*. Available at: http://tworiverspress.com/wp/english-nettles-reviewed-in-the-north/.

Stride Magazine, 2010. 'Some Uncut Pages about Roy Fisher': review by Martin Casely of *An Unofficial Roy Fisher*, ed. PR. Available at: http://www.stridebooks.co.uk/Stride%20mag2010/july%202010/caseley.fisher.htm.

Poetry Wales 46:3, Winter 2010–2011. 'Editorial: Viva la Poesía' by Zoë Skoulding contains commentary on *Poetry and Translation: The Art of the Impossible*.

Tony Williams's Poetry Blog, entry for Tuesday 1st March 2011, contains a review by Sean O'Brien of *An Unofficial Roy Fisher*, ed. PR. Available at: http://aye-lass.blogspot.com/2011/03/obrien-on-fisher.html.

Times Literary Supplement 5633, 18th March 2011. 'Poetry': review by Justin Quinn of *Poetry and Translation: The Art of the Impossible*.

The Observer, 29th May 2011. Review by Frances Leviston of *Bernard Spencer: Complete Poetry, Translations and Selected Prose*, ed. PR. Available at: https://www.theguardian.com/books/2011/may/29/complete-poetry-bernard-spencer-review.

Eyewear blog, 8th June 2011. Review by Todd Swift of *Reading Poetry: An Anthology*, ed. PR. Available at: http://toddswift.blogspot.co.uk/2011/06/review-reading-poetry.html.

Times Literary Supplement, 1st July 2011. 'Now Not-Beating': review by Robert Wells of *Bernard Spencer: Complete Poetry, Translations and Selected Prose*, ed. PR.

Poetry London 69, Summer 2011. Review by D.M. Black of *Poetry and Translation: The Art of the Impossible*.

London Review of Books 33:22, November 2011. 'The Analyst is Always Right': review by Mark Ford of *Bernard Spencer: Complete Poetry, Translations and Selected Prose*, ed. PR. 23-25.

The Use of English 63:1, Autumn 2011. Review by David Cooke of *Bernard Spencer: Complete Poetry, Translations and Selected Prose*, ed. PR. Available at: http://www2.le.ac.uk/offices/english-association/schools/teaching-poetry/poetry-portal-1/reviews-1/uereviews#bernard-spencer-complete-poetry.

The Bowwow Shop blog, c. 2011. 'Always Abroad': review by Paul Rossiter of *Bernard Spencer: Complete Poetry, Translations and Selected Prose*, ed. PR. Available at: http://www.bowwowshop.org.uk/page80.htm.

Welcome to the Seawall (Ron Slate's website), 6th December 2011. Joshua Weiner on *Bernard Spencer: Complete Poetry, Translations and Selected Prose*, ed. PR. Available at: http://www.ronslate.com/twenty_poets_recommend_new_recent_titles.

Notre Dame Review 33, Winter 2011/Spring 2012. 'Roy Fisher: The Vernacular Landscape, Jazz, and the Poem as Problem': review by Todd Nathan Thorpe of *An Unofficial Roy Fisher*, ed. PR. 234-246. Available at http://ndreview.nd.edu/assets/60038/thorpe_review.pdf.

PN Review 203, 38:3, January-February 2012. 'To Stand Against Chaos': review by James Sutherland-Smith of *Bernard Spencer: Complete Poetry, Translations and Selected Prose*, ed. PR. Excerpt available at: http://www.jamessutherland-smith.co.uk/pp005.shtml.

Times Literary Supplement, 24th February 2012. 'With Impure Lips': review by Thea Lenarduzzi of Antonia Pozzi, *Poems*, trans. PR.

PN Review 204, 38:4, March-April 2012. 'No Single Place to Be': review by Peter Riley of *An Unofficial Roy Fisher*, ed. PR.

The London Magazine, April–May 2012. 'In Our Own Hard Times': review by Andrew Mangham of *A Mutual Friend*, ed. PR.

Metamorphoses 20:1, Spring 2012. Review by Gregary J. Racz of *Poetry and Translation: The Art of the Impossible*. Available at: https://www.smith.edu/metamorphoses/issues/links/racz.pdf.

Translation and Literature 21:2, June 2012. Review by Adam Piette of *Poetry and Translation: The Art of the Impossible*. 275-282.

Poetry Wales, 48:1, Summer 2012. Review by Kym Martindale of *The Returning Sky*.

The Poetry Review 102:3, Autumn 2012. Review by Todd Swift of *The Returning Sky*.

Blackbox Manifold, ed. Alex Houen and Adam Piette, Issue 9, December 2012. "Peter Robinson at Sixty", ed. Adam Piette. This contains an interview with John Kerrigan (see Section E above); Alison Blair-Underwood, 'A Memoir: The Cambridge Poetry Festival'; Aidan Semmens, 'A Memoir: *Perfect Bound*'; Peter Swaab, 'Commissioning a Poem'; Adam Clarke-Williams, 'A Correspondance' [sic]; and a review by Ian Brinton of *The Returning Sky*. Also included are a selection of early and recent poems by PR, and poems for PR by eleven poets.

Available at: http://www.manifold.group.shef.ac.uk/issue9/index9.html.
Poetry London, 2012. Review by Sue Hubbard of *The Returning Sky*. Available at: http://www.suehubbard.com/index.php?mact=News,cntnt01,detail,0 &cntnt01articleid=244& cntnt01returnid=59.
Agenda 46:3, 2012. 'Turning and Returning': review by Belinda Cooke of *The Returning Sky*. Available at: http://www.agendapoetry.co.uk/documents/RetrospectivesWebReviews.pdf.
Agenda c. 2012. Review by Belinda Cooke of *Poetry and Translation: The Art of the Impossible*. Available at: http://www.agendapoetry.co.uk/documents/SissonOnlineessays.pdf.
The Use of English, 64, 2012. Review by Jeremy Tambling of *A Mutual Friend*, ed. PR.
The Fortnightly Review, June 2013. Peter Riley, 'An Introductory Note' [to 'Peter Robinson: Six New Poems']. Available at: http://fortnightly review.co.uk/2013/06/poems-peter-robinson/.
The Oxford Companion to Modern Poetry (2nd ed.), ed. Jeremy Noel-Todd (Oxford: Oxford University Press, 2013). 'Peter Robinson', entry by the editor. 523.
The Guardian, 18th February 2013. 'Poem of the Week: "Otterspool Prom" by Peter Robinson'. Commentary on the poem by Carol Rumens. Available at: https://www.theguardian.com/books/2013/feb/18/poem-week-peter-robinson-otterspool-prom.
Notre Dame Review 36, Summer/Fall 2013. 'The Poems of Antonia Pozzi': review by Wallis Wilde-Menozzi of *The Poems of Antonia Pozzi*, trans. PR. Available at: http://ndreview.nd.edu/assets/105009/wilde_menozzi.pdf.
The London Magazine, February/March 2014. 'From *Poets' Tales*': review by David Cooke of *Foreigners, Drunks and Babies*. Available at: http://blogs.reading.ac.uk/english-at-reading/2014/02/06/foreigners-drunks-and-babies/.
Stride Magazine, 2014: 'Back to Birmingham': review by Martin Caseley of *An Easily Bewildered Child*, Roy Fisher, ed. PR.
Acumen 80, September 2014. Review by Belinda Cooke of *Like the Living End*.
Pages (Robert Sheppard's blogzine), 6th October 2014. 'On a Note of Roy Fisher Concerning Christopher Middleton': commentary on a passage from *An Easily Bewildered Child*, Roy Fisher, ed. PR. Available at: http://robertsheppard.blogspot.co.uk/2014/10/robert-sheppard-on-note-of-roy-fisher.html.
Tears in the Fence blog, 20th October 2014. Review by Ian Brinton of *The Oxford Handbook of Contemporary British and Irish Poetry*, ed. PR. Available at: https://tearsinthefence.com/tag/peter-robinson/.

Review of English Studies 65:272, November 2014. Review by Peter Barry of *The Oxford Handbook of Contemporary British and Irish Poetry*, ed. PR.
Isola di Rifiuti (John Latta's blog), 18th November 2014. Contains an extended commentary on *An Easily Bewildered Child*, Roy Fisher, ed. PR. Available at: http://isola-di-rifiuti.blogspot.co.uk/2014/11/roy-fishers-easily-bewildered-child.html.
Under the Radar 13, 2014. Review by Michael Thomas of *Like the Living End*.
The Fortnightly Reviews: Poetry Notes 2012–2014, Peter Riley (Les Brouzils, France: The Fortnightly Review, 2015). "Worrying Around England", 245-263. Includes reviews of *The Returning Sky* and *Like the Living End* (plus reviews of books by John Welch). Available (entitled "Poetry of the Second Person") at http://fortnightlyreview.co.uk/2013/11/robinson-welch/.
Tears in the Fence blog, 18th January 2015. Review by Ian Brinton of *Buried Music*. Available at: https://tearsinthefence.com/2015/01/.
The Manchester Review, January 2015. Review by Ian Pople of *An Easily Bewildered Child*, Roy Fisher, ed. PR. Available at: http://www.themanchesterreview.co.uk/?p=4491.
The Manchester Review, March 2015. Review by Ian Pople of *Buried Music*. Available at: http://www.themanchesterreview.co.uk/?p=4553.
Litrefs Reviews (Tim Love's blog), 15th April 2015. Review of *The Returning Sky*. Available at: http://litrefsreviews.blogspot.co.uk/2015/04/the-returning-sky-by-peter-robinson.html.
Tears in the Fence blog, 29th November 2015. Review by Ian Brinton of *The Draft Will*. Available at: https://tearsinthefence.com/tag/peter-robinson/.
Alchetron [online encyclopaedia], no date, c. 2016. 'Peter Robinson (poet)'. Profile of PR and selected bibliography. Some misattributed book titles beneath image of PR. Available at: https://alchetron.com/Peter-Robinson-(poet)-368295-W#-.
Times Literary Supplement, 6th April 2016. 'Untormented': review by Charlie Louth of *The Rilke of Ruth Speirs*, ed. John Pilling and PR.
Tears in the Fence 63, Spring 2016. Review by Belinda Cooke of *Poems: Antonia Pozzi*, trans. PR.
Tears in the Fence blog, 29th August 2016. Review by Ian Brinton of *September in the Rain*. Available at: https://tearsinthefence.com/blog/.
The Manchester Review, October 2016. Review by Ian Pople of *Slakki*, Roy Fisher, ed. PR. Available at: http://www.themanchesterreview.co.uk/?p=6822.
The Guardian, 14th October 2016. 'A Collection with Extraordinary Vision': review by David Wheatley of *Slakki*, Roy Fisher, ed. PR. Available at: https://www.theguardian.com/books/2016/oct/14/slakki-new-and-neglected-poems-by-roy-fisher-review.

The Fortnightly Review, August 2016. 'Poetry Notes', Peter Riley. Includes a review of *The Rilke of Ruth Speirs*, ed. John Pilling and PR. Available at: http://fortnightlyreview.co.uk/2016/08/lorenzo-calogero/.

Stride Magazine Blogspot, entry for 9th November 2016. 'An Enjoyable Addendum': review by Simon Collings of *Slakki*, Roy Fisher, ed. PR.

Trinity Poets: An Anthology of Poems by Members of Trinity College, Cambridge, ed. Angela Leighton and Adrian Poole (Manchester: Carcanet Press, 2016). Profile of PR, 305-6.

The North 57, January 2017. Review by Ian McMillan of *Slakki*, Roy Fisher, ed. PR.

The London Magazine, February–March 2017. Review by Claire Crowther of *Slakki*, Roy Fisher, ed. PR.

Times Literary Supplement, 10th March 2017. 'The Apocrypha of Roy Fisher': review by William Wootten of *Slakki*, Roy Fisher, ed. PR.

Dundee University Review of the Arts, March 2017. Review by Shanley McConnell of *Slakki*, Roy Fisher, ed. PR. Available at: https://dura-dundee.org.uk/2017/03/31/slakki-new-neglected-poems/.

The London Magazine, April/May 2017. 'The Past Beneath our Feet': review by Ian Brinton of *September in the Rain* and *CP*. Available at: https://www.thelondonmagazine.org/tag/ian-brinton/.

The Manchester Review, May 2017. Review by Ian Pople of *CP*. Available at: http://www.themanchesterreview.co.uk/?p=7508.

The Interpreter's House 65, June 2017. 'Menial Caretaker of a Real': review by Martin Malone of *CP*.

Poetry Review 107:1, Spring 2017. Review by Carol Rumens of *Slakki*, Roy Fisher, ed. PR.

Dundee Review of the Arts, March 2017. Review by Beth MacDonough of *Buried Music*. Available at: https://dura-dundee.org.uk/2017/03/30/buried-music/.

The High Window, 3rd June 2017. Review by Keith Hutson of *Slakki*, Roy Fisher, ed. PR. Available at: https://thehighwindowpress.com/2017/06/03/reviews-for-summer-2017/.

Contemporanul: Ideea Europeană [Romania], Anul XXVIII, 6:783, June 2017. 'Peregrinările lui Peter Robinson', a profile of PR with particular reference to *CP*, by Roxana Ghiță.

The Rift in the Lute: Attuning Poetry and Philosophy, Maximilian de Gaynesford (Oxford: Oxford University Press, 2017). References to PR on 22, 29.

The Ogham Stone blog, 21st October 2017. 'A Poetry Reading with Peter Robinson': a brief account of PR's reading at Limerick City Library by Kaitlynn McShea. Available at: https://theoghamstoneul.com/2017/10/21/a-poetry-reading-with-peter-robinson/.

Journal of Poetics Research 8, 2017. Review by Will May of *CP*. Available at: http://poeticsresearch.com/article/will-may-reviews-peter-robinsons-collected-poems/.

The High Window 8, December 2017. Review by Tom Phillips of *CP*. Available at: https://thehighwindowpress.com/category/reviews/.

English: Journal of the English Association, 67:259, Winter 2018. Martin Dodsworth, '*Dormiveglia* in Peter Robinson's Poetry'.

The Manchester Review, January 2019. Review by Ian Pople of *Ravishing Europa*. Available at: http://www.themanchesterreview.co.uk/?p=10066.

The High Window, March 2019. Review by Andy Houwen of *Ravishing Europa*. Available at: https://thehighwindowpress.com/category/reviews/.

The London Magazine, April 2019. Review by Ian Brinton of *Ravishing Europa* and *The Sound Sense of Poetry*.

The Manchester Review, February 2019. Review by Ian Pople of Roy Fisher, *A Furnace* (Flood Editions, ed. PR). Available at: http://www.themanchesterreview.co.uk/?p=10360.

The Times Literary Supplement, 3rd July 2019. Brief review by David Wheatley of Roy Fisher, *A Furnace* (Flood Editions, ed. PR).

PN Review 248, 45:6, July-August 2019. 'Belonging's Tainted Now': review by Tim Dooley of *Ravishing Europa*.

Tears in the Fence blog, 9th March 2020. Review by Ian Brinton of *Bonjour Mr Inshaw*. Available at: https://tearsinthefence.com/2020/03/09/bonjour-mr-inshaw-poetry-by-peter-robinson-paintings-by-david-inshaw-two-rivers-press/.

Agenda 53:4, 2020. Review by James Harpur of *Bonjour Mr Inshaw*.

The High Window, May 2020. Review by Louise Warren of *Bonjour Mr Inshaw*. Available at: https://thehighwindowpress.com/category/reviews/. (You'll have to scroll down a bit.)

Two Rivers Press blog, entry for 11th May 2020. 'Poet of the Week: 6. Peter Robinson'. Brief profile of PR, plus reflections by him on how much of his work 'can be understood as an exploration of the word "repair"', and two poems: 'At Slader's Yard' and 'This Other Lifetime'. Available at: https://tworiverspress.com/2020/05/11/poet-of-the-week-6-peter-robinson/.

Martyn Crucefix website, 7th September 2020. 'Counting Clouds', review of *Bonjour Mr Inshaw*. Available at: https://martyncrucefix.com/2020/07/09/quickdraw-review-counting-clouds-poems-by-peter-robinson-paintings-by-david-inshaw/.

Poetry Salzburg Review 36, Autumn/Winter 2020. Review by Keith Hutson of *Bonjour Mr Inshaw*.

12. Archive Holdings

Selections of Peter Robinson's literary manuscripts, typescripts, corrected proofs, autograph correspondence, and sound recordings are held by the British Library, the John Rylands Library at the University of Manchester, the Brotherton Library at the University of Leeds, the Centro Manoscritti at the University of Pavia, the University of Sheffield Library, Hull History Centre, Special Collections at the University of Reading, the Beinecke Library at Yale University, and the Thomas J. Dodd Research Center, University of Connecticut Libraries. For further details about some of the material held in British collections, see the Location Register of Twentieth-Century English Manuscripts: http://www.unicorn.reading.ac.uk/uhtbin/cgisirsi/?ps=VE93NK8HiQ/MAIN-LIB/127670002/5/0.

Notes on contributors

Ian Brinton co-edits *Tears in the Fence* and *SNOW* and is closely involved with the Modern Poetry Archive at the University of Cambridge. His edition of the poems of Andrew Crozier was published by Carcanet and an account of post-1990 poetry by C.U.P.. Recent publications have included translations of poems from the French of Yves Bonnefoy, Francis Ponge and Philippe Jaccottet (Oystercatcher Press) and his translations of Stéphane Mallarmé appeared from Muscaliet Press in September 2019. He has edited two volumes of essays about the post-modernist Cambridge poet J. H. Prynne.

Peter Carpenter's 'New and Selected Poems', *Just Like That*, (Smith/Doorstop) came out in 2012, and a chapbook *Peace Camp* (Maquette) in 2015; these follow five previous collections. He is a regular essayist and reviewer for many journals including *Agenda, The North, Poetry Wales* and *The Use of English*. He has co-directed Worple Press since 1997, editing and publishing more than sixty poetry and arts titles. He has taught creative writing for many organisations including the Arvon Foundation and the Royal Academy. He contributed to Iain Sinclair's *London: City of Disappearances* and features in *London Orbital*. His next collection, *Get In*, is being published by Smith/Doorstep in 2022, and he is currently finishing a book about David Bowie.

Tony Crowley is Professor of English at the University of Leeds; a native of Liverpool, his recent publications include *Scouse: A Social and Cultural History* (Liverpool University Press, 2012) and *The Liverpool English Dictionary: A record of the language of Liverpool 1850-2015 on Historical Principles* (Liverpool University Press, 2017).

Martin Dodsworth is an Emeritus Professor of English of the University of London. He has edited the journal of the English Association, *English*, and has also served as chair of the Association. He reviewed poetry for the Guardian in the seventies and eighties, including Peter Robinson's early volumes, and has published reviews and articles in *Essays in Criticism* over the years. He contributed to Peter Robinson's symposium on Geoffrey Hill (1985) and a further essay on Hill appeared in 2020 in a collection edited by Andrew Michael Roberts for Shearsman.

Andrew Houwen has been an associate professor at Tokyo Woman's Christian University since 2018, having gone there two years earlier as a JSPS fellow. His research focuses on comparative literature, especially the relationships between Japanese and English poetry. His article on 'Ezra Pound's Early Cantos and His Translation of *Takasago*' was awarded the Ezra Pound Society Article Prize in 2014. His first academic monograph, *Ezra Pound's Japan*, was published by Bloomsbury in 2021. He also translates poetry: his translations with Chikako Nihei of Naka Tarō, *Music*, were brought out with Isobar Press in 2018. He is now collaborating with Peter Robinson on a new edition of Ibaragi Noriko's poems, some of which have appeared in *Modern Poetry in Translation*.

Miki Iwata is a professor of English literature at Rikkyo University, Japan. She received her PhD from Tohoku University in 2001, for her study of W. B. Yeats's drama and Irish cultural nationalism under the supervision of Peter Robinson. Her research interests cover a wide range of modern British and Irish plays, from Shakespeare to Oscar Wilde and Yeats, focusing particularly on the politics of family representations. Her recent publications include *Rival Brothers in British and Irish Drama* (Shohakusha Publishing, 2017, written in Japanese), 'Brothers Lost, Sisters Found: The Verbal Construction of Sisterhood in *Twelfth Night*' (2019), and 'Tony Lumpkin in and out of Sweet Auburn: The Literary Topography of Oliver Goldsmith's *She Stoops to Conquer*' (2020).

James Peake was born in Wimbledon and educated at Bristol University and Trinity College, Dublin. He has worked in trade publishing for several years, predominantly for Penguin Random House and Pan Macmillan as well as independents and leading literary agencies. His first poetry collection *Reaction Time of Glass* (Two Rivers Press) was published in 2019. He lives in London with his wife and son.

Piers Pennington completed his doctoral studies at Corpus Christi College, Oxford. He is co-editor of *Geoffrey Hill and his Contexts* (2011) and *Poetry & the Dictionary* (2020).

Tom Phillips teaches creative writing at Sofia University St Kliment Ohridski, Bulgaria, and has published a number of articles on the representation of SE Europe in English-language writing. His poetry has been published in a wide range of journals, anthologies and pamphlets, as well as in the full-length collections *Recreation Ground* (Two Rivers Press, 2012) and *Unknown Translations* (Scalino, 2016). He is the founding editor of *Balkan Poetry Today* and has translated a wide range of contemporary Bulgarian poetry.

Adam Piette is a Professor of Modern Literature at the University of Sheffield. He is the author of *Remembering and the Sound of Words: Mallarmé, Proust, Joyce, Beckett* (OUP 1996), *Imagination at War: British Fiction and Poetry, 1939–1945* (Macmillan, 1995), and *The Literary Cold War, 1945 to Vietnam* (EUP, 2009). He co-edited with Mark Rawlinson *The Edinburgh Companion to Twentieth-century British and American War Literature* (EUP, 2012) and is co-editor with Alex Houen of the poetry journal *Blackbox Manifold*. He co-edited with Katy Price *The Salt Companion to Peter Robinson* (Salt, 2007).

Elaine Randell is a widely published poet and prose writer. Her most recent work, *The Meaning of Things*, was published by Shearsman Books in 2017. Currently she is working in the new territory of crime fiction. She continues to work in private practice as a child psychotherapist and within the Church of England at Canterbury Cathedral. She lives on Romney Marsh and also has a home in rural Turkey. She is an enthusiastic gardener in both countries and lives with her husband, a flock of Soay sheep, chickens and three English Setters.

Anna Saroldi is a doctoral student at the English Faculty of the University of Oxford. She graduated with distinction from the same university (MSt in French and Italian), and has previously obtained her BA and MA from the Università di Pavia (Italy), where she was a member of the Scuola Superiore IUSS and of the Almo Collegio Borromeo. She works on translation, self-translation, translingualism and heteroglossia, especially concerning poetical practice. She has presented papers on authors such as Jorie Graham, Louise Labé, Jhumpa Lahiri, Jacqueline Risset and Amelia Rosselli. Her article on Lahiri's Italian prose writing was featured in *Quaderni Borromaici* (2017) and her contribution on the poetry of Risset will appear in the proceedings of the conference 'Translation and Lyrical Tradition between Italy and France'.

Derek Slade prepared a comprehensive bibliography of Roy Fisher for *The Thing About Roy Fisher* (ed. John Kerrigan and Peter Robinson,

Liverpool University Press, 2000), with an update covering the years 2000–2010 published in *An Unofficial Roy Fisher* (ed. Peter Robinson, Shearsman Books, 2010). A further updated version is due to be published in digital form as part of the Roy Fisher Archive, Sheffield University. He also contributed a bibliography of secondary materials to *An Andrew Crozier Reader* (ed. Ian Brinton, Carcanet Press, 2012).

Matthew Sperling is the author of two novels, *Astroturf* (2018) and *Viral* (2020), both published by riverrun books, and of *Visionary Philology: Geoffrey Hill and the Study of Words* (2014), published by Oxford University Press. He is Lecturer in Literature in English from 1900 to the present at University College London, and previously worked at the Universities of Oxford and Reading.

Alison Stone completed her PhD on 'Contemporary British Poetry and The Objectivists' at Exeter University in 2017. Her research interests span twentieth century poetry and poetics, especially modernist inheritances and neo-modernism in anglophone literature. She has a particular interest in the ways artistic collaborations can be uncovered in archives, and was AHRC IPS Fellow at the Harry Ransom Center in Texas in 2014. She teaches as an associate lecturer at Exeter and Plymouth Universities.

www.ingramcontent.com/pod-product-compliance
Lightning Source LLC
Chambersburg PA
CBHW032018230426
43671CB00005B/128